NOW THAT YOU'VE PICKED UP THIS BOOK...
...THE CASHIER IS RIGHT OVER THERE.
Grin

TENSHI JA NAI!!

Translation –Akira Tsubasa
Lettering – Jennifer Skarupa
Design – Team Pokopen
Editor – Jake Forbes

A Go! Comi manga

Published by Go! Media Entertainment, LLC

Tenshi Ja Nai!! 2 © 2004 Takako Shigematsu/ Akitashoten.
Originally published in Japan in 2004 by AKITASHOTEN CO, LTD., Tokyo.
English translation rights arranged with AKITASHOTEN CO., LTD.
through TOHAN CORPORATION, Tokyo.

English Text © 2006 Go! Media Entertainment, LLC. All rights reserved.

Visit us online at www.gocomi.com
e-mail: info@gocomi.com

ISBN 0-9768957-5-7

First printed in January 2006

1 2 3 4 5 6 7 8 9

Manufactured in the United States of America

TENSHI JA NAI!!

I'm No Angel!

Volume 2

Story and Art by
Takako Shigematsu

go!comi

Concerning Honorifics

At Go! Comi, we do our best to ensure that our translations read seamlessly in English while respecting the original Japanese language and culture. To this end, the original honorifics (the suffixes found at the end of characters' names) remain intact. In Japan, where politeness and formality are more integrated into every aspect of the language, honorifics give a better understanding of character relationships. They can be used to indicate both respect and affection. Whether a person addresses someone by first name or last name also indicates how close their relationship is.

Here are some of the honorifics you might encounter in this book:

-san: This is the most common and neutral of honorifics. The polite way to address someone you're not on close terms with is to use "-san." It's kind of like Mr. or Ms., except you can use "-san" with first or last names as easily as family names.

-chan: Used for friendly familiarity, mostly applied towards young women and girls.

-kun: Like "-chan," it's an informal suffix for friends and classmates, only "-kun" is usually associated with boys. It can also be used in a professional environment by someone addressing a subordinate.

-sama: Indicates a great deal of respect or admiration.

Sempai: In school, "sempai" is used to refer to an upperclassman or club leader. It can also be used in the workplace by a new employee to address a mentor or staff member with seniority.

Sensei: Teachers, doctors, writers or any master of a trade are referred to as "sensei." When addressing a manga creator, the polite thing to do is attach "-sensei" to the manga-ka's name (as in Shigematsu-sensei).

[blank]: Not using an honorific when addressing someone indicates that the speaker has permission to speak intimately with the other person. This relationship is usually reserved for close friends and family.

TENSHI JA NAI!!

CONTENTS

VOL .2

Hikaru Takabayashi

The reluctant star of the series. Hikaru wants nothing more than to be left alone, but ever since she transferred to the prestigious Seika Academy, she's been stuck in the spotlight. Being roommates with a cross-dressing pop idol is bad enough, but now Izumi is blackmailing her into helping with his modeling job. Will Hikaru ever catch a break?

Izumi Kido

Izumi is one of the hottest new female pop idols in Japan. The only problem is...she's a guy! Only two people knew his secret—Yasukuni, his bodyguard and childhood friend, and Akizuki his manager. When Hikaru finds out, Izumi blackmails her into helping him maintain his secret. Izumi needs the modeling money to pay off his father's medical bills.

Yasukuni Inukai

Yasukuni is fiercely loyal to Izumi. A bastard child disowned by his father, Izumi is the only family he has. Now that Hikaru has won his trust, he's taken to looking out for her, as well. Much of his past remains a mystery, such as why he's missing his right eye. He does double duty as the school janitor so he can always be close to Izumi.

SUMIKKO

Momochi

Akizuki

Hikaru's best friend in the world. Yasukuni takes care of her while Hikaru's at school.

Star reporter for the school paper, Momochi is always on the lookout for gossip!

President of the Akizuki Talent Agency and Izumi's manager.

Cast of Characters

Wall of Memories

A New School

When her mom and step-dad move to France, Hikaru transfers to her mother's alma mater, the prestigious Seika Academy, an all-girls finishing school.

Childhood memories

When she was seven years old, Hikaru modeled in a series of ads. Her jealous classmates picked on her relentlessly so now Hikaru's greatest wish is to be left alone.

BLACKMAIL!!!

To keep Hikaru quiet and in order to enlist her help, Izumi and Yasukuni blackmail Hikaru with naked photos.

She's a GUY!?

Hikaru discovers that her roommate, Izumi, is actually a guy!

Hikaru turns out to be a blessing in surprise for Izumi. Having a female conspirator by his side helps him maintain his cover in the trickiest circumstances.

Izumi's Confidant

When Fans Attack!

It's not easy being a celebrity on campus. Half the students worship Izumi, the other half resent her. And Hikaru's stuck in the middle!

A Shocking Past

After being betrayed and left for broke, Izumi's father attempted to commit suicide but ended up in a coma. Now Izumi has to work as a model to pay off his dad's medical bills.

TENSHI JA NAI!!
I'm No Angel!

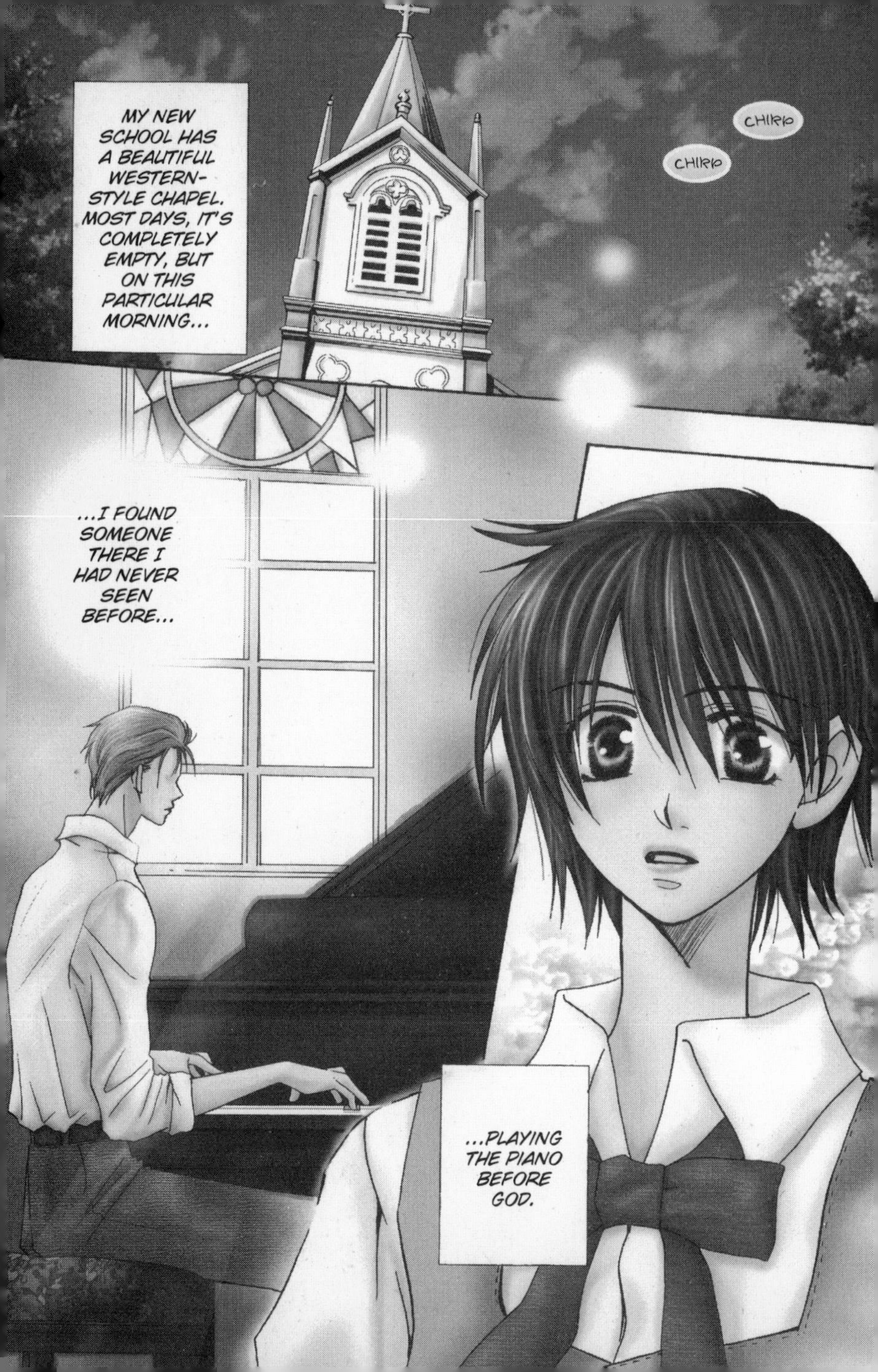
CHIRP
CHIRP
MY NEW SCHOOL HAS A BEAUTIFUL WESTERN-STYLE CHAPEL. MOST DAYS, IT'S COMPLETELY EMPTY, BUT ON THIS PARTICULAR MORNING...
...I FOUND SOMEONE THERE I HAD NEVER SEEN BEFORE...
...PLAYING THE PIANO BEFORE GOD.

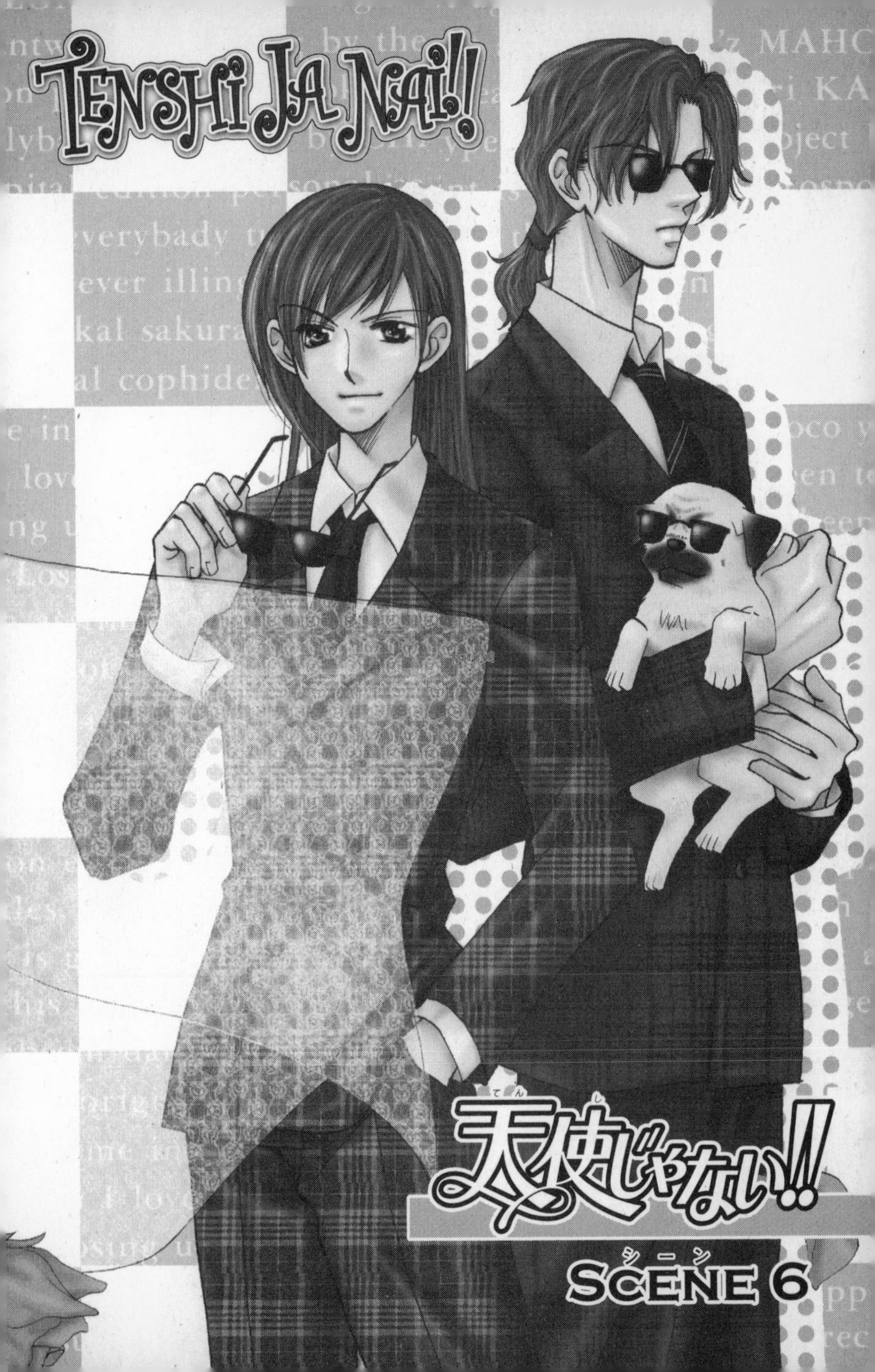
TENSHI JA NAI!!
天使じゃない!!
SCENE 6

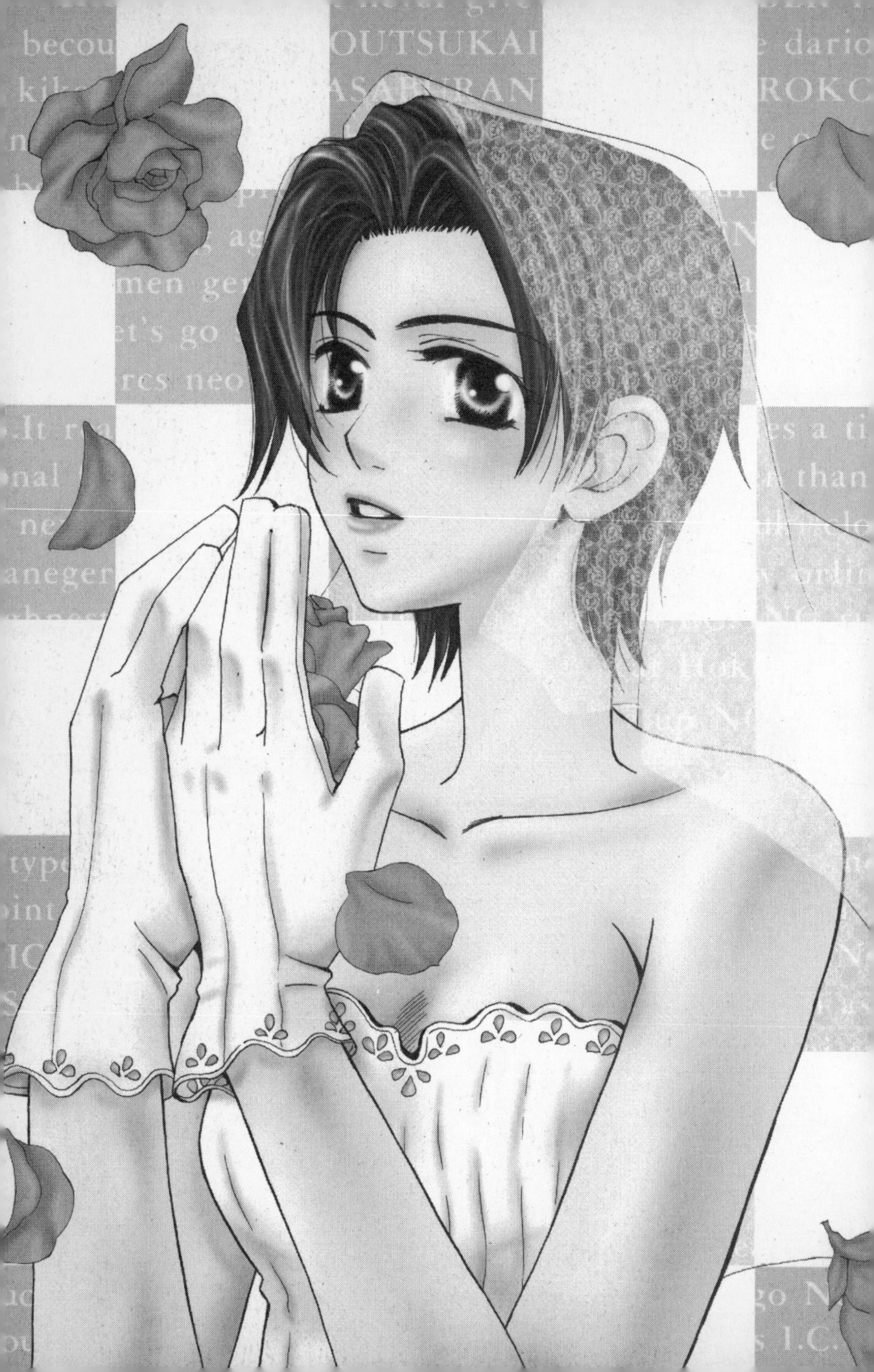

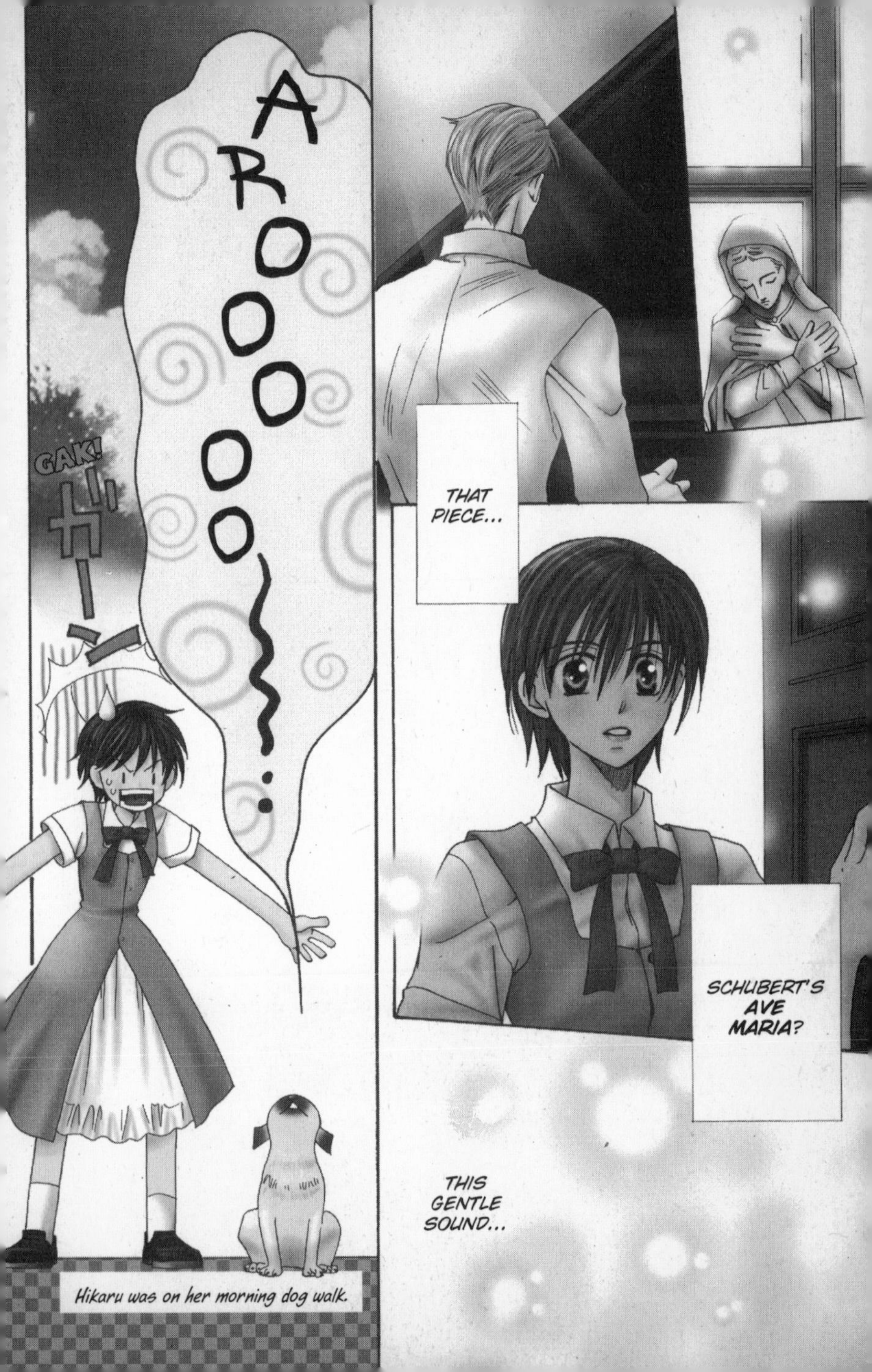
THAT PIECE...
SCHUBERT'S AVE MARIA?
THIS GENTLE SOUND...
AROOOOO~...
GAK!
ガーン
Hikaru was on her morning dog walk.

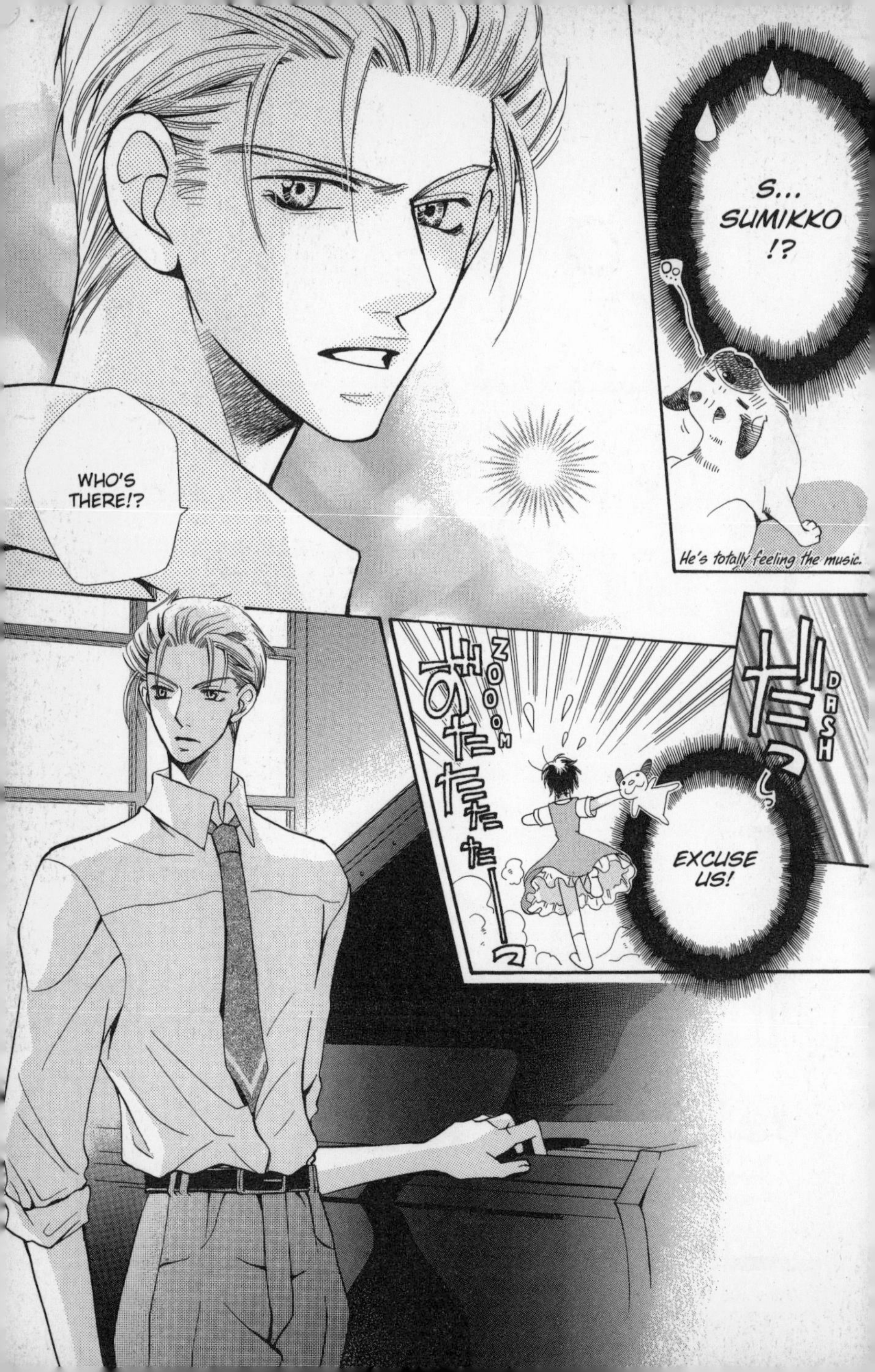

S... SUMIKKO !?
He's totally feeling the music.
WHO'S THERE!?
DASH
EXCUSE US!
ZOOOOM

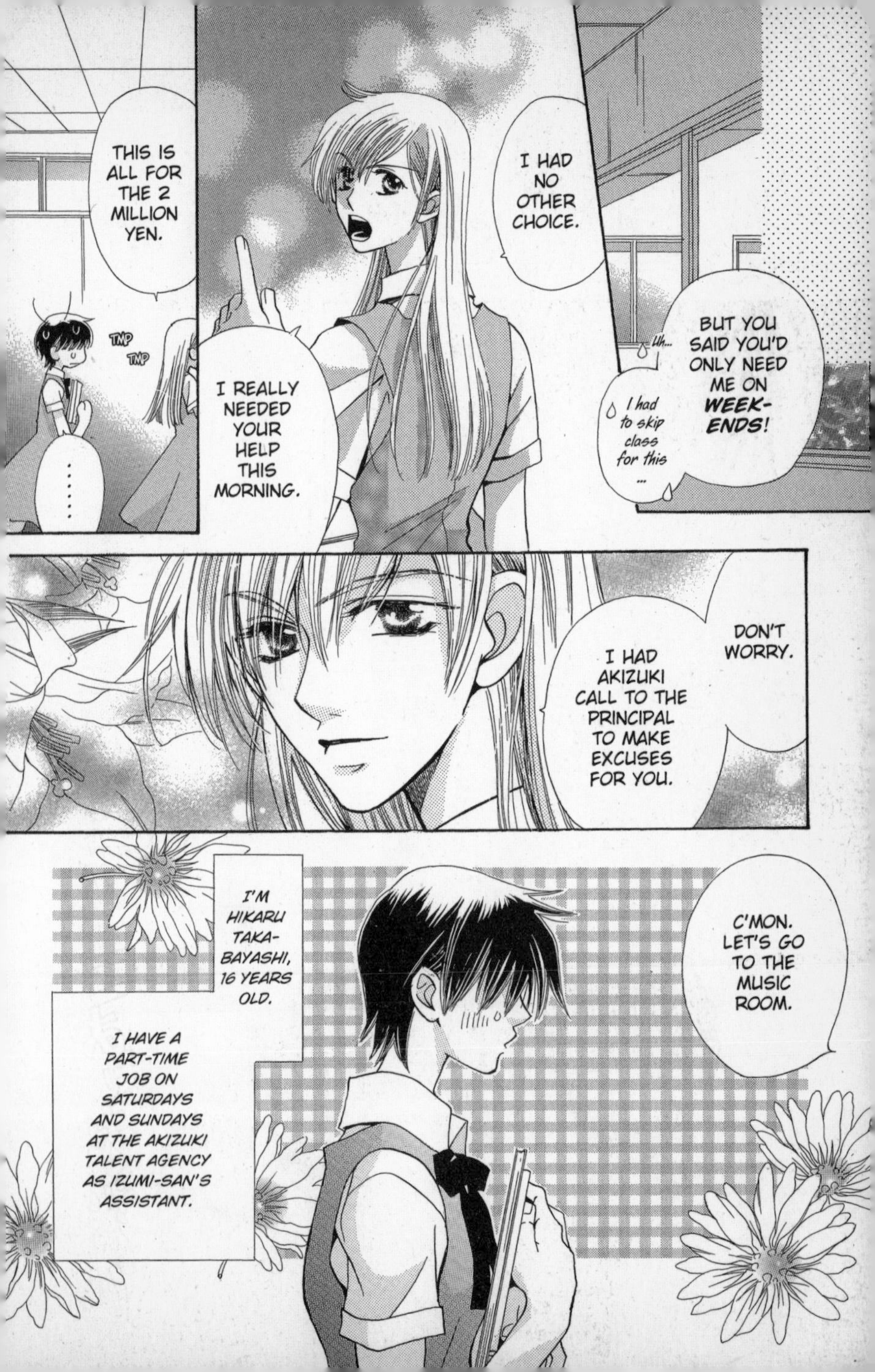
BUT YOU SAID YOU'D ONLY NEED ME ON **WEEK-ENDS**!
Uh...
I had to skip class for this ...
I HAD NO OTHER CHOICE.
I REALLY NEEDED YOUR HELP THIS MORNING.
THIS IS ALL FOR THE 2 MILLION YEN.
TMP
TMP
......
DON'T WORRY.
I HAD AKIZUKI CALL TO THE PRINCIPAL TO MAKE EXCUSES FOR YOU.
C'MON. LET'S GO TO THE MUSIC ROOM.
I'M HIKARU TAKA-BAYASHI, 16 YEARS OLD.
I HAVE A PART-TIME JOB ON SATURDAYS AND SUNDAYS AT THE AKIZUKI TALENT AGENCY AS IZUMI-SAN'S ASSISTANT.

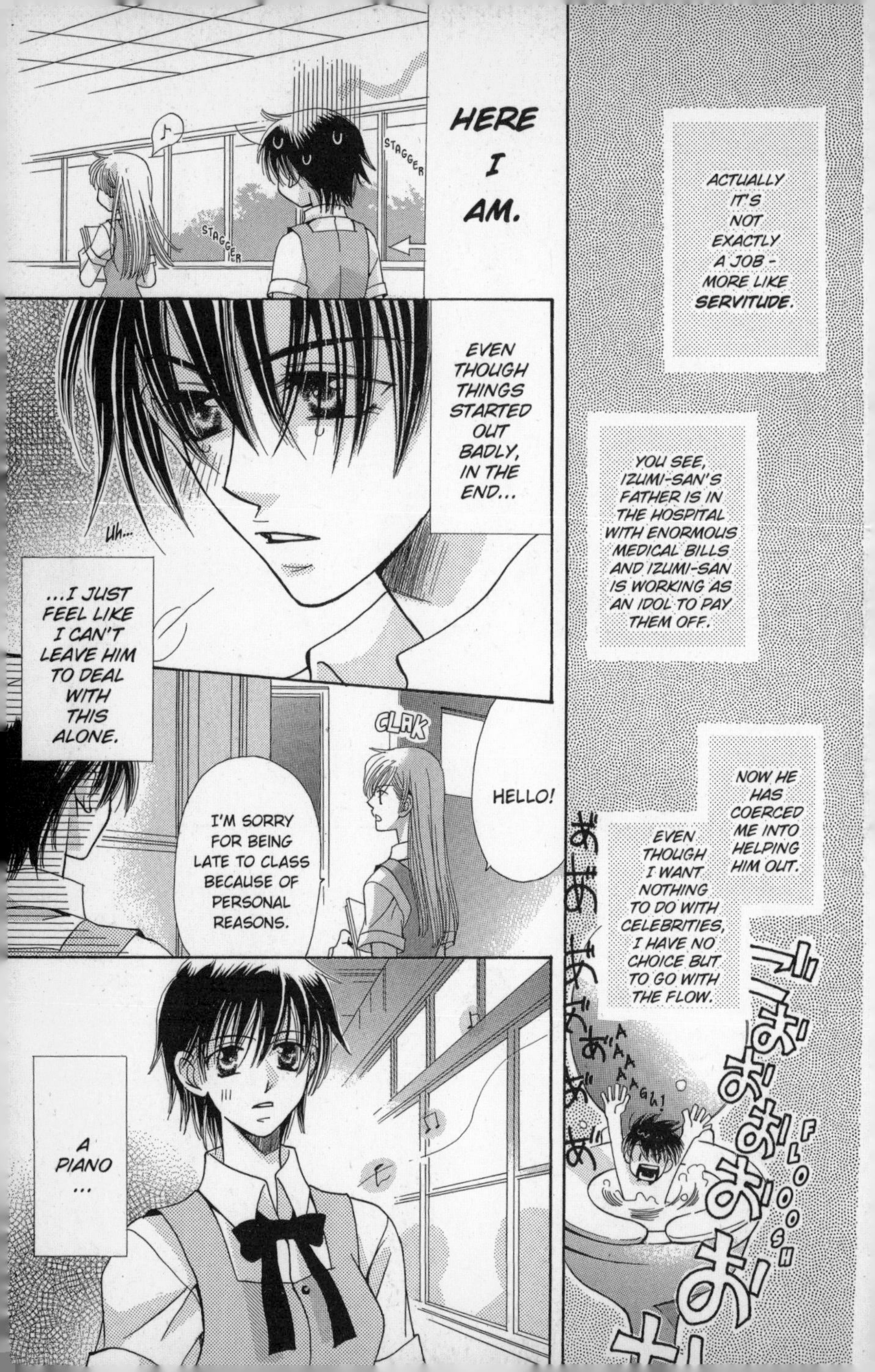
ACTUALLY IT'S NOT EXACTLY A JOB - MORE LIKE SERVITUDE.
YOU SEE, IZUMI-SAN'S FATHER IS IN THE HOSPITAL WITH ENORMOUS MEDICAL BILLS AND IZUMI-SAN IS WORKING AS AN IDOL TO PAY THEM OFF.
NOW HE HAS COERCED ME INTO HELPING HIM OUT.
EVEN THOUGH I WANT NOTHING TO DO WITH CELEBRITIES, I HAVE NO CHOICE BUT TO GO WITH THE FLOW.
AAAARGH!
FLOOOSH
HERE I AM.
STAGGER
STAGGER
♪
EVEN THOUGH THINGS STARTED OUT BADLY, IN THE END...
Uh...
...I JUST FEEL LIKE I CAN'T LEAVE HIM TO DEAL WITH THIS ALONE.
HELLO!
CLAK
I'M SORRY FOR BEING LATE TO CLASS BECAUSE OF PERSONAL REASONS.
A PIANO ...

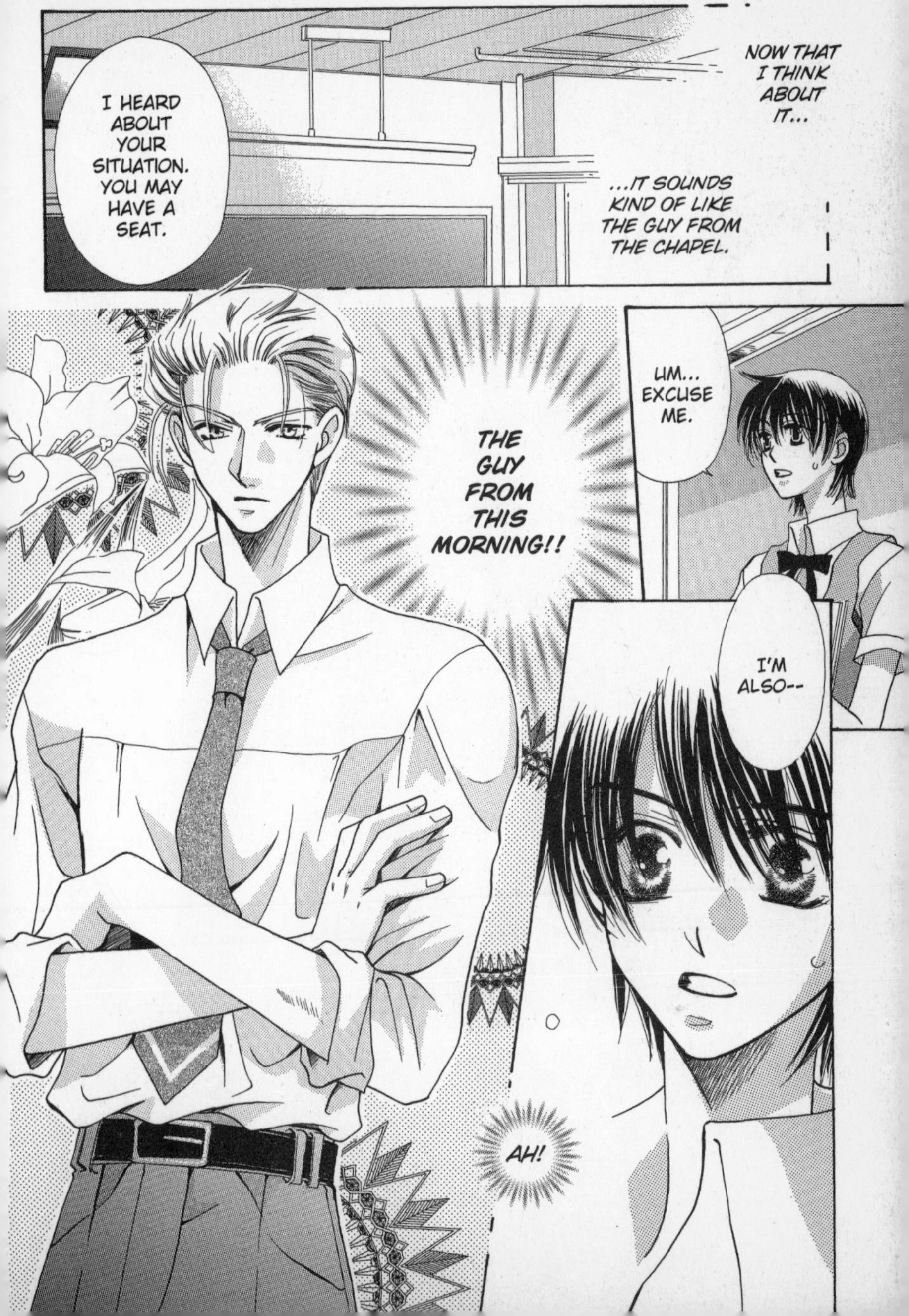
NOW THAT I THINK ABOUT IT...
...IT SOUNDS KIND OF LIKE THE GUY FROM THE CHAPEL.
I HEARD ABOUT YOUR SITUATION. YOU MAY HAVE A SEAT.
UM... EXCUSE ME.
I'M ALSO--
AH!
THE GUY FROM THIS MORNING!!

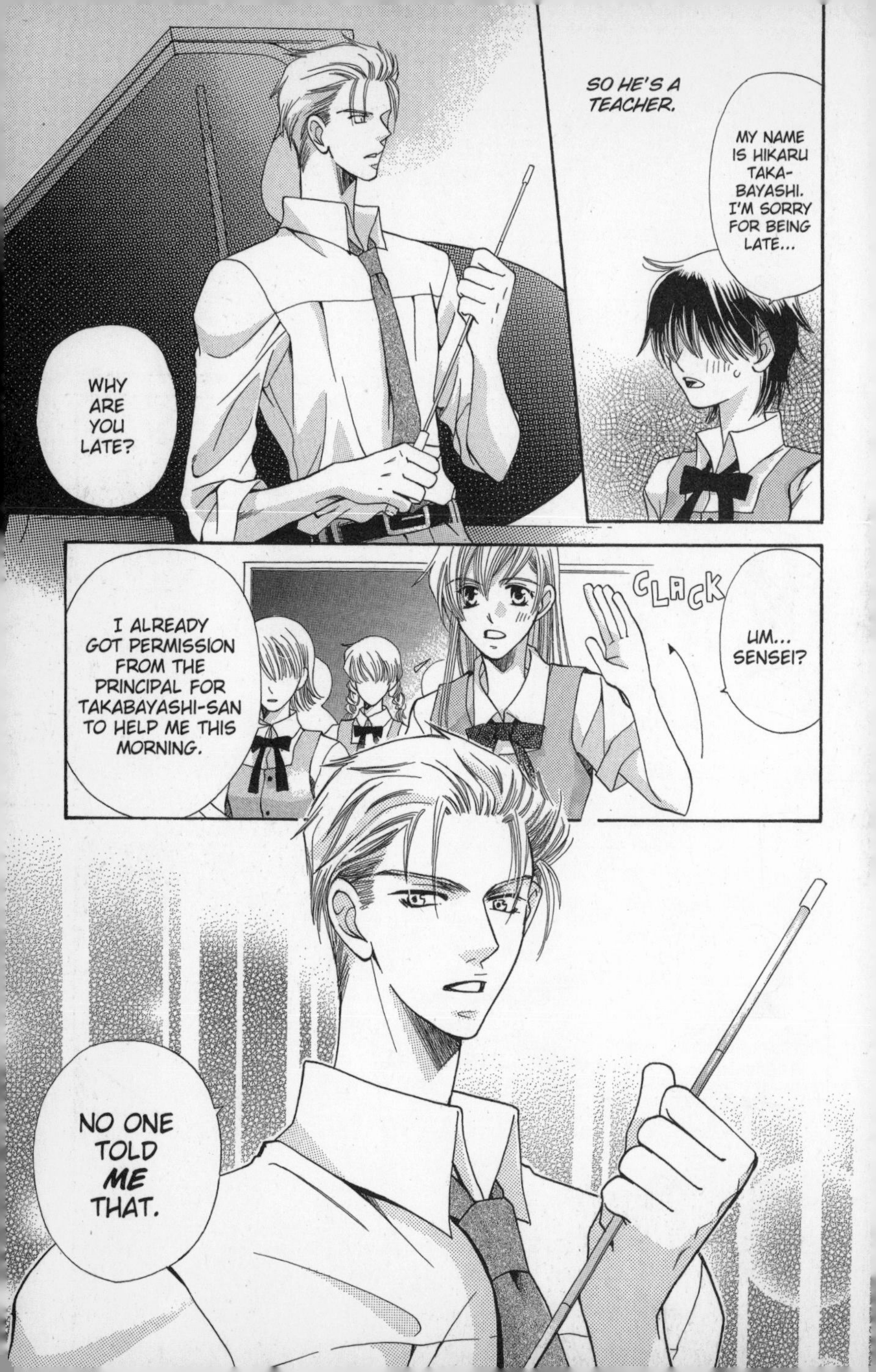
SO HE'S A TEACHER.
MY NAME IS HIKARU TAKA-BAYASHI. I'M SORRY FOR BEING LATE...
WHY ARE YOU LATE?
UM... SENSEI?
CLACK
I ALREADY GOT PERMISSION FROM THE PRINCIPAL FOR TAKABAYASHI-SAN TO HELP ME THIS MORNING.
NO ONE TOLD *ME* THAT.

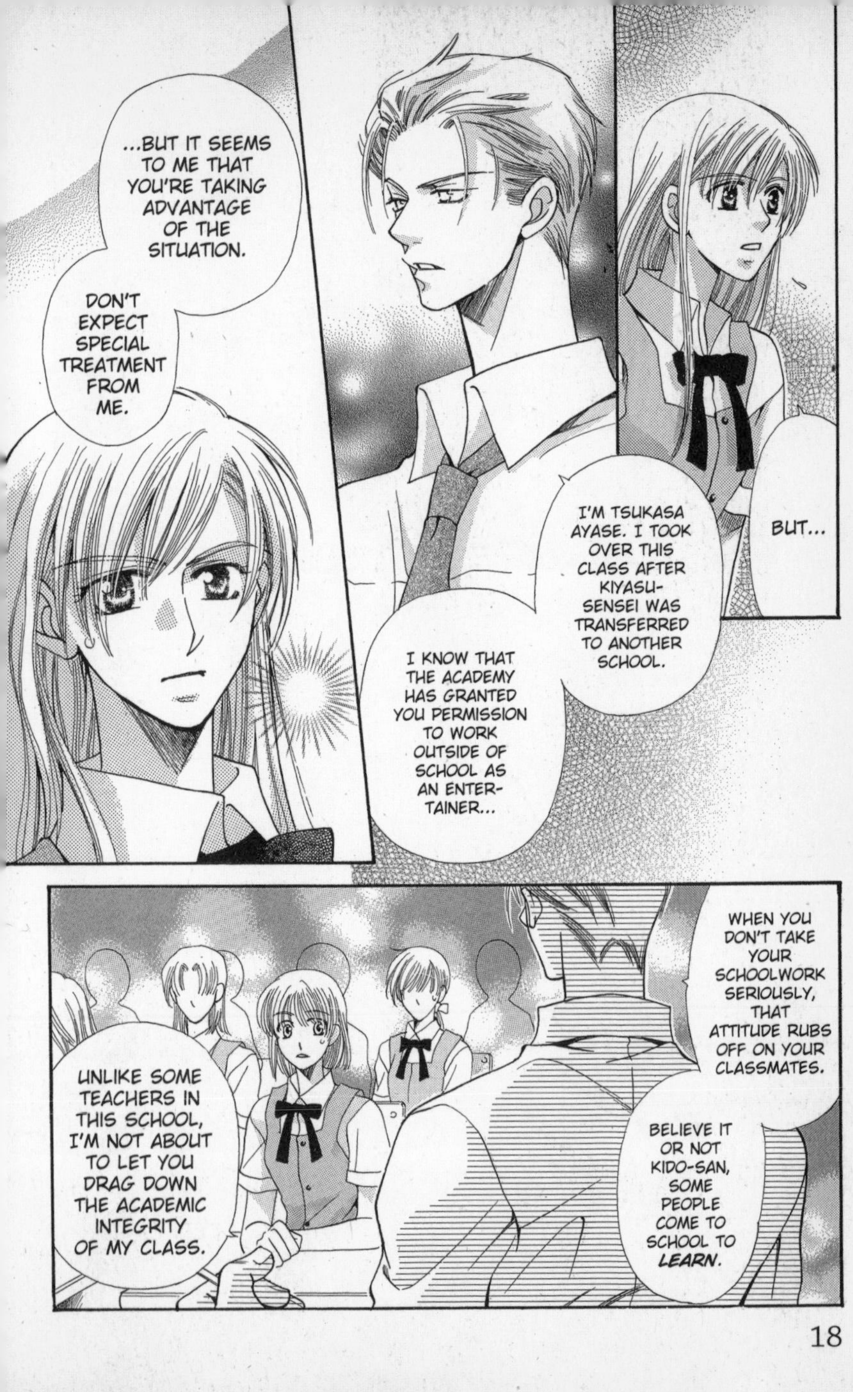
BUT...
I'M TSUKASA AYASE. I TOOK OVER THIS CLASS AFTER KIYASU-SENSEI WAS TRANSFERRED TO ANOTHER SCHOOL.
I KNOW THAT THE ACADEMY HAS GRANTED YOU PERMISSION TO WORK OUTSIDE OF SCHOOL AS AN ENTER-TAINER...
...BUT IT SEEMS TO ME THAT YOU'RE TAKING ADVANTAGE OF THE SITUATION.
DON'T EXPECT SPECIAL TREATMENT FROM ME.
WHEN YOU DON'T TAKE YOUR SCHOOLWORK SERIOUSLY, THAT ATTITUDE RUBS OFF ON YOUR CLASSMATES.
BELIEVE IT OR NOT KIDO-SAN, SOME PEOPLE COME TO SCHOOL TO ***LEARN***.
UNLIKE SOME TEACHERS IN THIS SCHOOL, I'M NOT ABOUT TO LET YOU DRAG DOWN THE ACADEMIC INTEGRITY OF MY CLASS.

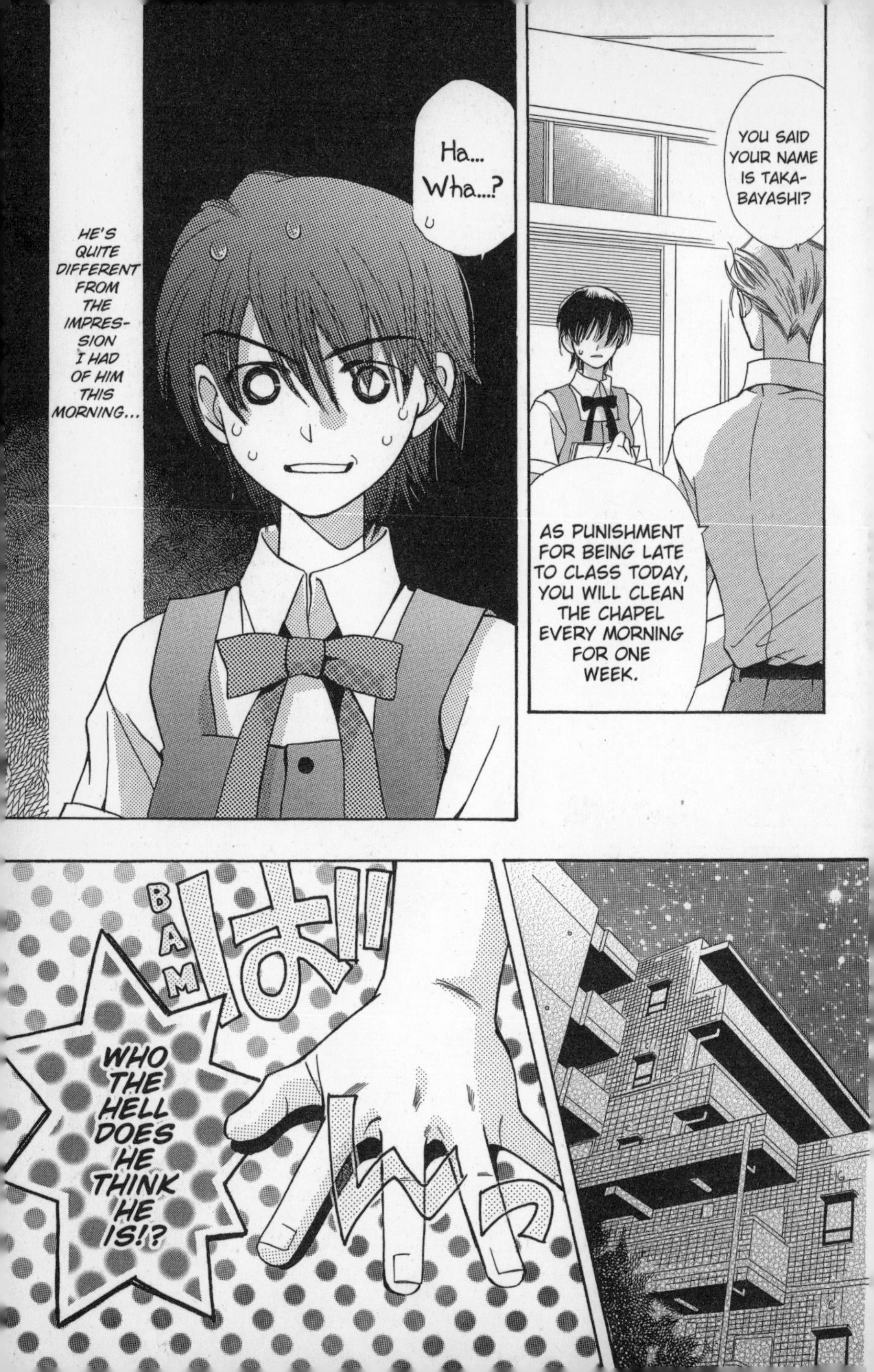
YOU SAID YOUR NAME IS TAKA-BAYASHI?
AS PUNISHMENT FOR BEING LATE TO CLASS TODAY, YOU WILL CLEAN THE CHAPEL EVERY MORNING FOR ONE WEEK.
Ha... Wha...?
HE'S QUITE DIFFERENT FROM THE IMPRES-SION I HAD OF HIM THIS MORNING...
BAM
WHO THE HELL DOES HE THINK HE IS!?

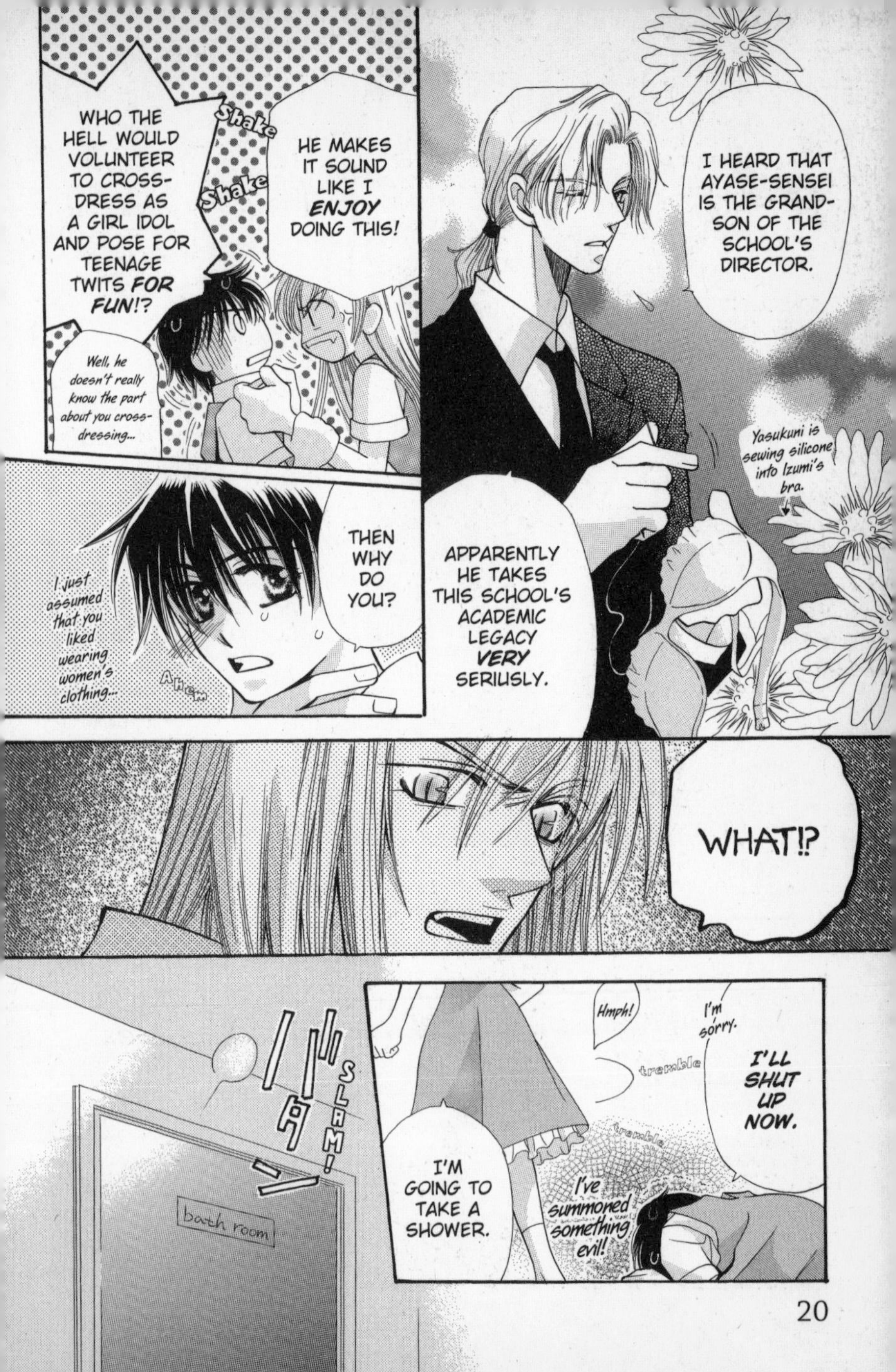
I HEARD THAT AYASE-SENSEI IS THE GRAND-SON OF THE SCHOOL'S DIRECTOR.
APPARENTLY HE TAKES THIS SCHOOL'S ACADEMIC LEGACY VERY SERIUSLY.
Yasukuni is sewing silicone into Izumi's bra.
HE MAKES IT SOUND LIKE I ENJOY DOING THIS!
Shake
Shake
WHO THE HELL WOULD VOLUNTEER TO CROSS-DRESS AS A GIRL IDOL AND POSE FOR TEENAGE TWITS FOR FUN!?
Well, he doesn't really know the part about you cross-dressing...
THEN WHY DO YOU?
I just assumed that you liked wearing women's clothing...
Ahem
WHAT!?
I'm sorry.
I'LL SHUT UP NOW.
Hmph!
tremble
tremble
I've summoned something evil!
I'M GOING TO TAKE A SHOWER.
SLAM!
bath room

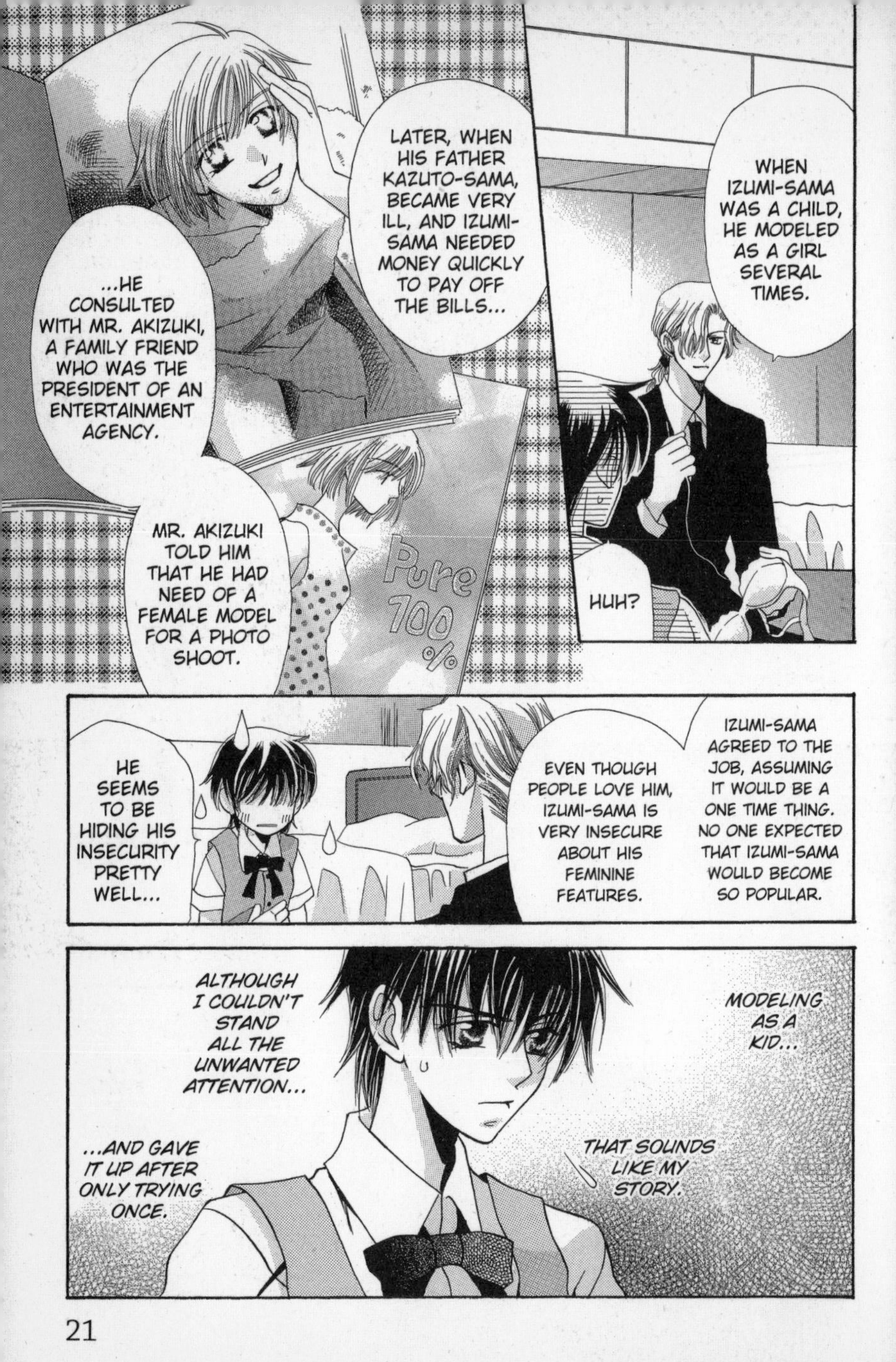
WHEN IZUMI-SAMA WAS A CHILD, HE MODELED AS A GIRL SEVERAL TIMES.
HUH?
LATER, WHEN HIS FATHER KAZUTO-SAMA, BECAME VERY ILL, AND IZUMI-SAMA NEEDED MONEY QUICKLY TO PAY OFF THE BILLS...
...HE CONSULTED WITH MR. AKIZUKI, A FAMILY FRIEND WHO WAS THE PRESIDENT OF AN ENTERTAINMENT AGENCY.
Pure 100%
MR. AKIZUKI TOLD HIM THAT HE HAD NEED OF A FEMALE MODEL FOR A PHOTO SHOOT.
IZUMI-SAMA AGREED TO THE JOB, ASSUMING IT WOULD BE A ONE TIME THING. NO ONE EXPECTED THAT IZUMI-SAMA WOULD BECOME SO POPULAR.
EVEN THOUGH PEOPLE LOVE HIM, IZUMI-SAMA IS VERY INSECURE ABOUT HIS FEMININE FEATURES.
HE SEEMS TO BE HIDING HIS INSECURITY PRETTY WELL...
MODELING AS A KID...
ALTHOUGH I COULDN'T STAND ALL THE UNWANTED ATTENTION...
THAT SOUNDS LIKE MY STORY.
...AND GAVE IT UP AFTER ONLY TRYING ONCE.

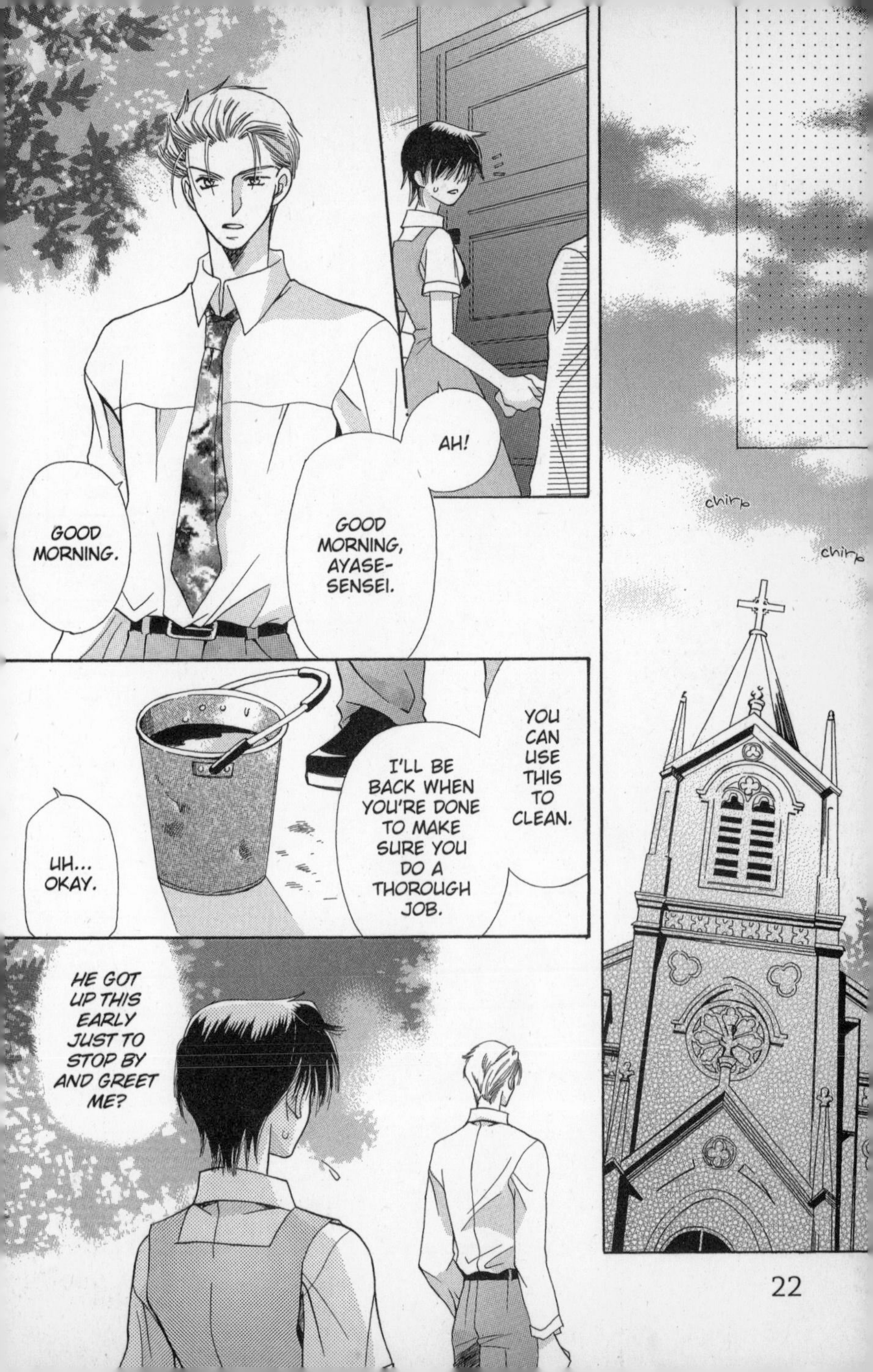
chirp
chirp
AH!
GOOD MORNING, AYASE-SENSEI.
GOOD MORNING.
YOU CAN USE THIS TO CLEAN.
I'LL BE BACK WHEN YOU'RE DONE TO MAKE SURE YOU DO A THOROUGH JOB.
UH... OKAY.
HE GOT UP THIS EARLY JUST TO STOP BY AND GREET ME?

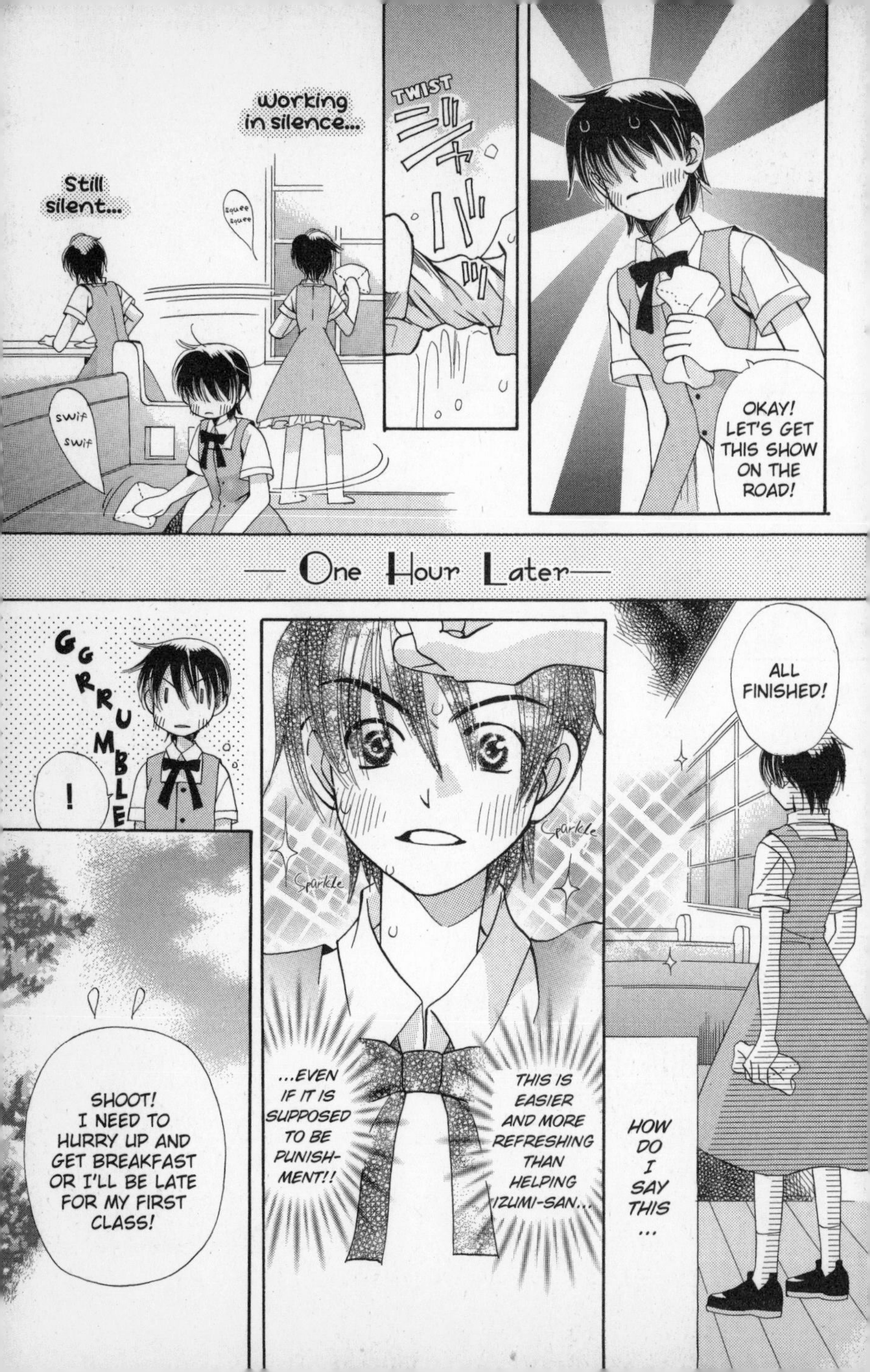
OKAY! LET'S GET THIS SHOW ON THE ROAD!
TWIST
Working in silence...
squee squee
Still silent...
swif swif
One Hour Later
ALL FINISHED!
HOW DO I SAY THIS...
THIS IS EASIER AND MORE REFRESHING THAN HELPING IZUMI-SAN...
...EVEN IF IT IS SUPPOSED TO BE PUNISHMENT!!
Sparkle
Sparkle
GGRRUMBLE
!
SHOOT! I NEED TO HURRY UP AND GET BREAKFAST OR I'LL BE LATE FOR MY FIRST CLASS!

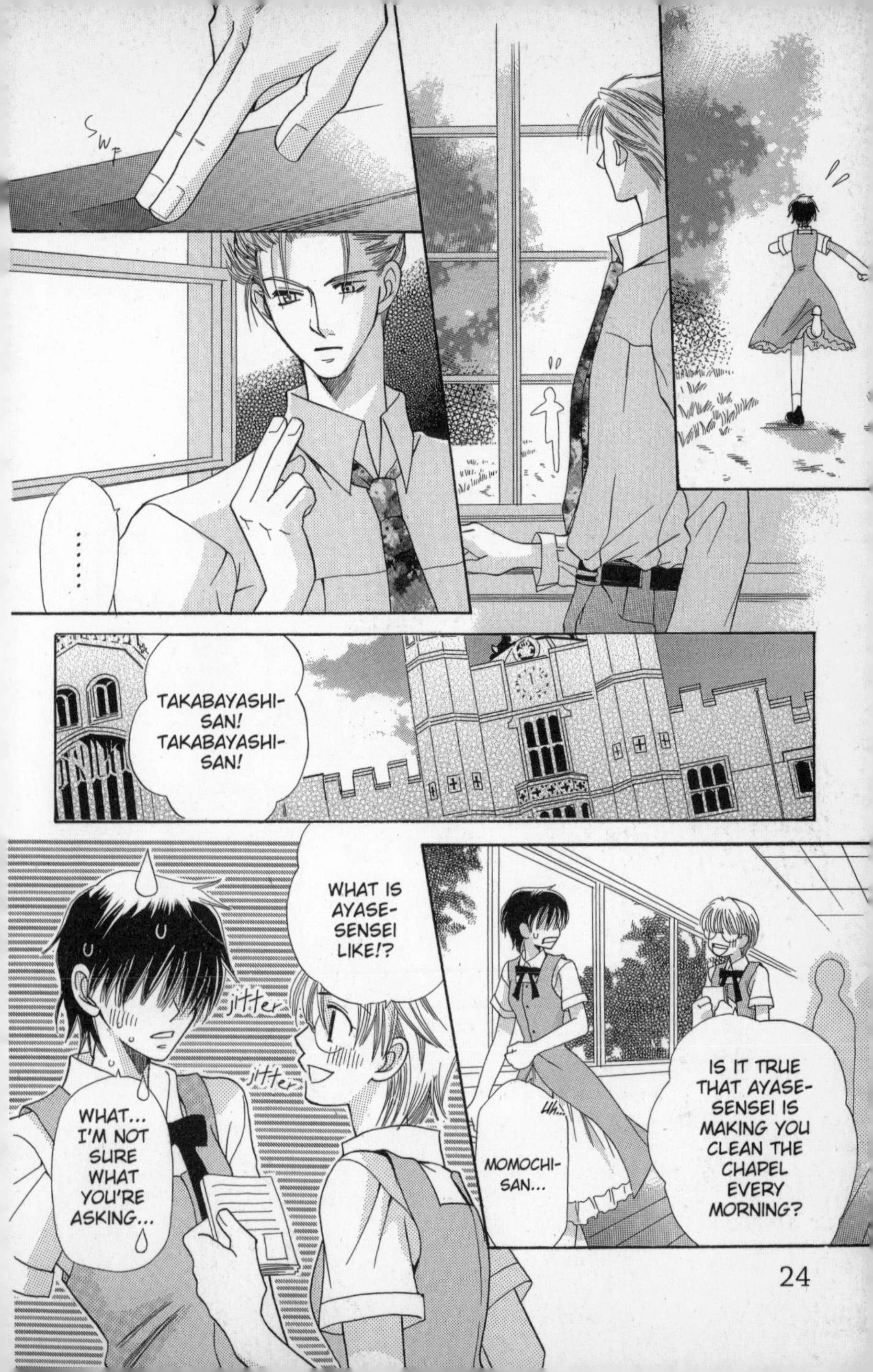
SWF
......
TAKABAYASHI-SAN! TAKABAYASHI-SAN!
IS IT TRUE THAT AYASE-SENSEI IS MAKING YOU CLEAN THE CHAPEL EVERY MORNING?
uh...
MOMOCHI-SAN...
WHAT IS AYASE-SENSEI LIKE!?
jitter
jitter
WHAT... I'M NOT SURE WHAT YOU'RE ASKING...

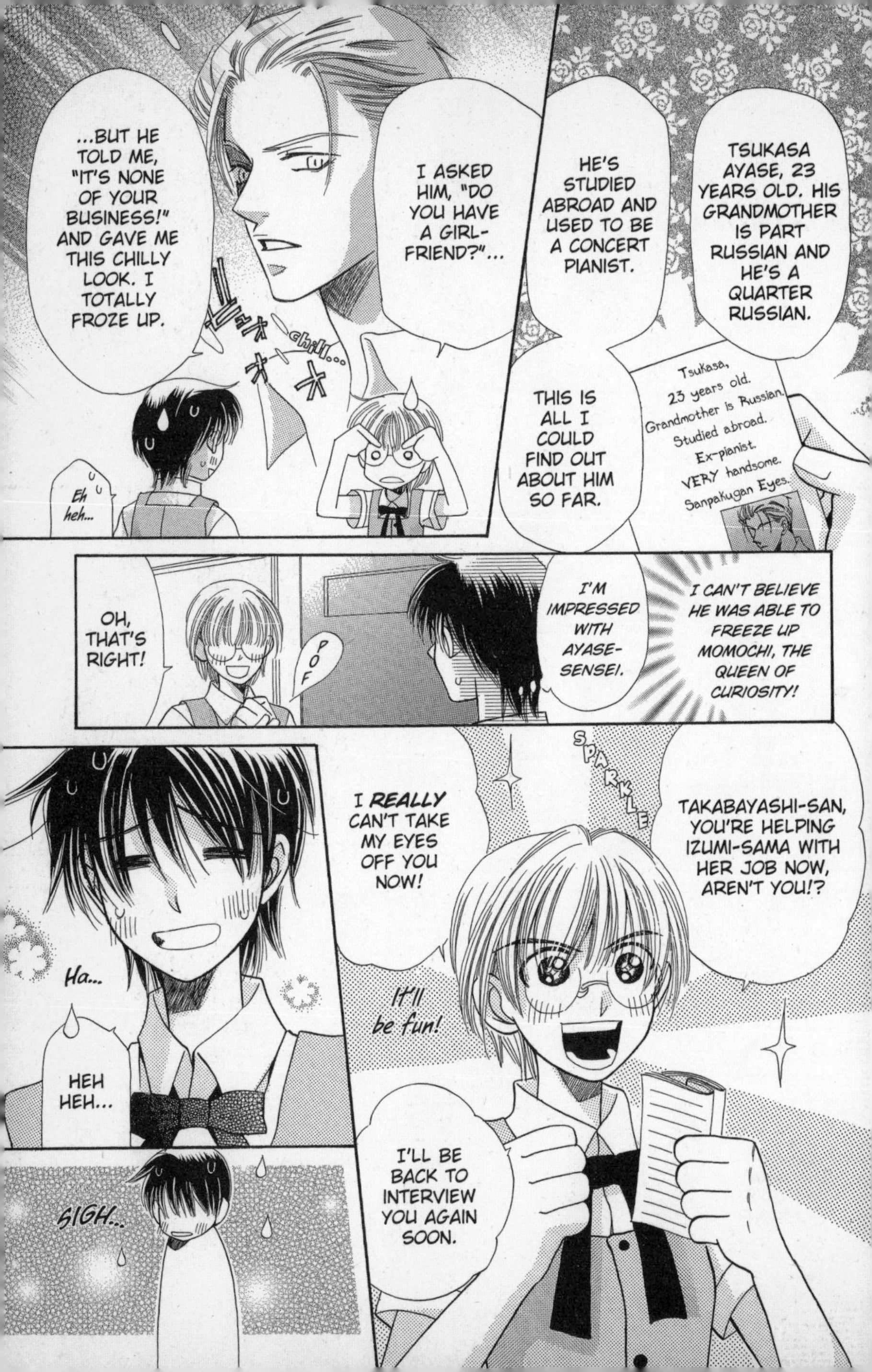
TSUKASA AYASE, 23 YEARS OLD. HIS GRANDMOTHER IS PART RUSSIAN AND HE'S A QUARTER RUSSIAN.
HE'S STUDIED ABROAD AND USED TO BE A CONCERT PIANIST.
Tsukasa, 23 years old. Grandmother is Russian. Studied abroad. Ex-pianist. VERY handsome. Sanpakugan Eyes.
THIS IS ALL I COULD FIND OUT ABOUT HIM SO FAR.
I ASKED HIM, "DO YOU HAVE A GIRL-FRIEND?"...
...BUT HE TOLD ME, "IT'S NONE OF YOUR BUSINESS!" AND GAVE ME THIS CHILLY LOOK. I TOTALLY FROZE UP.
chill...
Eh heh...
I CAN'T BELIEVE HE WAS ABLE TO FREEZE UP MOMOCHI, THE QUEEN OF CURIOSITY!
I'M IMPRESSED WITH AYASE-SENSEI.
POF
OH, THAT'S RIGHT!
TAKABAYASHI-SAN, YOU'RE HELPING IZUMI-SAMA WITH HER JOB NOW, AREN'T YOU!?
SPARKLE
I REALLY CAN'T TAKE MY EYES OFF YOU NOW!
It'll be fun!
I'LL BE BACK TO INTERVIEW YOU AGAIN SOON.
Ha...
HEH HEH...
SIGH...

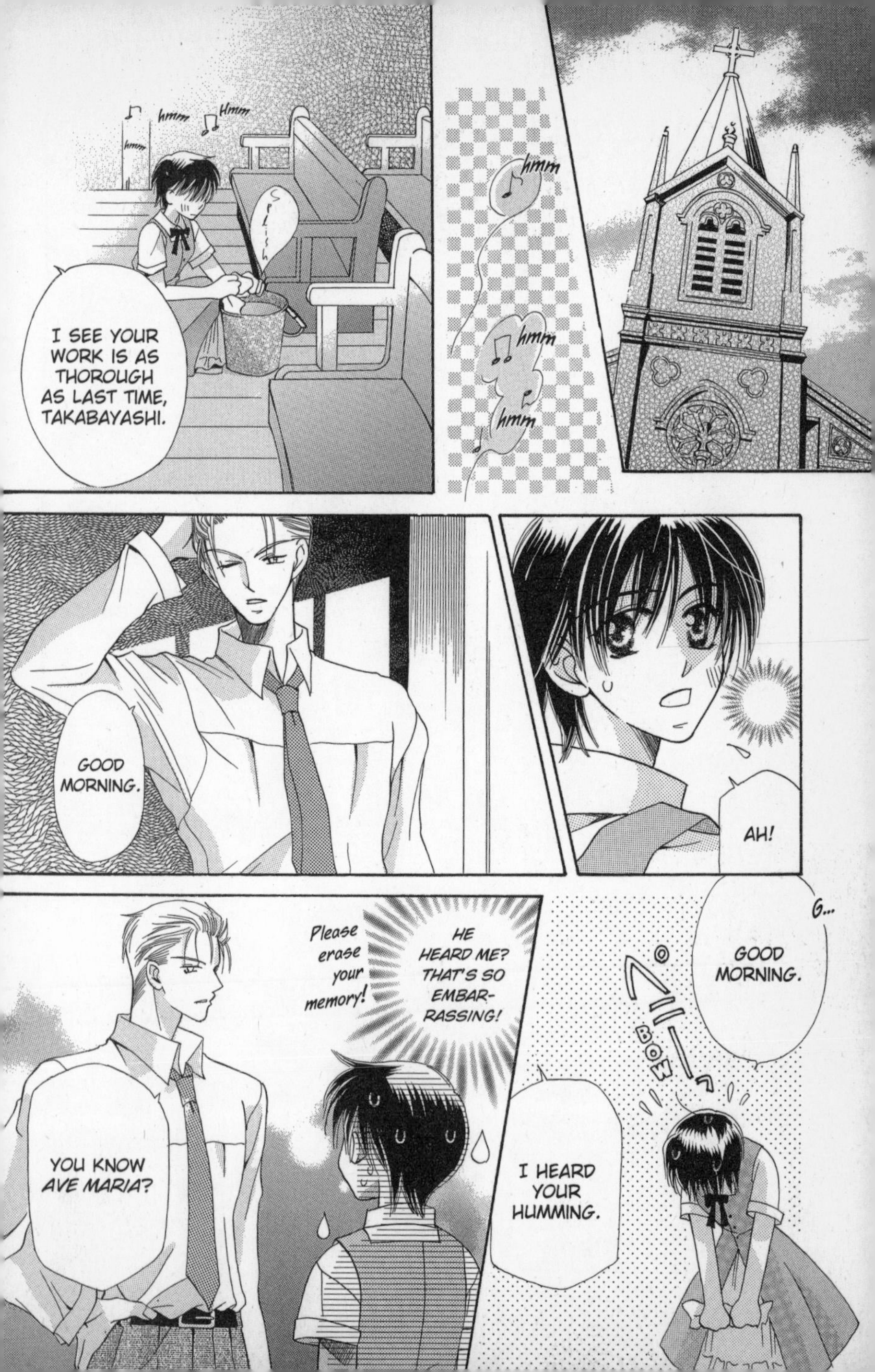
hmm
hmm
hmm
hmm
hmm
Hmm
splish
I SEE YOUR WORK IS AS THOROUGH AS LAST TIME, TAKABAYASHI.
AH!
GOOD MORNING.
G...
GOOD MORNING.
BOW
I HEARD YOUR HUMMING.
HE HEARD ME? THAT'S SO EMBARRASSING!
Please erase your memory!
YOU KNOW AVE MARIA?

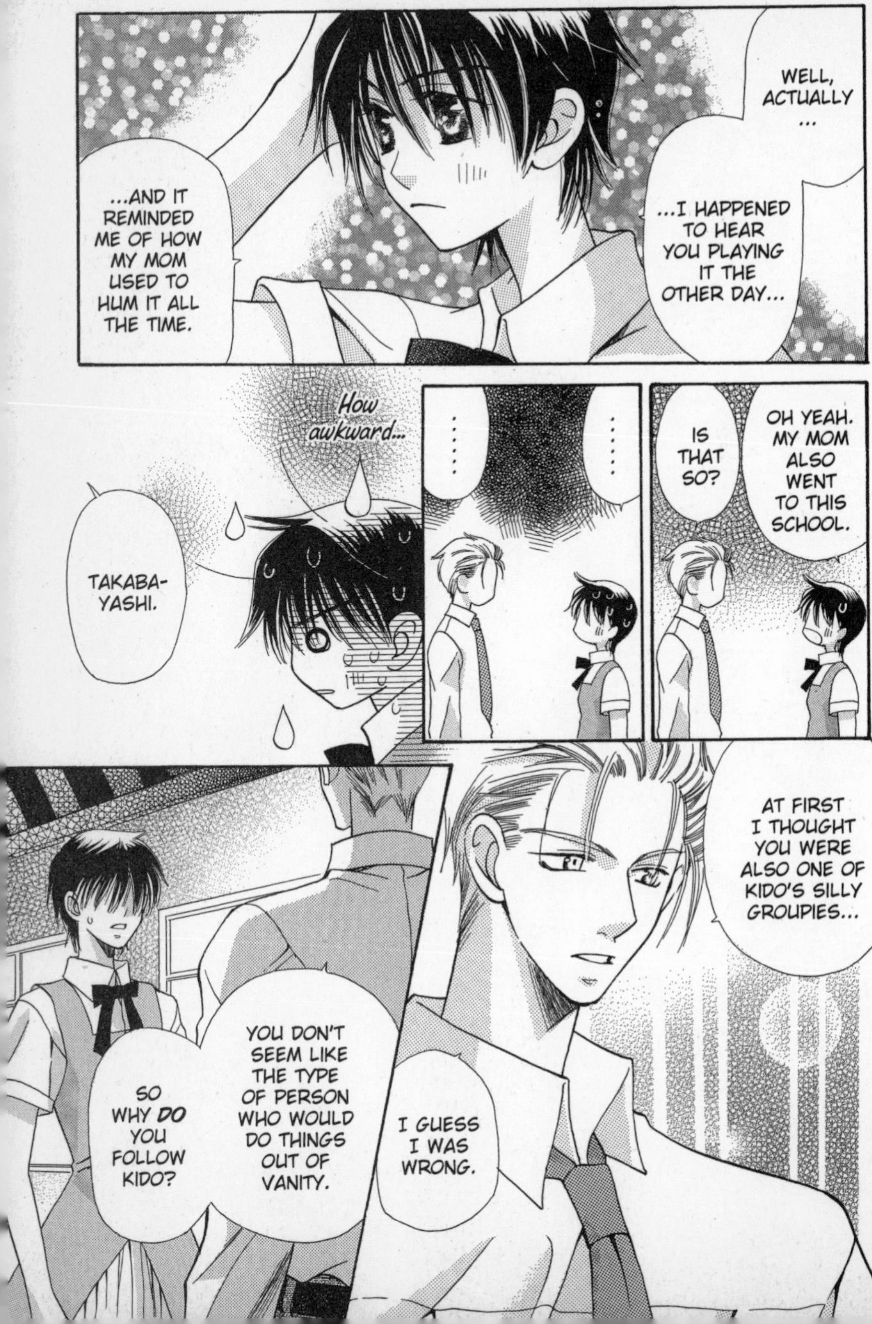
WELL, ACTUALLY ...
...I HAPPENED TO HEAR YOU PLAYING IT THE OTHER DAY...
...AND IT REMINDED ME OF HOW MY MOM USED TO HUM IT ALL THE TIME.
OH YEAH. MY MOM ALSO WENT TO THIS SCHOOL.
IS THAT SO?
......
......
How awkward...
TAKABA-YASHI.
AT FIRST I THOUGHT YOU WERE ALSO ONE OF KIDO'S SILLY GROUPIES...
I GUESS I WAS WRONG.
YOU DON'T SEEM LIKE THE TYPE OF PERSON WHO WOULD DO THINGS OUT OF VANITY.
SO WHY *DO* YOU FOLLOW KIDO?

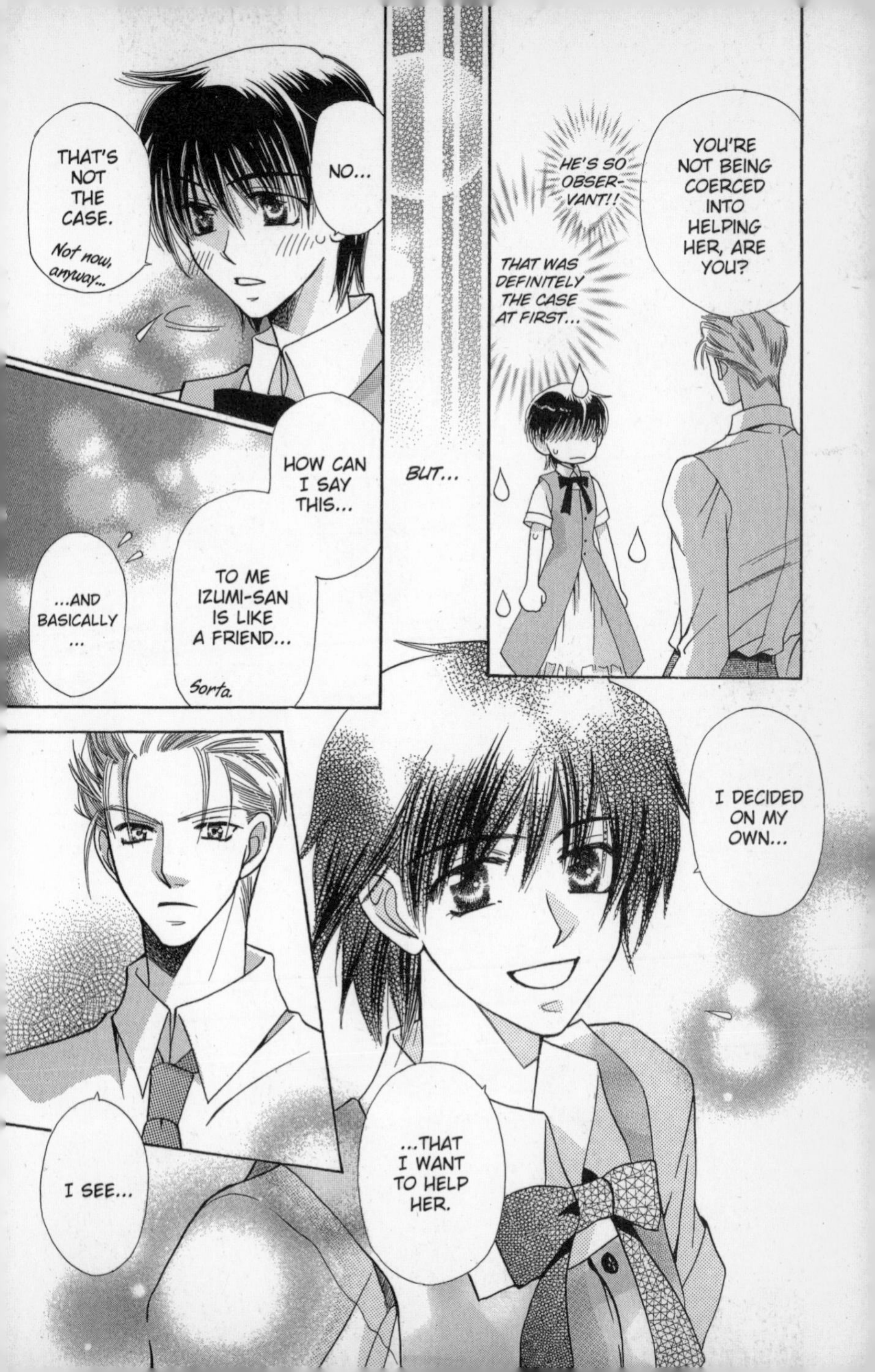

YOU'RE NOT BEING COERCED INTO HELPING HER, ARE YOU?
HE'S SO OBSERVANT!!
THAT WAS DEFINITELY THE CASE AT FIRST...
BUT...
NO...
THAT'S NOT THE CASE.
Not now, anyway...
HOW CAN I SAY THIS...
TO ME IZUMI-SAN IS LIKE A FRIEND...
Sorta.
...AND BASICALLY ...
I DECIDED ON MY OWN...
...THAT I WANT TO HELP HER.
I SEE...

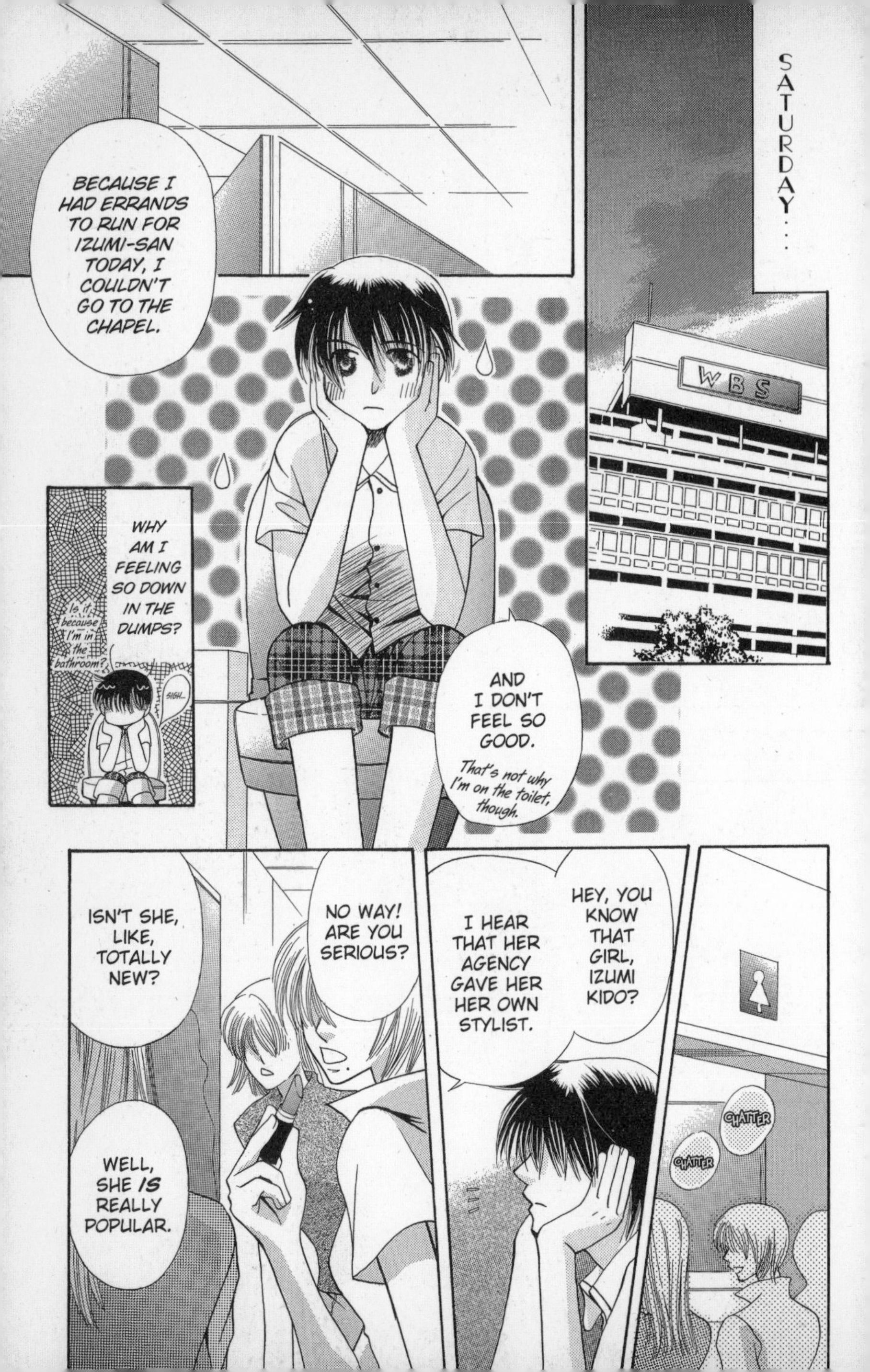
SATURDAY...
BECAUSE I HAD ERRANDS TO RUN FOR IZUMI-SAN TODAY, I COULDN'T GO TO THE CHAPEL.
AND I DON'T FEEL SO GOOD.
That's not why I'm on the toilet, though.
WHY AM I FEELING SO DOWN IN THE DUMPS?
Is it because I'm in the bathroom?
SIGH...
CHATTER
CHATTER
HEY, YOU KNOW THAT GIRL, IZUMI KIDO?
I HEAR THAT HER AGENCY GAVE HER HER OWN STYLIST.
NO WAY! ARE YOU SERIOUS?
ISN'T SHE, LIKE, TOTALLY NEW?
WELL, SHE IS REALLY POPULAR.

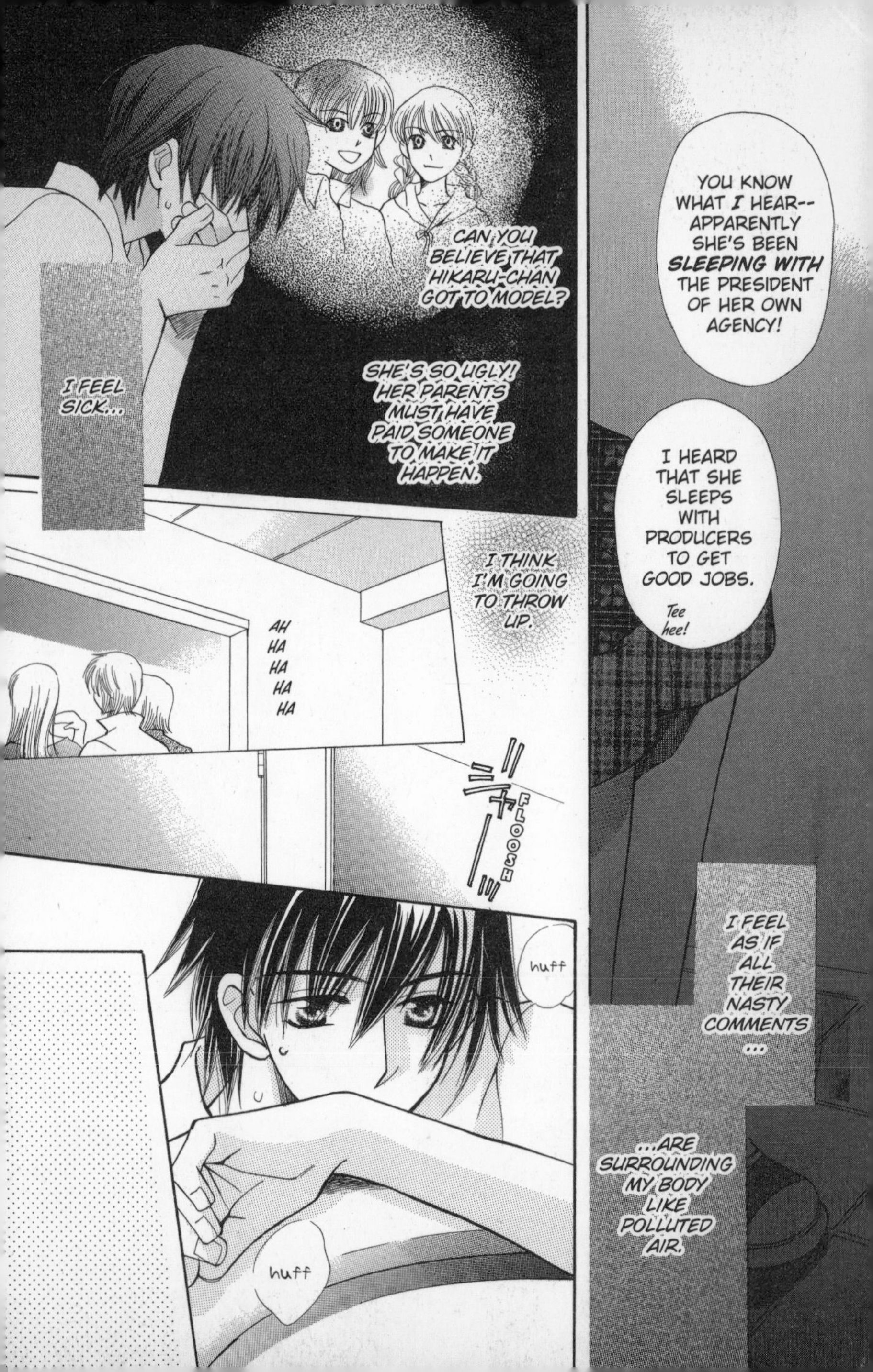
YOU KNOW WHAT I HEAR-- APPARENTLY SHE'S BEEN SLEEPING WITH THE PRESIDENT OF HER OWN AGENCY!
I HEARD THAT SHE SLEEPS WITH PRODUCERS TO GET GOOD JOBS.
Tee hee!
I FEEL AS IF ALL THEIR NASTY COMMENTS...
...ARE SURROUNDING MY BODY LIKE POLLUTED AIR.
CAN YOU BELIEVE THAT HIKARU-CHAN GOT TO MODEL?
SHE'S SO UGLY! HER PARENTS MUST HAVE PAID SOMEONE TO MAKE IT HAPPEN.
I FEEL SICK...
I THINK I'M GOING TO THROW UP.
AH HA HA HA HA
FLOOSH
huff
huff

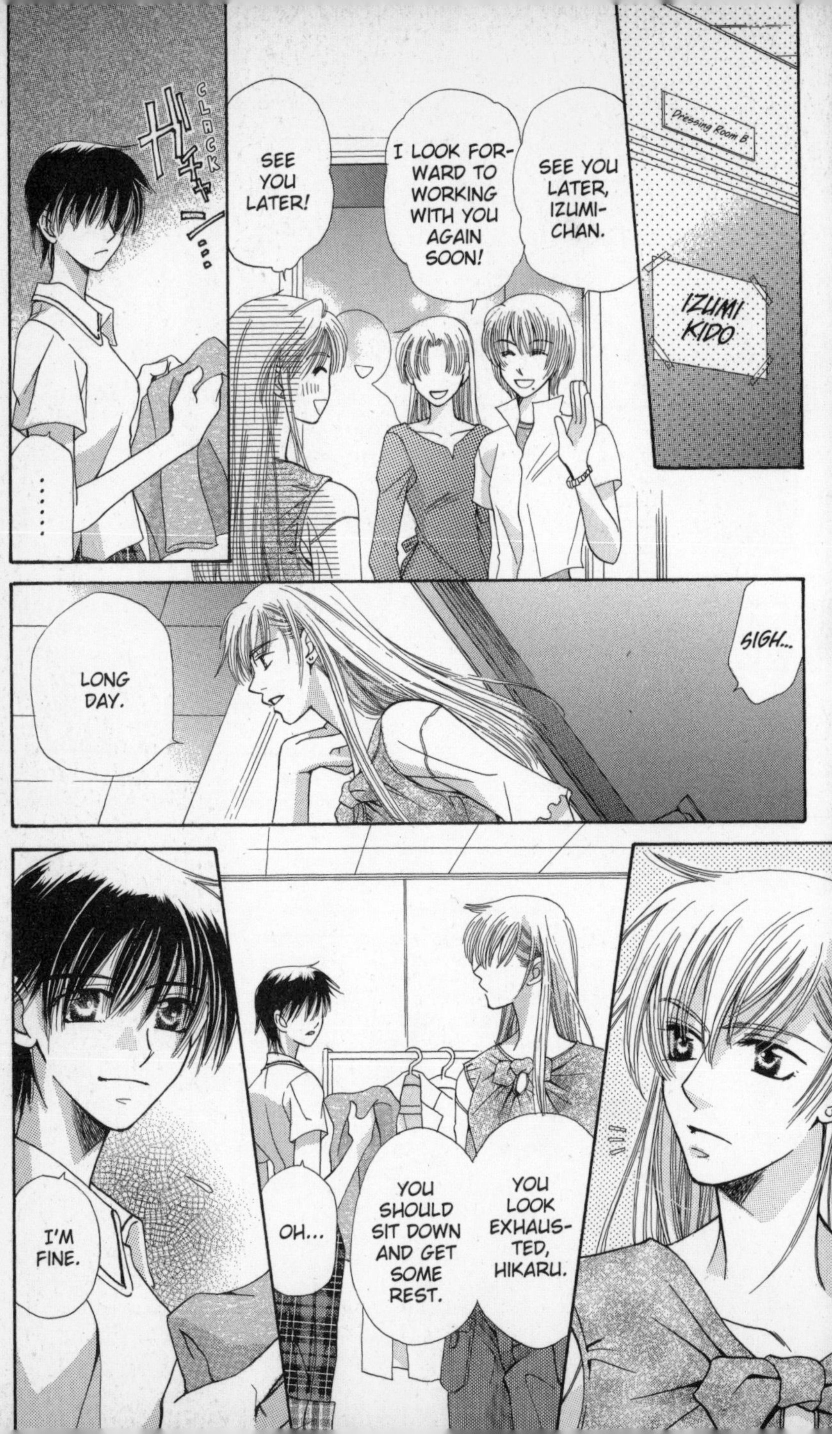
Dressing Room B
IZUMI KIDO
SEE YOU LATER, IZUMI-CHAN.
I LOOK FORWARD TO WORKING WITH YOU AGAIN SOON!
SEE YOU LATER!
CLACK
......
SIGH...
LONG DAY.
YOU LOOK EXHAUSTED, HIKARU.
YOU SHOULD SIT DOWN AND GET SOME REST.
OH...
I'M FINE.

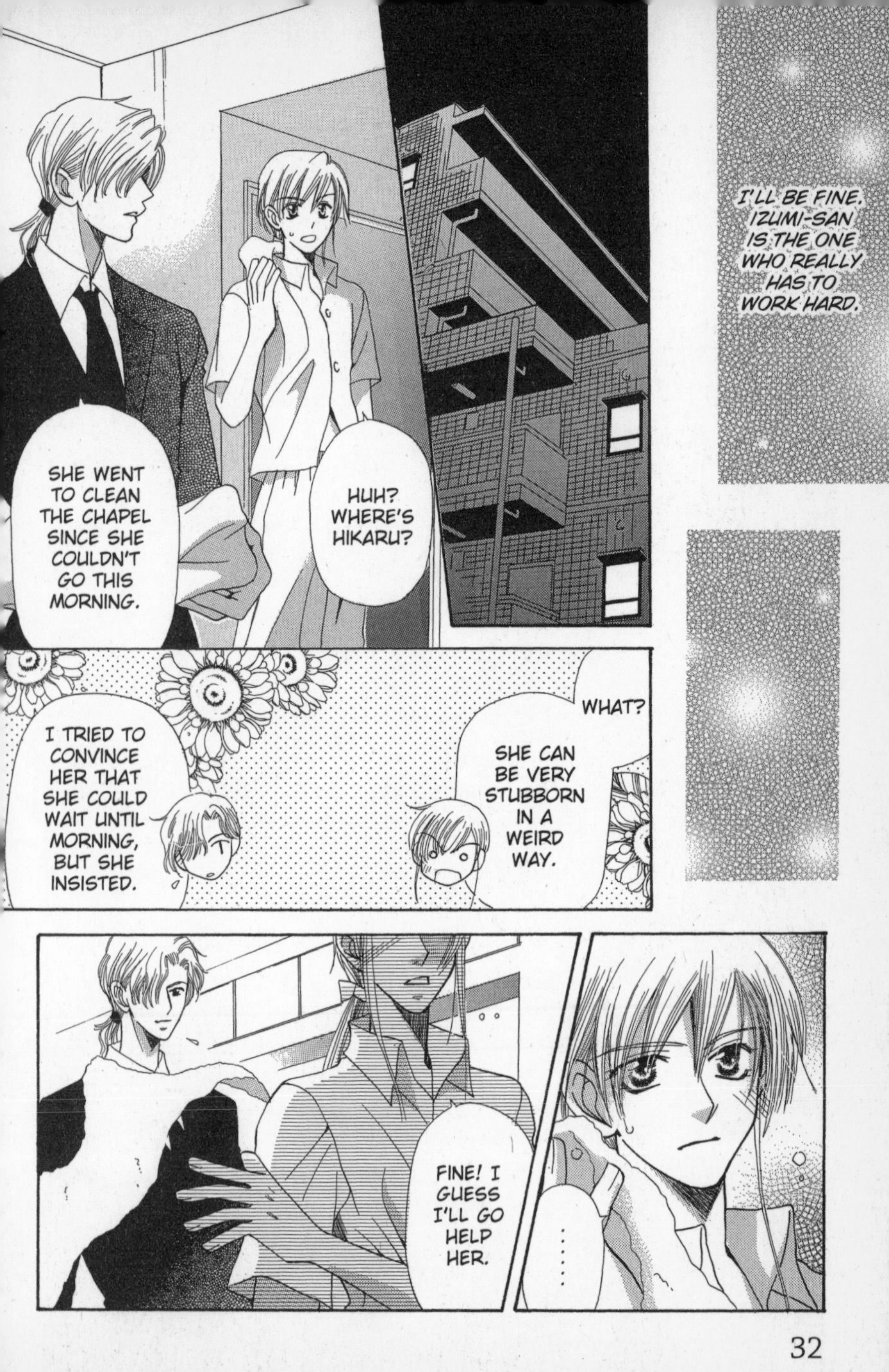
I'LL BE FINE. IZUMI-SAN IS THE ONE WHO REALLY HAS TO WORK HARD.
HUH? WHERE'S HIKARU?
SHE WENT TO CLEAN THE CHAPEL SINCE SHE COULDN'T GO THIS MORNING.
WHAT?
SHE CAN BE VERY STUBBORN IN A WEIRD WAY.
I TRIED TO CONVINCE HER THAT SHE COULD WAIT UNTIL MORNING, BUT SHE INSISTED.
......
FINE! I GUESS I'LL GO HELP HER.

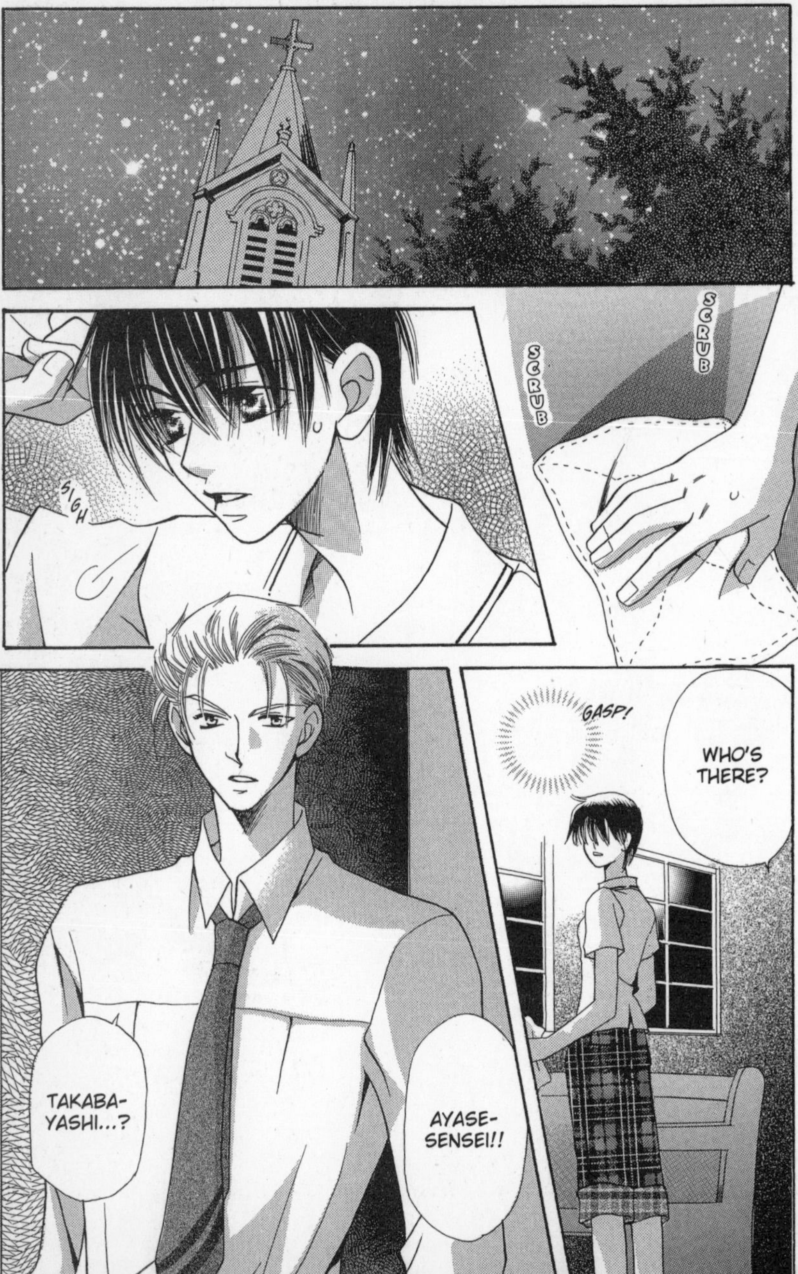
SCRUB
SCRUB
SIGH
GASP!
WHO'S THERE?
AYASE-SENSEI!!
TAKABA-YASHI...?

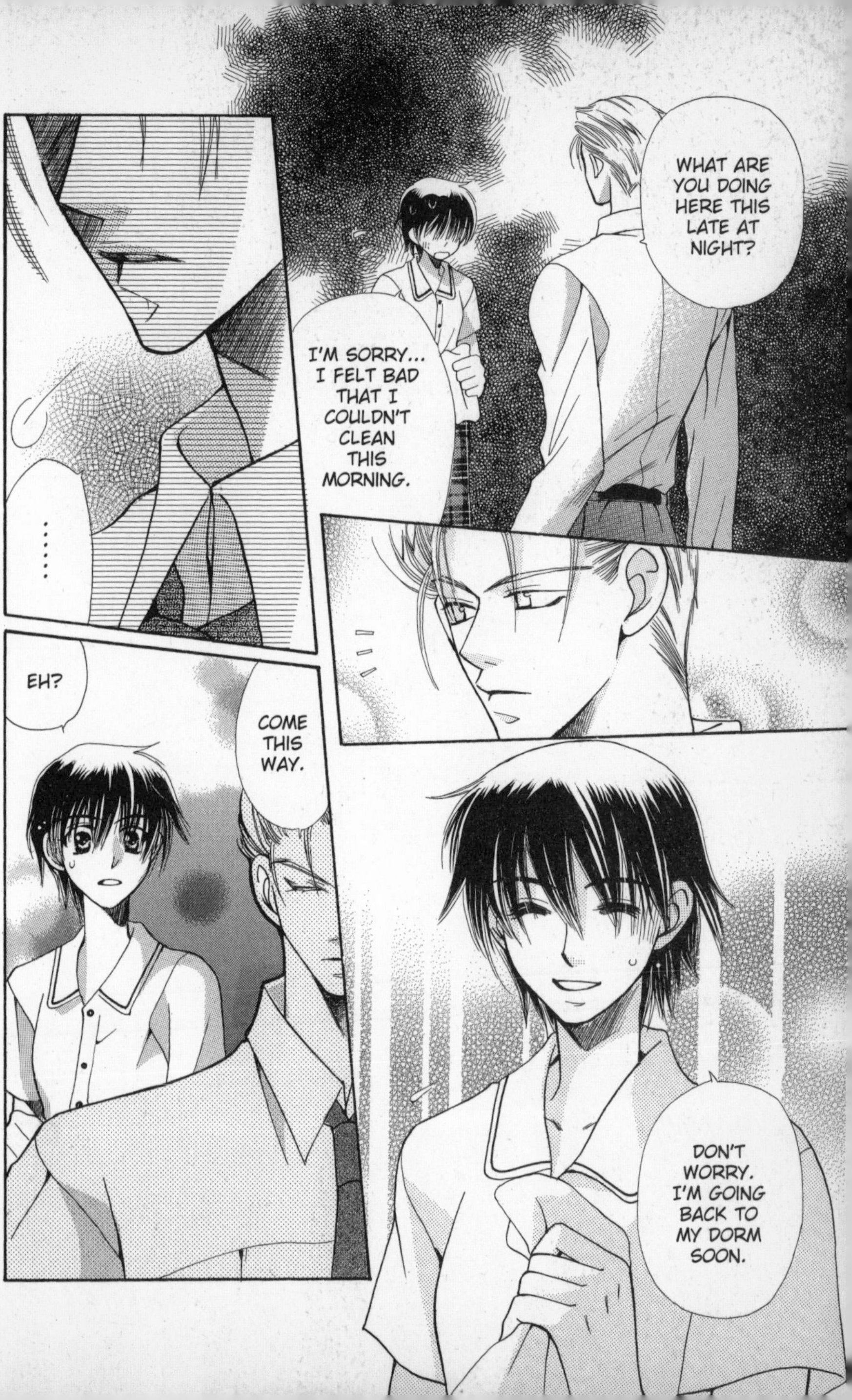
WHAT ARE YOU DOING HERE THIS LATE AT NIGHT?
I'M SORRY... I FELT BAD THAT I COULDN'T CLEAN THIS MORNING.
......
DON'T WORRY. I'M GOING BACK TO MY DORM SOON.
COME THIS WAY.
EH?

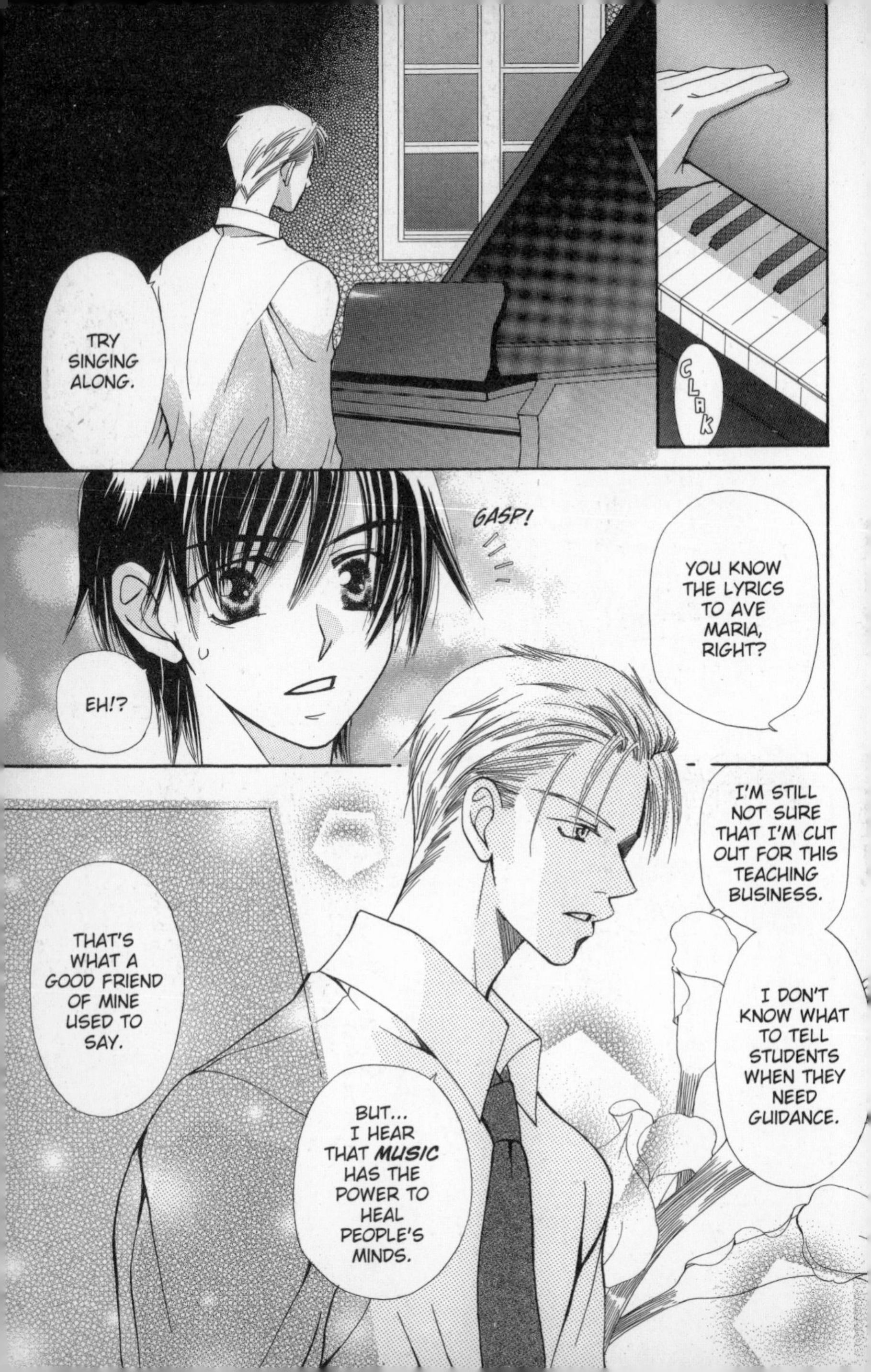
CLAK
TRY SINGING ALONG.
YOU KNOW THE LYRICS TO AVE MARIA, RIGHT?
GASP!
EH!?
I'M STILL NOT SURE THAT I'M CUT OUT FOR THIS TEACHING BUSINESS.
I DON'T KNOW WHAT TO TELL STUDENTS WHEN THEY NEED GUIDANCE.
BUT... I HEAR THAT *MUSIC* HAS THE POWER TO HEAL PEOPLE'S MINDS.
THAT'S WHAT A GOOD FRIEND OF MINE USED TO SAY.

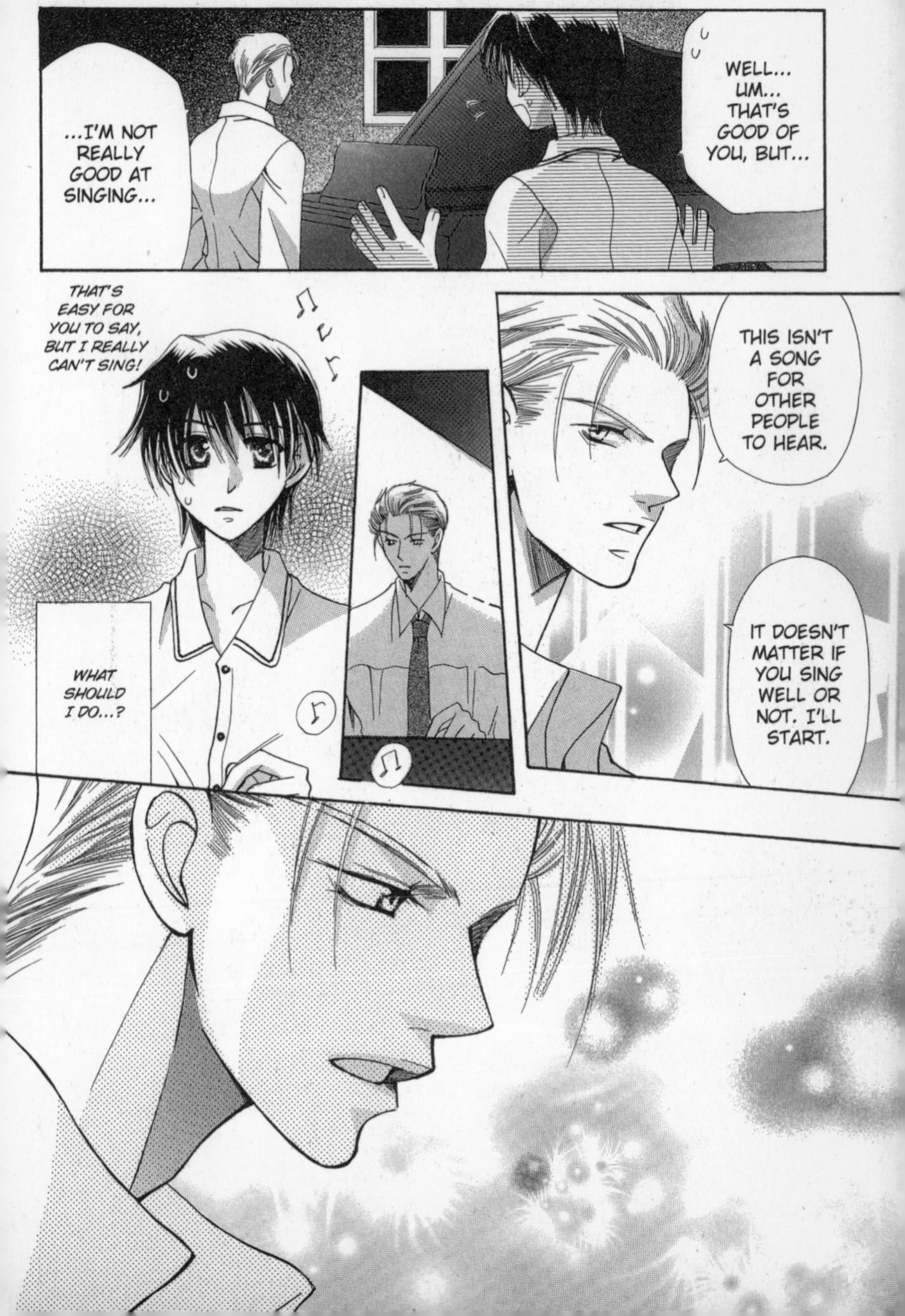
WELL... UM... THAT'S GOOD OF YOU, BUT...
...I'M NOT REALLY GOOD AT SINGING...
THIS ISN'T A SONG FOR OTHER PEOPLE TO HEAR.
IT DOESN'T MATTER IF YOU SING WELL OR NOT. I'LL START.
THAT'S EASY FOR YOU TO SAY, BUT I REALLY CAN'T SING!
WHAT SHOULD I DO...?

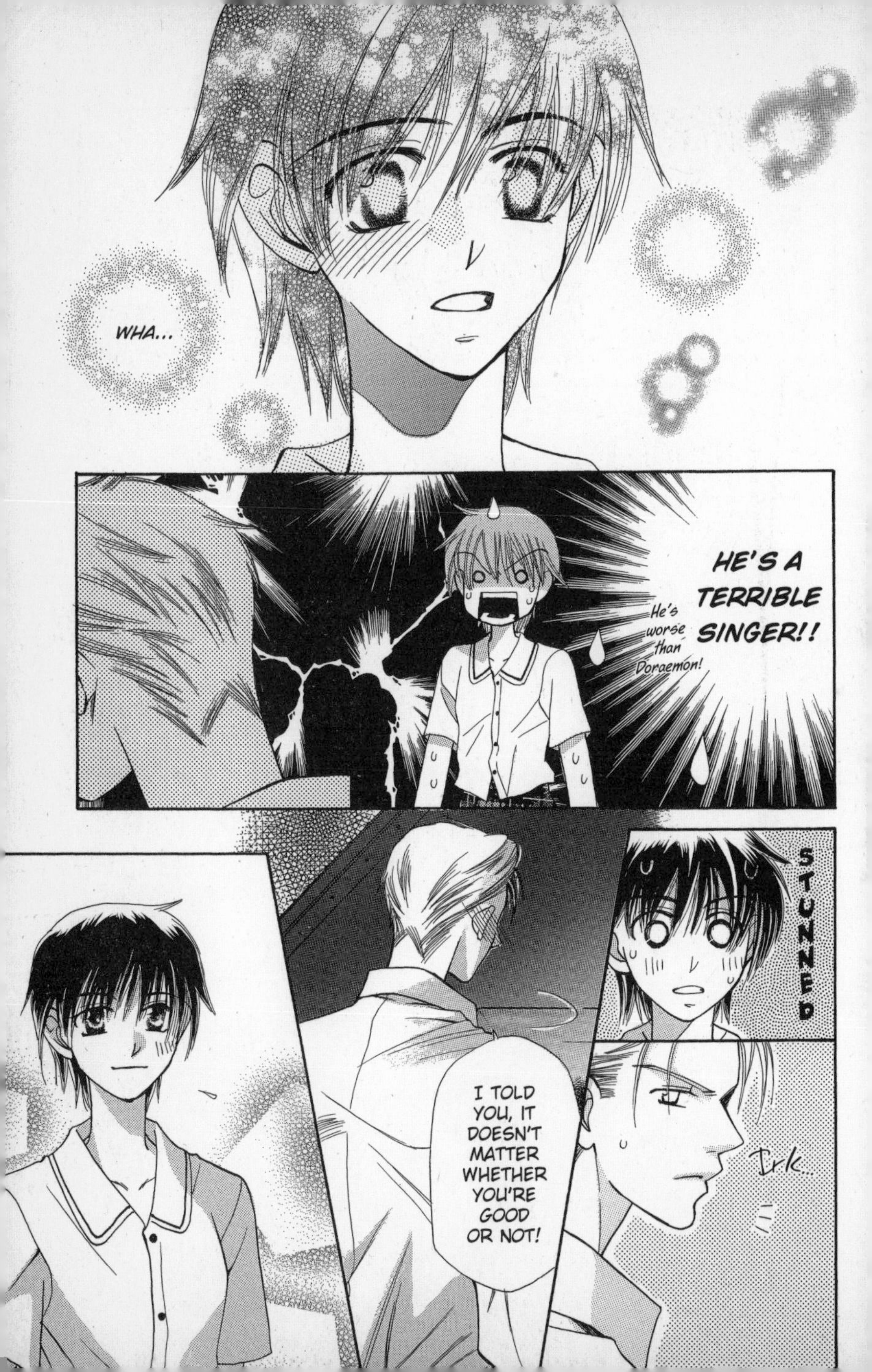
WHA...
HE'S A TERRIBLE SINGER!!
He's worse than Doraemon!
STUNNED
I TOLD YOU, IT DOESN'T MATTER WHETHER YOU'RE GOOD OR NOT!
Urk...

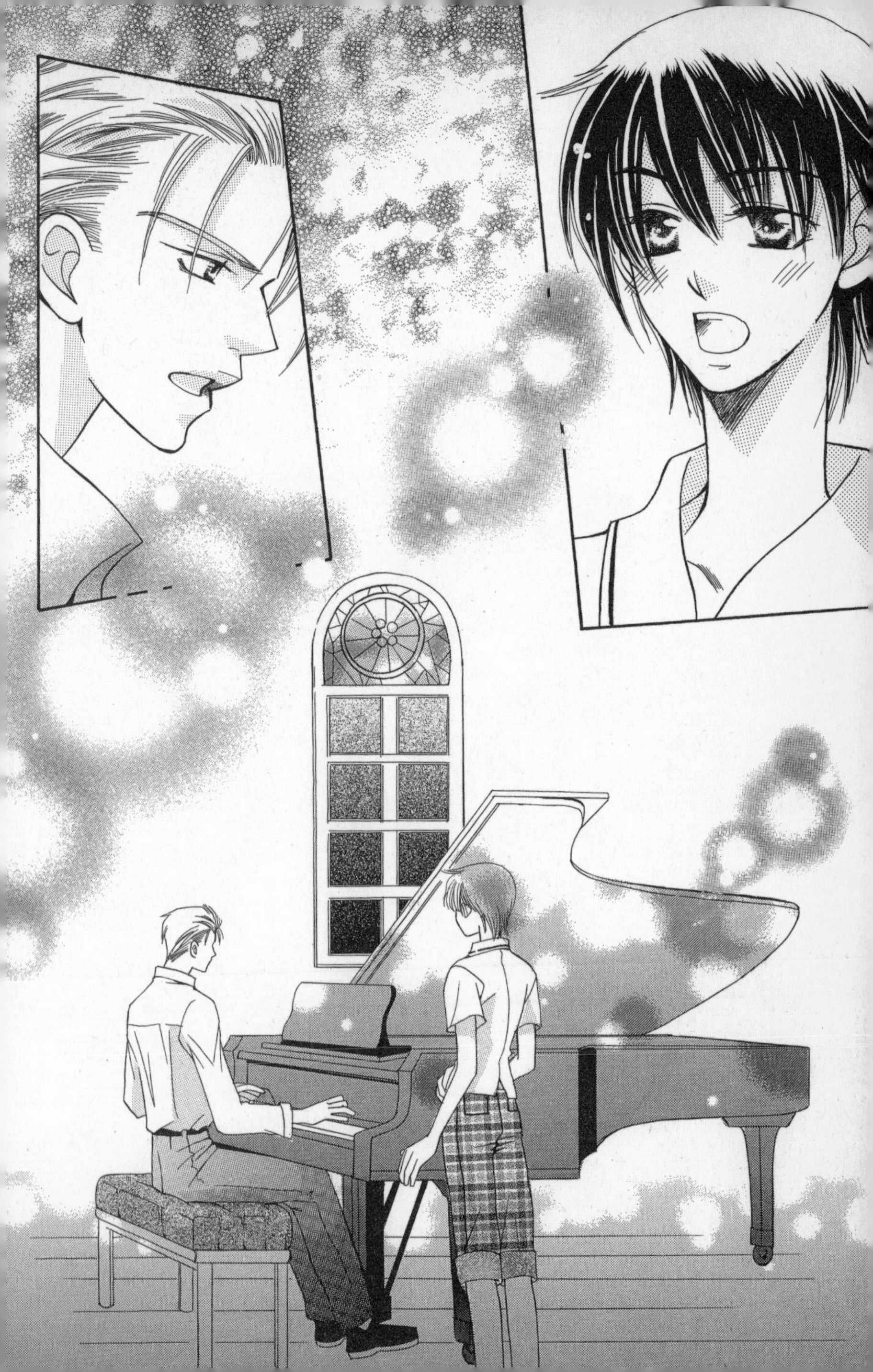

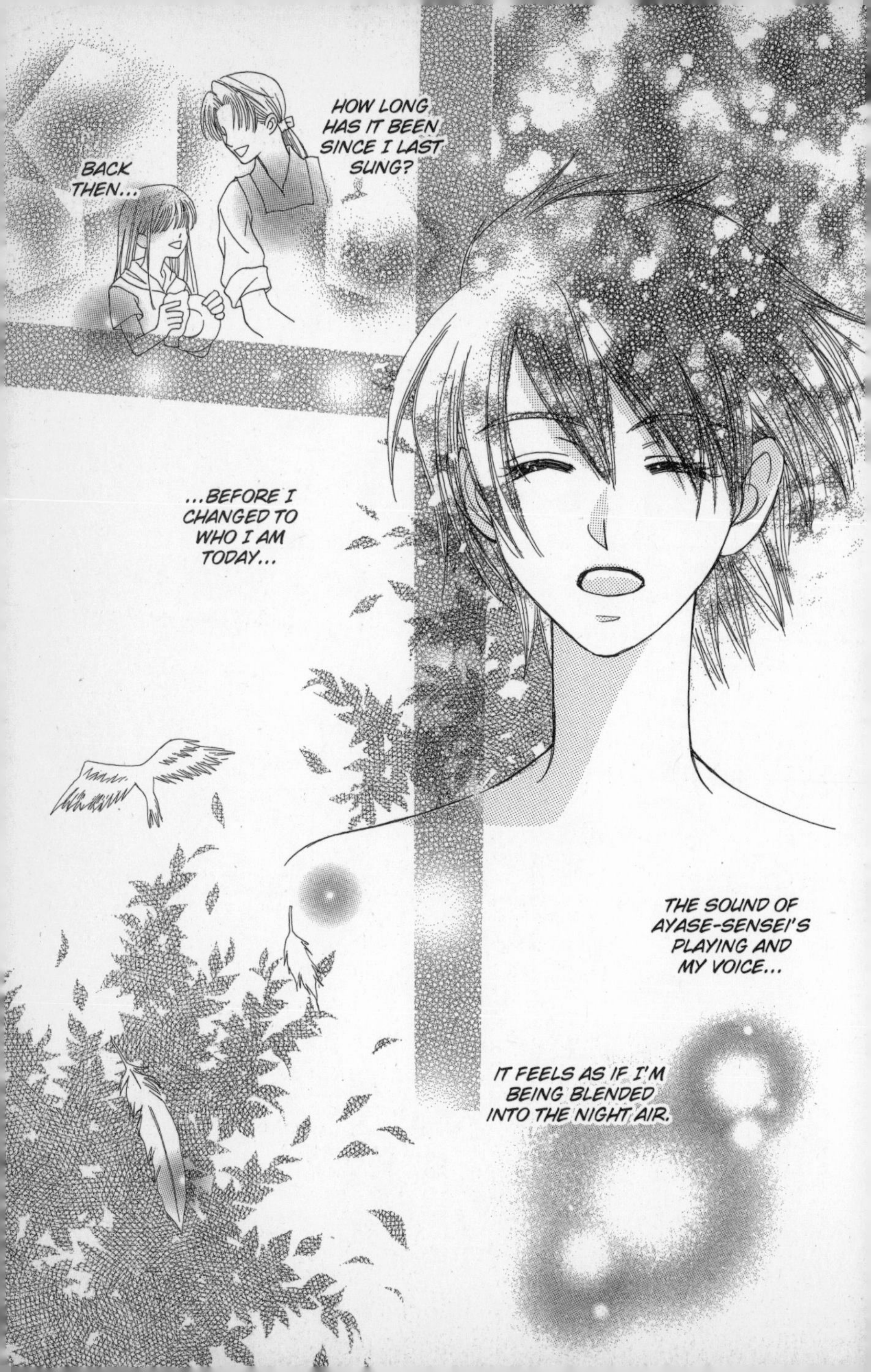
HOW LONG HAS IT BEEN SINCE I LAST SUNG?
BACK THEN...
...BEFORE I CHANGED TO WHO I AM TODAY...
THE SOUND OF AYASE-SENSEI'S PLAYING AND MY VOICE...
IT FEELS AS IF I'M BEING BLENDED INTO THE NIGHT AIR.

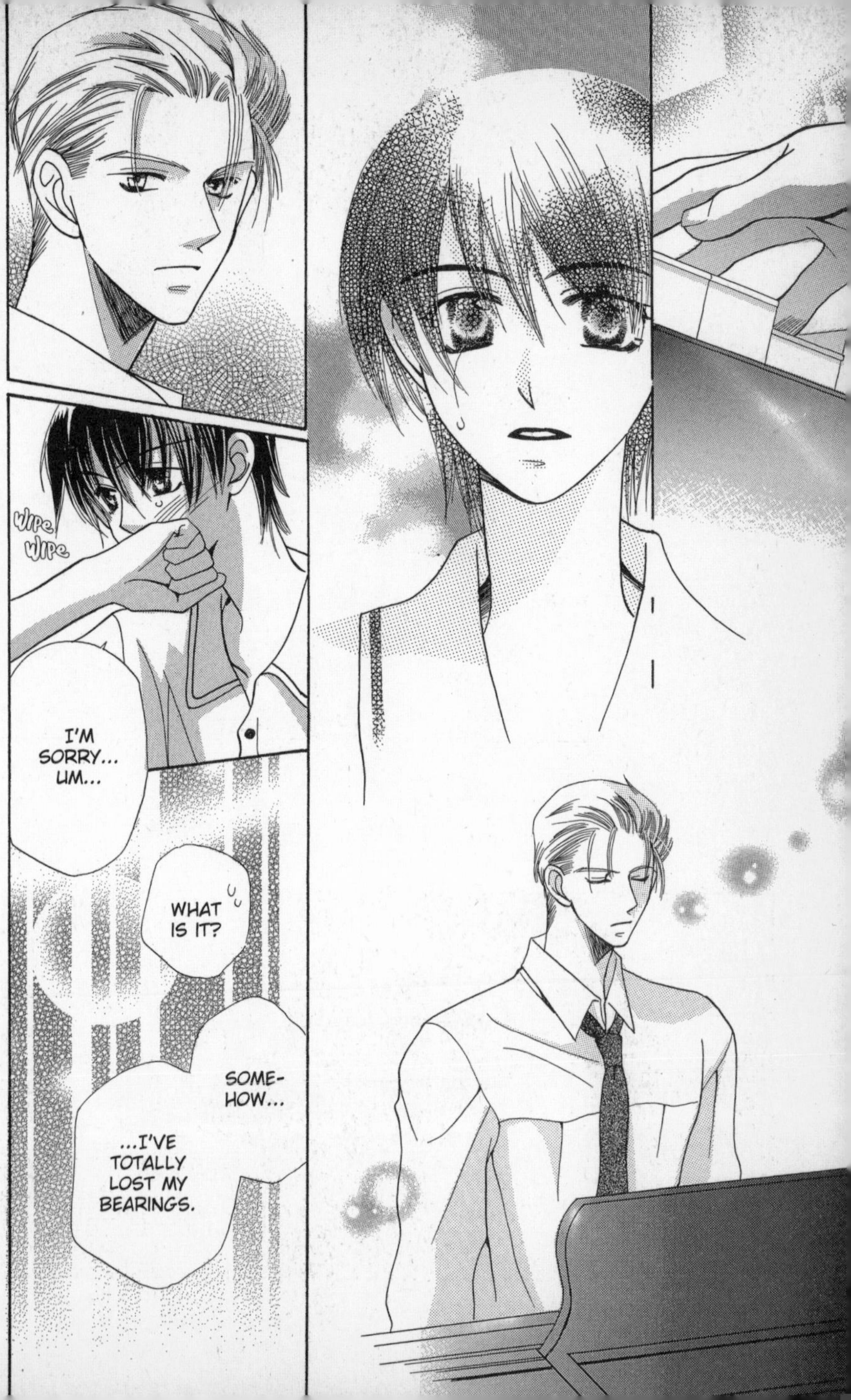
WIPE WIPE
I'M SORRY... UM...
WHAT IS IT?
SOME-HOW...
...I'VE TOTALLY LOST MY BEARINGS.

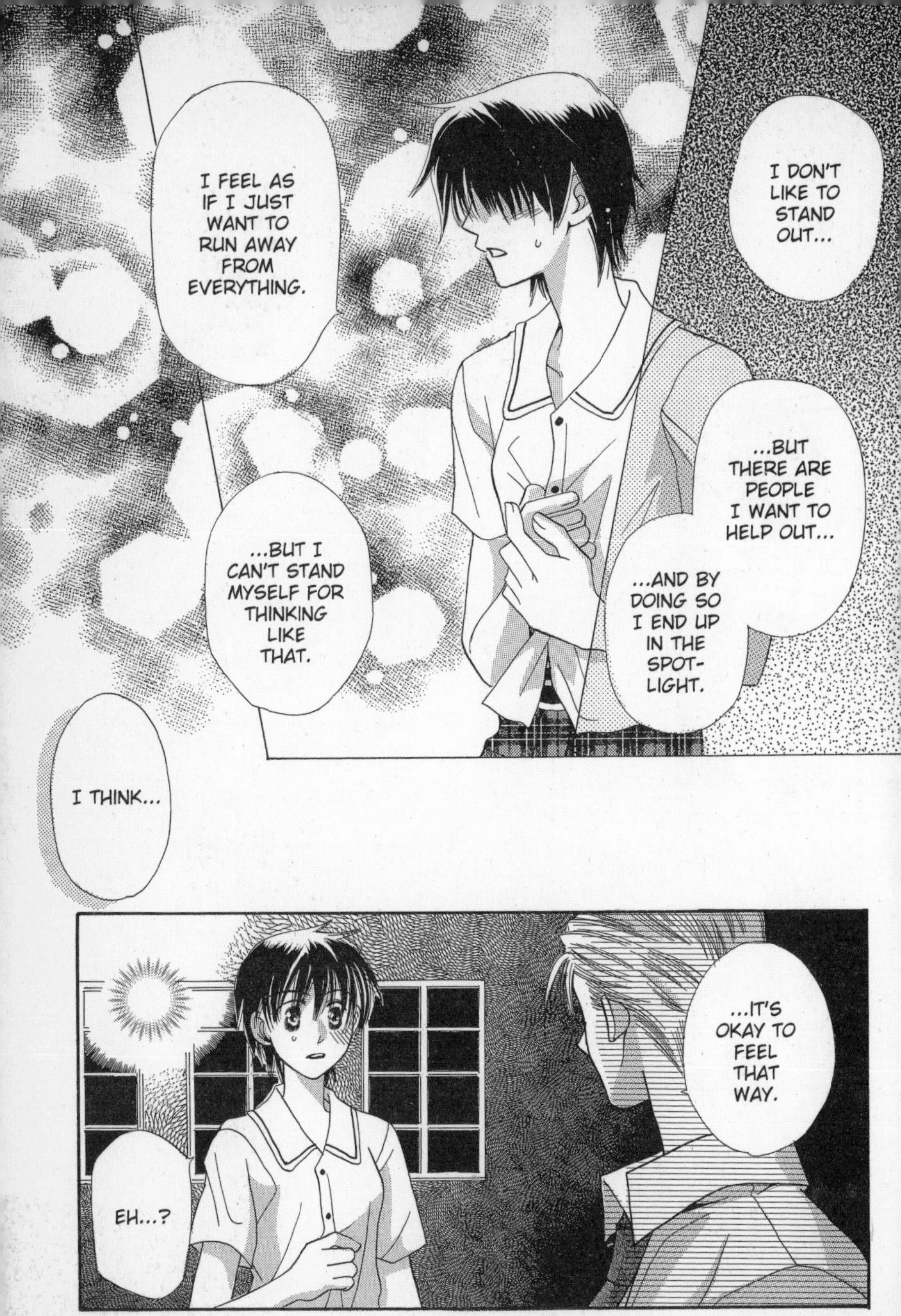
I DON'T LIKE TO STAND OUT...
...BUT THERE ARE PEOPLE I WANT TO HELP OUT...
...AND BY DOING SO I END UP IN THE SPOT-LIGHT.
I FEEL AS IF I JUST WANT TO RUN AWAY FROM EVERYTHING.
...BUT I CAN'T STAND MYSELF FOR THINKING LIKE THAT.
I THINK...
...IT'S OKAY TO FEEL THAT WAY.
EH...?

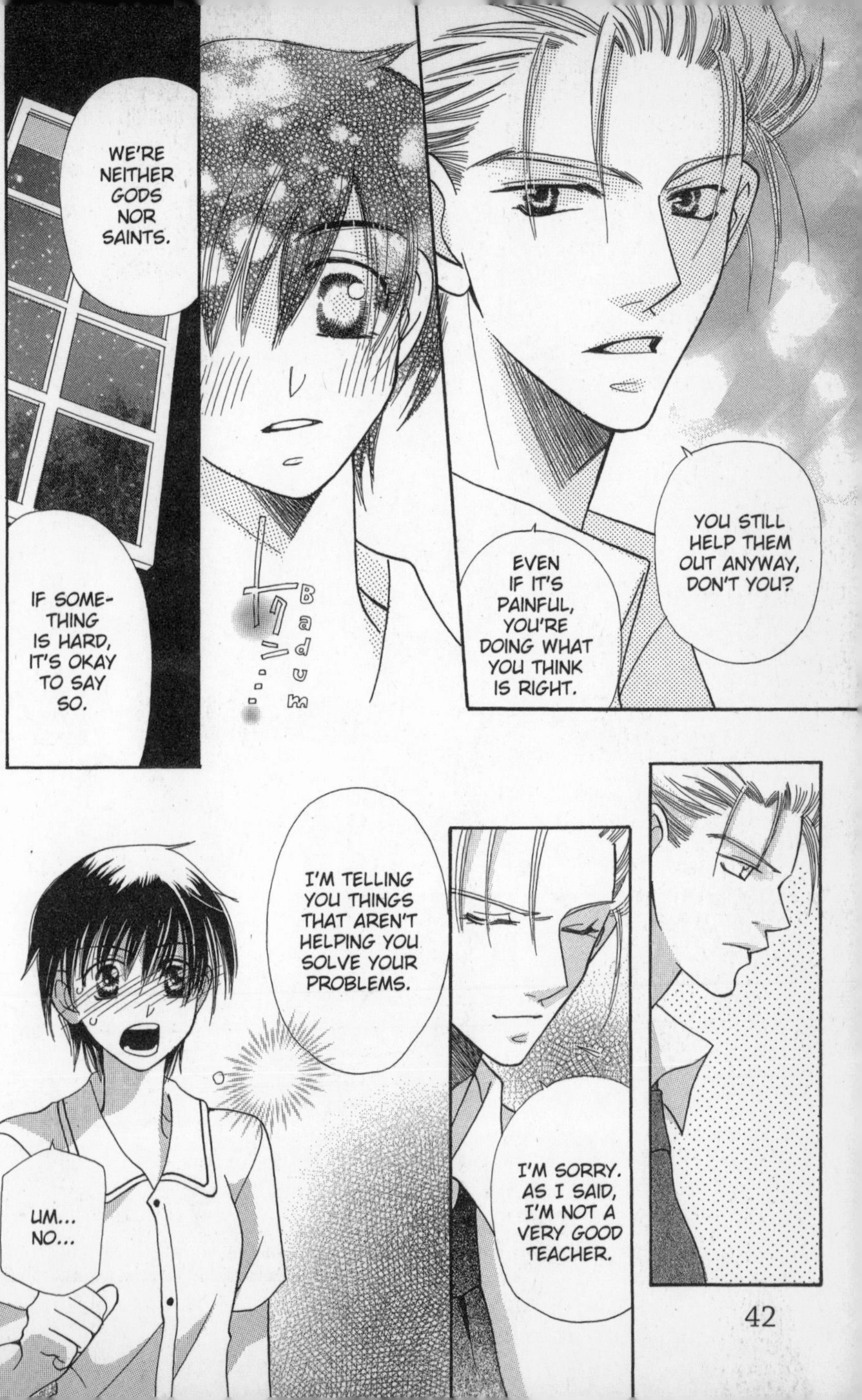
YOU STILL HELP THEM OUT ANYWAY, DON'T YOU?
EVEN IF IT'S PAINFUL, YOU'RE DOING WHAT YOU THINK IS RIGHT.
Badum...
WE'RE NEITHER GODS NOR SAINTS.
IF SOME-THING IS HARD, IT'S OKAY TO SAY SO.
I'M TELLING YOU THINGS THAT AREN'T HELPING YOU SOLVE YOUR PROBLEMS.
I'M SORRY. AS I SAID, I'M NOT A VERY GOOD TEACHER.
UM... NO...

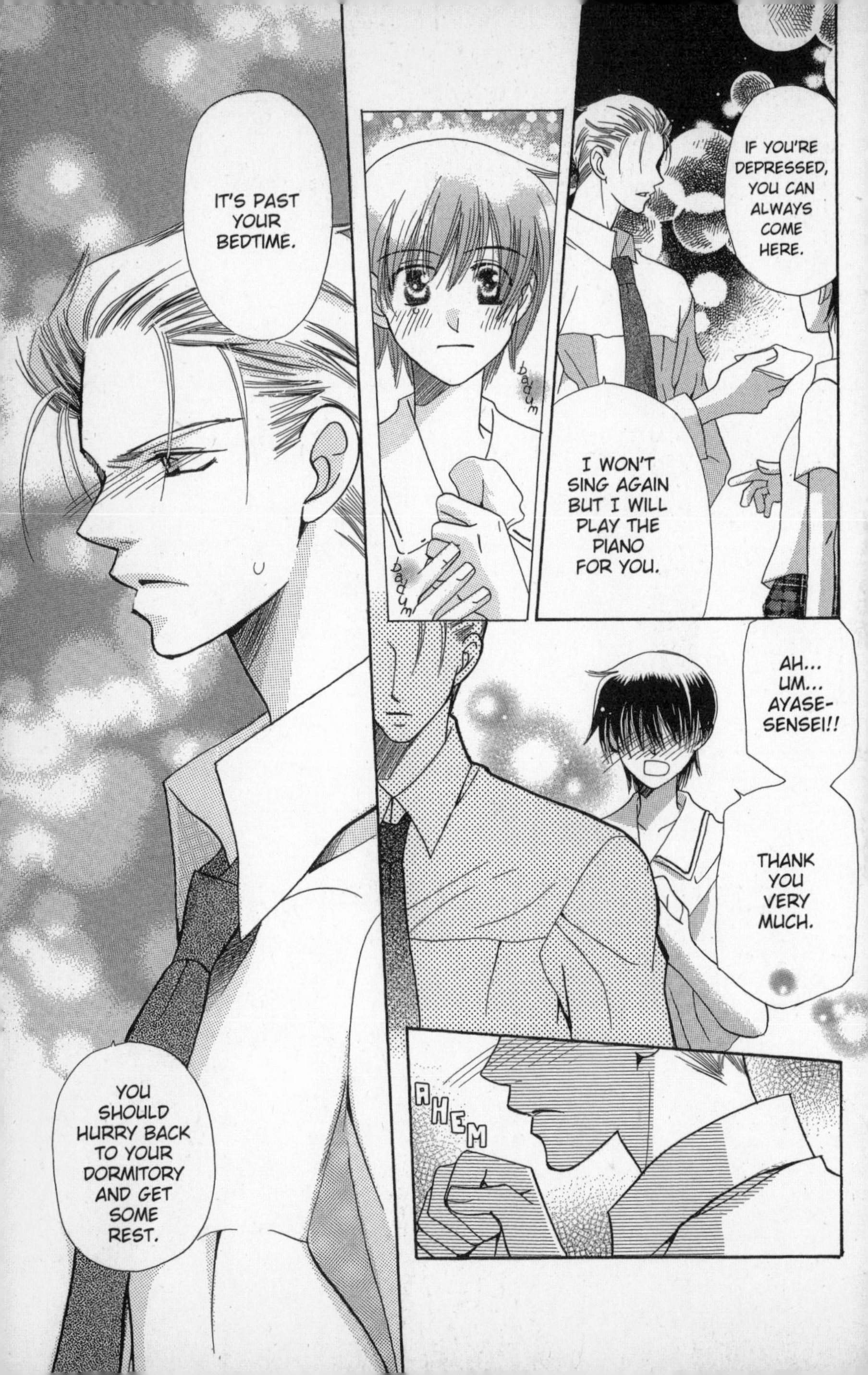
IF YOU'RE DEPRESSED, YOU CAN ALWAYS COME HERE.
I WON'T SING AGAIN BUT I WILL PLAY THE PIANO FOR YOU.
badum
badum
AH... UM... AYASE-SENSEI!!
THANK YOU VERY MUCH.
AHEM
IT'S PAST YOUR BEDTIME.
YOU SHOULD HURRY BACK TO YOUR DORMITORY AND GET SOME REST.

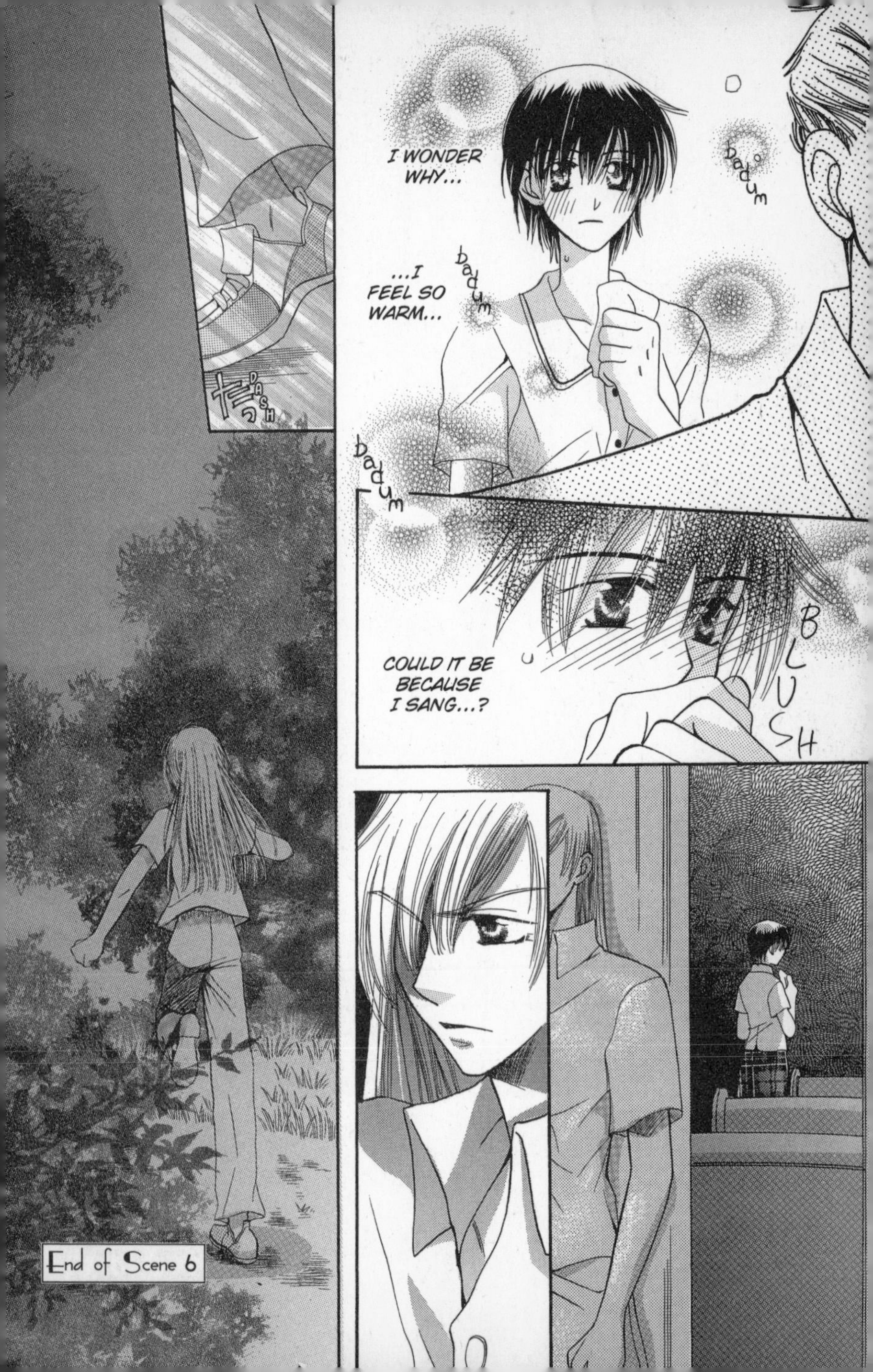
badum
I WONDER WHY...
...I FEEL SO WARM...
badum
badum
COULD IT BE BECAUSE I SANG...?
BLUSH
DASH
End of Scene 6

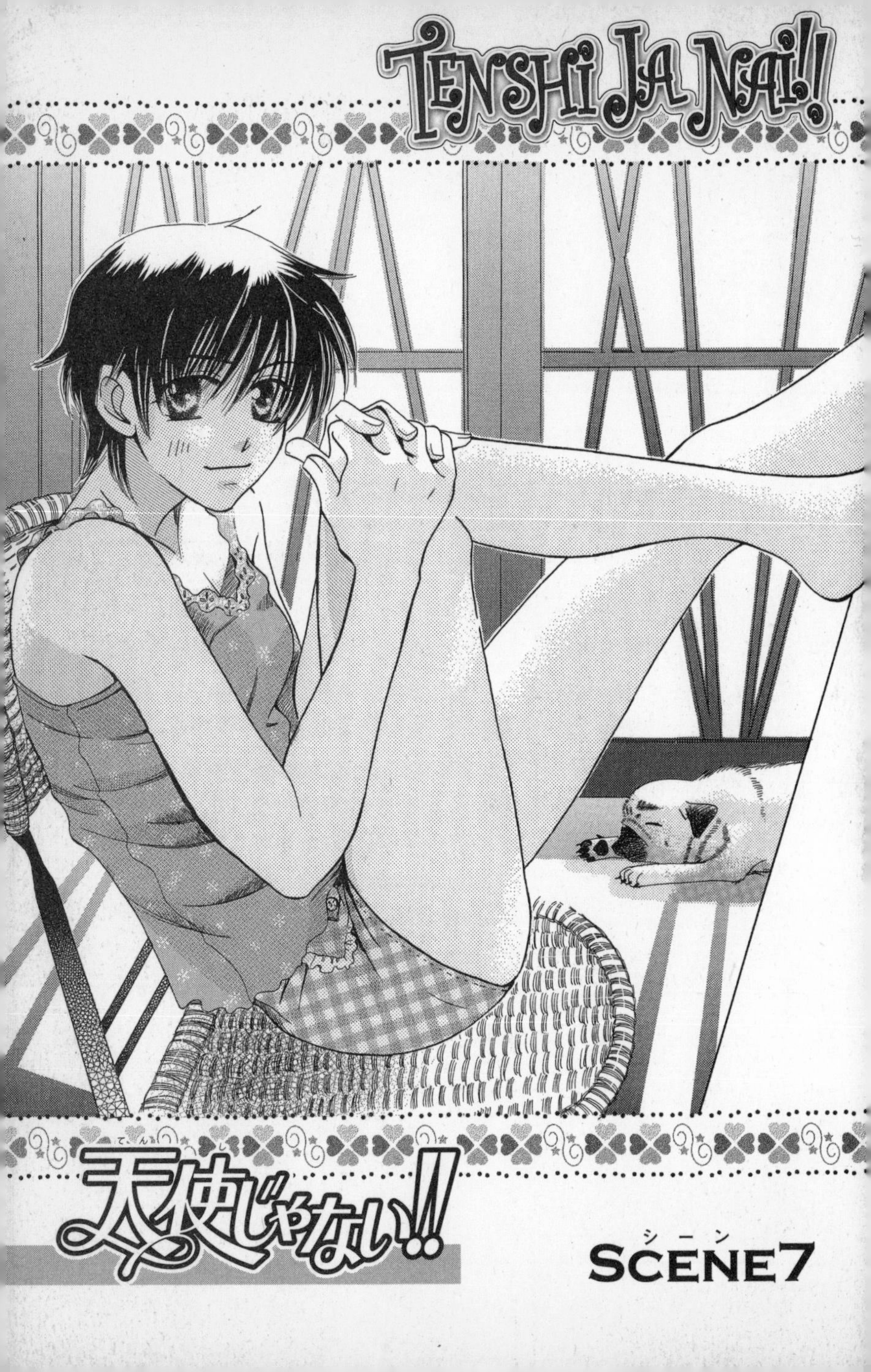
TENSHI JA NAI!!
天使じゃない!!
SCENE7

UH, SURE.

WE NEED TO LEAVE SOON. COULD YOU PLEASE GO GET IZUMI-SAMA?

HIKARU-SAN.

UNTIL YASUKUNI-SAN ASKED ME TO GO LOOK FOR IZUMI-SAN IN THE BACKYARD...

!?

IZUMI-SAN...

...I NEVER REALIZED JUST HOW INSANE THINGS COULD GET WHEN YOU LIVE WITH A CELEBRITY.

Howdy!

Hajimemashite! Long time no see! Vol 2 is out at last! I'm so happy that I get to see you again. This success is thanks to your ongoing support!! I hope that you will continue to support me!! (BOW) I just fell on my Knees to beg you!

46

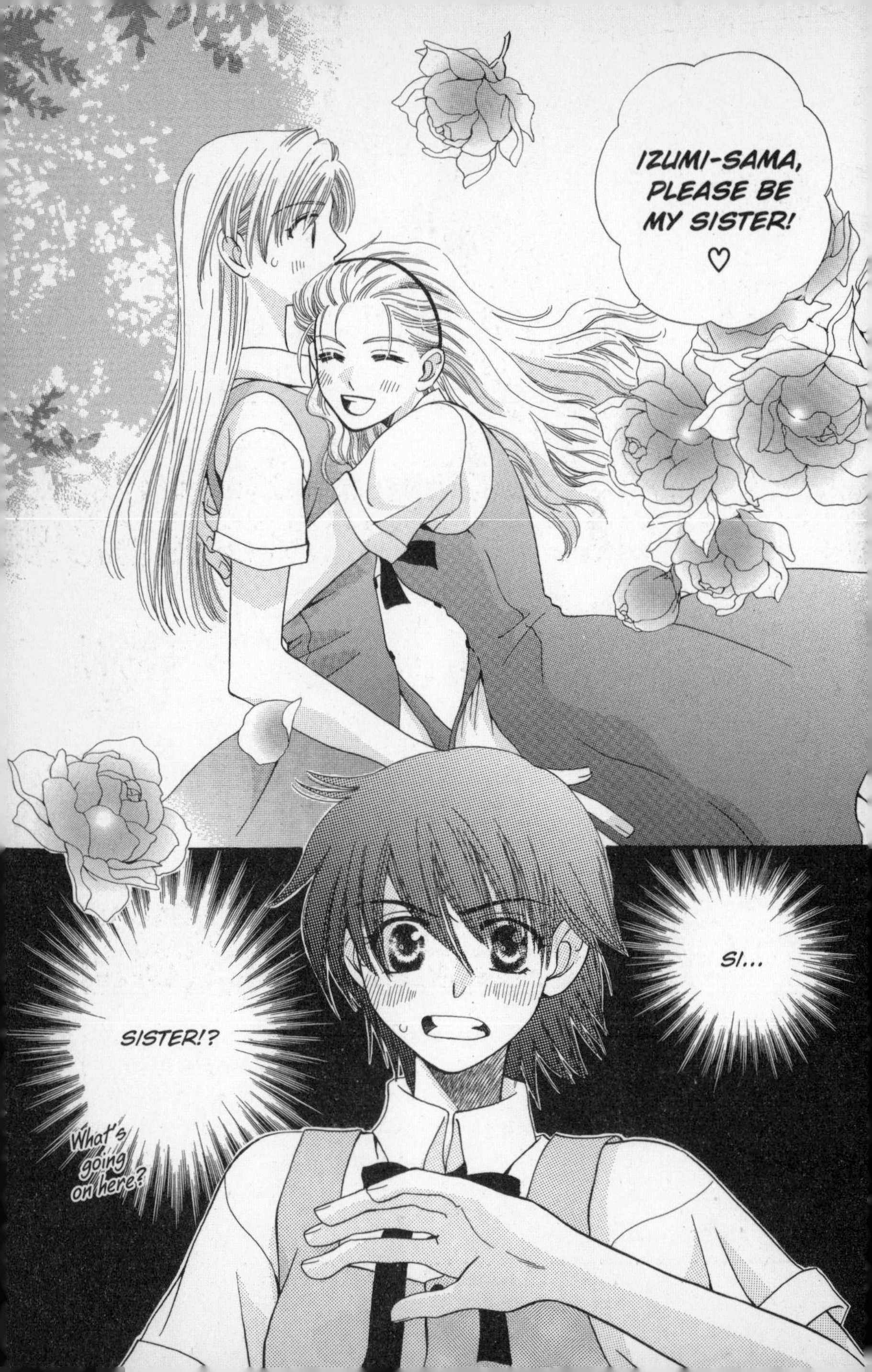
IZUMI-SAMA, PLEASE BE MY SISTER! ♡
SI...
SISTER!?
What's going on here?

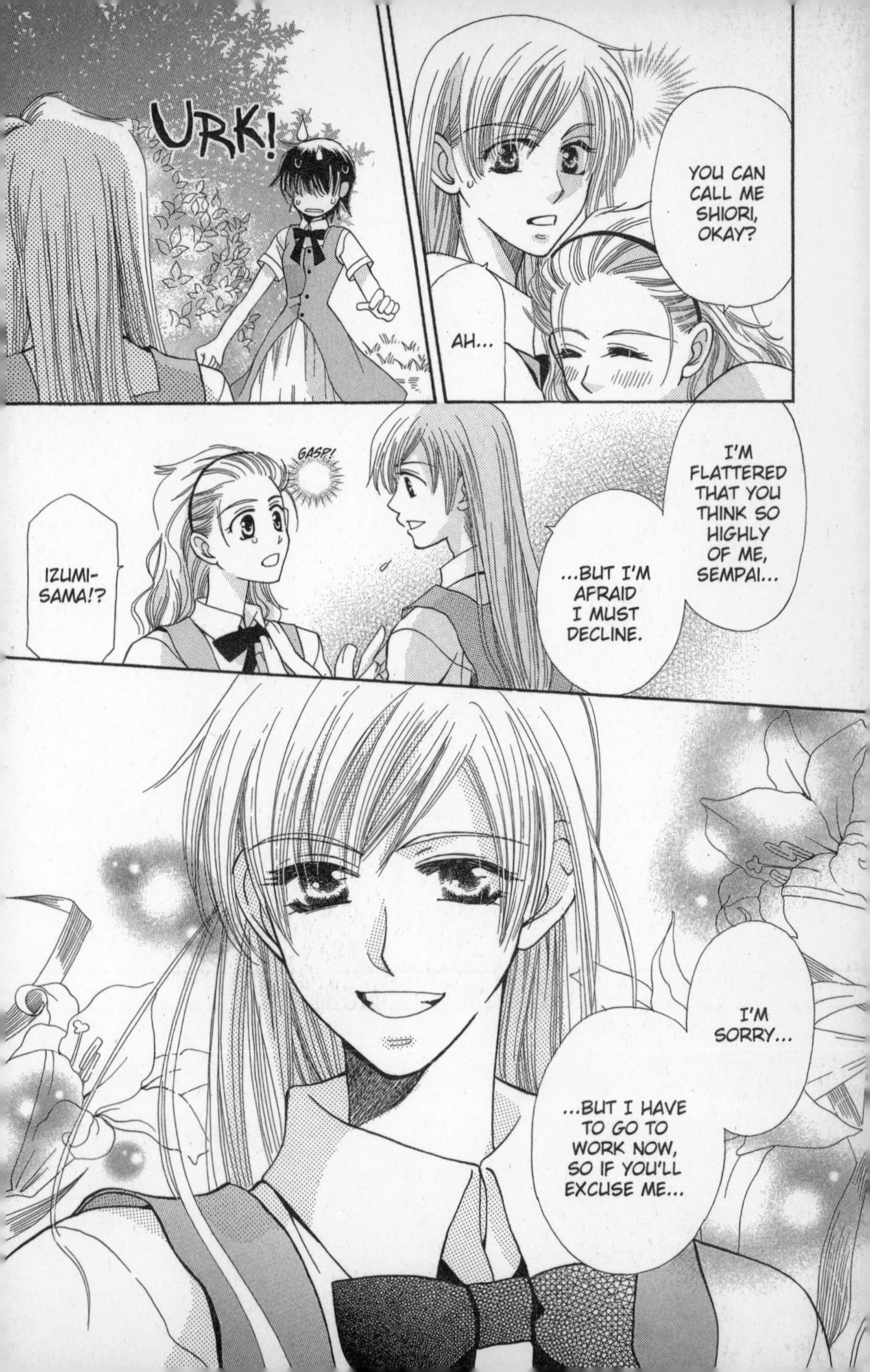
YOU CAN CALL ME SHIORI, OKAY?
AH...
URK!
I'M FLATTERED THAT YOU THINK SO HIGHLY OF ME, SEMPAI...
...BUT I'M AFRAID I MUST DECLINE.
GASP!
IZUMI-SAMA!?
I'M SORRY...
...BUT I HAVE TO GO TO WORK NOW, SO IF YOU'LL EXCUSE ME...

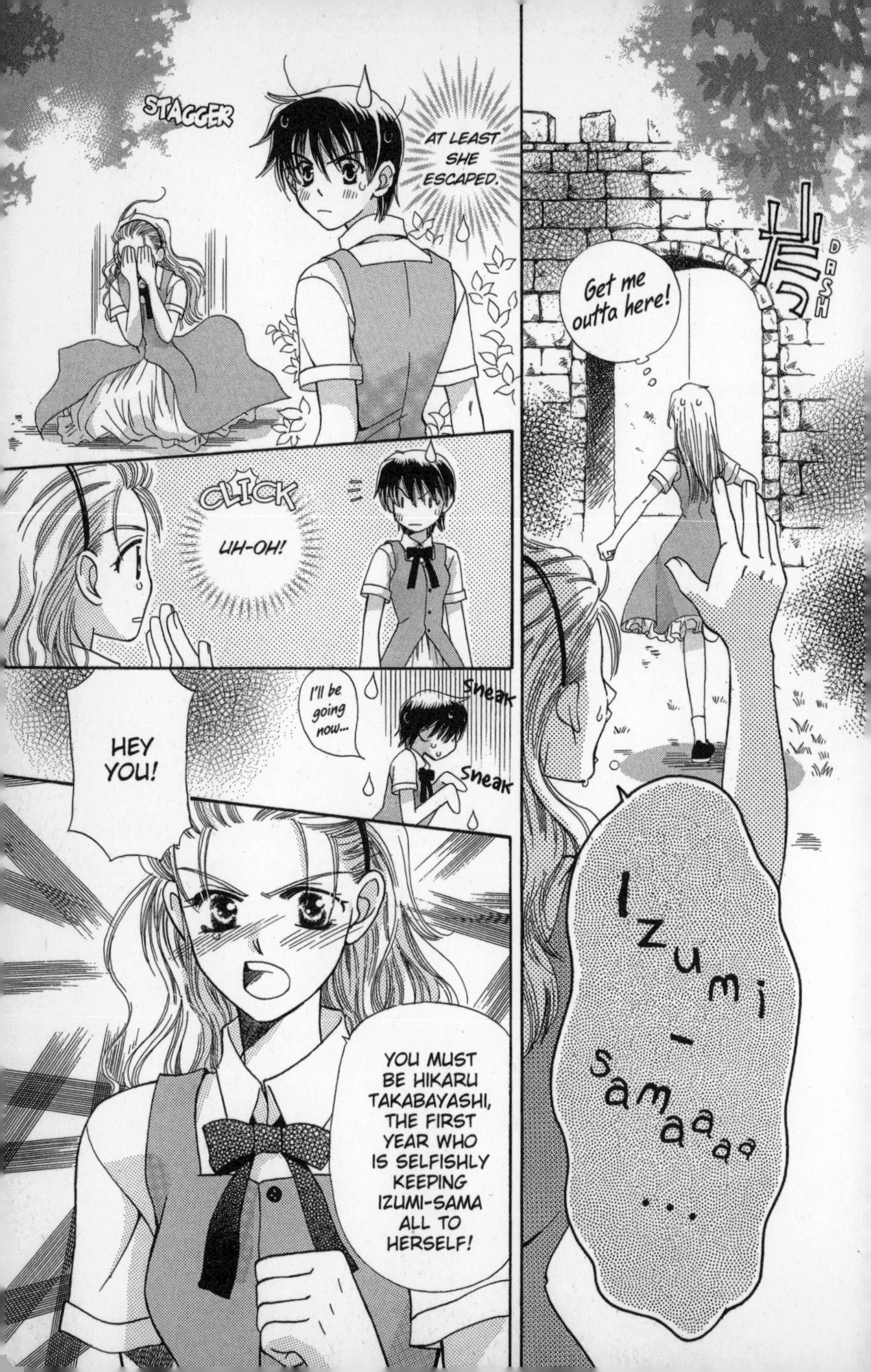
DASH
Get me outta here!
Izumi-samaaaa...
AT LEAST SHE ESCAPED.
STAGGER
CLICK
UH-OH!
Sneak
I'll be going now...
Sneak
HEY YOU!
YOU MUST BE HIKARU TAKABAYASHI, THE FIRST YEAR WHO IS SELFISHLY KEEPING IZUMI-SAMA ALL TO HERSELF!

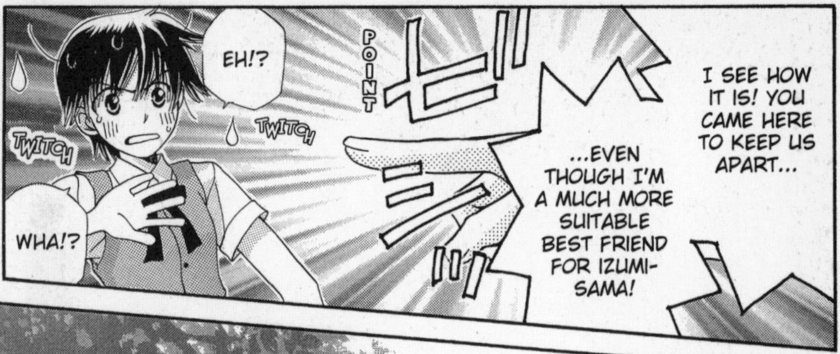
I SEE HOW IT IS! YOU CAME HERE TO KEEP US APART...
...EVEN THOUGH I'M A MUCH MORE SUITABLE BEST FRIEND FOR IZUMI-SAMA!
POINT
EH!?
TWITCH
TWITCH
WHA!?
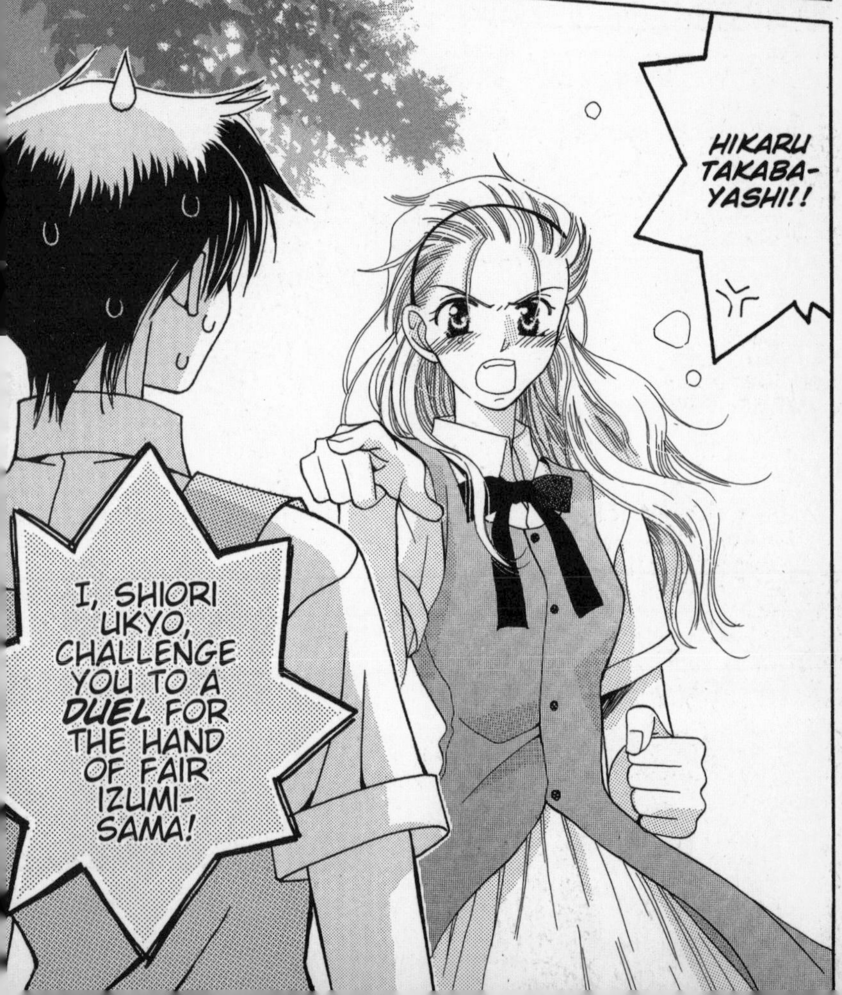
HIKARU TAKABA-YASHI!!
I, SHIORI UKYO, CHALLENGE YOU TO A *DUEL* FOR THE HAND OF FAIR IZUMI-SAMA!

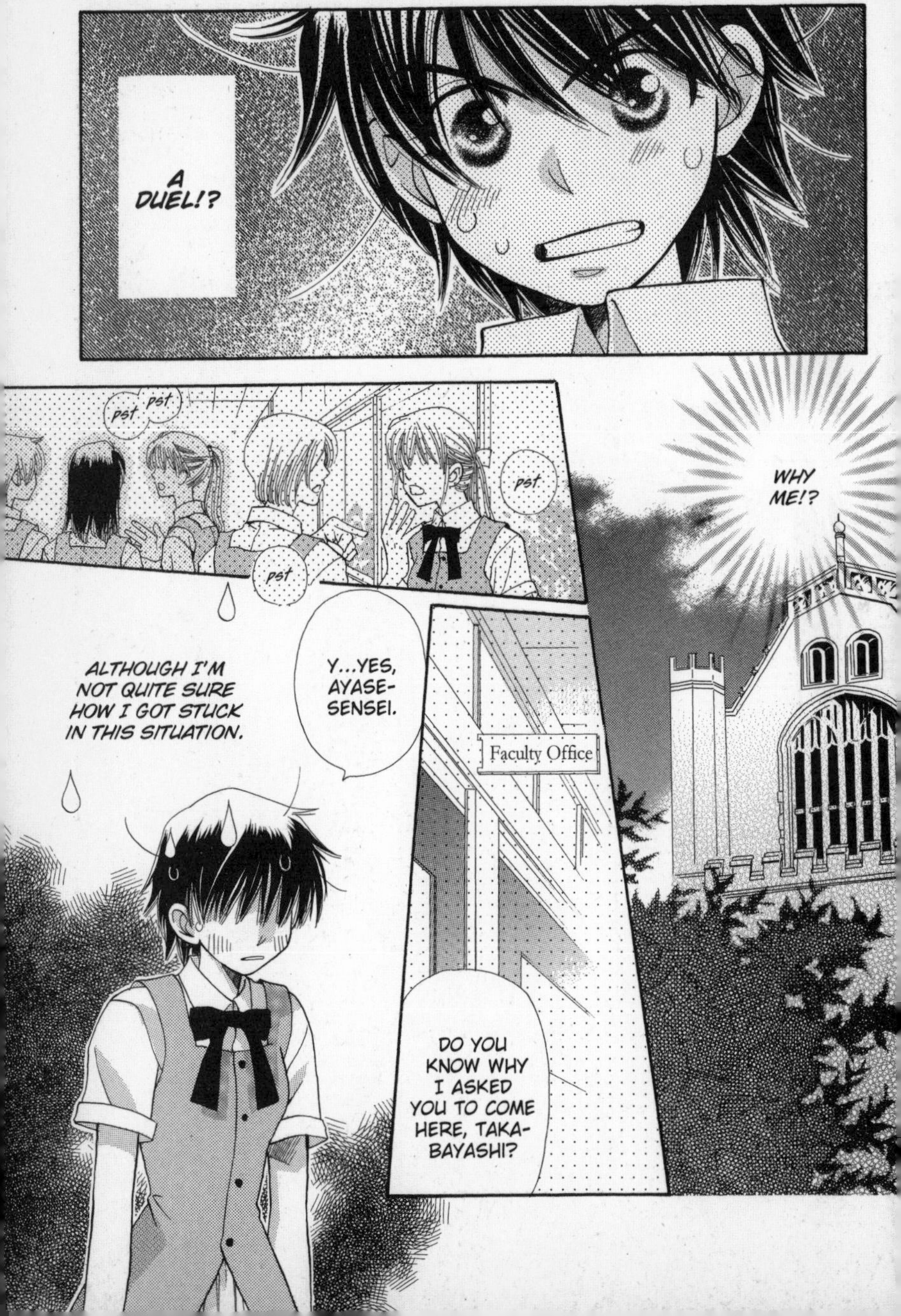

A DUEL!?
WHY ME!?
pst pst
pst
pst
pst
Faculty Office
DO YOU KNOW WHY I ASKED YOU TO COME HERE, TAKA-BAYASHI?
Y...YES, AYASE-SENSEI.
ALTHOUGH I'M NOT QUITE SURE HOW I GOT STUCK IN THIS SITUATION.

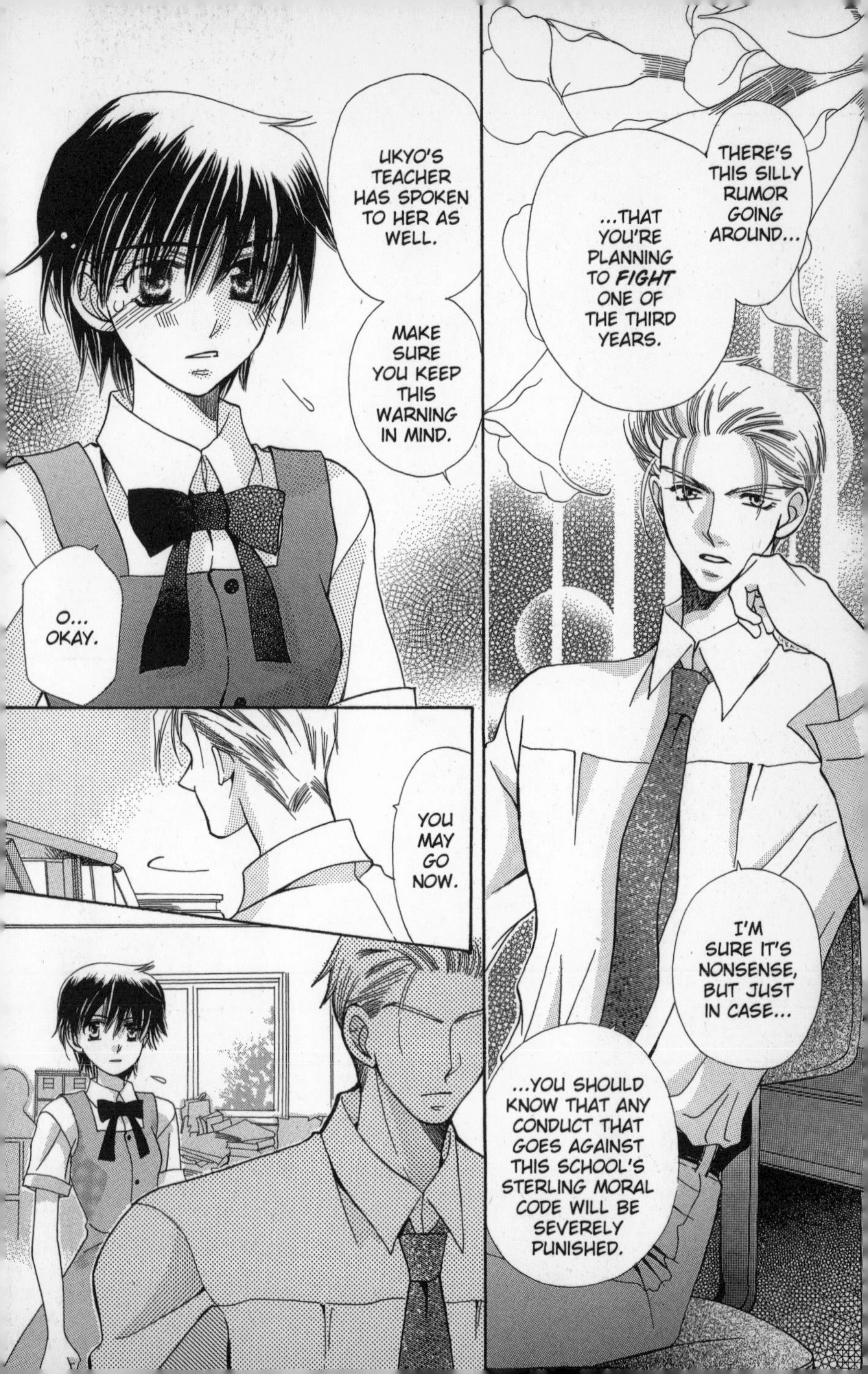
THERE'S THIS SILLY RUMOR GOING AROUND...
...THAT YOU'RE PLANNING TO **FIGHT** ONE OF THE THIRD YEARS.
I'M SURE IT'S NONSENSE, BUT JUST IN CASE...
...YOU SHOULD KNOW THAT ANY CONDUCT THAT GOES AGAINST THIS SCHOOL'S STERLING MORAL CODE WILL BE SEVERELY PUNISHED.
UKYO'S TEACHER HAS SPOKEN TO HER AS WELL.
MAKE SURE YOU KEEP THIS WARNING IN MIND.
O... OKAY.
YOU MAY GO NOW.

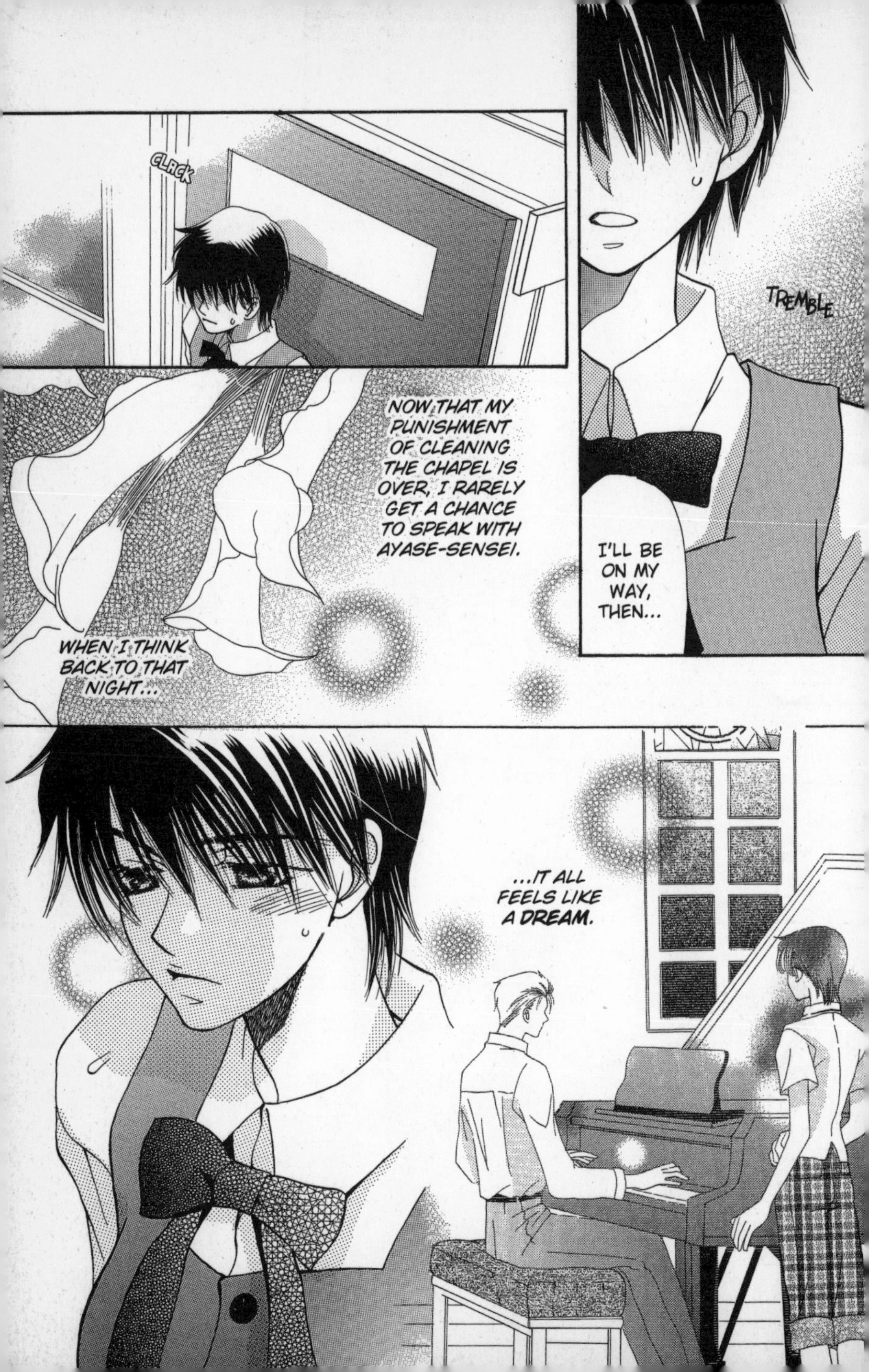
TREMBLE
I'LL BE ON MY WAY, THEN...
CLACK
NOW THAT MY PUNISHMENT OF CLEANING THE CHAPEL IS OVER, I RARELY GET A CHANCE TO SPEAK WITH AYASE-SENSEI.
WHEN I THINK BACK TO THAT NIGHT...
...IT ALL FEELS LIKE A DREAM.

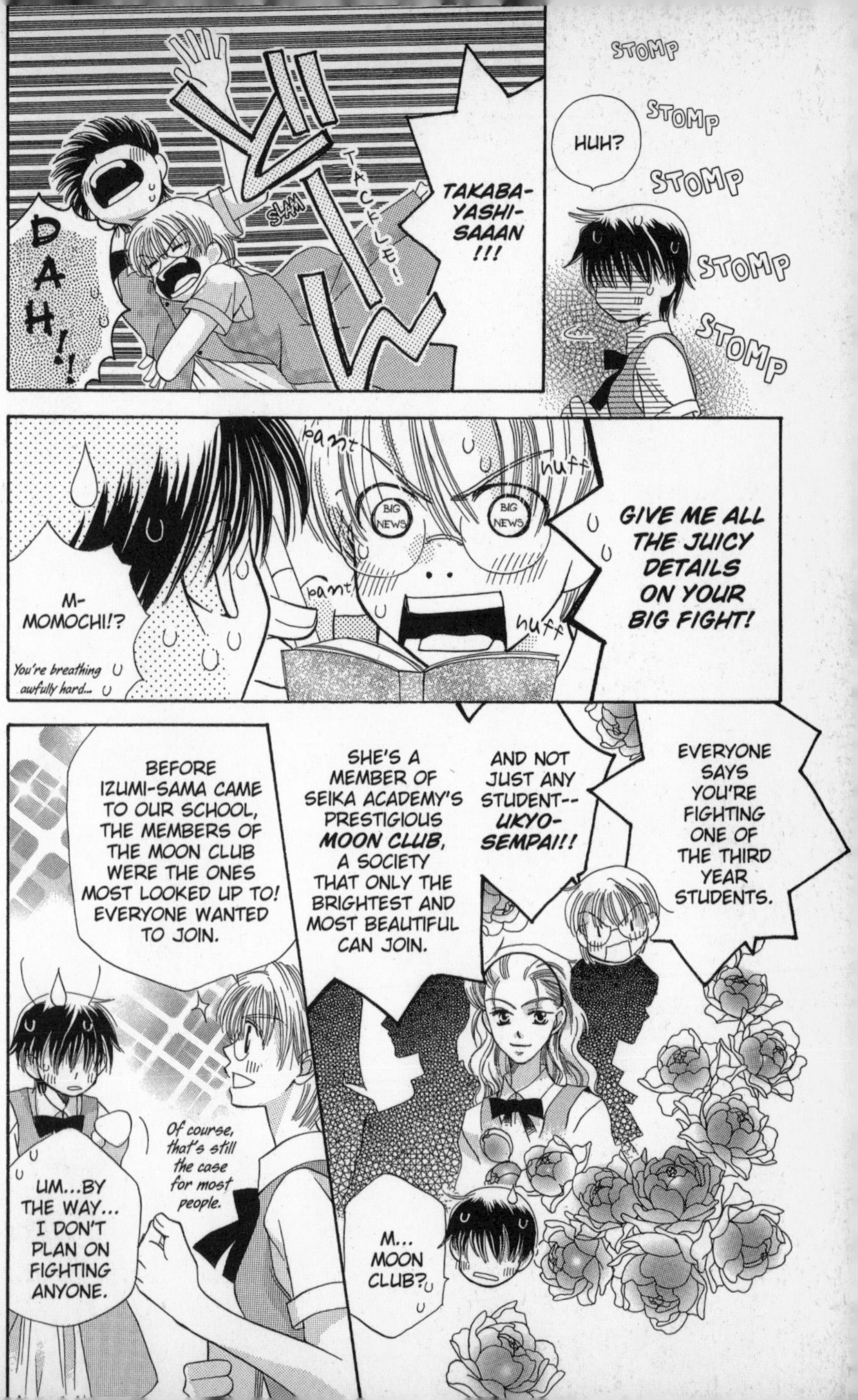
STOMP
STOMP
STOMP
STOMP
STOMP
HUH?
TAKABA-YASHI-SAAAN!!!
TACKLE!
SLAM
DAH!!
GIVE ME ALL THE JUICY DETAILS ON YOUR BIG FIGHT!
huff
huff
BIG NEWS
BIG NEWS
pant
pant
M-MOMOCHI!?
You're breathing awfully hard...
EVERYONE SAYS YOU'RE FIGHTING ONE OF THE THIRD YEAR STUDENTS.
AND NOT JUST ANY STUDENT--UKYO-SEMPAI!!
SHE'S A MEMBER OF SEIKA ACADEMY'S PRESTIGIOUS MOON CLUB, A SOCIETY THAT ONLY THE BRIGHTEST AND MOST BEAUTIFUL CAN JOIN.
M... MOON CLUB?
BEFORE IZUMI-SAMA CAME TO OUR SCHOOL, THE MEMBERS OF THE MOON CLUB WERE THE ONES MOST LOOKED UP TO! EVERYONE WANTED TO JOIN.
Of course, that's still the case for most people.
UM...BY THE WAY... I DON'T PLAN ON FIGHTING ANYONE.

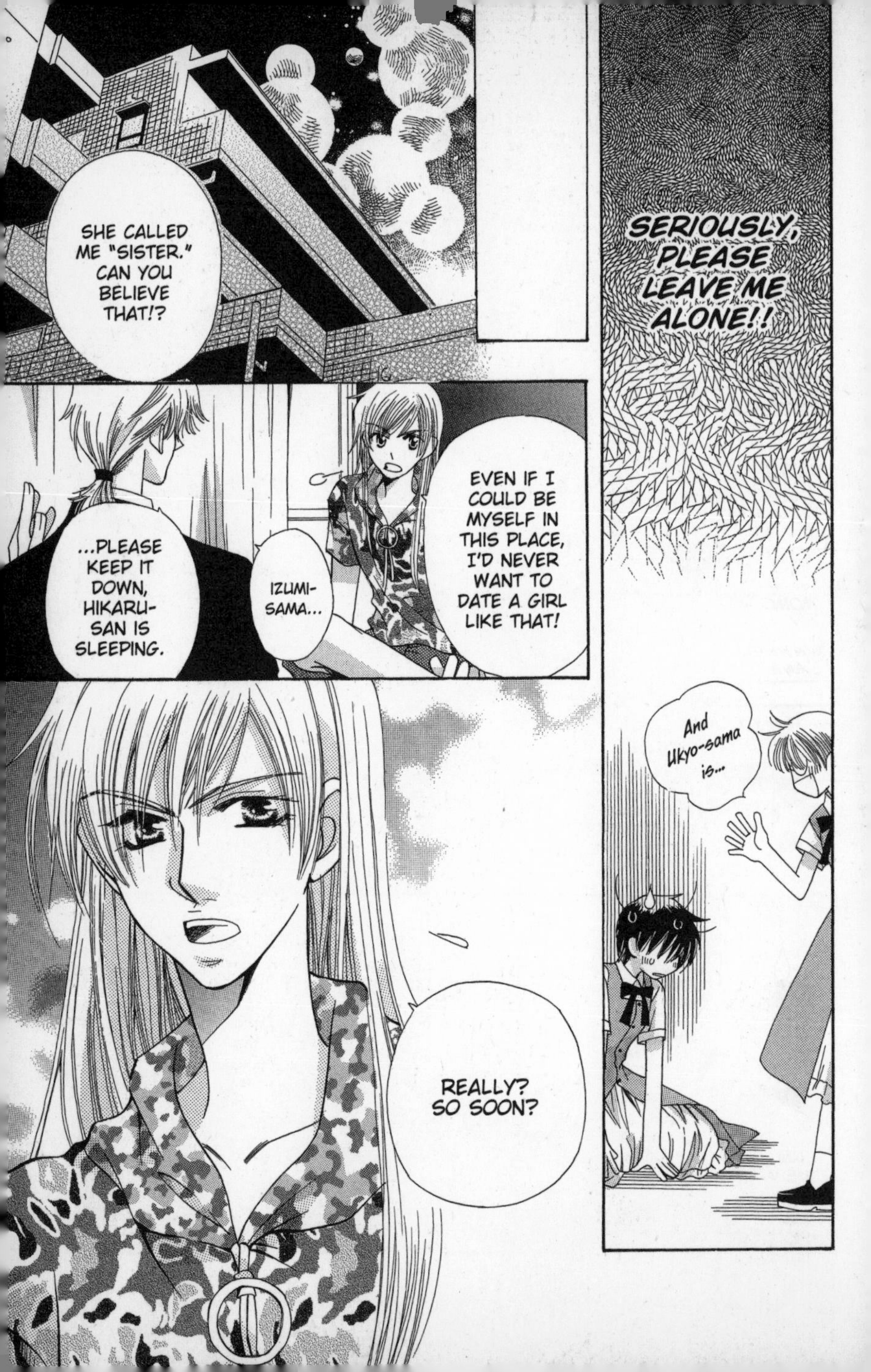
SERIOUSLY, PLEASE LEAVE ME ALONE!!
And Ukyo-sama is...
SHE CALLED ME "SISTER." CAN YOU BELIEVE THAT!?
EVEN IF I COULD BE MYSELF IN THIS PLACE, I'D NEVER WANT TO DATE A GIRL LIKE THAT!
IZUMI-SAMA...
...PLEASE KEEP IT DOWN, HIKARU-SAN IS SLEEPING.
REALLY? SO SOON?

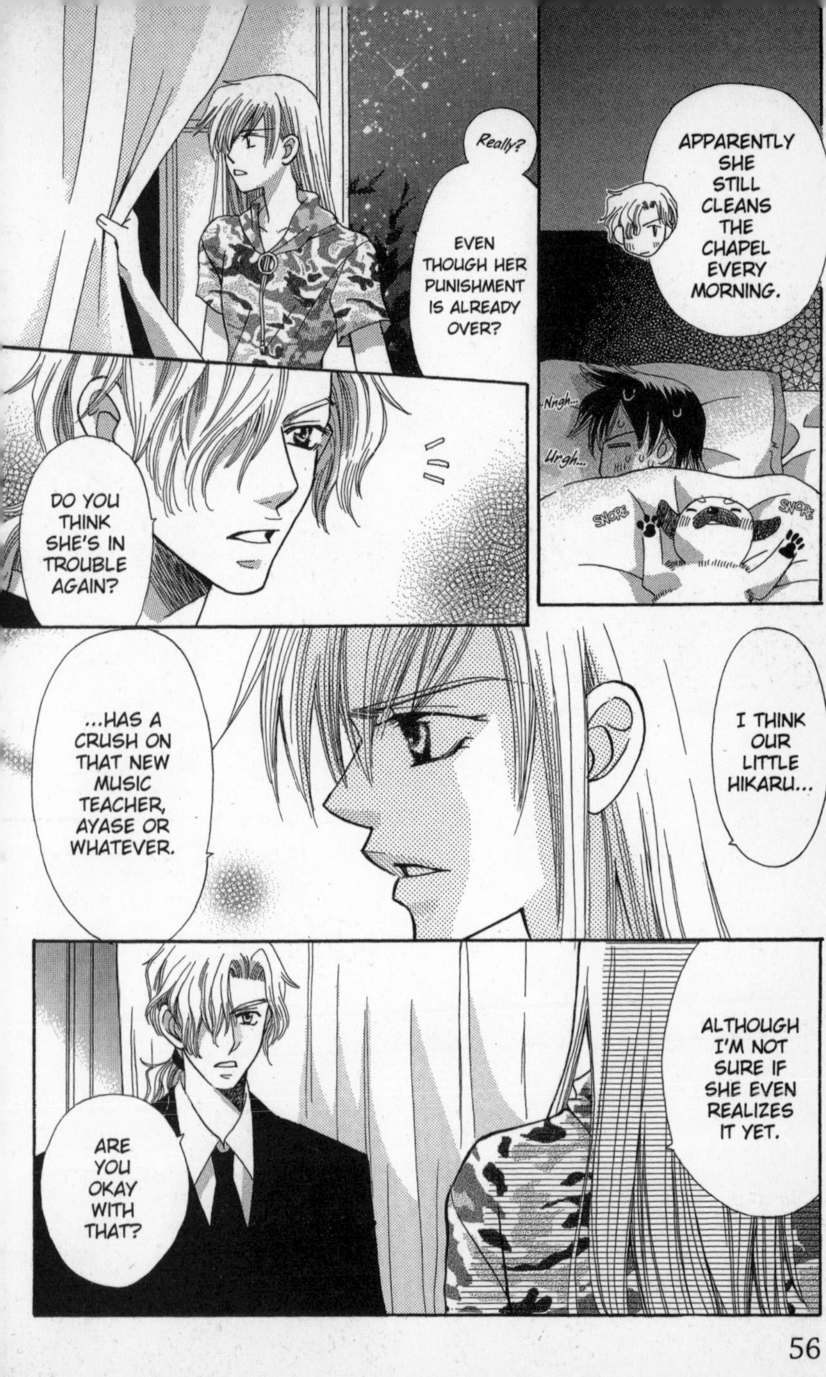
APPARENTLY SHE STILL CLEANS THE CHAPEL EVERY MORNING.
Really?
EVEN THOUGH HER PUNISHMENT IS ALREADY OVER?
DO YOU THINK SHE'S IN TROUBLE AGAIN?
Nngh...
Urgh...
SNORE
SNORE
I THINK OUR LITTLE HIKARU...
...HAS A CRUSH ON THAT NEW MUSIC TEACHER, AYASE OR WHATEVER.
ALTHOUGH I'M NOT SURE IF SHE EVEN REALIZES IT YET.
ARE YOU OKAY WITH THAT?

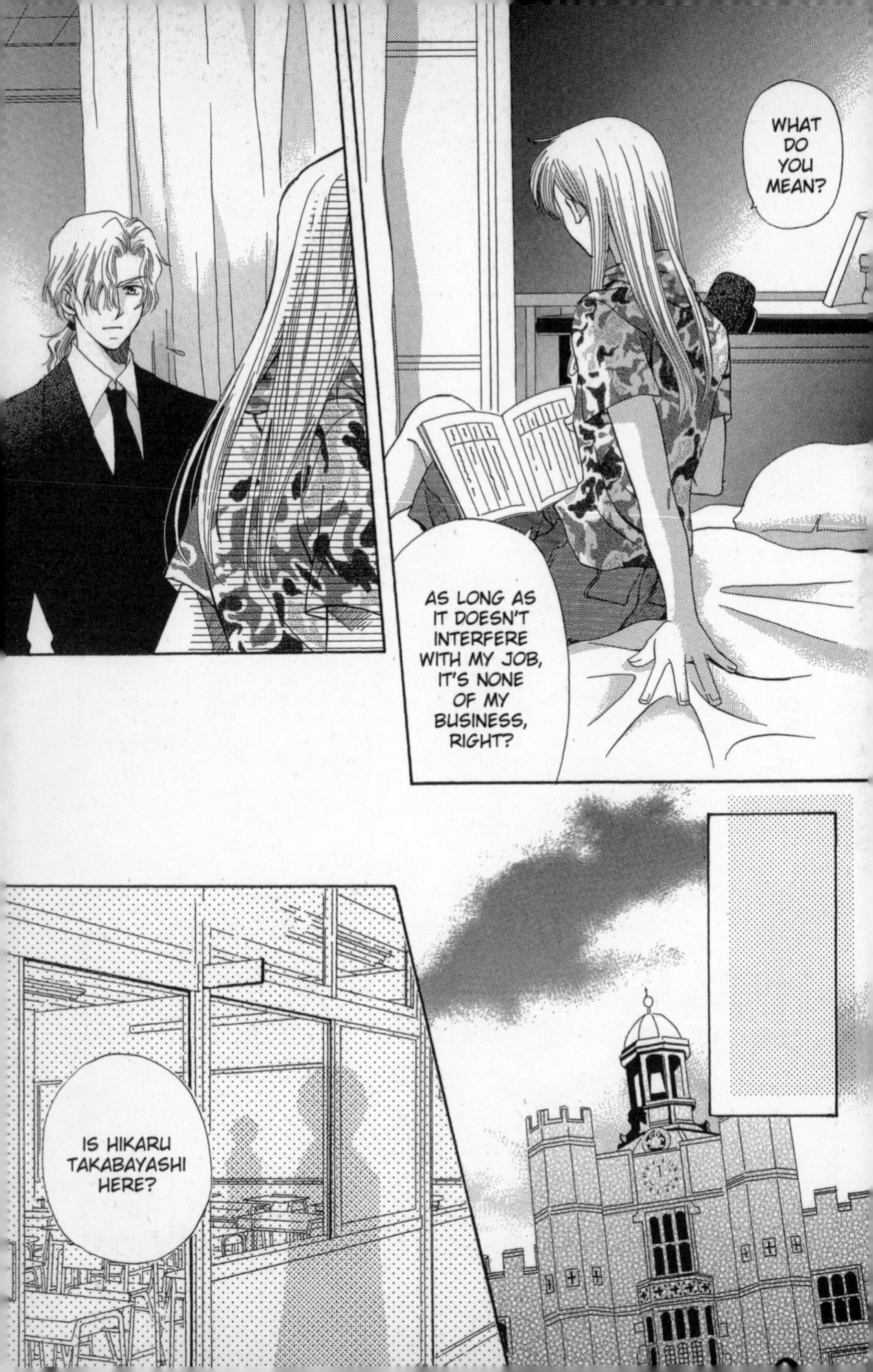
WHAT DO YOU MEAN?
AS LONG AS IT DOESN'T INTERFERE WITH MY JOB, IT'S NONE OF MY BUSINESS, RIGHT?
IS HIKARU TAKABAYASHI HERE?

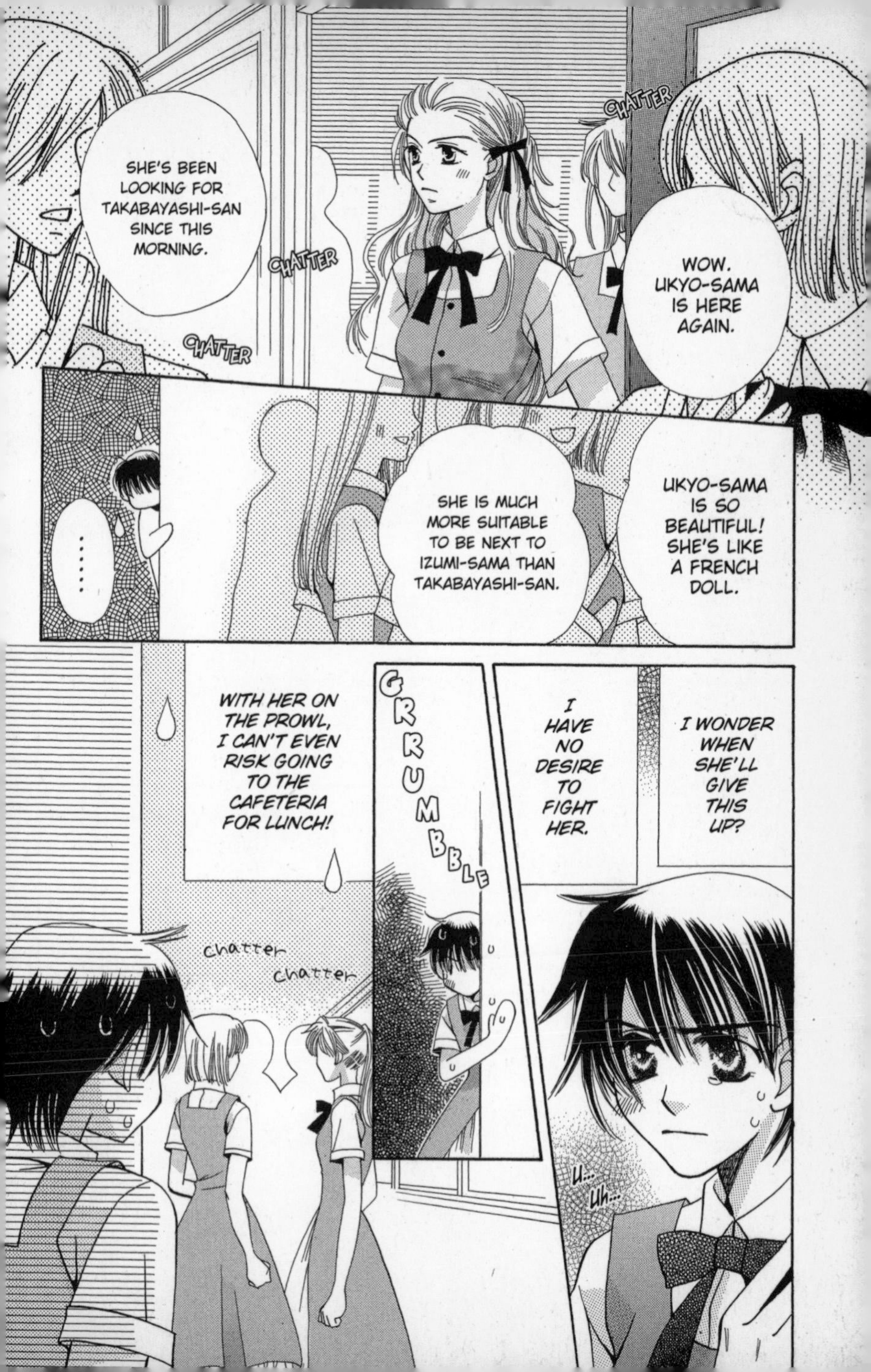
CHATTER
WOW. UKYO-SAMA IS HERE AGAIN.
CHATTER
SHE'S BEEN LOOKING FOR TAKABAYASHI-SAN SINCE THIS MORNING.
CHATTER
UKYO-SAMA IS SO BEAUTIFUL! SHE'S LIKE A FRENCH DOLL.
SHE IS MUCH MORE SUITABLE TO BE NEXT TO IZUMI-SAMA THAN TAKABAYASHI-SAN.
......
I WONDER WHEN SHE'LL GIVE THIS UP?
I HAVE NO DESIRE TO FIGHT HER.
U... Uh...
GRRUMBBLE
WITH HER ON THE PROWL, I CAN'T EVEN RISK GOING TO THE CAFETERIA FOR LUNCH!
chatter
chatter

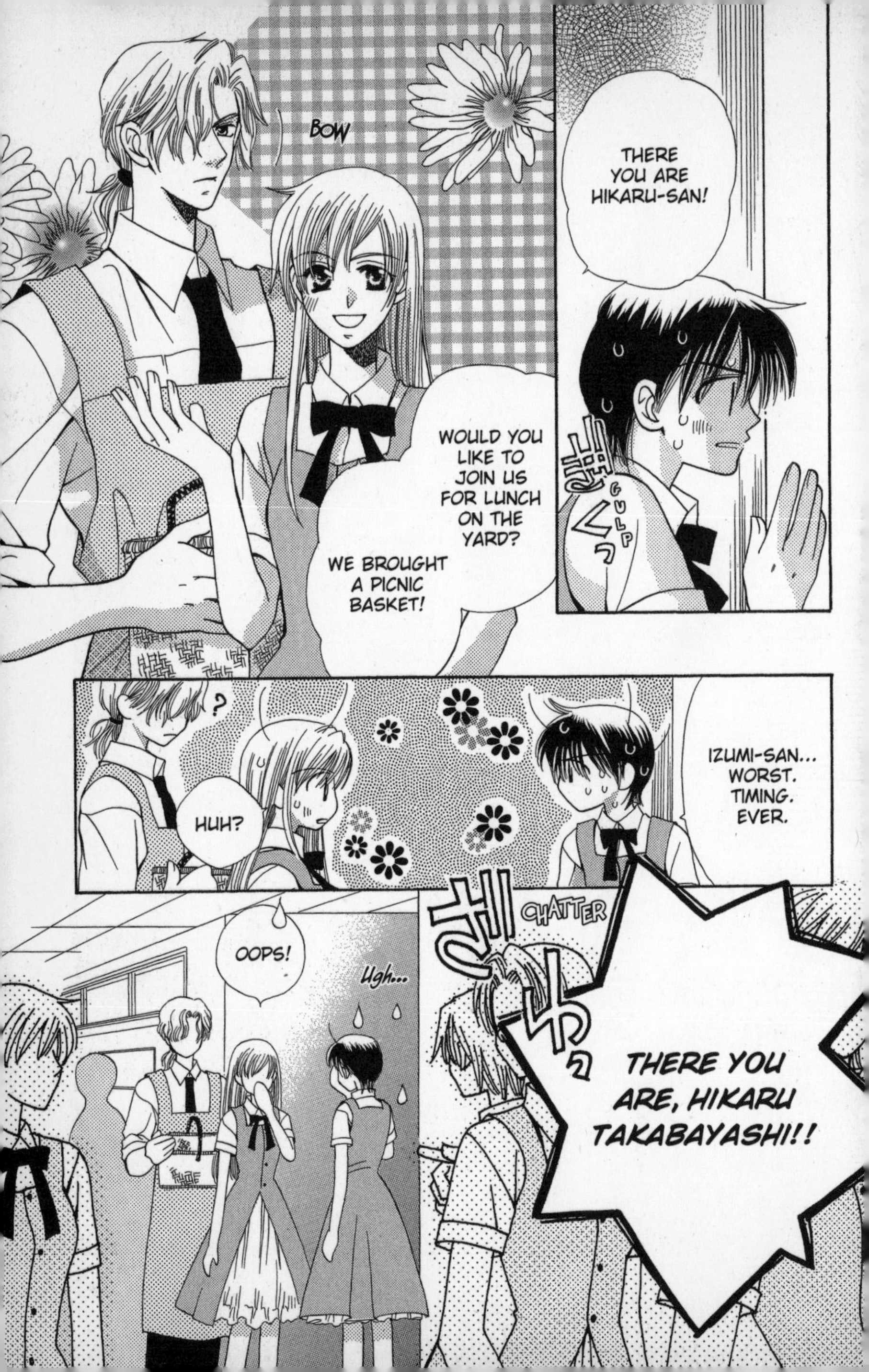
THERE YOU ARE HIKARU-SAN!
GULP
BOW
WOULD YOU LIKE TO JOIN US FOR LUNCH ON THE YARD?
WE BROUGHT A PICNIC BASKET!
IZUMI-SAN... WORST. TIMING. EVER.
HUH?
?
CHATTER
THERE YOU ARE, HIKARU TAKABAYASHI!!
OOPS!
Ugh...

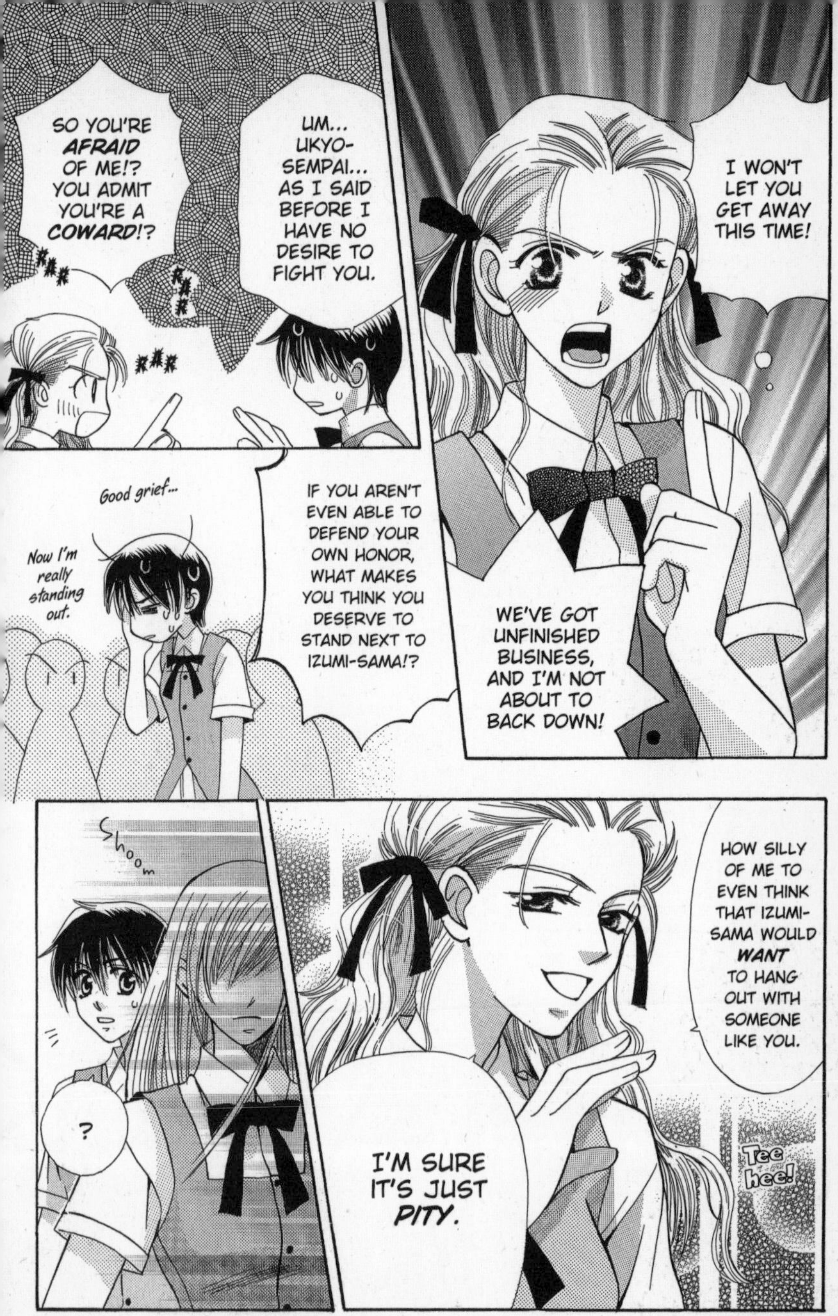
I WON'T LET YOU GET AWAY THIS TIME!
WE'VE GOT UNFINISHED BUSINESS, AND I'M NOT ABOUT TO BACK DOWN!
UM... UKYO-SEMPAI... AS I SAID BEFORE I HAVE NO DESIRE TO FIGHT YOU.
SO YOU'RE AFRAID OF ME!? YOU ADMIT YOU'RE A COWARD!?
RAR
RAR
RAR
IF YOU AREN'T EVEN ABLE TO DEFEND YOUR OWN HONOR, WHAT MAKES YOU THINK YOU DESERVE TO STAND NEXT TO IZUMI-SAMA!?
Good grief...
Now I'm really standing out.
HOW SILLY OF ME TO EVEN THINK THAT IZUMI-SAMA WOULD WANT TO HANG OUT WITH SOMEONE LIKE YOU.
I'M SURE IT'S JUST PITY.
Tee hee!
Shoom
?

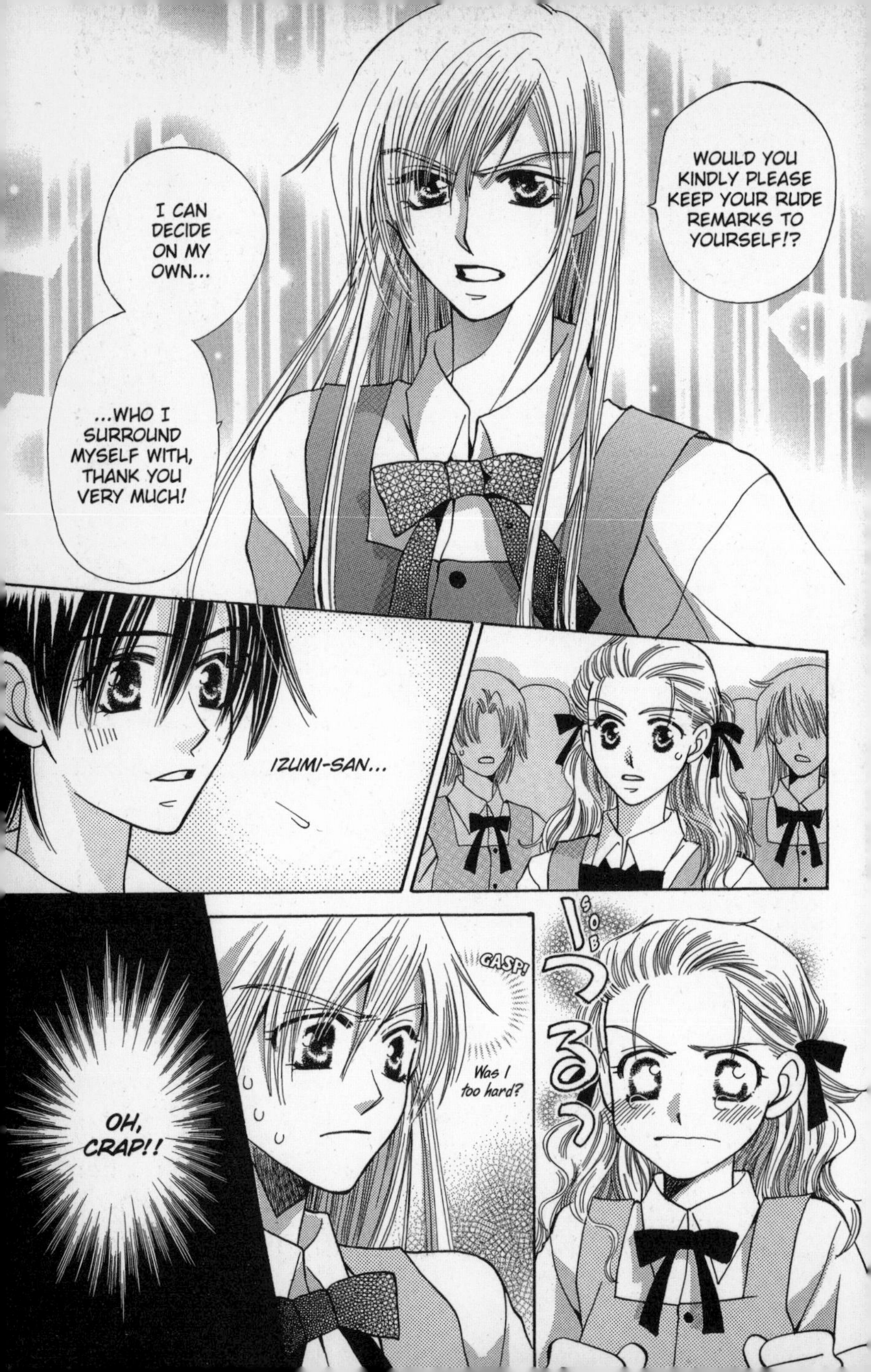
WOULD YOU KINDLY PLEASE KEEP YOUR RUDE REMARKS TO YOURSELF!?
I CAN DECIDE ON MY OWN...
...WHO I SURROUND MYSELF WITH, THANK YOU VERY MUCH!
IZUMI-SAN...
SOB
GASP!
Was I too hard?
OH, CRAP!!

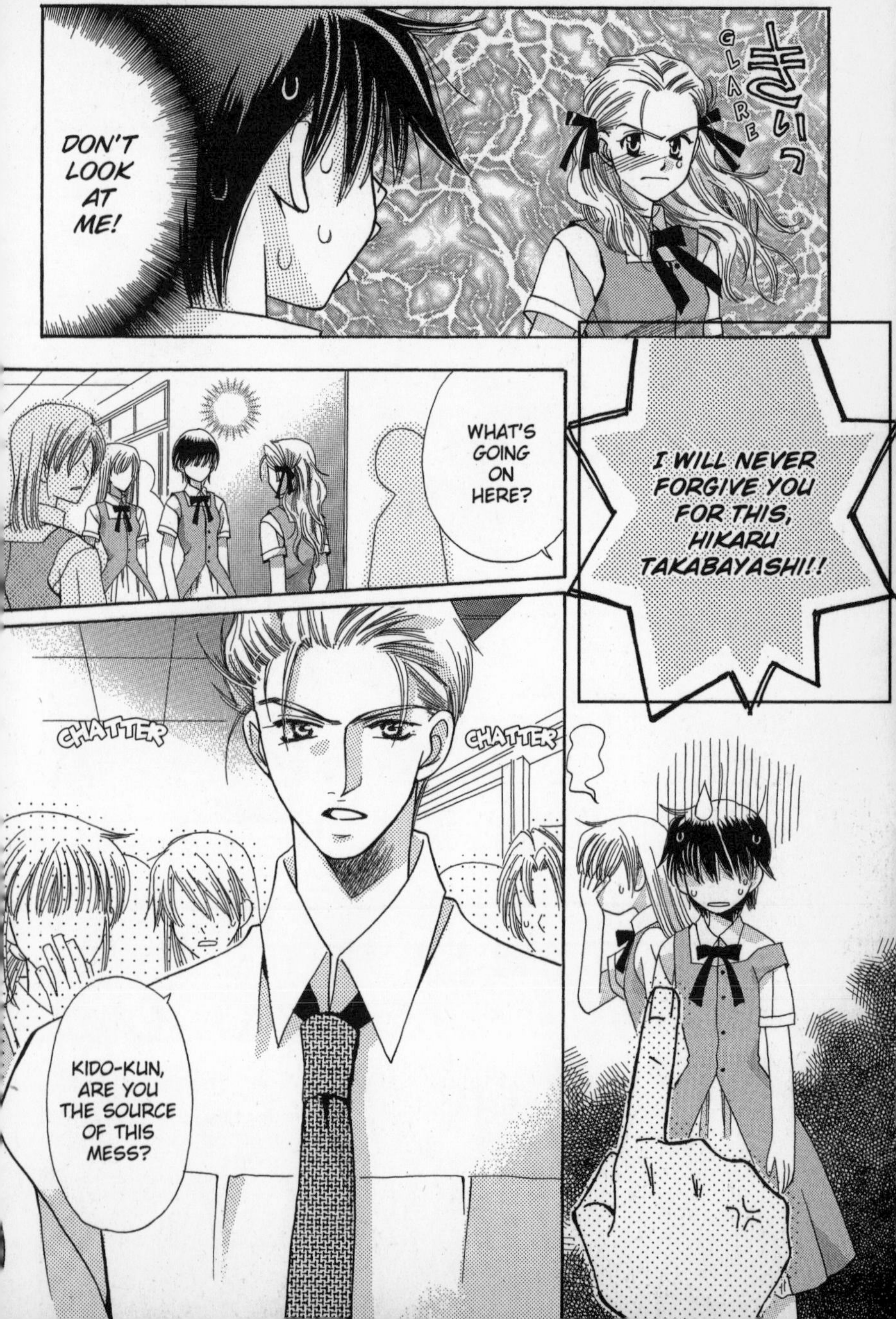
きーっ
GLARE
DON'T LOOK AT ME!
I WILL NEVER FORGIVE YOU FOR THIS, HIKARU TAKABAYASHI!!
WHAT'S GOING ON HERE?
CHATTER
CHATTER
KIDO-KUN, ARE YOU THE SOURCE OF THIS MESS?

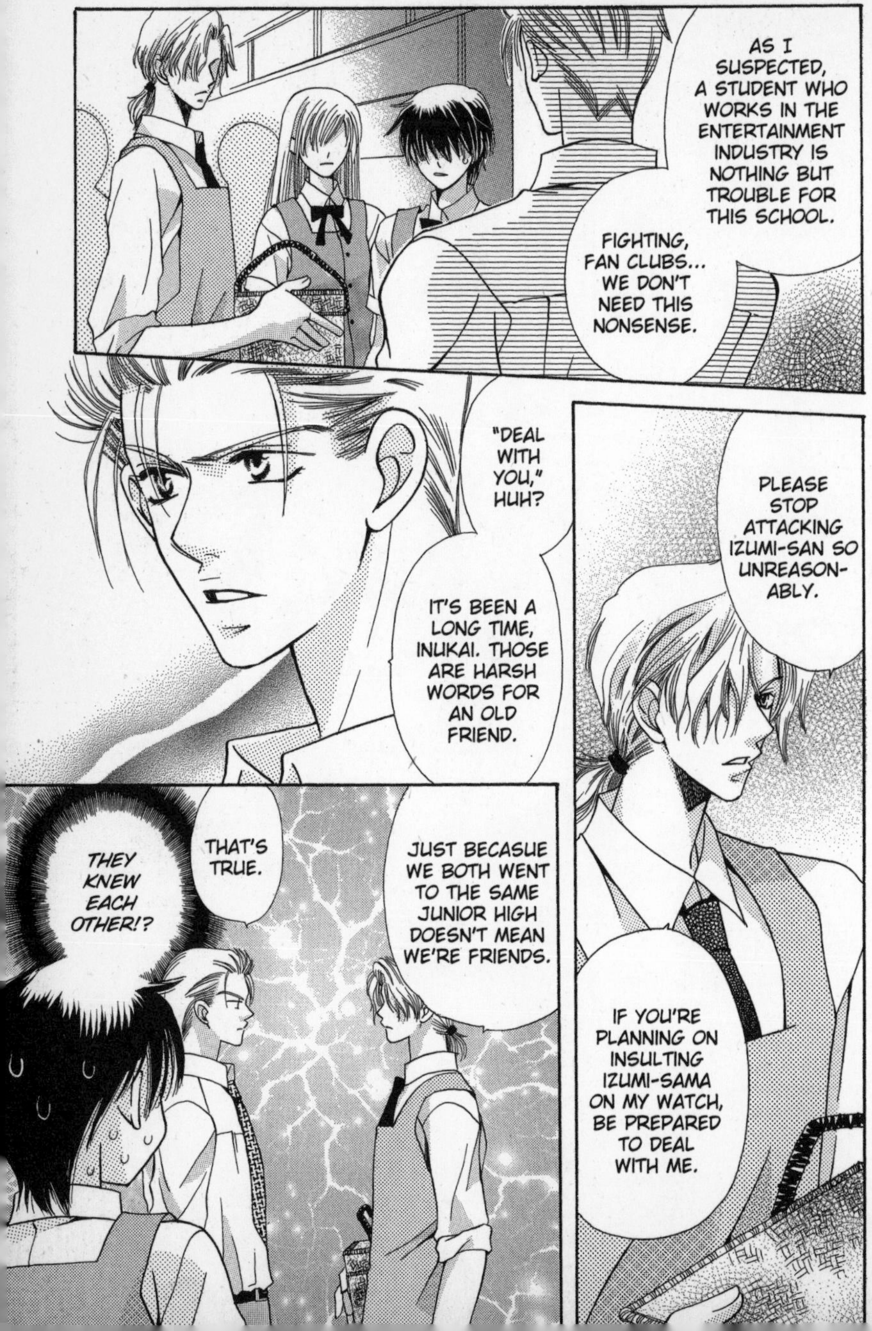
AS I SUSPECTED, A STUDENT WHO WORKS IN THE ENTERTAINMENT INDUSTRY IS NOTHING BUT TROUBLE FOR THIS SCHOOL.
FIGHTING, FAN CLUBS... WE DON'T NEED THIS NONSENSE.
PLEASE STOP ATTACKING IZUMI-SAN SO UNREASON-ABLY.
IF YOU'RE PLANNING ON INSULTING IZUMI-SAMA ON MY WATCH, BE PREPARED TO DEAL WITH ME.
"DEAL WITH YOU," HUH?
IT'S BEEN A LONG TIME, INUKAI. THOSE ARE HARSH WORDS FOR AN OLD FRIEND.
THAT'S TRUE.
JUST BECASUE WE BOTH WENT TO THE SAME JUNIOR HIGH DOESN'T MEAN WE'RE FRIENDS.
THEY KNEW EACH OTHER!?

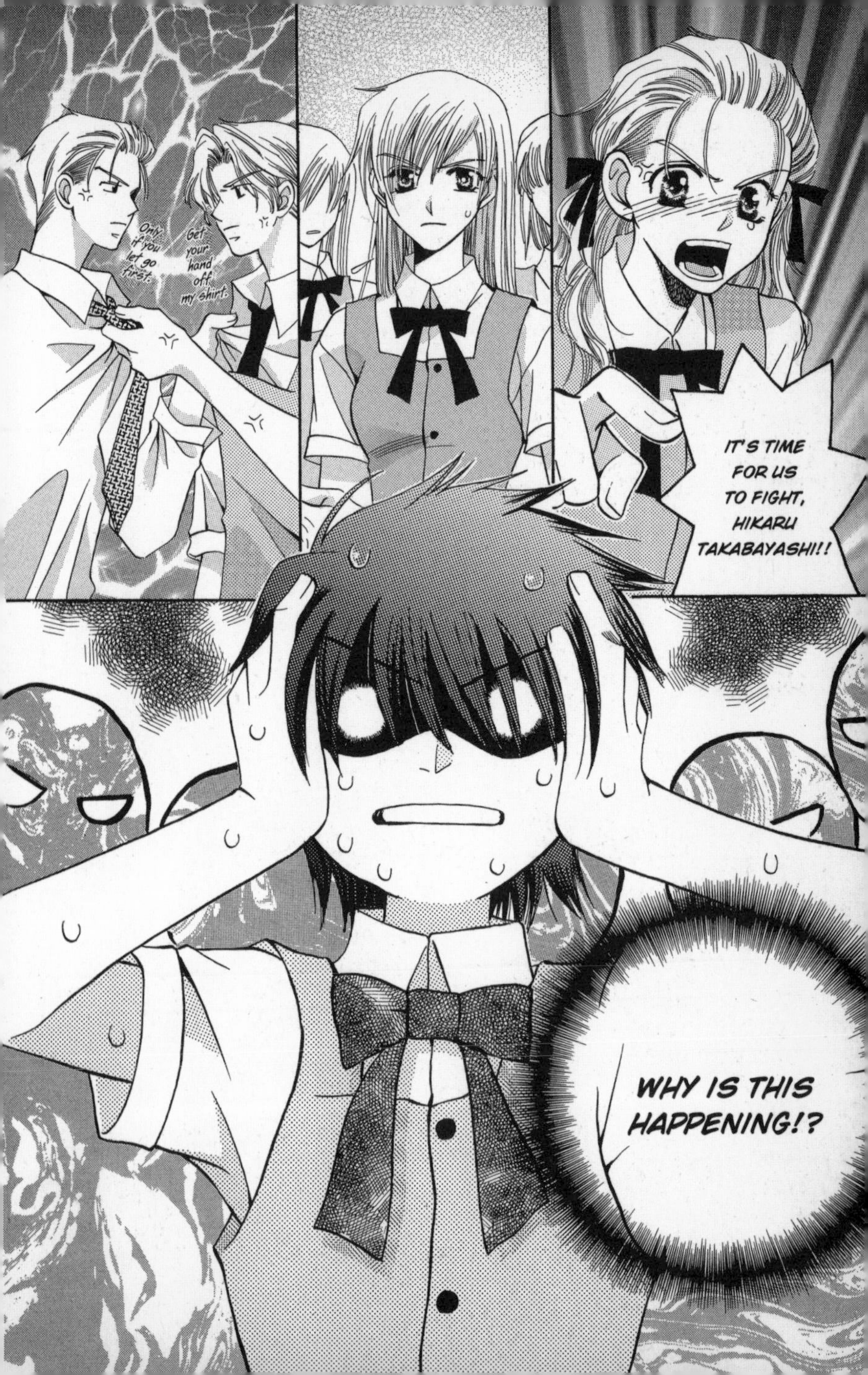
IT'S TIME FOR US TO FIGHT, HIKARU TAKABAYASHI!!
Get your hand off my shirt.
Only if you let go first.
WHY IS THIS HAPPENING!?

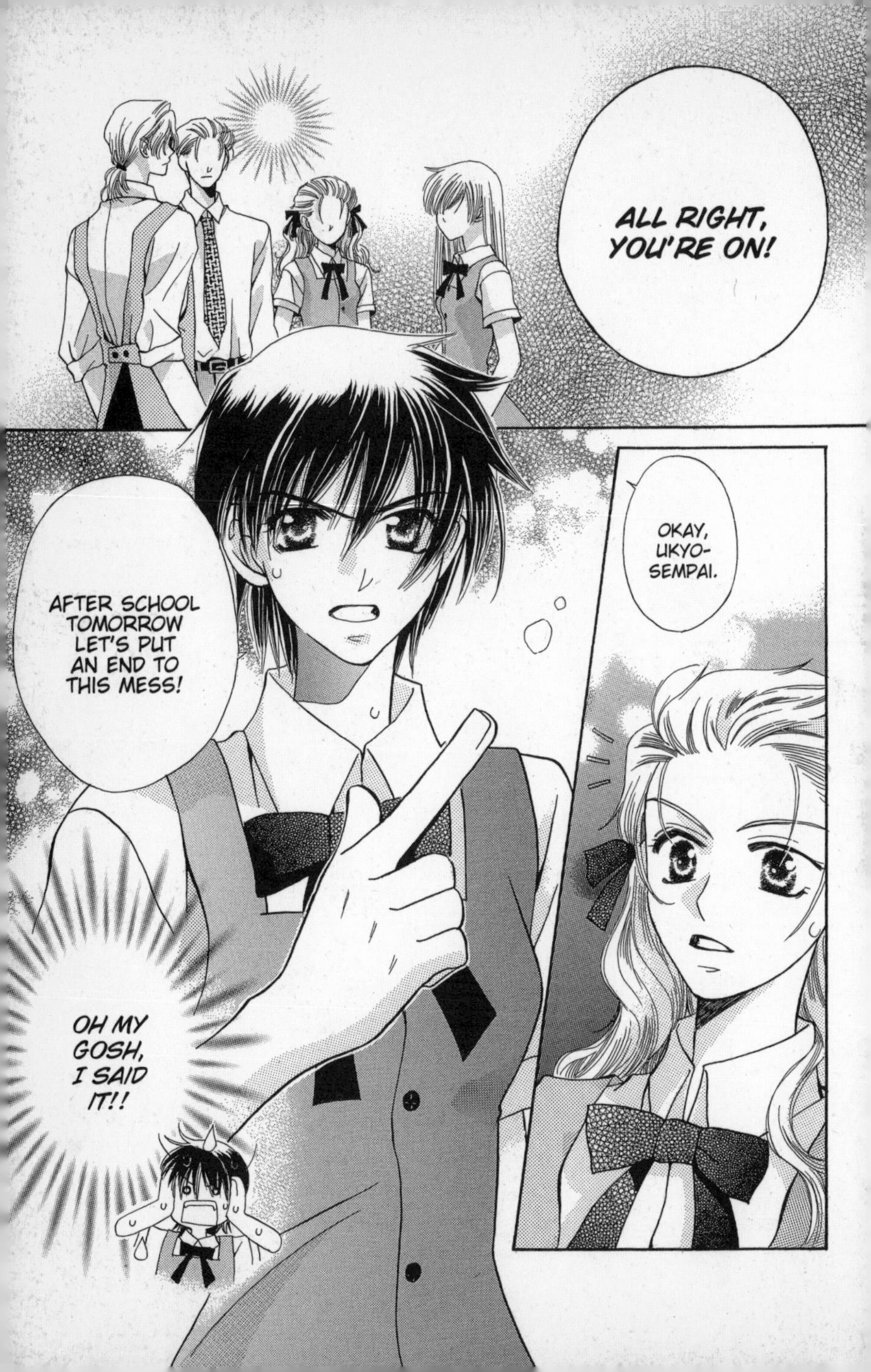
ALL RIGHT, YOU'RE ON!
OKAY, UKYO-SEMPAI.
AFTER SCHOOL TOMORROW LET'S PUT AN END TO THIS MESS!
OH MY GOSH, I SAID IT!!

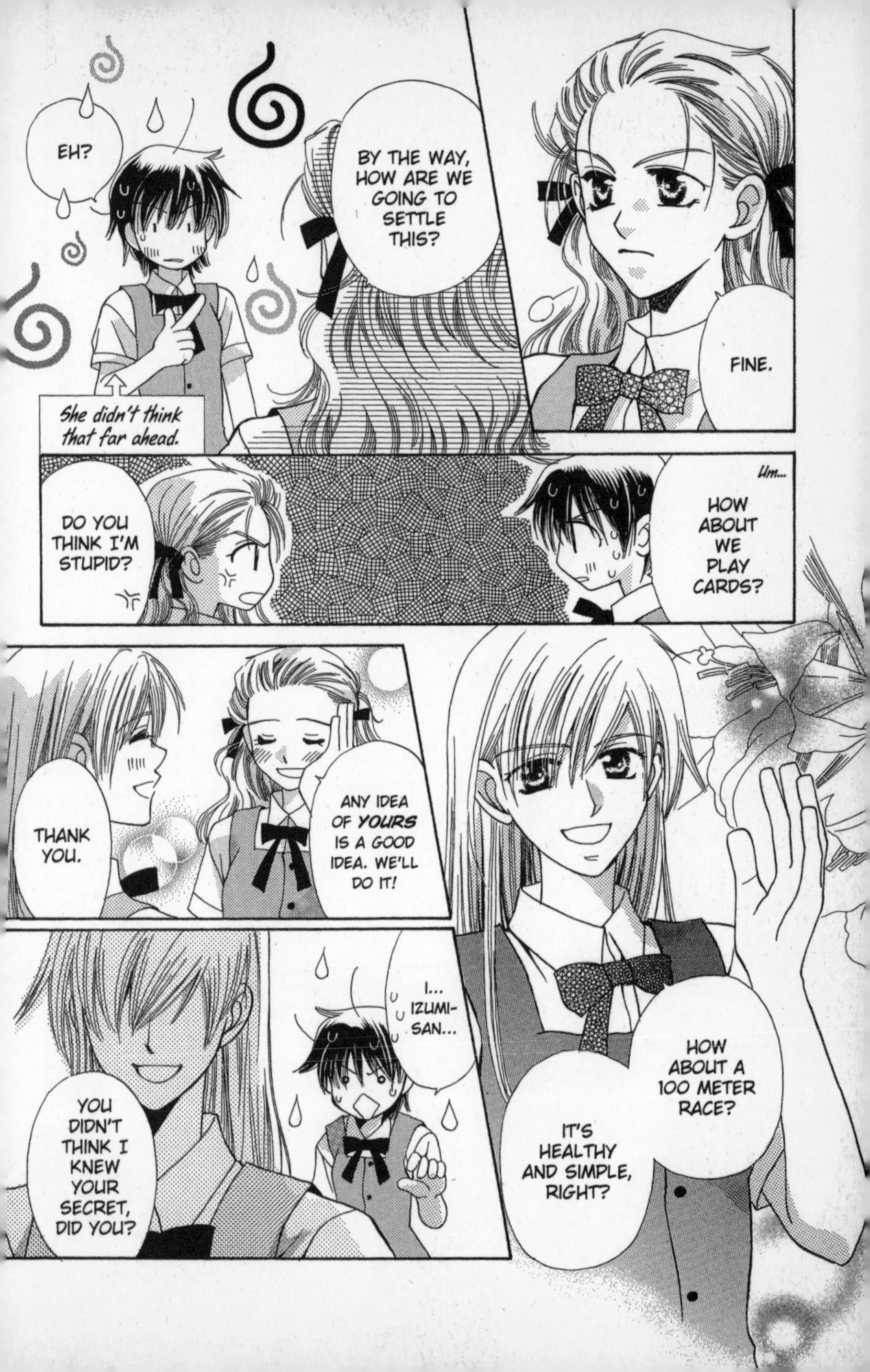
FINE.
BY THE WAY, HOW ARE WE GOING TO SETTLE THIS?
EH?
She didn't think that far ahead.
Um...
HOW ABOUT WE PLAY CARDS?
DO YOU THINK I'M STUPID?
HOW ABOUT A 100 METER RACE?
IT'S HEALTHY AND SIMPLE, RIGHT?
ANY IDEA OF *YOURS* IS A GOOD IDEA. WE'LL DO IT!
THANK YOU.
I... IZUMI-SAN...
YOU DIDN'T THINK I KNEW YOUR SECRET, DID YOU?

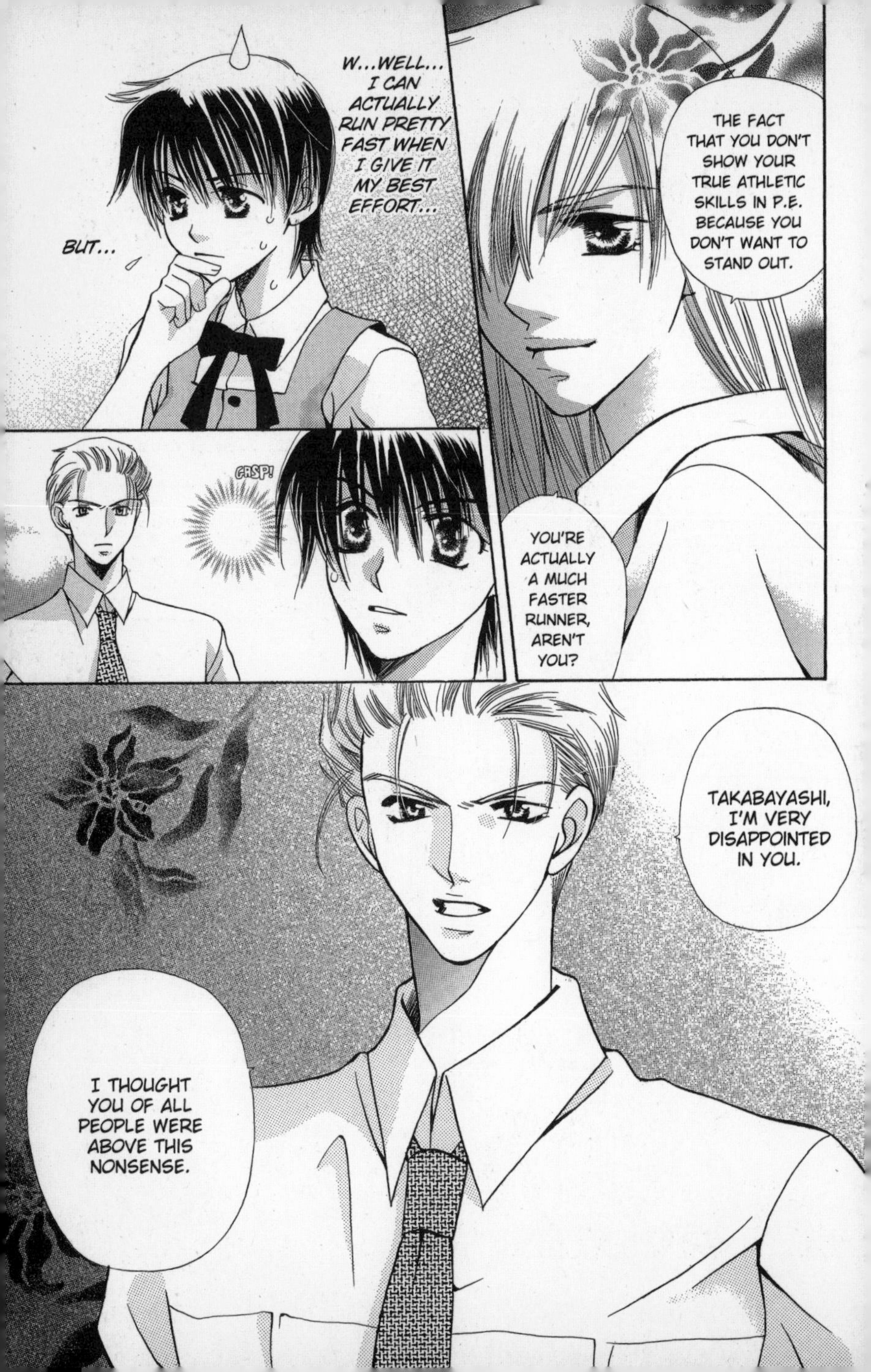
THE FACT THAT YOU DON'T SHOW YOUR TRUE ATHLETIC SKILLS IN P.E. BECAUSE YOU DON'T WANT TO STAND OUT.
YOU'RE ACTUALLY A MUCH FASTER RUNNER, AREN'T YOU?
W...WELL... I CAN ACTUALLY RUN PRETTY FAST WHEN I GIVE IT MY BEST EFFORT...
BUT...
GASP!
TAKABAYASHI, I'M VERY DISAPPOINTED IN YOU.
I THOUGHT YOU OF ALL PEOPLE WERE ABOVE THIS NONSENSE.

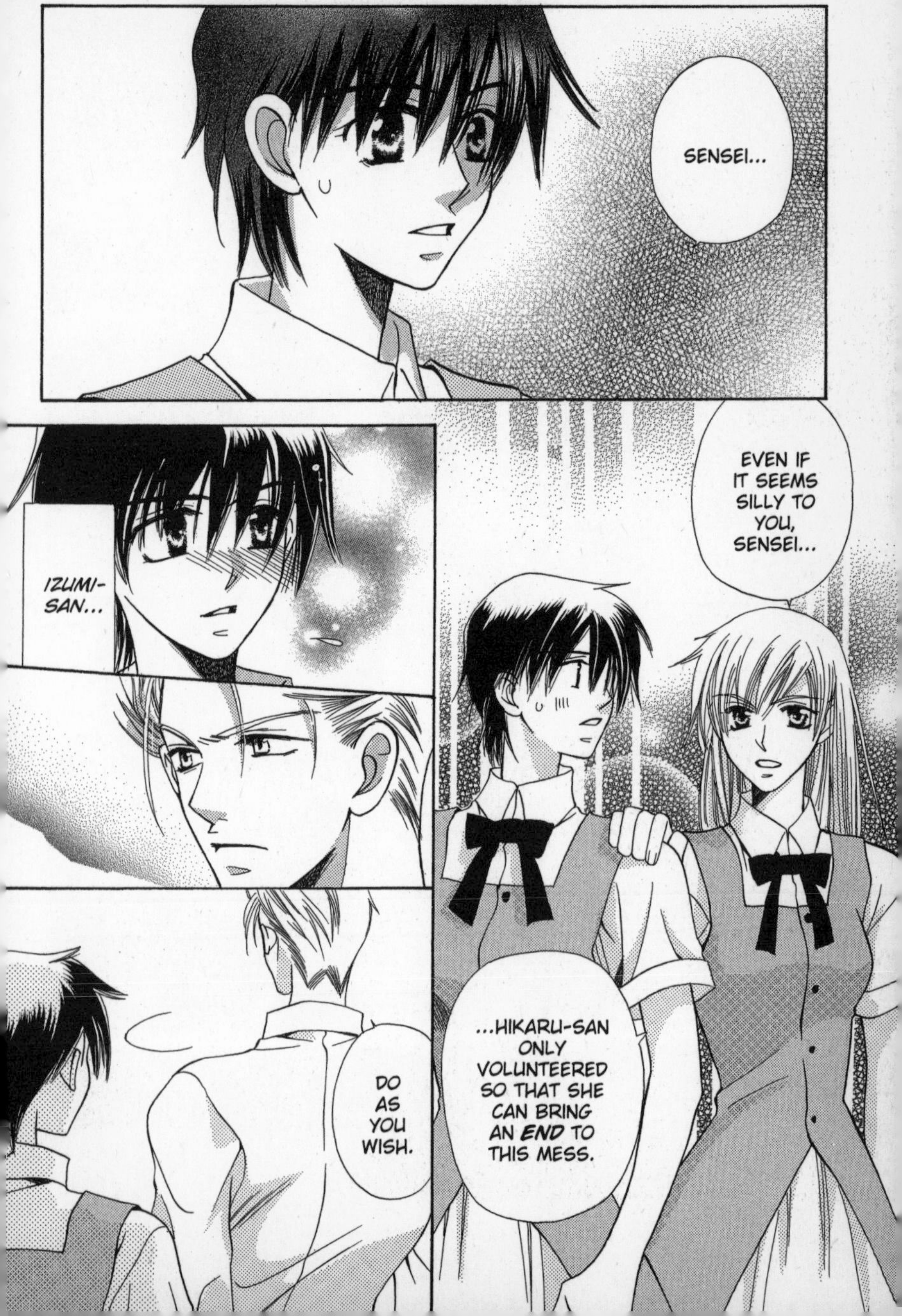
SENSEI...
EVEN IF IT SEEMS SILLY TO YOU, SENSEI...
...HIKARU-SAN ONLY VOLUNTEERED SO THAT SHE CAN BRING AN *END* TO THIS MESS.
IZUMI-SAN...
DO AS YOU WISH.

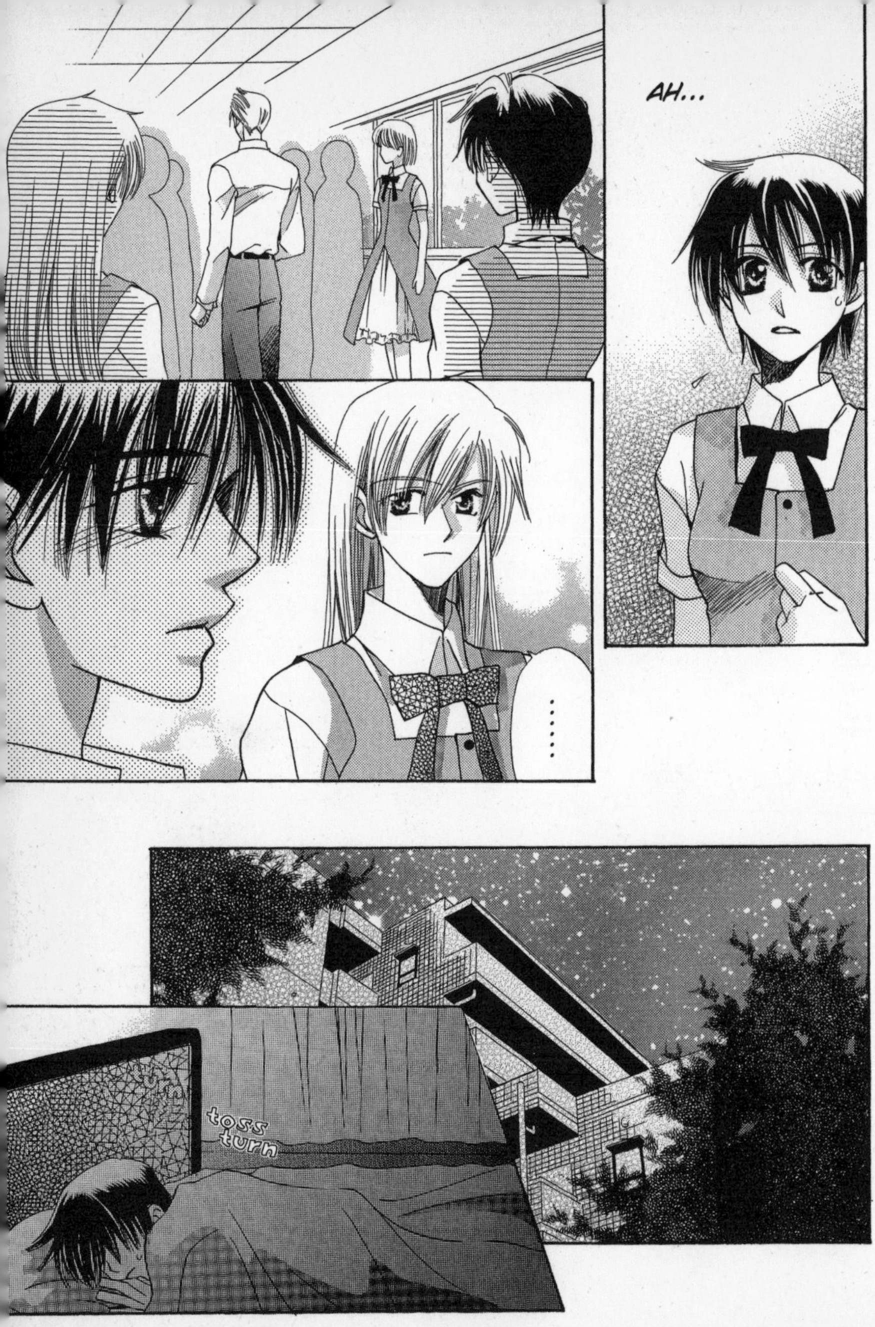
AH...
......
toss
turn

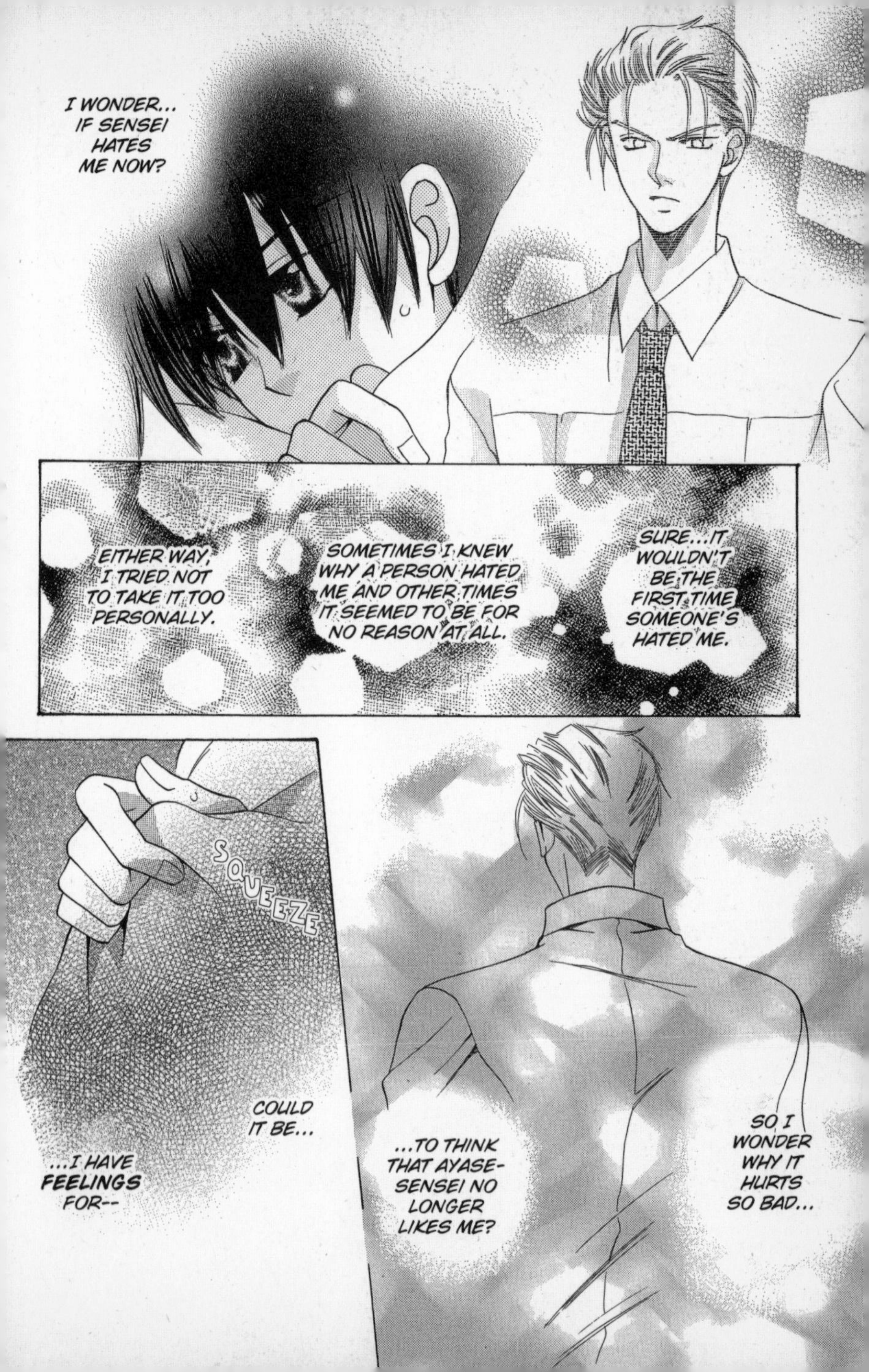
I WONDER... IF SENSEI HATES ME NOW?
SURE...IT WOULDN'T BE THE FIRST TIME SOMEONE'S HATED ME.
SOMETIMES I KNEW WHY A PERSON HATED ME AND OTHER TIMES IT SEEMED TO BE FOR NO REASON AT ALL.
EITHER WAY, I TRIED NOT TO TAKE IT TOO PERSONALLY.
SO I WONDER WHY IT HURTS SO BAD...
...TO THINK THAT AYASE-SENSEI NO LONGER LIKES ME?
SQUEEZE
COULD IT BE...
...I HAVE FEELINGS FOR--

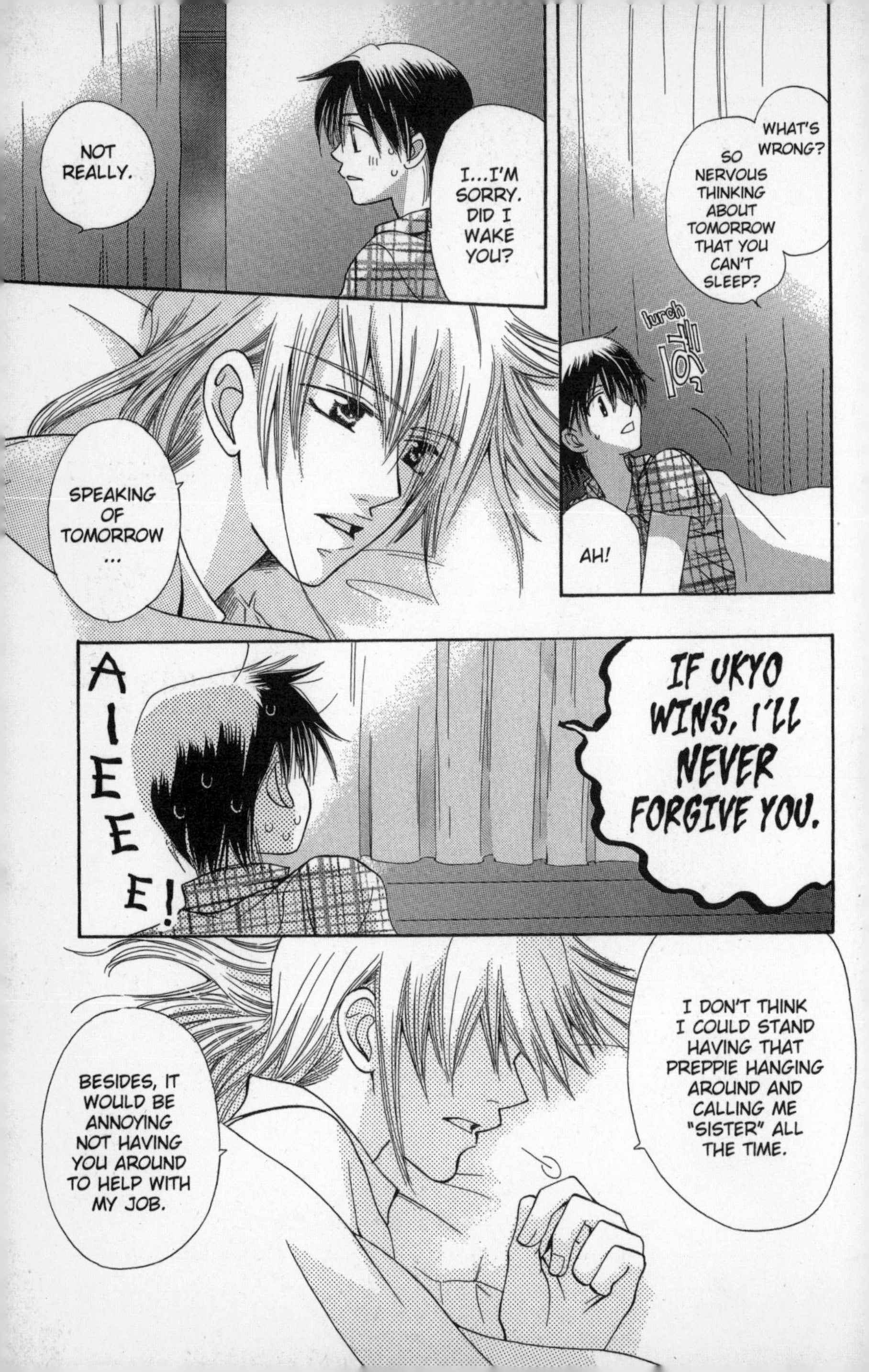
WHAT'S WRONG?
SO NERVOUS THINKING ABOUT TOMORROW THAT YOU CAN'T SLEEP?
lurch
AH!
I...I'M SORRY. DID I WAKE YOU?
NOT REALLY.
SPEAKING OF TOMORROW ...
IF UKYO WINS, I'LL NEVER FORGIVE YOU.
AIEEEE!
I DON'T THINK I COULD STAND HAVING THAT PREPPIE HANGING AROUND AND CALLING ME "SISTER" ALL THE TIME.
BESIDES, IT WOULD BE ANNOYING NOT HAVING YOU AROUND TO HELP WITH MY JOB.

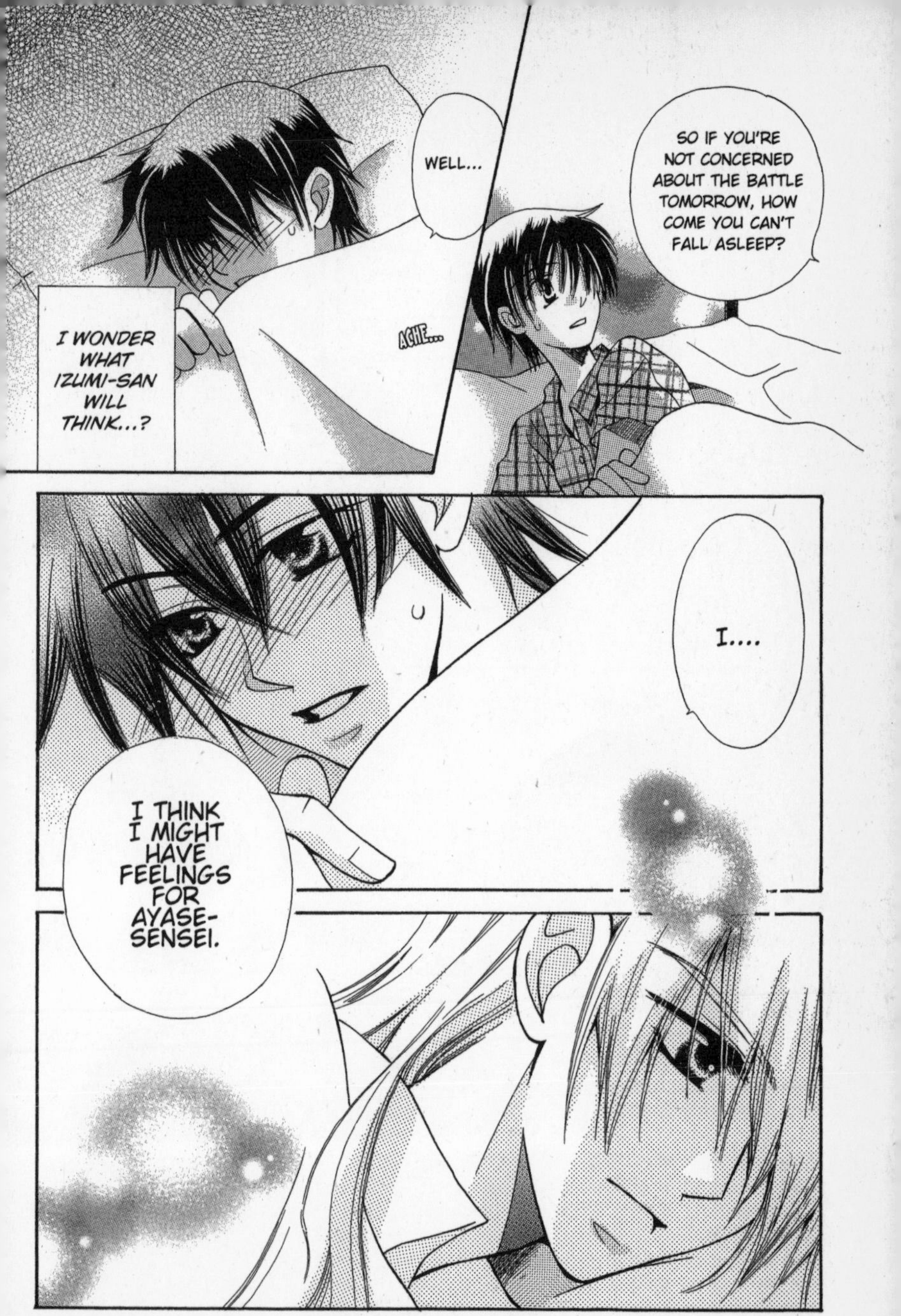
SO IF YOU'RE NOT CONCERNED ABOUT THE BATTLE TOMORROW, HOW COME YOU CAN'T FALL ASLEEP?
WELL...
ACHE...
I WONDER WHAT IZUMI-SAN WILL THINK...?
I....
I THINK I MIGHT HAVE FEELINGS FOR AYASE-SENSEI.

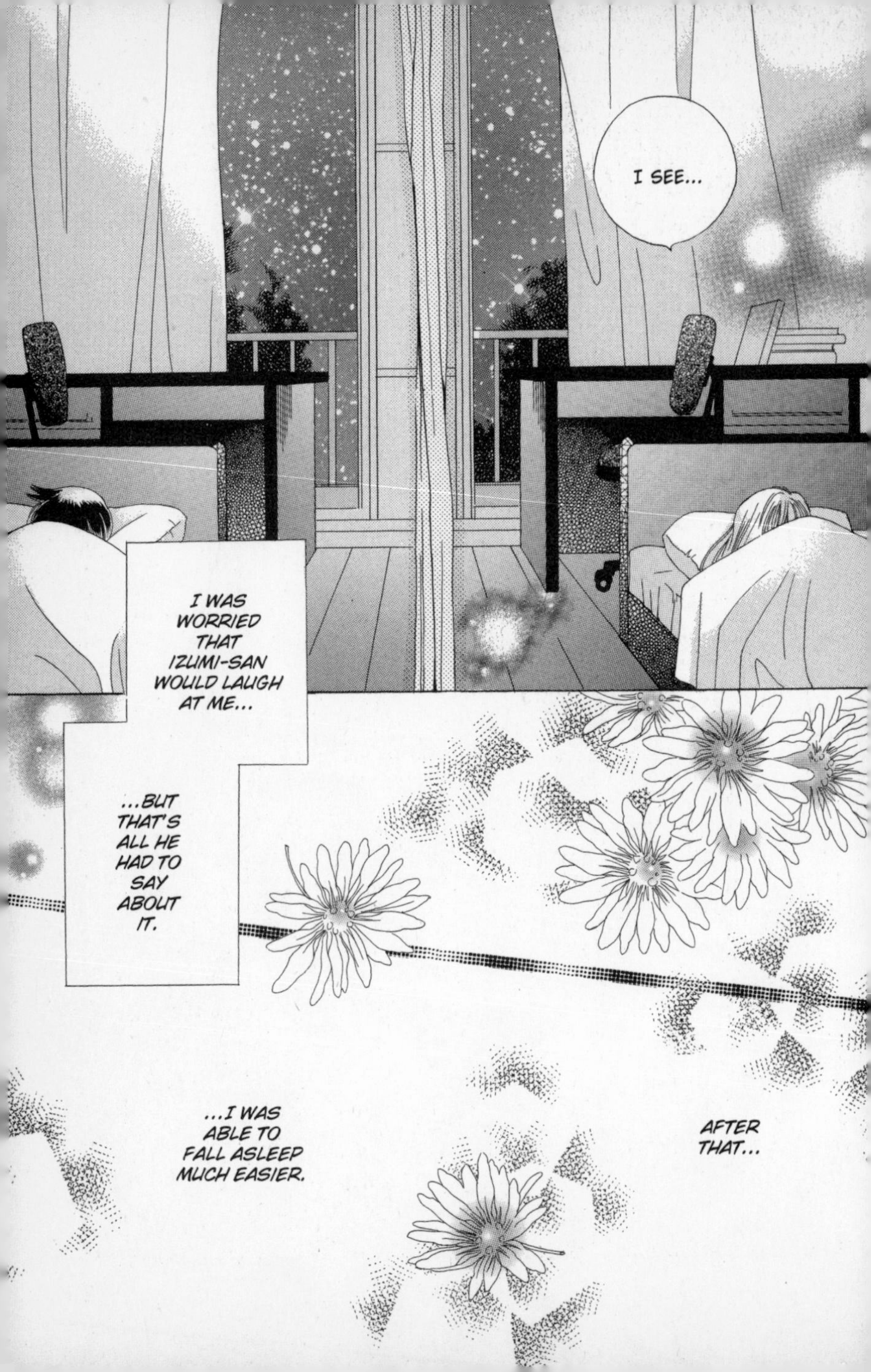
I SEE...
I WAS WORRIED THAT IZUMI-SAN WOULD LAUGH AT ME...
...BUT THAT'S ALL HE HAD TO SAY ABOUT IT.
AFTER THAT...
...I WAS ABLE TO FALL ASLEEP MUCH EASIER.

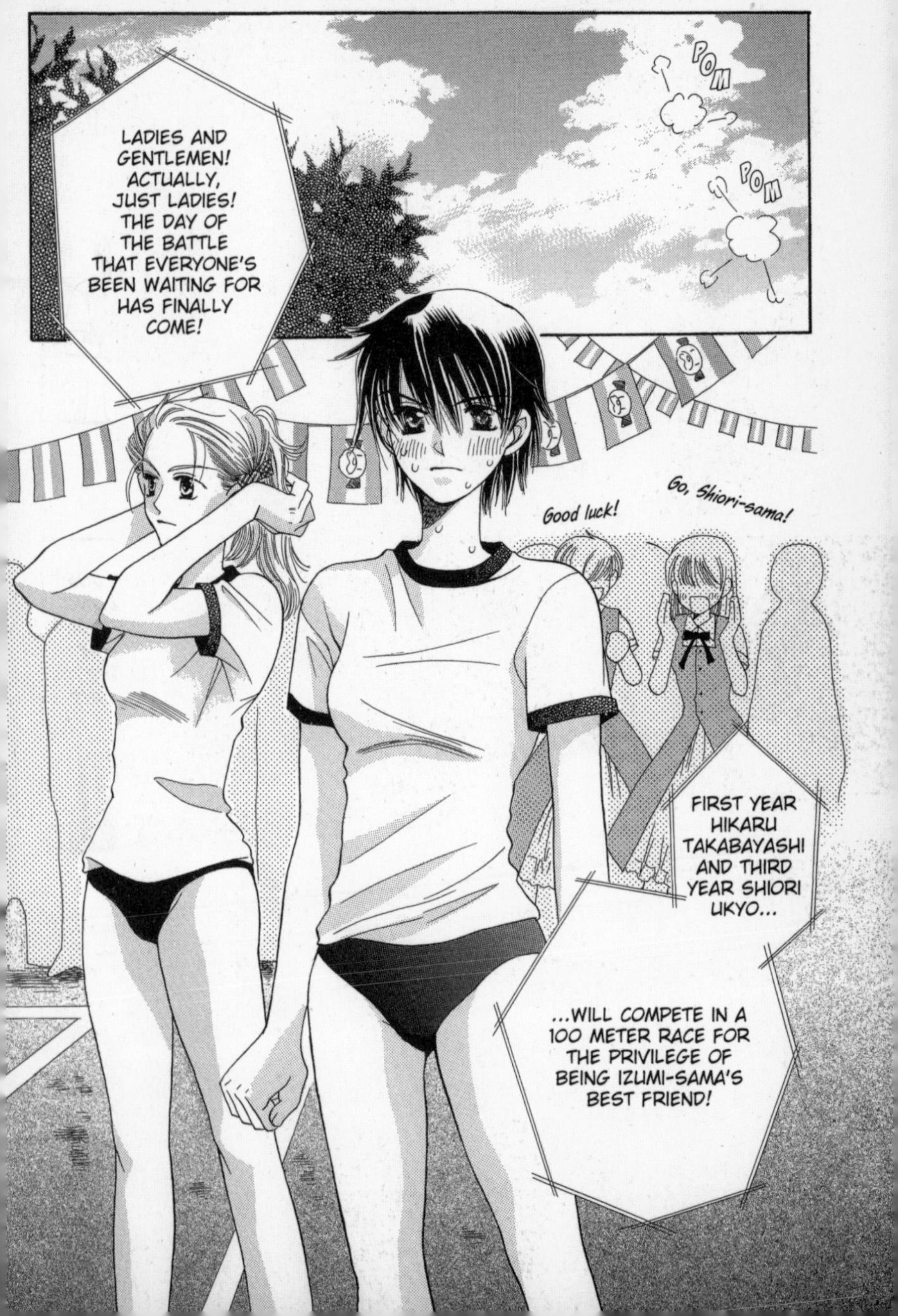
POM
POM
LADIES AND GENTLEMEN! ACTUALLY, JUST LADIES! THE DAY OF THE BATTLE THAT EVERYONE'S BEEN WAITING FOR HAS FINALLY COME!
Go, Shiori-sama!
Good luck!
FIRST YEAR HIKARU TAKABAYASHI AND THIRD YEAR SHIORI UKYO...
...WILL COMPETE IN A 100 METER RACE FOR THE PRIVILEGE OF BEING IZUMI-SAMA'S BEST FRIEND!

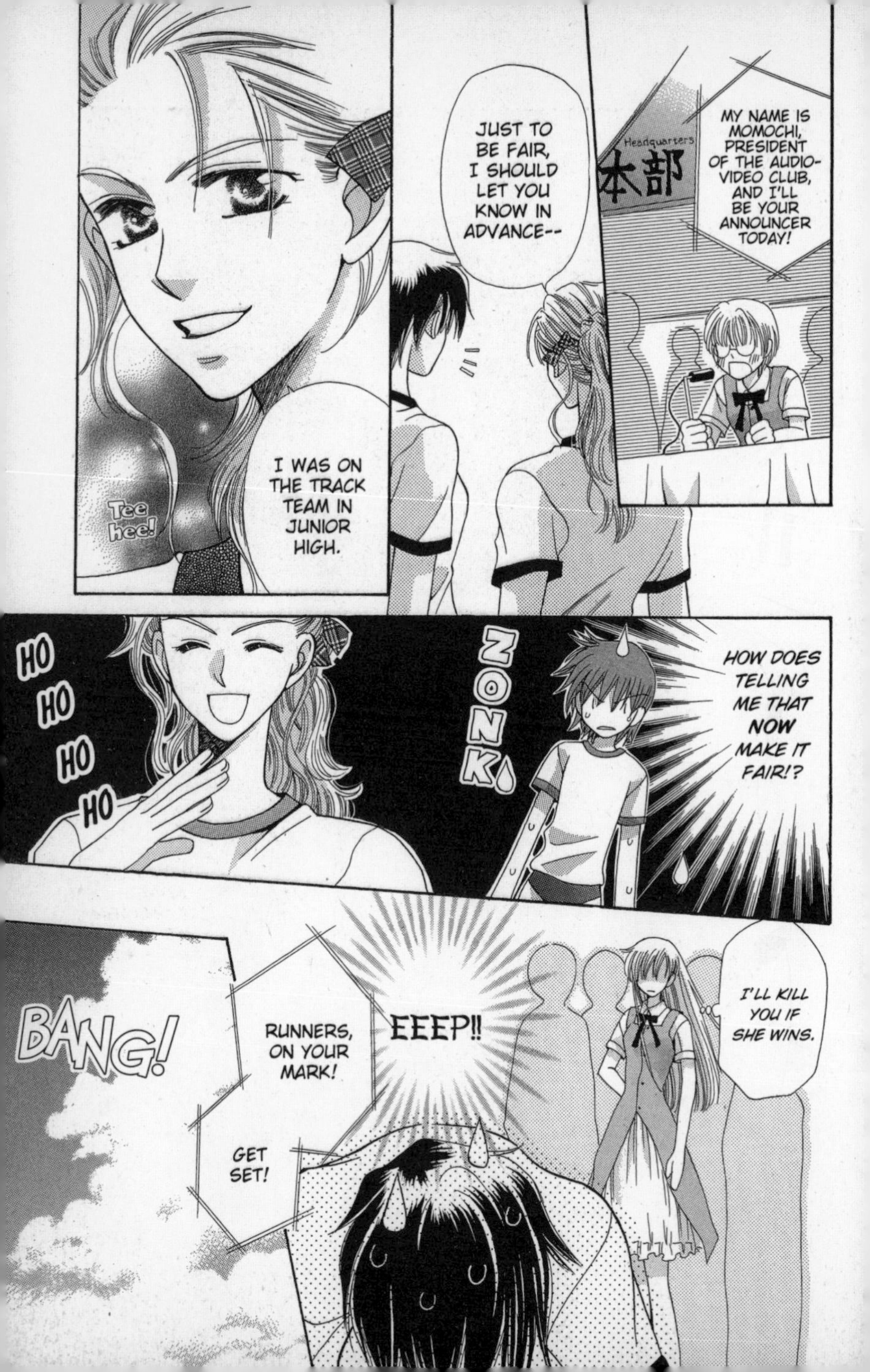
Headquarters
本部
MY NAME IS MOMOCHI, PRESIDENT OF THE AUDIO-VIDEO CLUB, AND I'LL BE YOUR ANNOUNCER TODAY!
JUST TO BE FAIR, I SHOULD LET YOU KNOW IN ADVANCE--
I WAS ON THE TRACK TEAM IN JUNIOR HIGH.
Tee hee!
HOW DOES TELLING ME THAT NOW MAKE IT FAIR!?
ZONK
HO HO HO HO HO
I'LL KILL YOU IF SHE WINS.
EEEP!!
RUNNERS, ON YOUR MARK!
GET SET!
BANG!

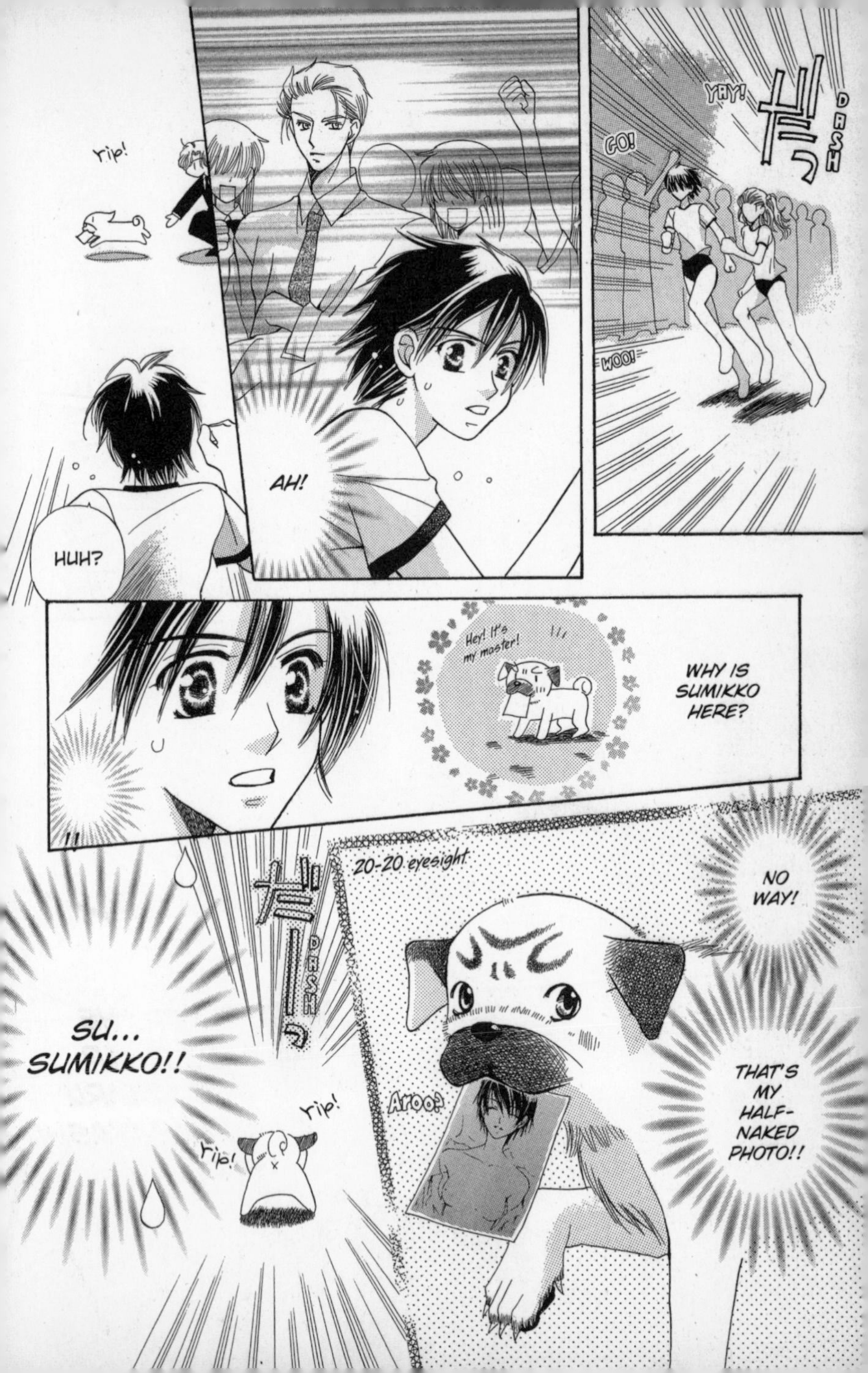
YAY!
DASH
GO!
WOO!
AH!
rip!
HUH?
Hey! It's my master!
WHY IS SUMIKKO HERE?
NO WAY!
THAT'S MY HALF-NAKED PHOTO!!
20-20 eyesight
Aroo?
DASH
SU... SUMIKKO!!
rip!
rip!

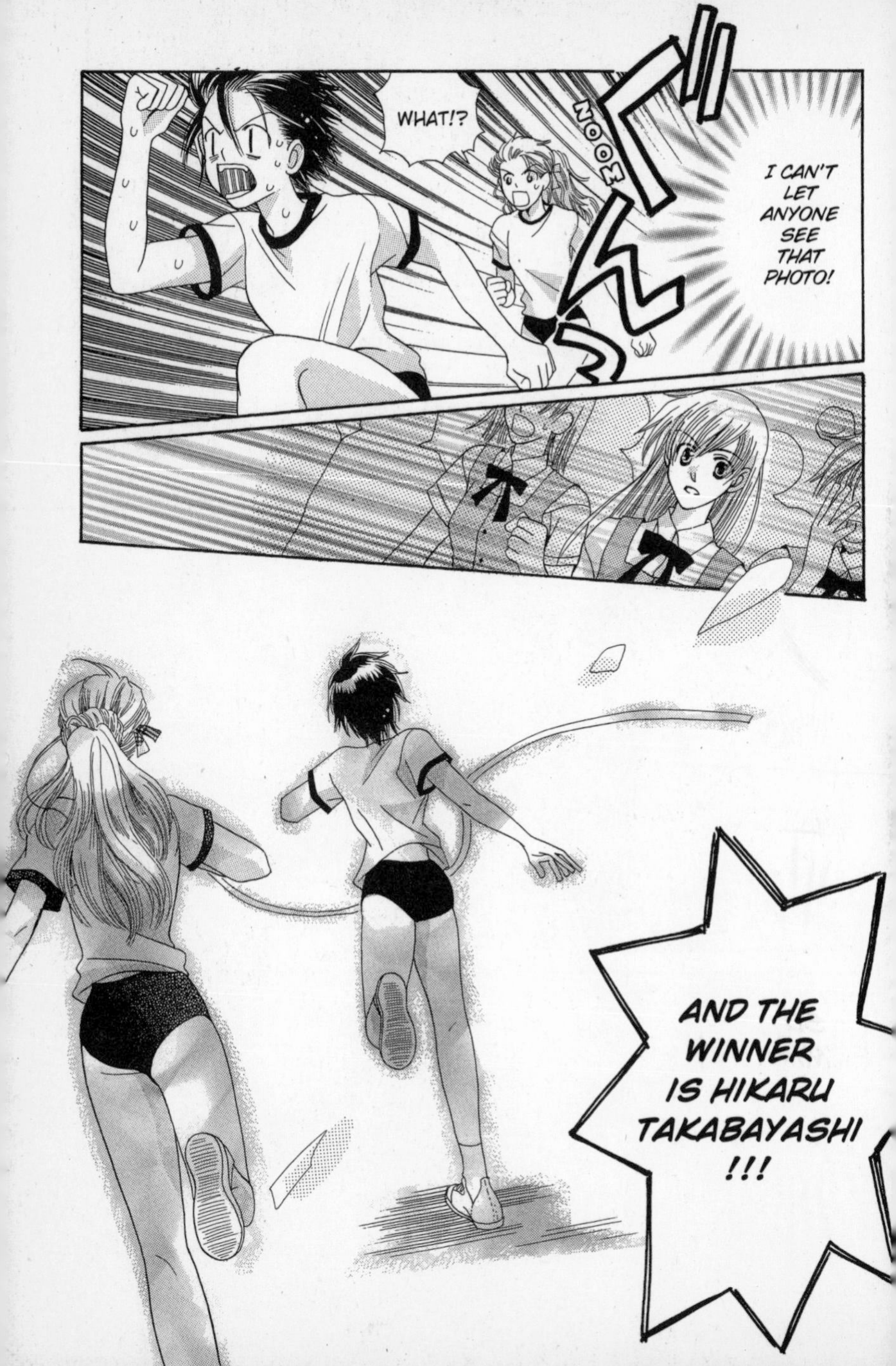
I CAN'T LET ANYONE SEE THAT PHOTO!
ZOOM
WHAT!?
AND THE WINNER IS HIKARU TAKABAYASHI !!!

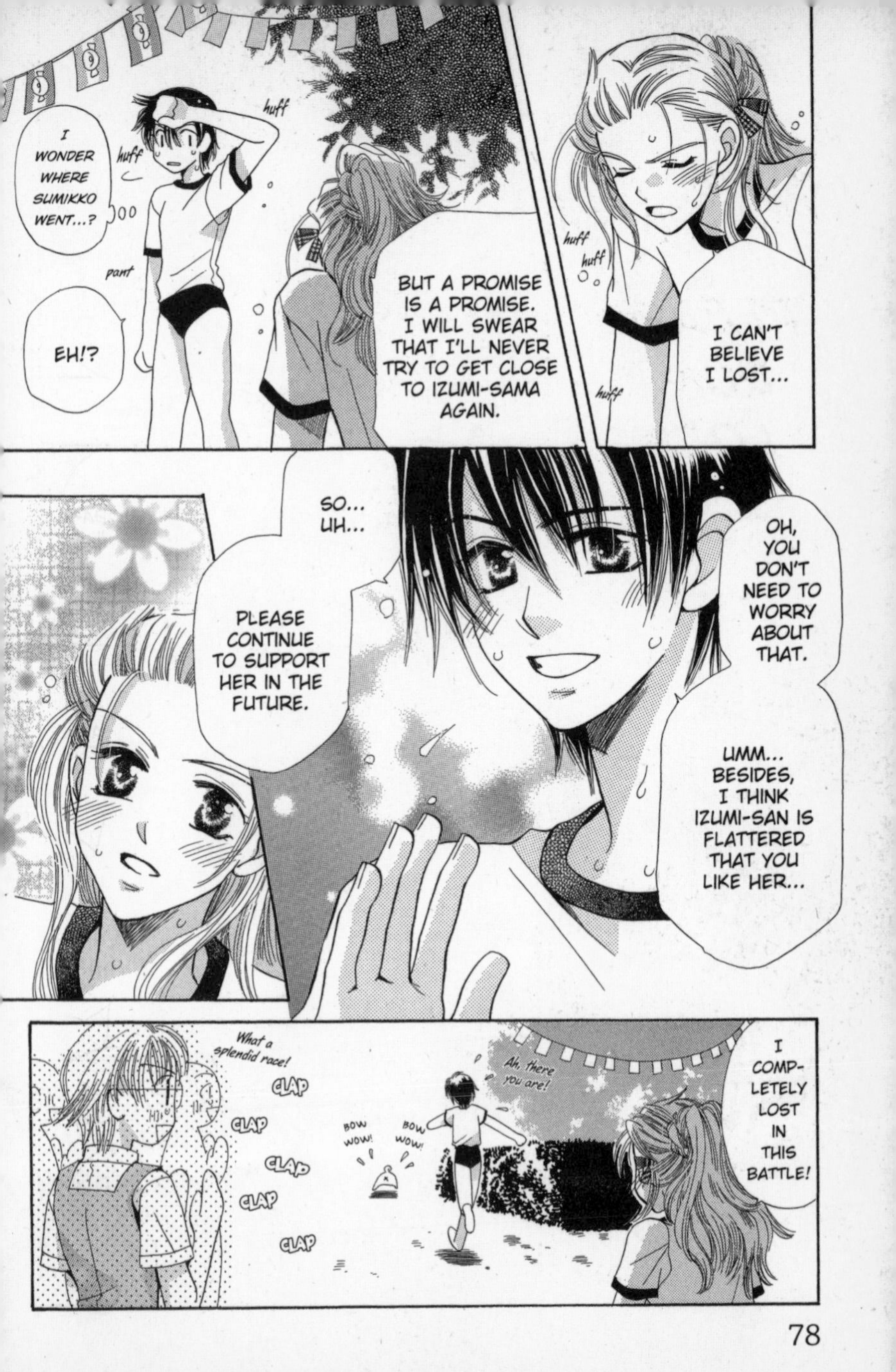
huff
huff
I CAN'T BELIEVE I LOST...
huff
huff
BUT A PROMISE IS A PROMISE. I WILL SWEAR THAT I'LL NEVER TRY TO GET CLOSE TO IZUMI-SAMA AGAIN.
huff
I WONDER WHERE SUMIKKO WENT...?
pant
EH!?
OH, YOU DON'T NEED TO WORRY ABOUT THAT.
UMM... BESIDES, I THINK IZUMI-SAN IS FLATTERED THAT YOU LIKE HER...
SO... UH...
PLEASE CONTINUE TO SUPPORT HER IN THE FUTURE.
I COMP-LETELY LOST IN THIS BATTLE!
Ah, there you are!
BOW WOW!
BOW WOW!
What a splendid race!
CLAP
CLAP
CLAP
CLAP
CLAP

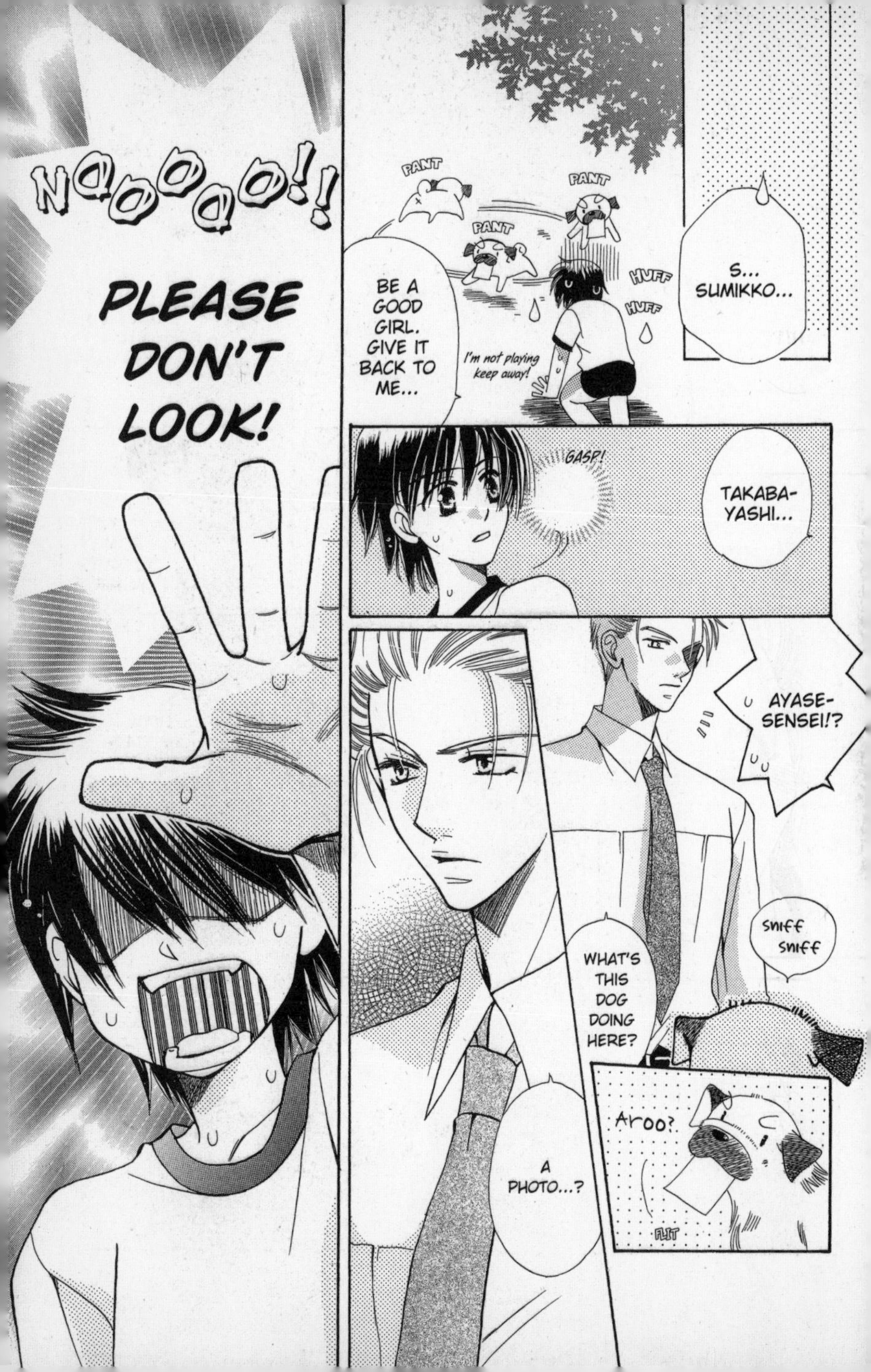
S... SUMIKKO...
HUFF HUFF
PANT
PANT
PANT
BE A GOOD GIRL. GIVE IT BACK TO ME...
I'm not playing keep away!
TAKABAYASHI...
GASP!
AYASE-SENSEI!?
sniff sniff
WHAT'S THIS DOG DOING HERE?
Aroo?
FLIT
A PHOTO...?
NOOOOO!!
PLEASE DON'T LOOK!

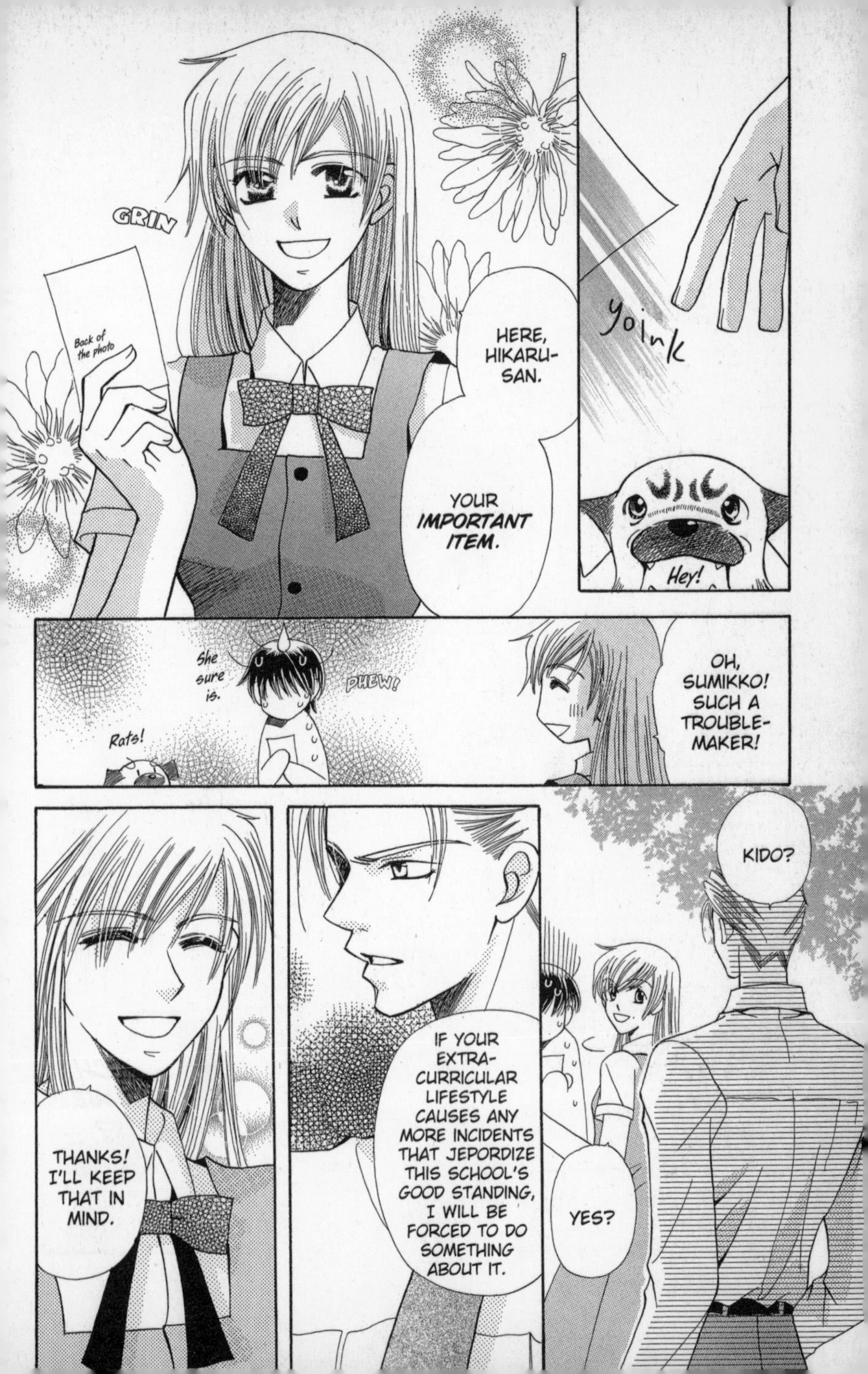
yoink
Hey!
HERE, HIKARU-SAN.
YOUR IMPORTANT ITEM.
GRIN
Back of the photo
OH, SUMIKKO! SUCH A TROUBLE-MAKER!
PHEW!
She sure is.
Rats!
KIDO?
YES?
IF YOUR EXTRA-CURRICULAR LIFESTYLE CAUSES ANY MORE INCIDENTS THAT JEPORDIZE THIS SCHOOL'S GOOD STANDING, I WILL BE FORCED TO DO SOMETHING ABOUT IT.
THANKS! I'LL KEEP THAT IN MIND.

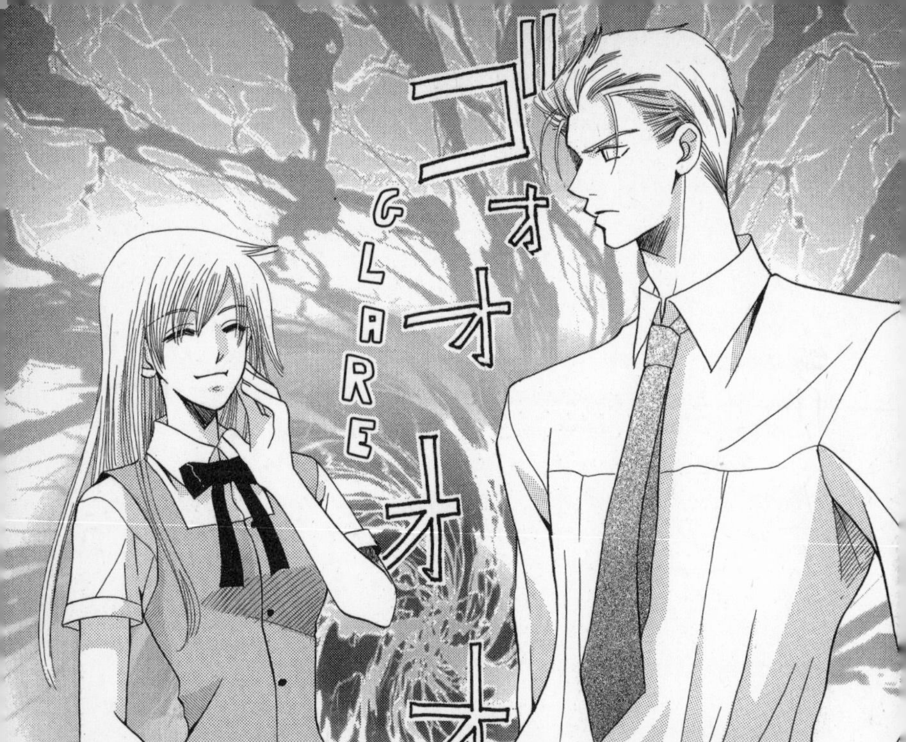
ゴォオオオオ
GLARE

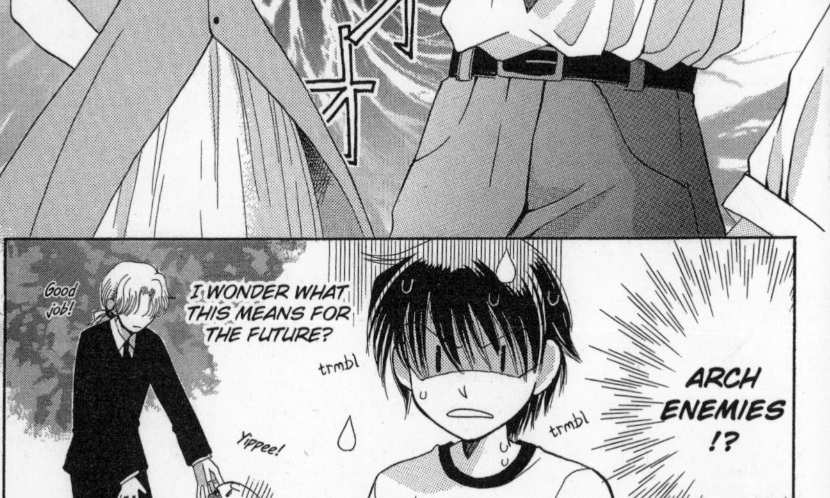
ARCH ENEMIES !?
trmbl
trmbl
SQUEEZE
I WONDER WHAT THIS MEANS FOR THE FUTURE?
Good job!
Yippee!

End of Scene 7

MY OBSESSIONS

I tend to get obsessed with things very easily. (laugh)
At the moment, I'm really much into custard pudding
from Haagen Dazs—it's happiness I can purchase at
convenience stores! As always, I'm still into Romance
novels, but lately I've been trying to read them in English,
as well. The problem is, my English language skills
have been terrible since my school years...
Nevertheless, I will press forward on a long journey
through romance literature that hasn't been translated...

VIDEO GAMES & ME

I've been feeling rather low on
energy lately, and ironically enough
it was in playing video games that
these symptoms showed up!
Just a few years ago I was the
type of gamer who could finish an
RPG in three days...(sob) Lately,
my body can't overcome sleepiness.
I have to do something to change
this!! Perhaps this is a sign that
I need to change my lifestyle!!
In order to correct my lack of
physical strength I'm going to
start exercising by walking my
dog and visiting temples!!

You know you're out of shape when you don't have
the energy to play video games like you used to!

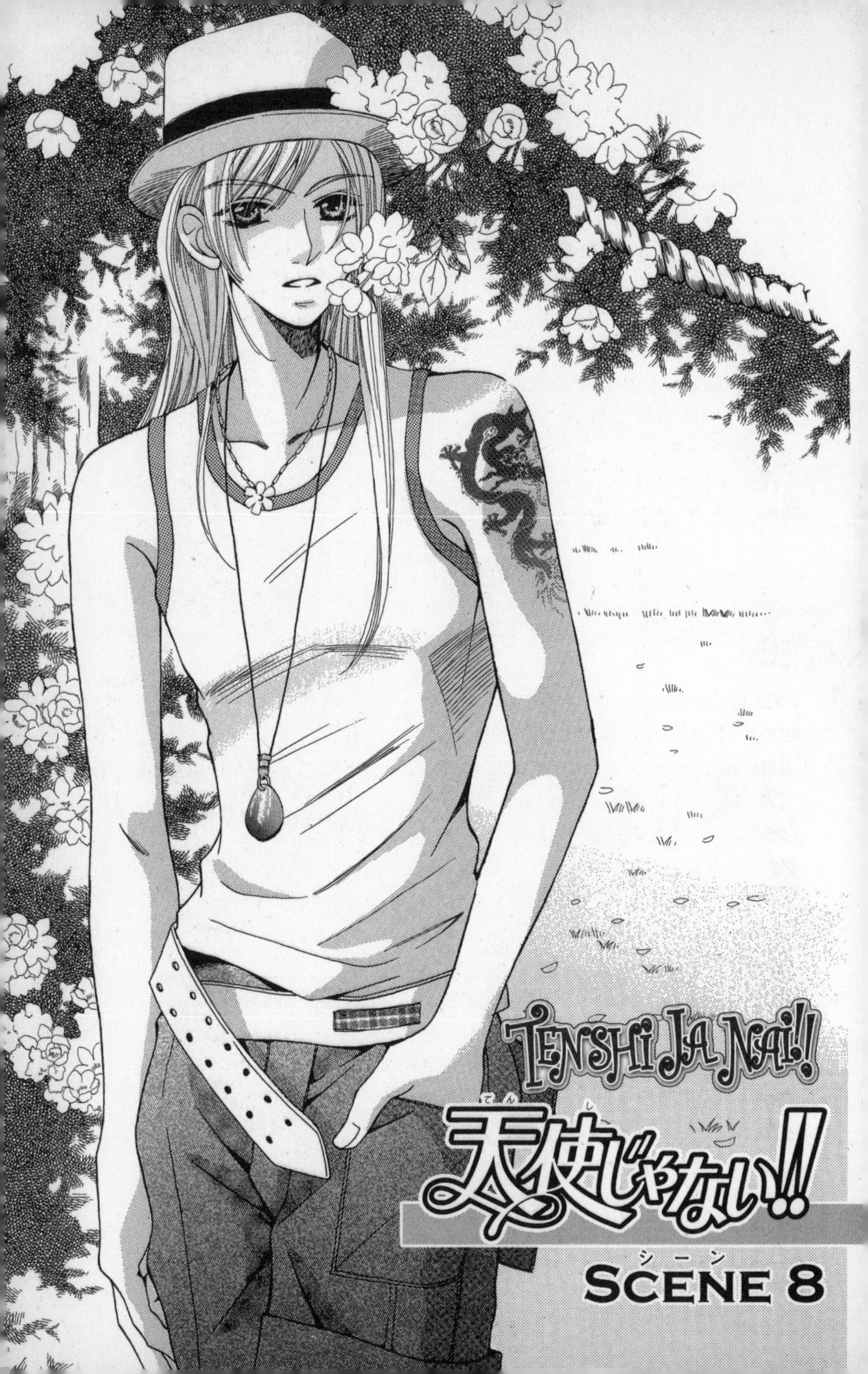
TENSHI JA NAI!!
天使じゃない!!
SCENE 8

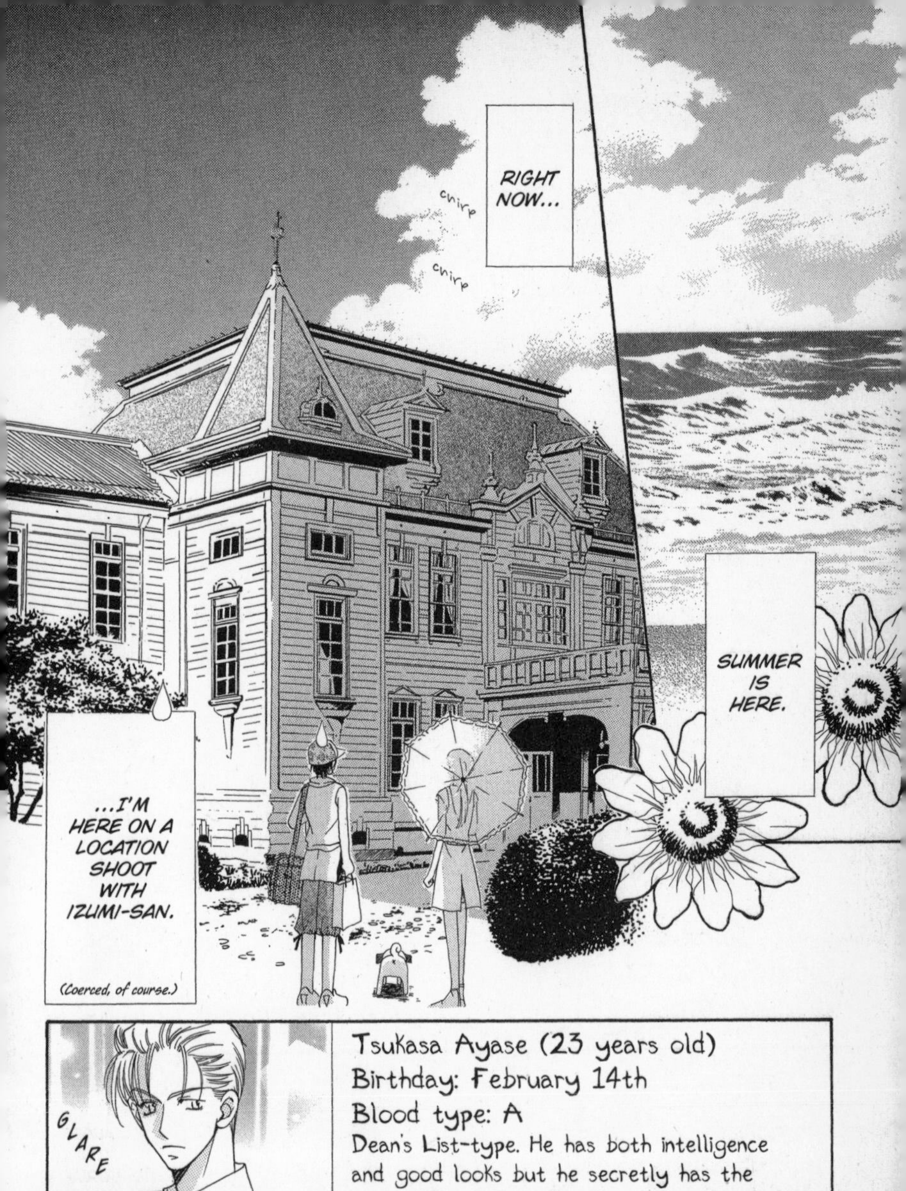
RIGHT NOW...
chirp
chirp
SUMMER IS HERE.
...I'M HERE ON A LOCATION SHOOT WITH IZUMI-SAN.
(Coerced, of course.)

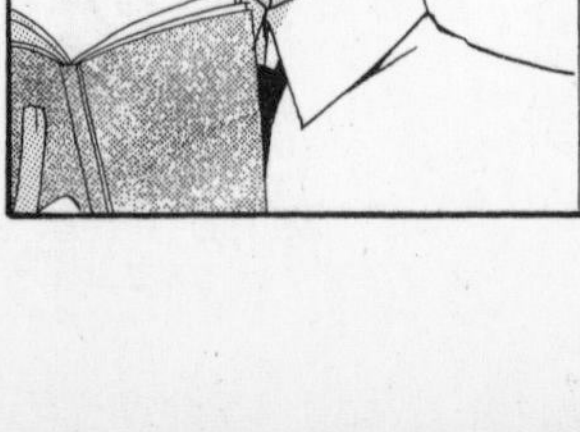
GLARE

Tsukasa Ayase (23 years old)
Birthday: February 14th
Blood type: A
Dean's List-type. He has both intelligence and good looks but he secretly has the soul of Giant from Doraemon. He appears to have shared a stormy past with Yasukuni...
(Although the author isn't even sure if she'll get around to revealing that stormy past...)

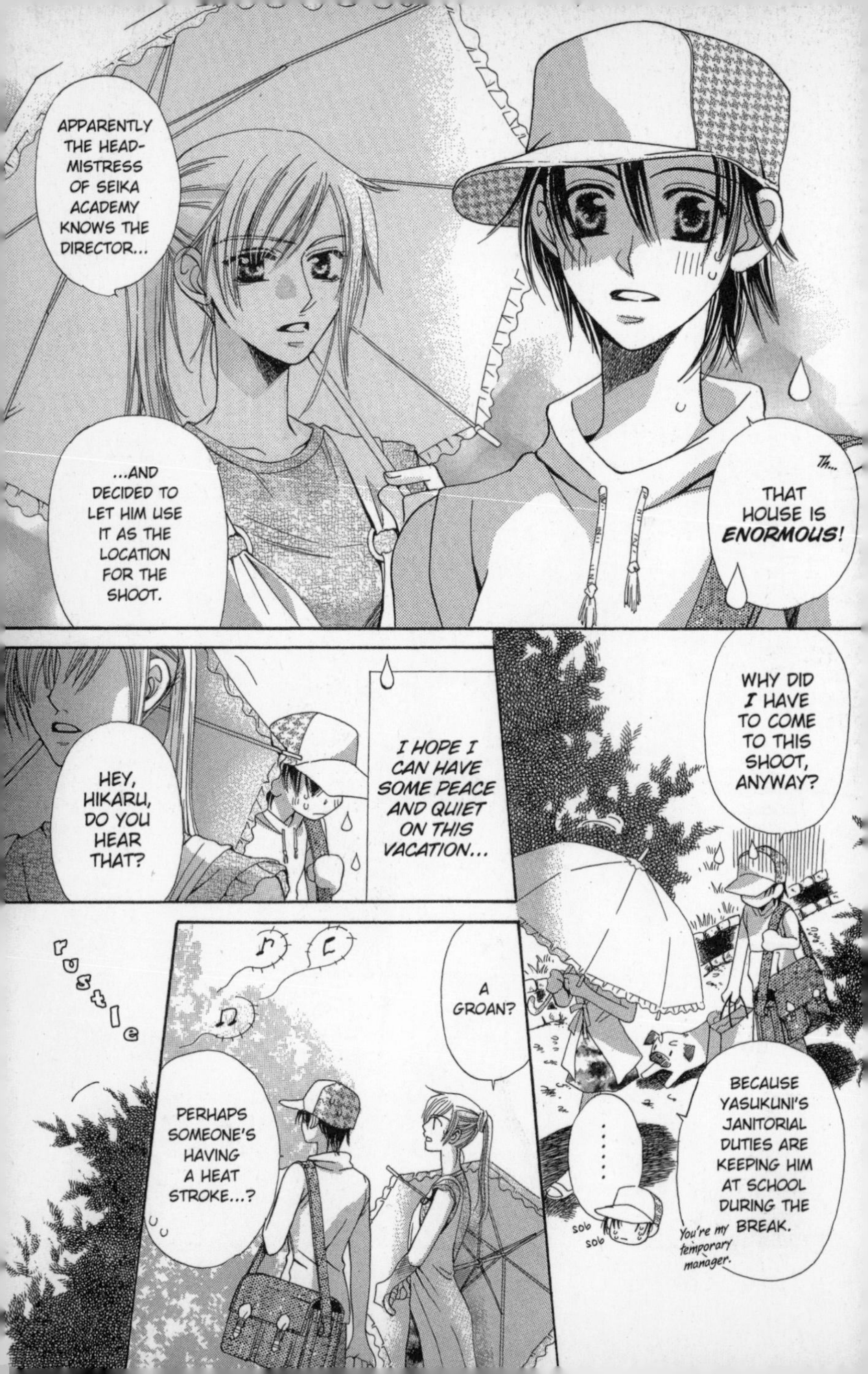
Th...
THAT HOUSE IS ENORMOUS!
APPARENTLY THE HEAD-MISTRESS OF SEIKA ACADEMY KNOWS THE DIRECTOR...
...AND DECIDED TO LET HIM USE IT AS THE LOCATION FOR THE SHOOT.
WHY DID I HAVE TO COME TO THIS SHOOT, ANYWAY?
BECAUSE YASUKUNI'S JANITORIAL DUTIES ARE KEEPING HIM AT SCHOOL DURING THE BREAK.
You're my temporary manager.
......
sob sob
I HOPE I CAN HAVE SOME PEACE AND QUIET ON THIS VACATION...
HEY, HIKARU, DO YOU HEAR THAT?
A GROAN?
PERHAPS SOMEONE'S HAVING A HEAT STROKE...?
rustle

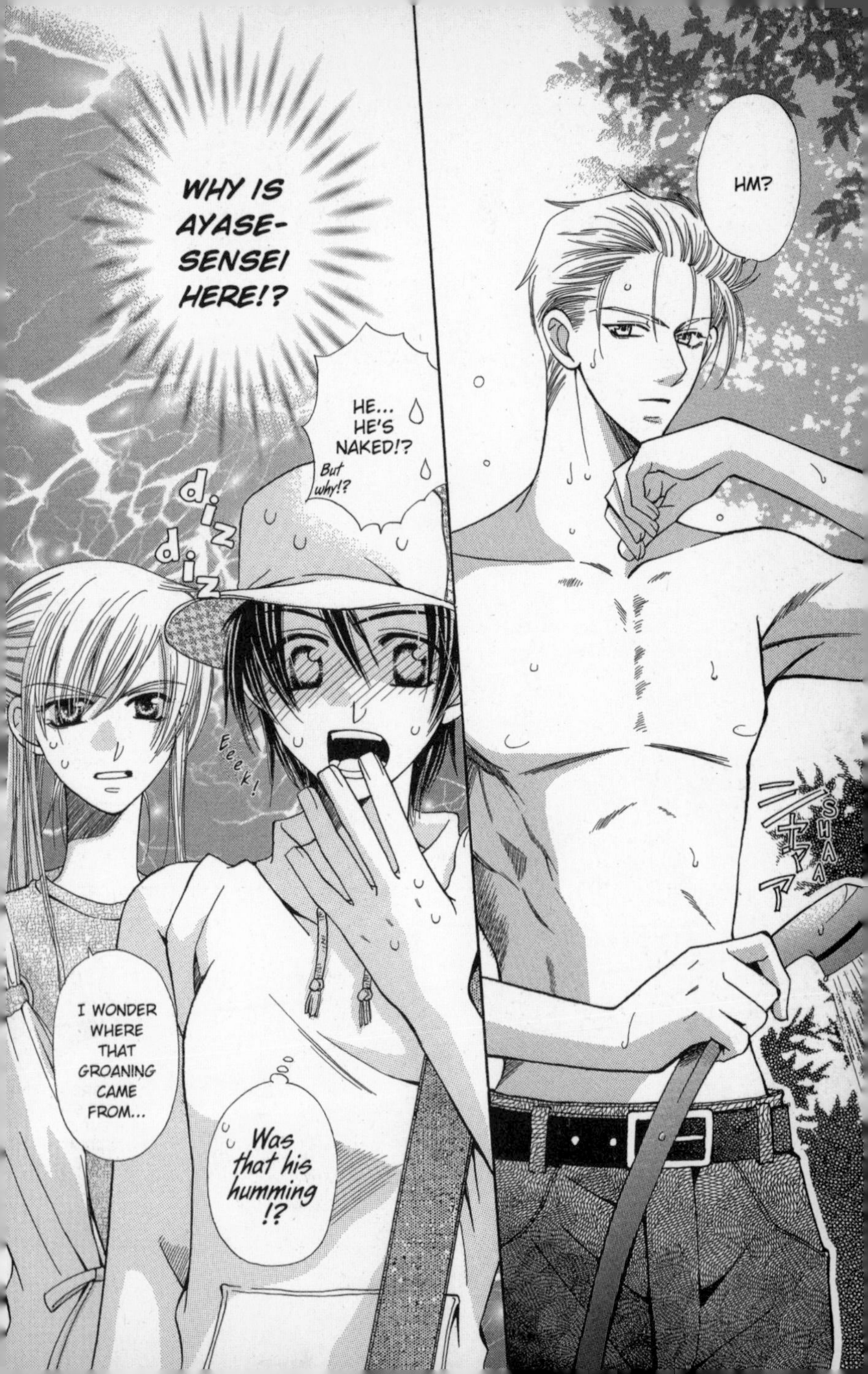
HM?
シャア
SHAA
WHY IS AYASE-SENSEI HERE!?
HE... HE'S NAKED!?
But why!?
diz diz
Eeeek!
Was that his humming!?
I WONDER WHERE THAT GROANING CAME FROM...

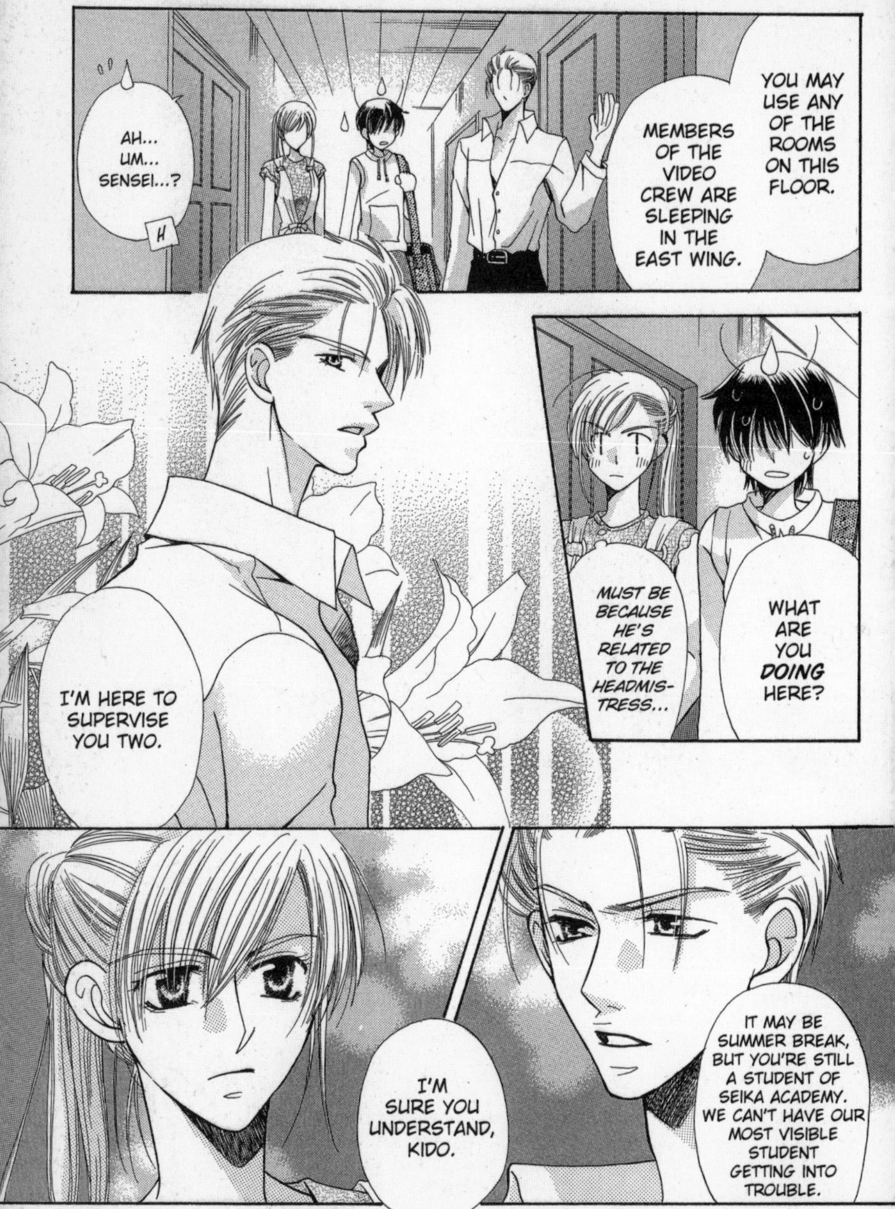
YOU MAY USE ANY OF THE ROOMS ON THIS FLOOR.
MEMBERS OF THE VIDEO CREW ARE SLEEPING IN THE EAST WING.
AH... UM... SENSEI...?
H
WHAT ARE YOU *DOING* HERE?
MUST BE BECAUSE HE'S RELATED TO THE HEADMIS-TRESS...
I'M HERE TO SUPERVISE YOU TWO.
IT MAY BE SUMMER BREAK, BUT YOU'RE STILL A STUDENT OF SEIKA ACADEMY. WE CAN'T HAVE OUR MOST VISIBLE STUDENT GETTING INTO TROUBLE.
I'M SURE YOU UNDERSTAND, KIDO.

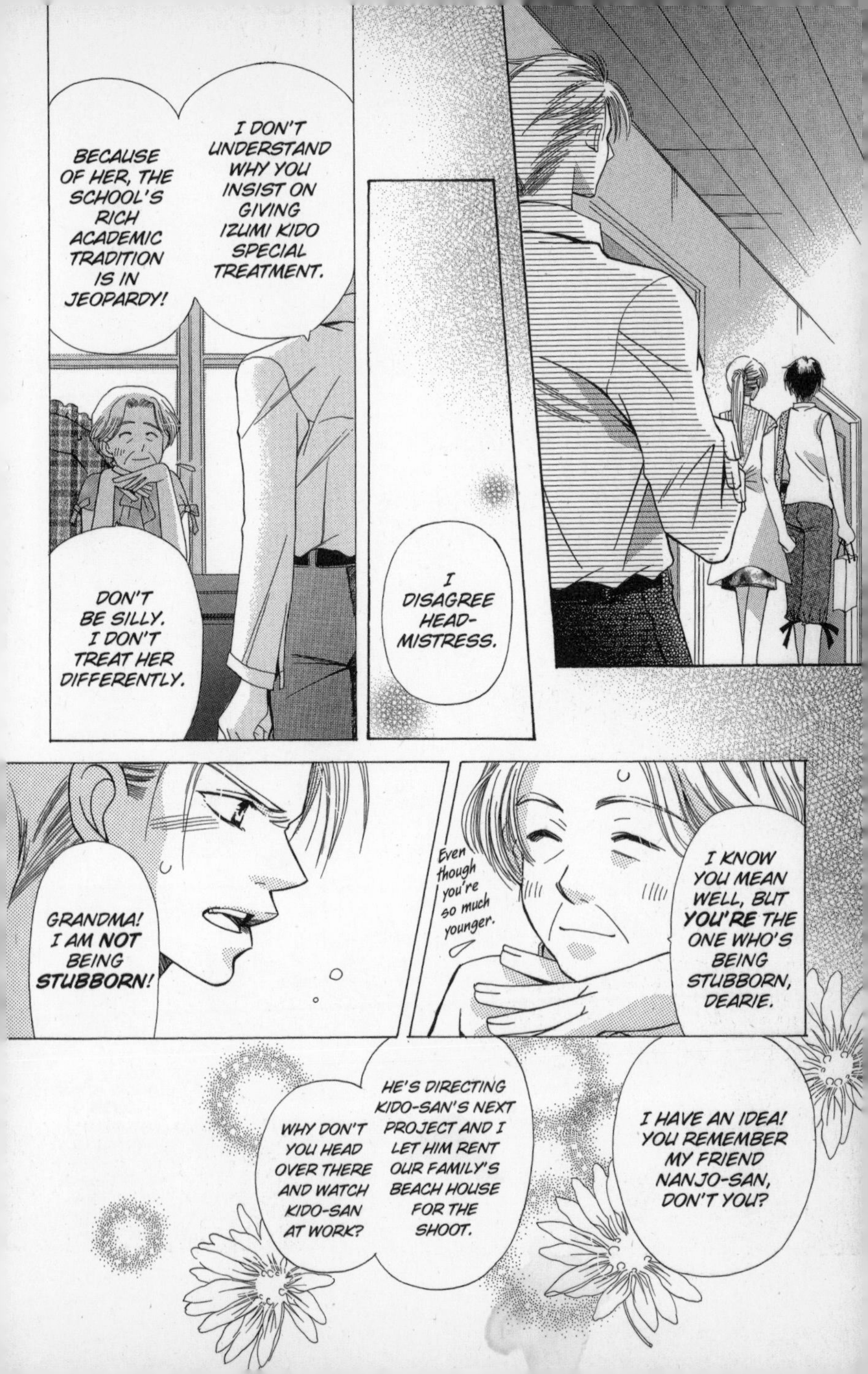

I DISAGREE HEAD-MISTRESS.
I DON'T UNDERSTAND WHY YOU INSIST ON GIVING IZUMI KIDO SPECIAL TREATMENT.
BECAUSE OF HER, THE SCHOOL'S RICH ACADEMIC TRADITION IS IN JEOPARDY!
DON'T BE SILLY. I DON'T TREAT HER DIFFERENTLY.
I KNOW YOU MEAN WELL, BUT YOU'RE THE ONE WHO'S BEING STUBBORN, DEARIE.
Even though you're so much younger.
GRANDMA! I AM NOT BEING STUBBORN!
I HAVE AN IDEA! YOU REMEMBER MY FRIEND NANJO-SAN, DON'T YOU?
HE'S DIRECTING KIDO-SAN'S NEXT PROJECT AND I LET HIM RENT OUR FAMILY'S BEACH HOUSE FOR THE SHOOT.
WHY DON'T YOU HEAD OVER THERE AND WATCH KIDO-SAN AT WORK?

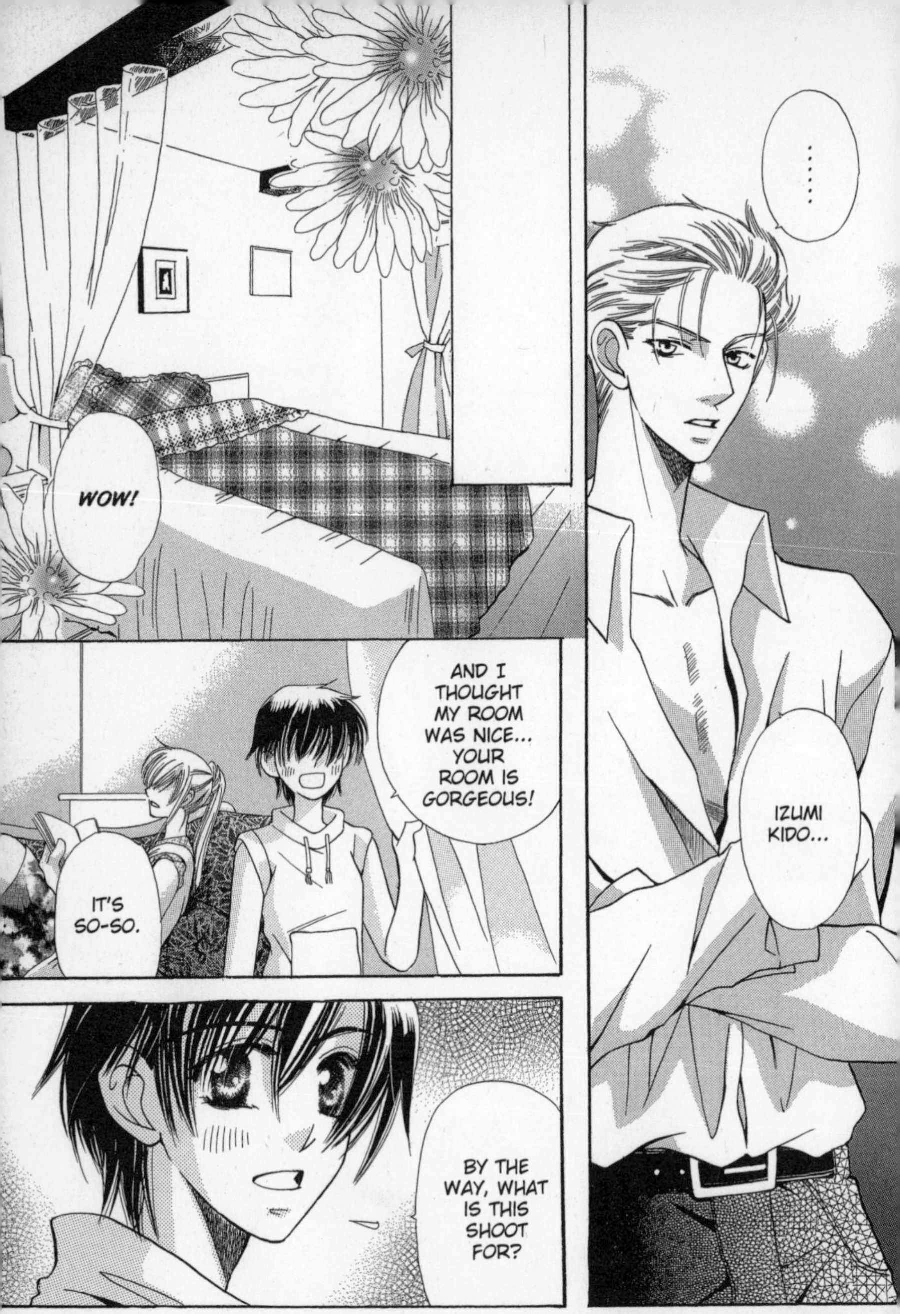
......
IZUMI KIDO...
WOW!
AND I THOUGHT MY ROOM WAS NICE... YOUR ROOM IS GORGEOUS!
IT'S SO-SO.
BY THE WAY, WHAT IS THIS SHOOT FOR?

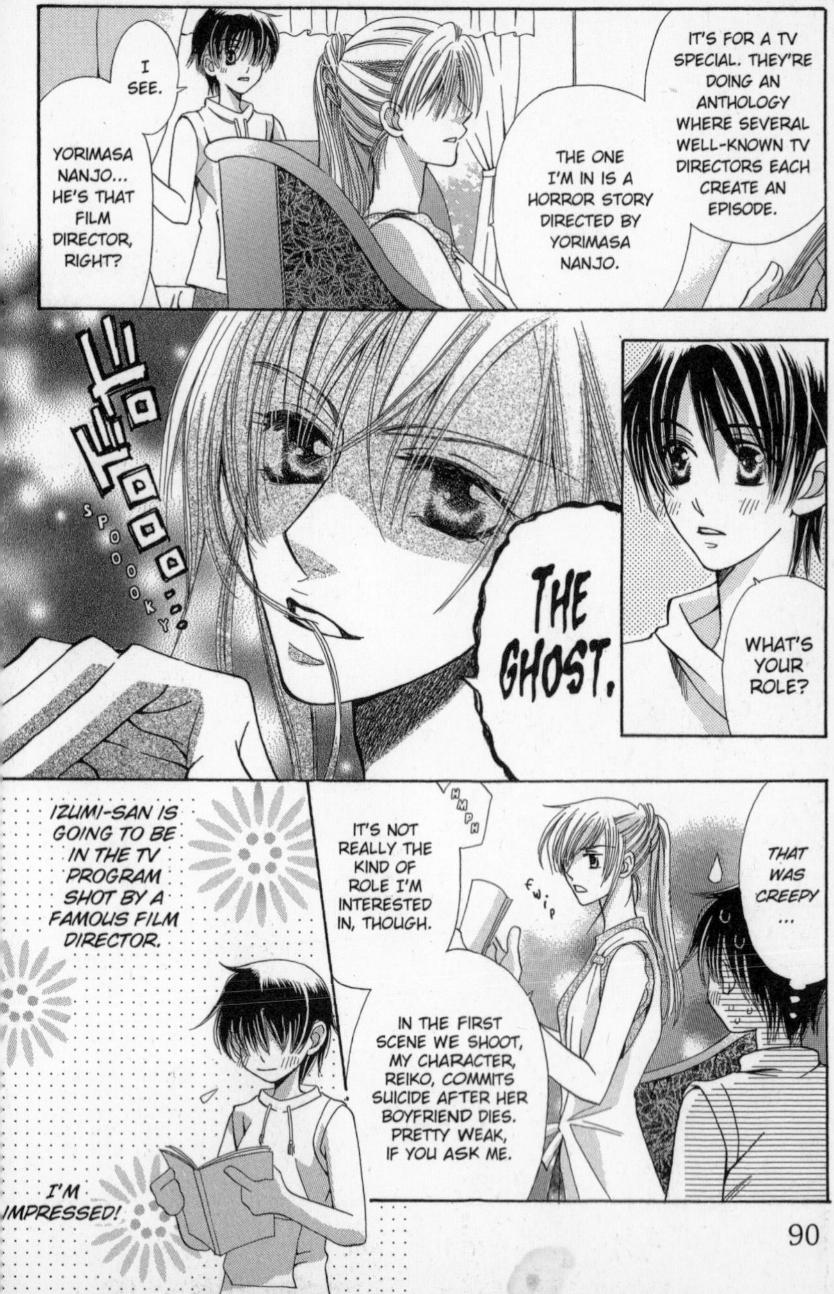
IT'S FOR A TV SPECIAL. THEY'RE DOING AN ANTHOLOGY WHERE SEVERAL WELL-KNOWN TV DIRECTORS EACH CREATE AN EPISODE.
THE ONE I'M IN IS A HORROR STORY DIRECTED BY YORIMASA NANJO.
I SEE.
YORIMASA NANJO... HE'S THAT FILM DIRECTOR, RIGHT?
WHAT'S YOUR ROLE?
THE GHOST.
SPOOOOKY
THAT WAS CREEPY...
HMPH
IT'S NOT REALLY THE KIND OF ROLE I'M INTERESTED IN, THOUGH.
fwip
IN THE FIRST SCENE WE SHOOT, MY CHARACTER, REIKO, COMMITS SUICIDE AFTER HER BOYFRIEND DIES. PRETTY WEAK, IF YOU ASK ME.
IZUMI-SAN IS GOING TO BE IN THE TV PROGRAM SHOT BY A FAMOUS FILM DIRECTOR.
I'M IMPRESSED!

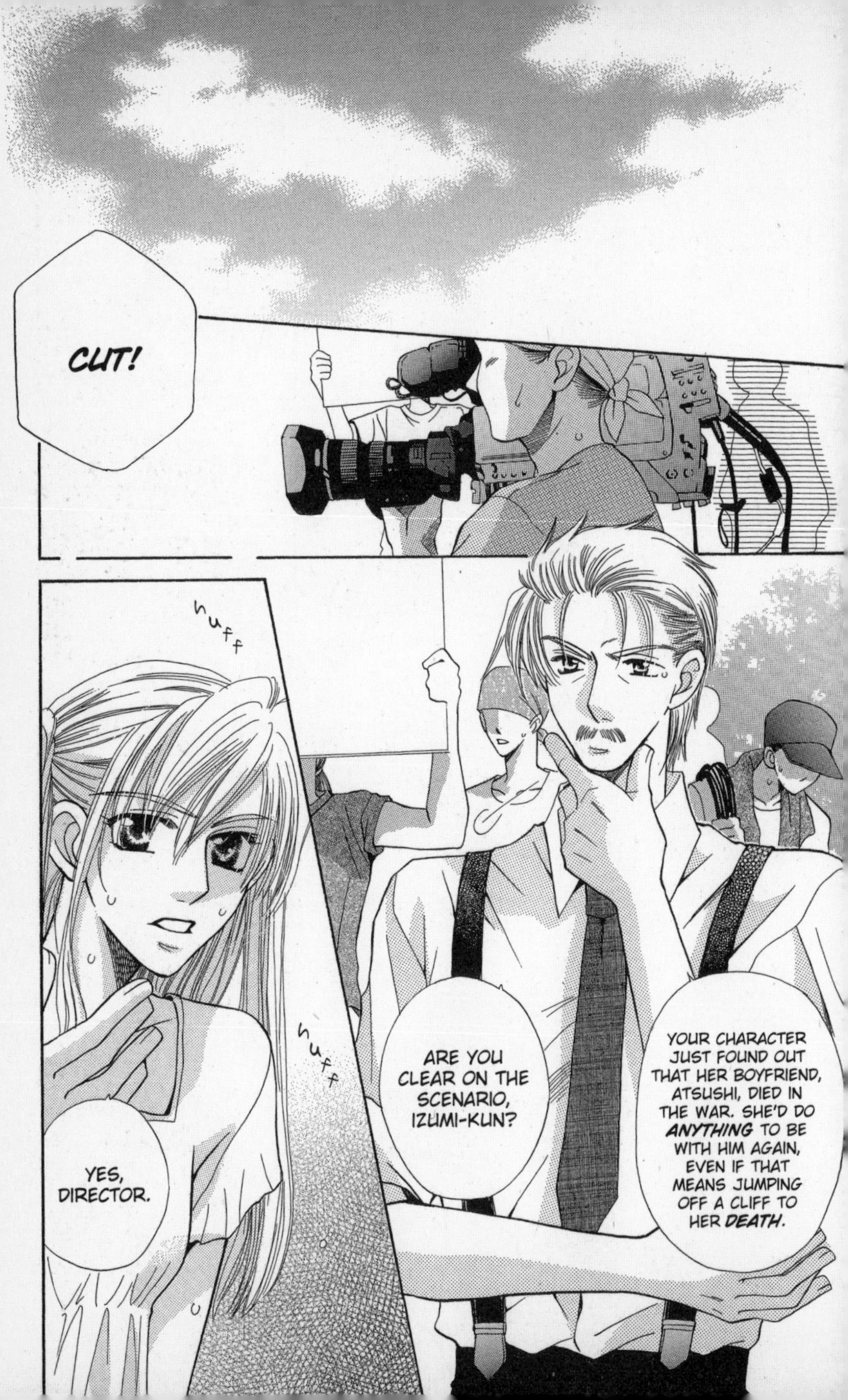
CUT!
YOUR CHARACTER JUST FOUND OUT THAT HER BOYFRIEND, ATSUSHI, DIED IN THE WAR. SHE'D DO ANYTHING TO BE WITH HIM AGAIN, EVEN IF THAT MEANS JUMPING OFF A CLIFF TO HER DEATH.
ARE YOU CLEAR ON THE SCENARIO, IZUMI-KUN?
huff
huff
YES, DIRECTOR.

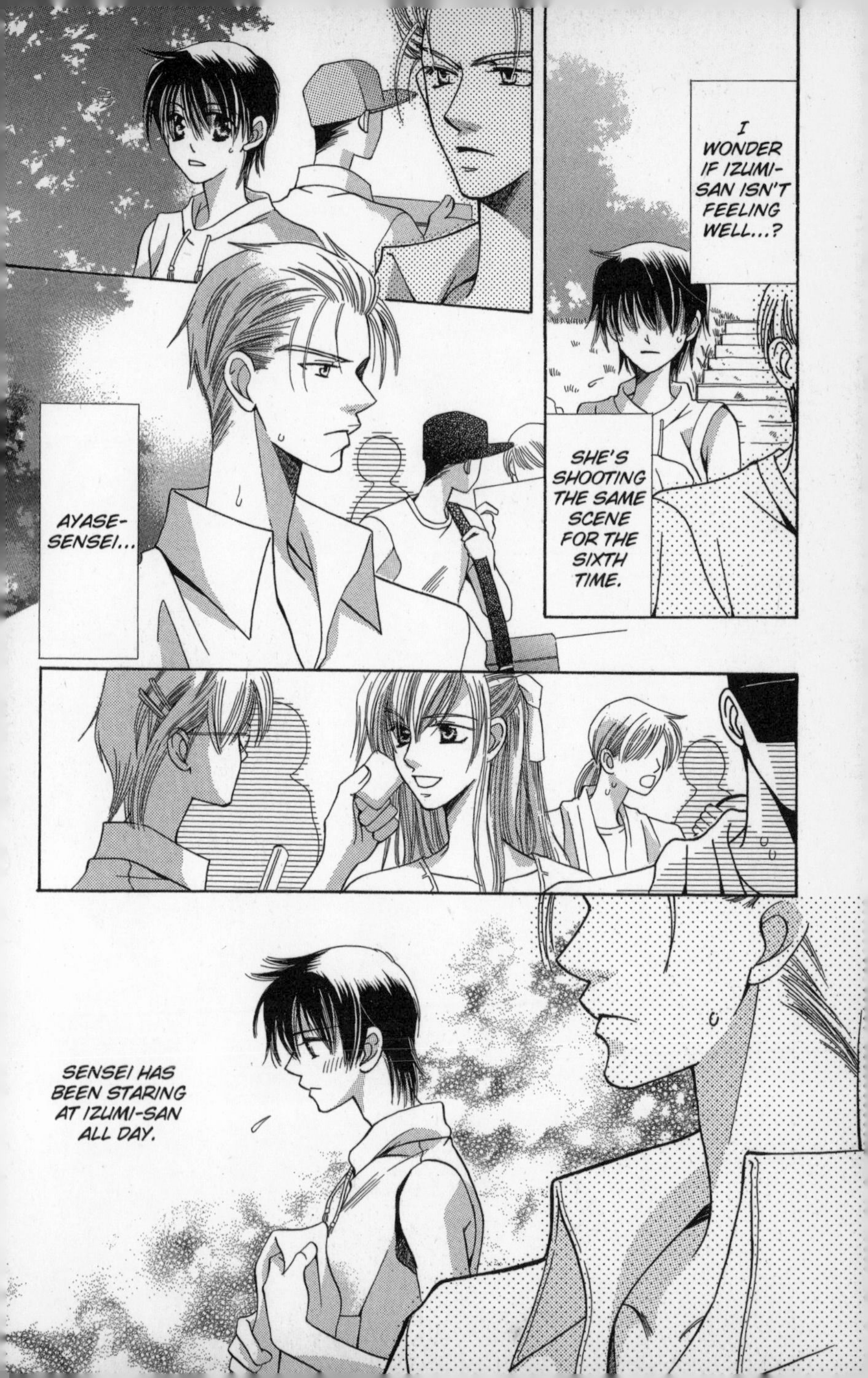
I WONDER IF IZUMI-SAN ISN'T FEELING WELL...?
SHE'S SHOOTING THE SAME SCENE FOR THE SIXTH TIME.
AYASE-SENSEI...
SENSEI HAS BEEN STARING AT IZUMI-SAN ALL DAY.

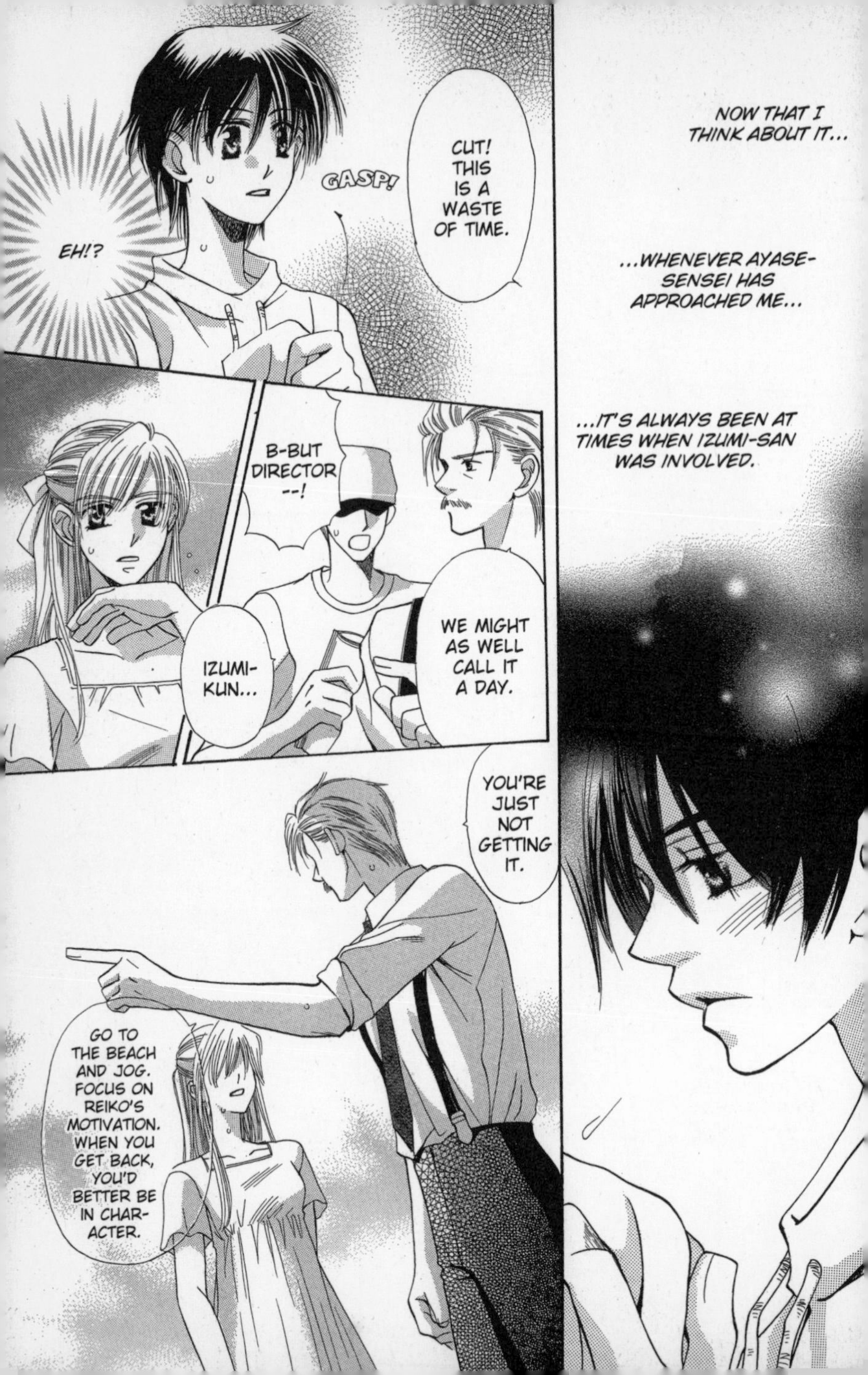
NOW THAT I THINK ABOUT IT...
...WHENEVER AYASE-SENSEI HAS APPROACHED ME...
...IT'S ALWAYS BEEN AT TIMES WHEN IZUMI-SAN WAS INVOLVED.
CUT! THIS IS A WASTE OF TIME.
GASP!
EH!?
B-BUT DIRECTOR --!
WE MIGHT AS WELL CALL IT A DAY.
IZUMI-KUN...
YOU'RE JUST NOT GETTING IT.
GO TO THE BEACH AND JOG. FOCUS ON REIKO'S MOTIVATION. WHEN YOU GET BACK, YOU'D BETTER BE IN CHARACTER.

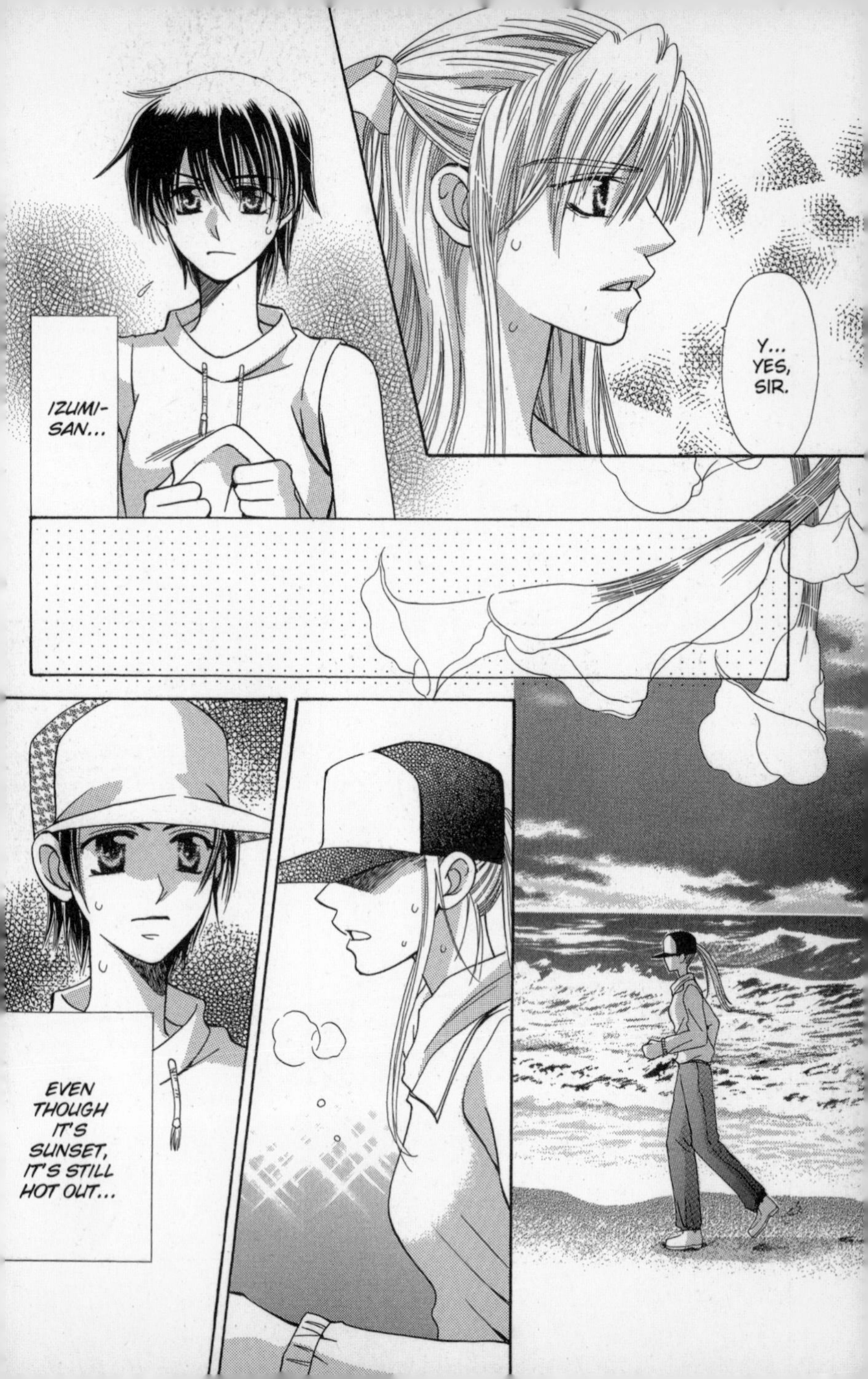
Y... YES, SIR.
IZUMI-SAN...
EVEN THOUGH IT'S SUNSET, IT'S STILL HOT OUT...

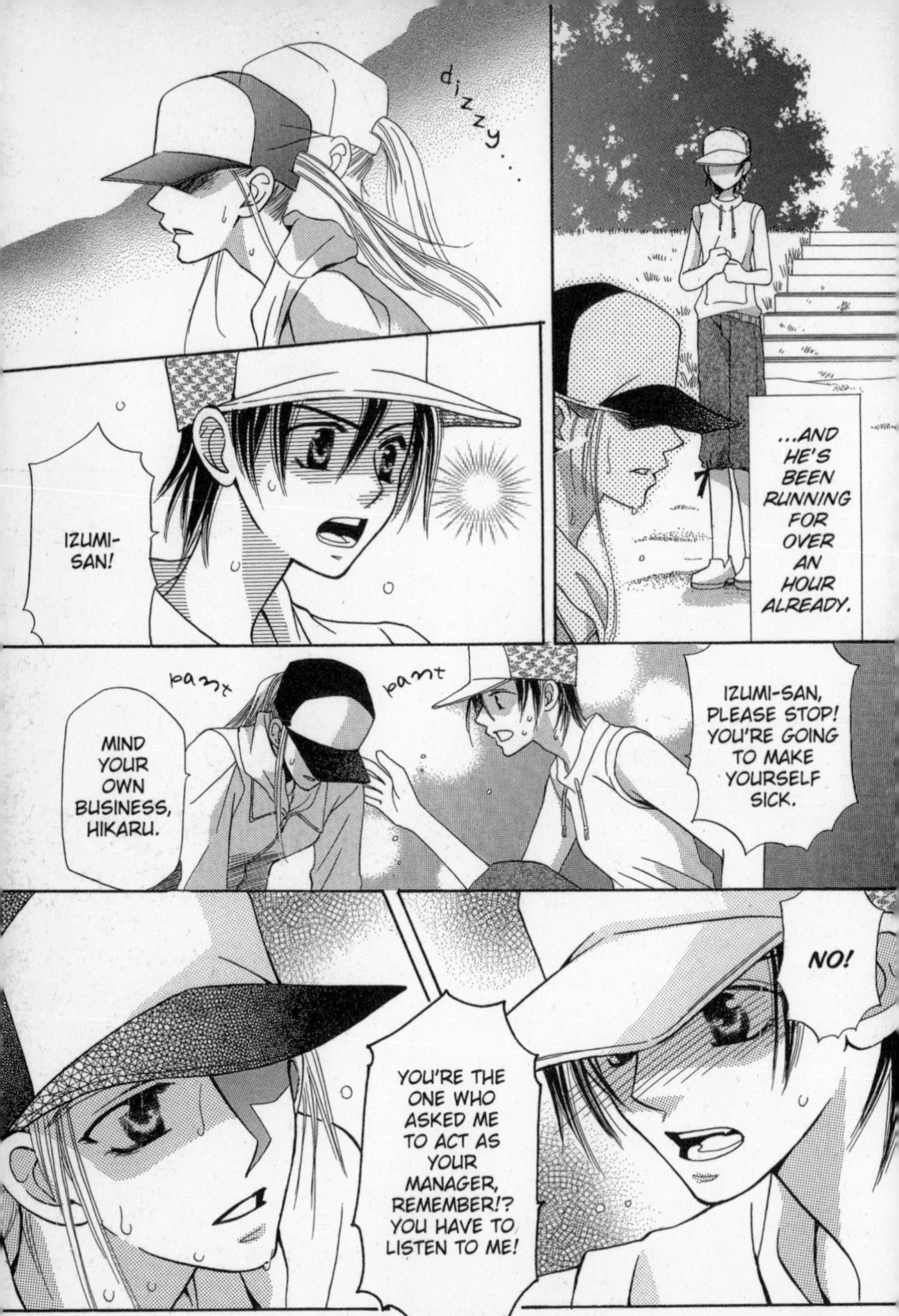
...AND HE'S BEEN RUNNING FOR OVER AN HOUR ALREADY.
dizzy...
IZUMI-SAN!
IZUMI-SAN, PLEASE STOP! YOU'RE GOING TO MAKE YOURSELF SICK.
pant
pant
MIND YOUR OWN BUSINESS, HIKARU.
NO!
YOU'RE THE ONE WHO ASKED ME TO ACT AS YOUR MANAGER, REMEMBER!? YOU HAVE TO LISTEN TO ME!

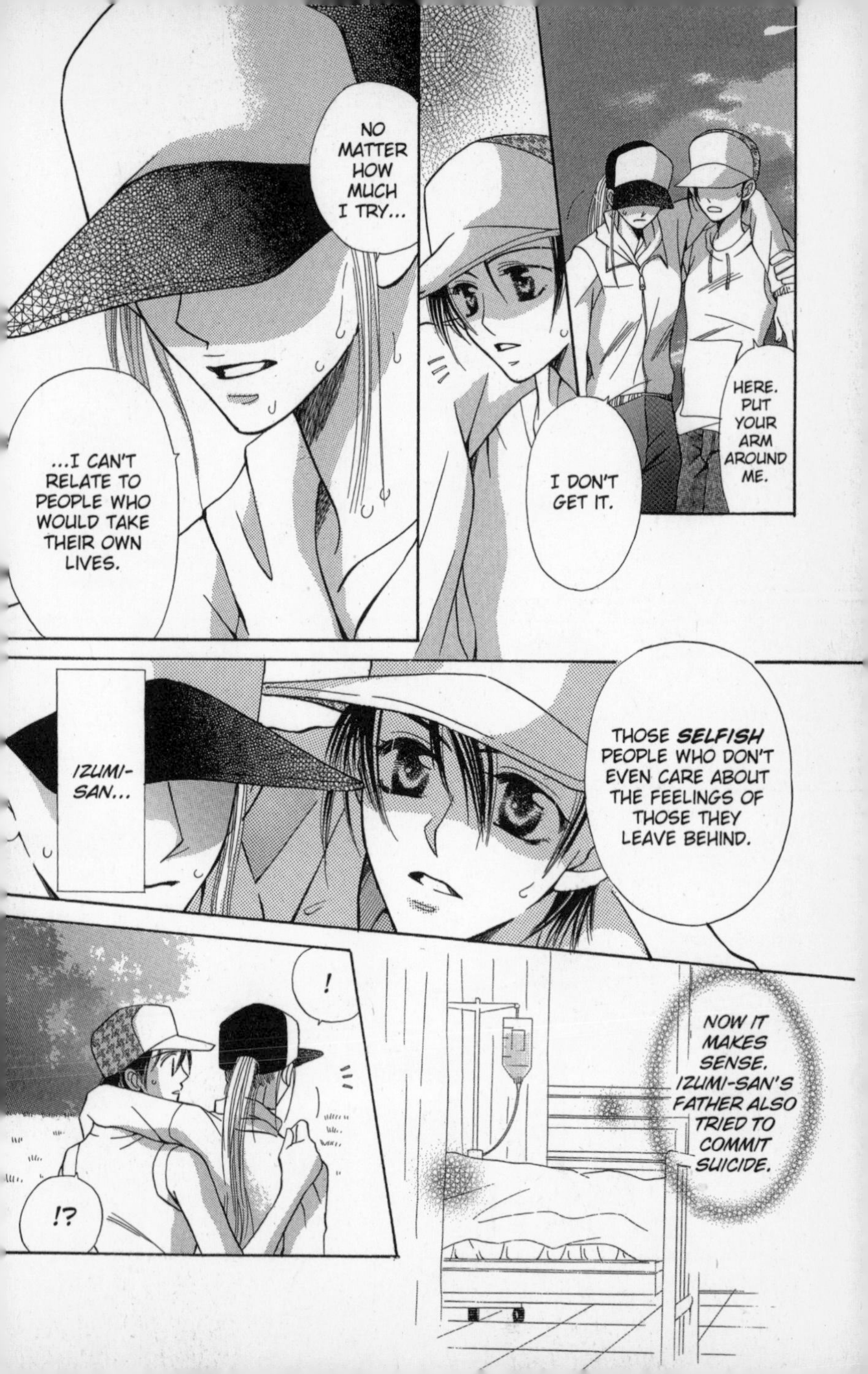
HERE. PUT YOUR ARM AROUND ME.
I DON'T GET IT.
NO MATTER HOW MUCH I TRY...
...I CAN'T RELATE TO PEOPLE WHO WOULD TAKE THEIR OWN LIVES.
THOSE **SELFISH** PEOPLE WHO DON'T EVEN CARE ABOUT THE FEELINGS OF THOSE THEY LEAVE BEHIND.
IZUMI-SAN...
NOW IT MAKES SENSE. IZUMI-SAN'S FATHER ALSO TRIED TO COMMIT SUICIDE.
!
!?

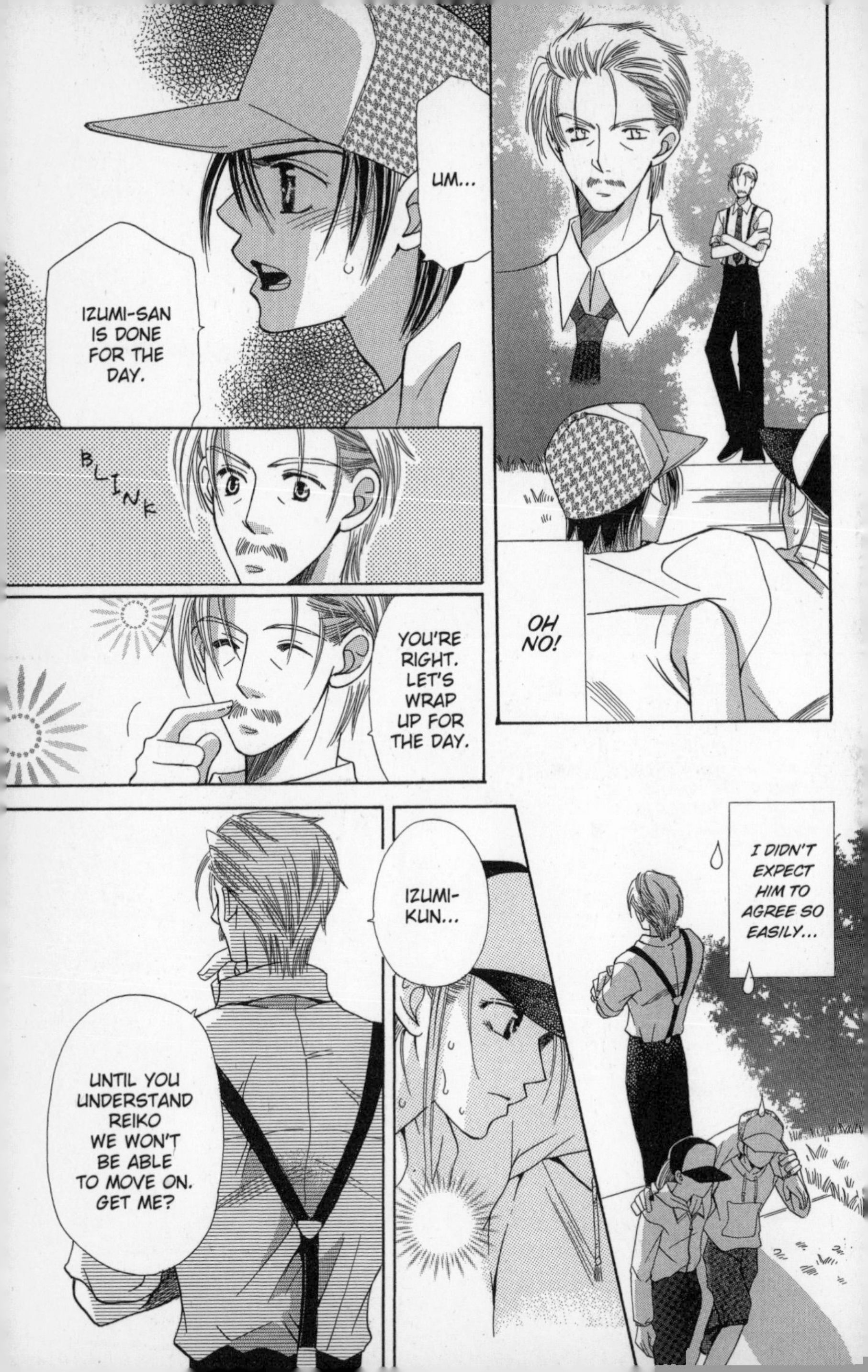
OH NO!
UM...
IZUMI-SAN IS DONE FOR THE DAY.
BLINK
YOU'RE RIGHT. LET'S WRAP UP FOR THE DAY.
I DIDN'T EXPECT HIM TO AGREE SO EASILY...
IZUMI-KUN...
UNTIL YOU UNDERSTAND REIKO WE WON'T BE ABLE TO MOVE ON. GET ME?

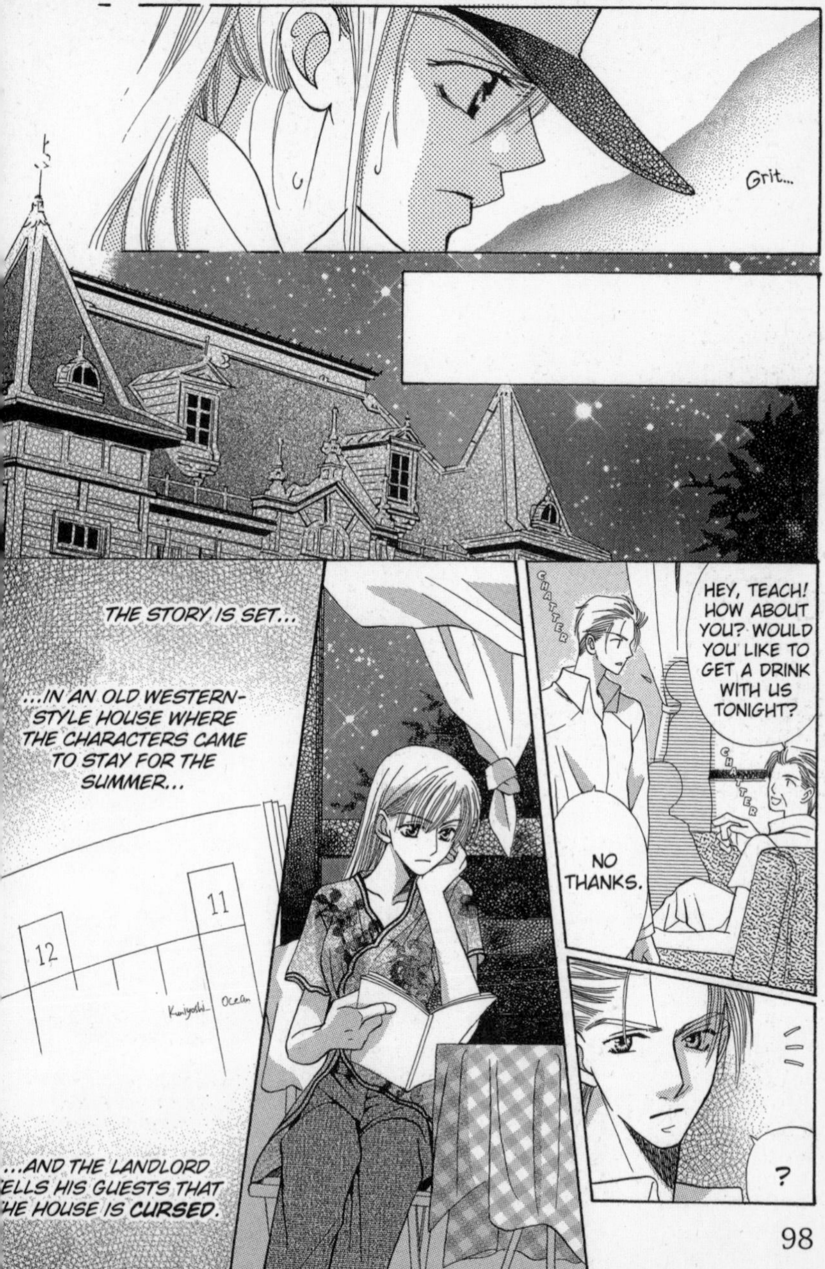
Grit...
CHATTER
HEY, TEACH! HOW ABOUT YOU? WOULD YOU LIKE TO GET A DRINK WITH US TONIGHT?
CHATTER
NO THANKS.
?
THE STORY IS SET...
...IN AN OLD WESTERN-STYLE HOUSE WHERE THE CHARACTERS CAME TO STAY FOR THE SUMMER...
11
12
Kuniyoshi
Ocean
...AND THE LANDLORD ELLS HIS GUESTS THAT HE HOUSE IS **CURSED**.

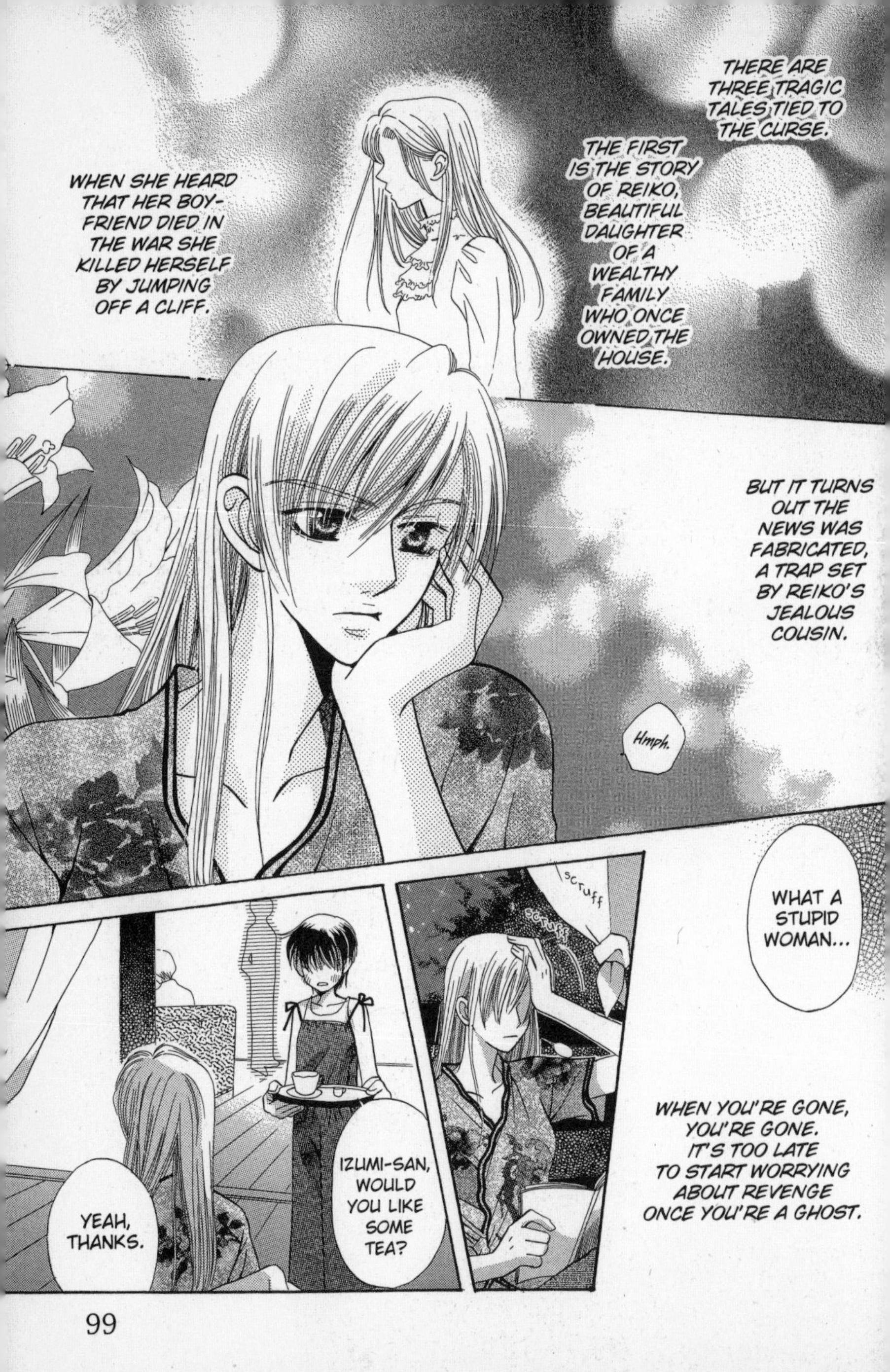
THERE ARE THREE TRAGIC TALES TIED TO THE CURSE.
THE FIRST IS THE STORY OF REIKO, BEAUTIFUL DAUGHTER OF A WEALTHY FAMILY WHO ONCE OWNED THE HOUSE.
WHEN SHE HEARD THAT HER BOY-FRIEND DIED IN THE WAR SHE KILLED HERSELF BY JUMPING OFF A CLIFF.
BUT IT TURNS OUT THE NEWS WAS FABRICATED, A TRAP SET BY REIKO'S JEALOUS COUSIN.
Hmph.
WHAT A STUPID WOMAN...
SCRUFF
SCRUFF
WHEN YOU'RE GONE, YOU'RE GONE. IT'S TOO LATE TO START WORRYING ABOUT REVENGE ONCE YOU'RE A GHOST.
IZUMI-SAN, WOULD YOU LIKE SOME TEA?
YEAH, THANKS.

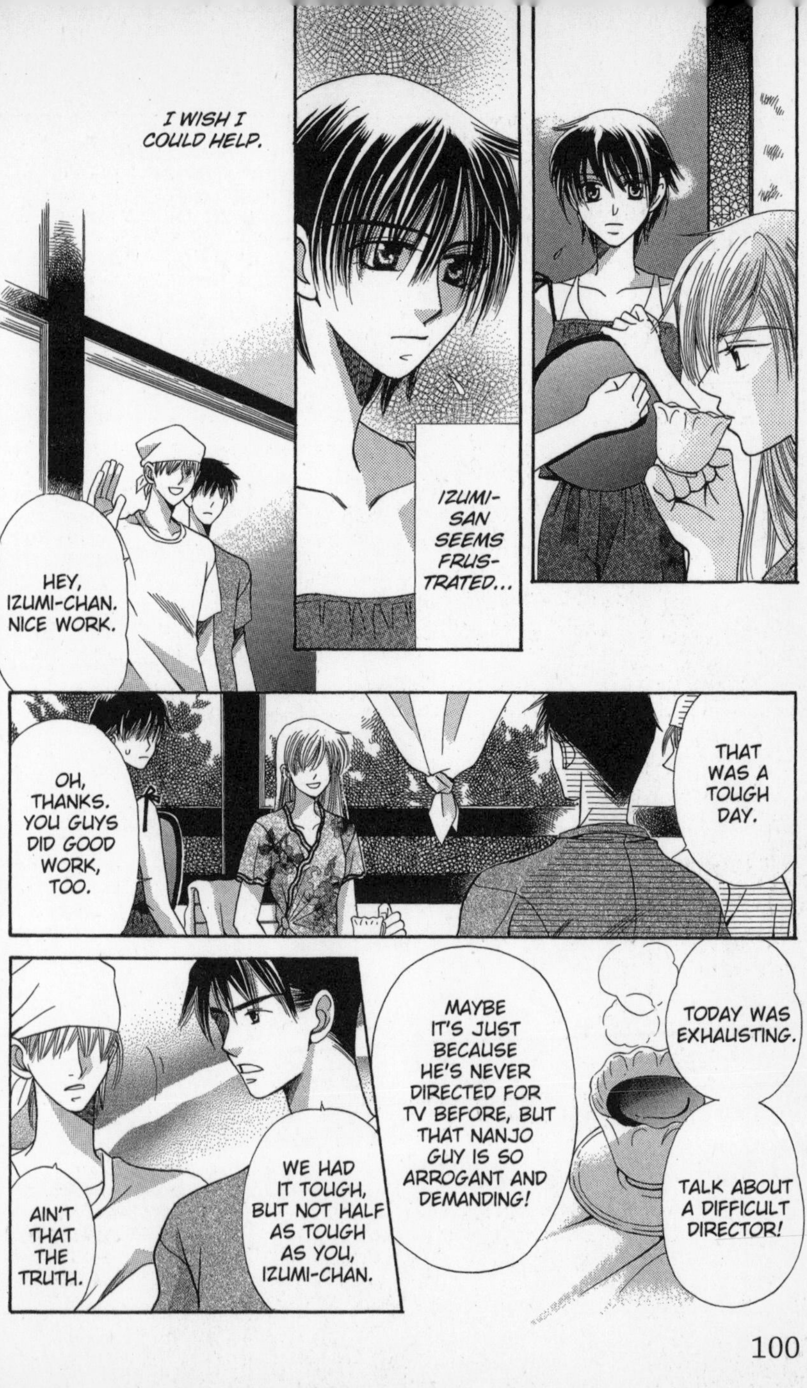
IZUMI-SAN SEEMS FRUS-TRATED...
I WISH I COULD HELP.
HEY, IZUMI-CHAN. NICE WORK.
THAT WAS A TOUGH DAY.
OH, THANKS. YOU GUYS DID GOOD WORK, TOO.
TODAY WAS EXHAUSTING.
TALK ABOUT A DIFFICULT DIRECTOR!
MAYBE IT'S JUST BECAUSE HE'S NEVER DIRECTED FOR TV BEFORE, BUT THAT NANJO GUY IS SO ARROGANT AND DEMANDING!
WE HAD IT TOUGH, BUT NOT HALF AS TOUGH AS YOU, IZUMI-CHAN.
AIN'T THAT THE TRUTH.

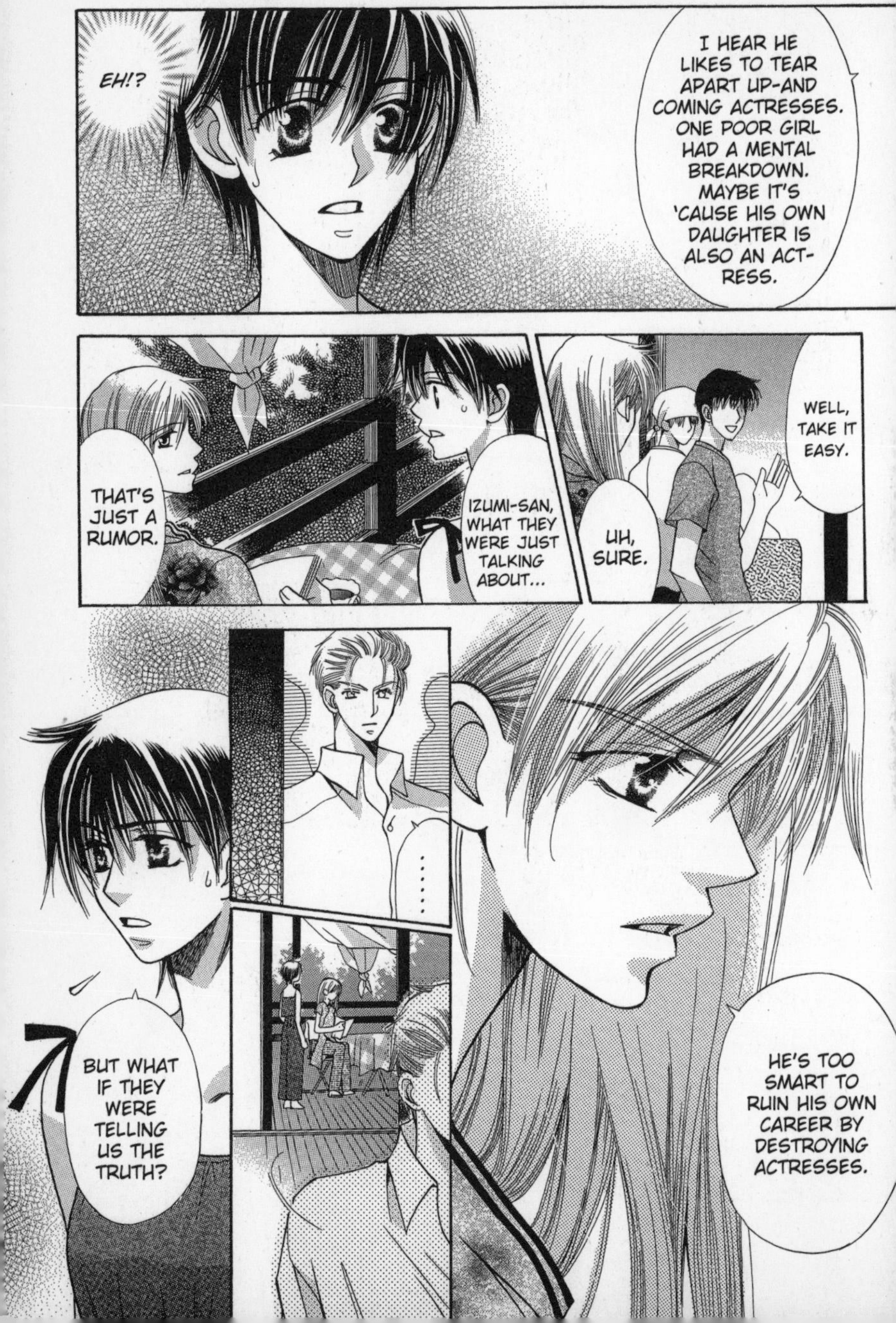
I HEAR HE LIKES TO TEAR APART UP-AND COMING ACTRESSES. ONE POOR GIRL HAD A MENTAL BREAKDOWN. MAYBE IT'S 'CAUSE HIS OWN DAUGHTER IS ALSO AN ACT-RESS.
EH!?
WELL, TAKE IT EASY.
UH, SURE.
IZUMI-SAN, WHAT THEY WERE JUST TALKING ABOUT...
THAT'S JUST A RUMOR.
HE'S TOO SMART TO RUIN HIS OWN CAREER BY DESTROYING ACTRESSES.
......
BUT WHAT IF THEY WERE TELLING US THE TRUTH?

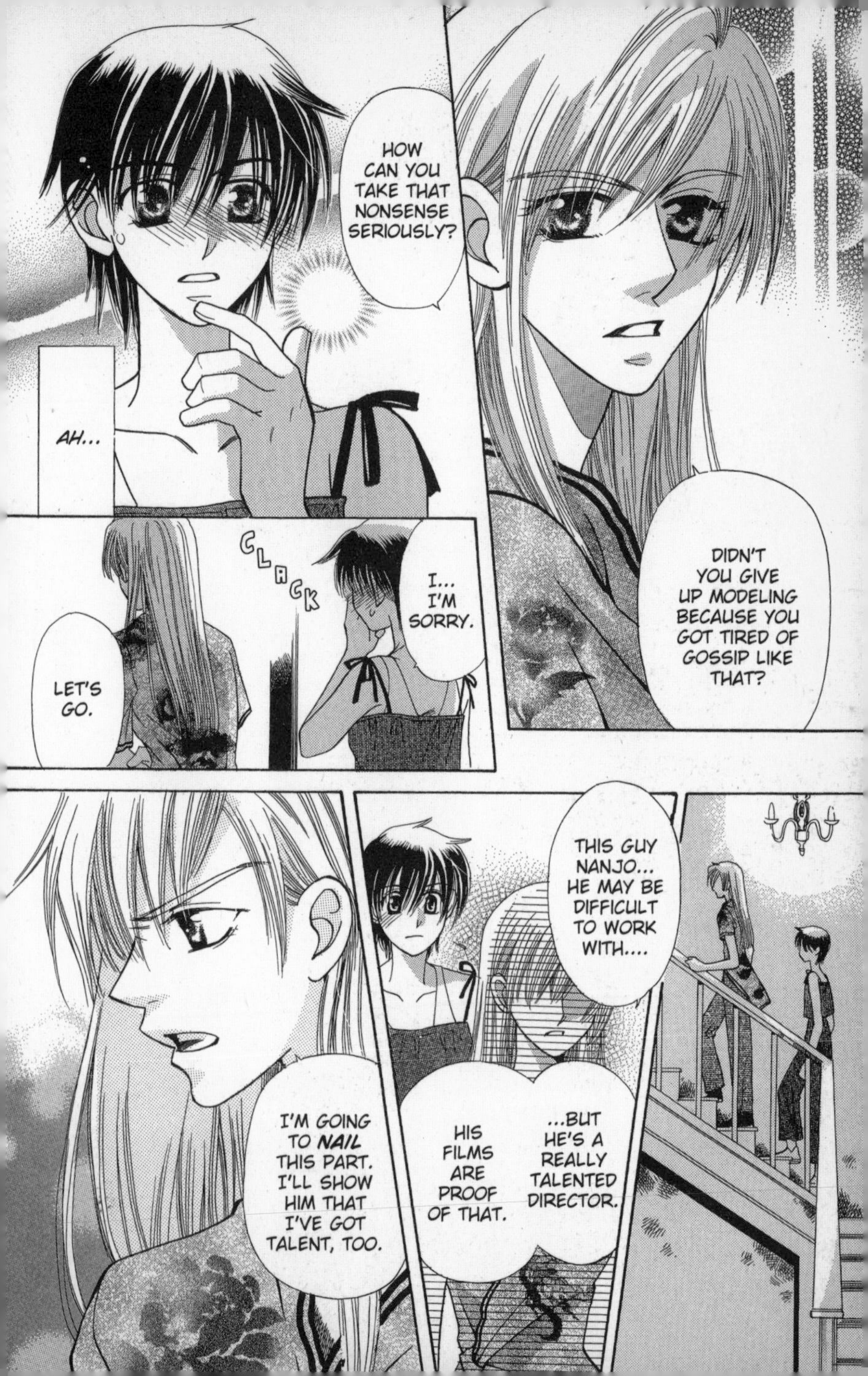
HOW CAN YOU TAKE THAT NONSENSE SERIOUSLY?
DIDN'T YOU GIVE UP MODELING BECAUSE YOU GOT TIRED OF GOSSIP LIKE THAT?
AH...
I... I'M SORRY.
CLACK
LET'S GO.
THIS GUY NANJO... HE MAY BE DIFFICULT TO WORK WITH....
...BUT HE'S A REALLY TALENTED DIRECTOR.
HIS FILMS ARE PROOF OF THAT.
I'M GOING TO *NAIL* THIS PART. I'LL SHOW HIM THAT I'VE GOT TALENT, TOO.

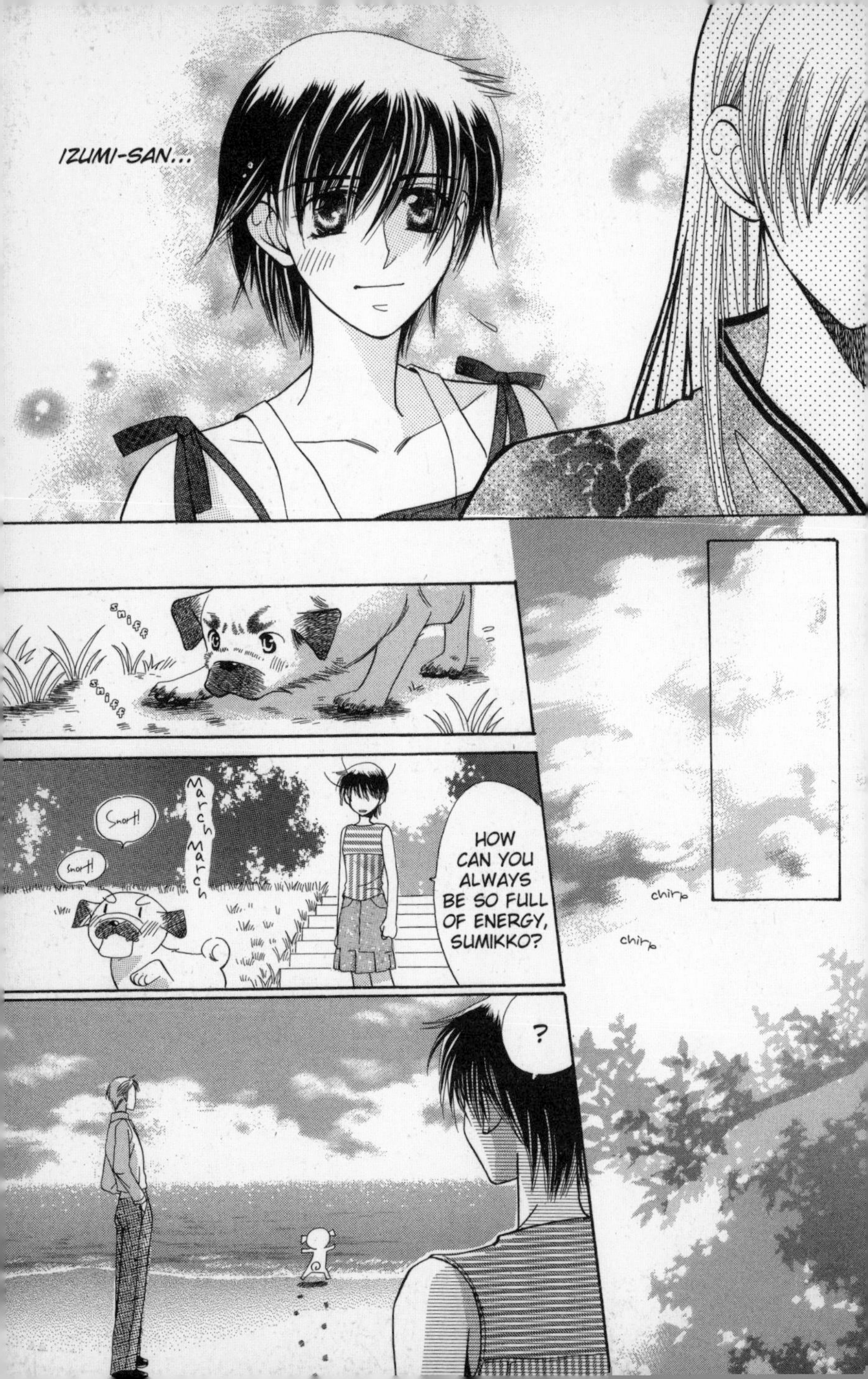
IZUMI-SAN...
chirp
chirp
sniff
sniff
HOW CAN YOU ALWAYS BE SO FULL OF ENERGY, SUMIKKO?
March March
Snort!
snort!
?

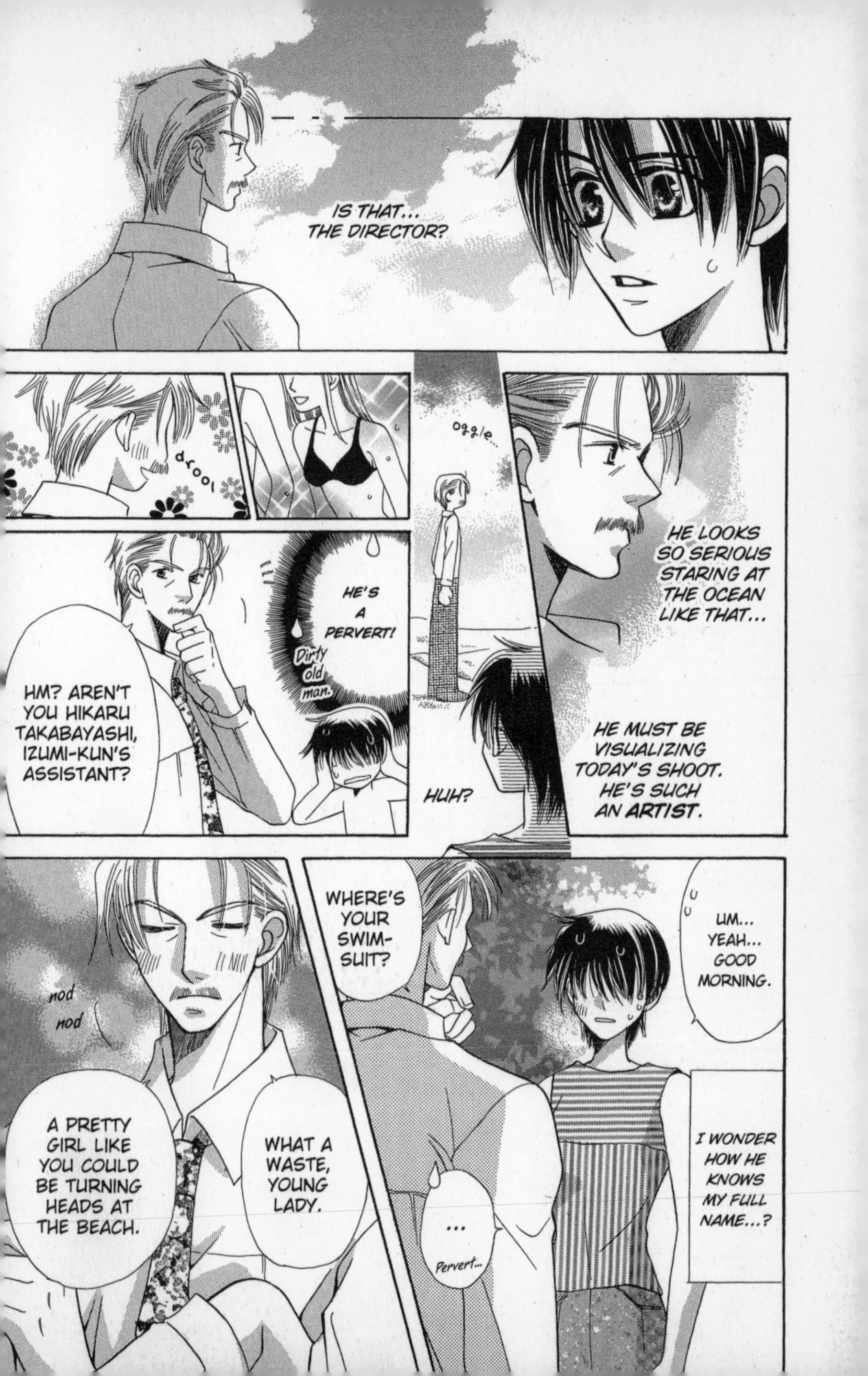
IS THAT... THE DIRECTOR?
HE LOOKS SO SERIOUS STARING AT THE OCEAN LIKE THAT...
oggle...
HE MUST BE VISUALIZING TODAY'S SHOOT. HE'S SUCH AN ARTIST.
HUH?
drool
HE'S A PERVERT!
Dirty old man.
HM? AREN'T YOU HIKARU TAKABAYASHI, IZUMI-KUN'S ASSISTANT?
UM... YEAH... GOOD MORNING.
WHERE'S YOUR SWIM-SUIT?
I WONDER HOW HE KNOWS MY FULL NAME...?
...
Pervert...
nod nod
WHAT A WASTE, YOUNG LADY.
A PRETTY GIRL LIKE YOU COULD BE TURNING HEADS AT THE BEACH.

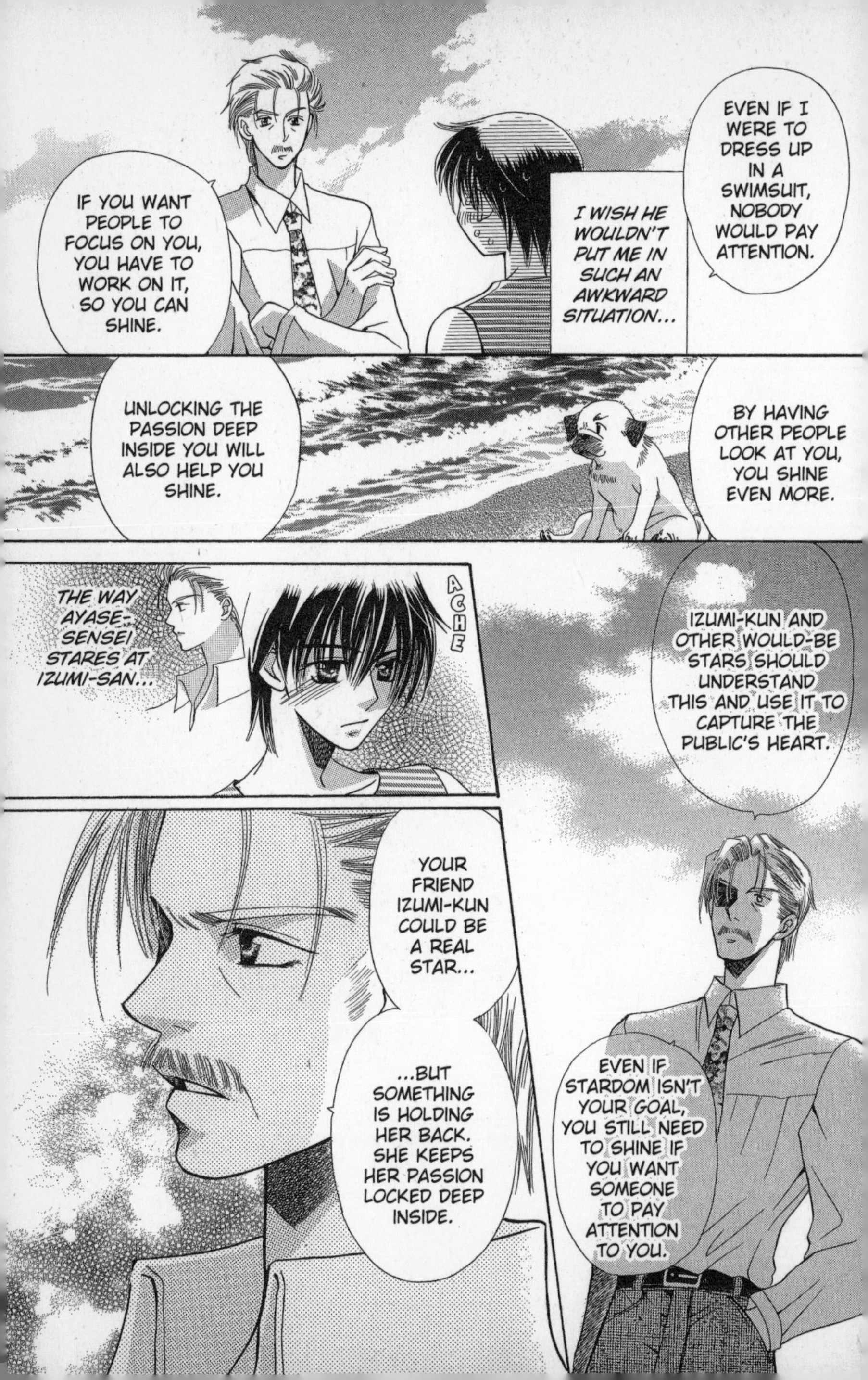
EVEN IF I WERE TO DRESS UP IN A SWIMSUIT, NOBODY WOULD PAY ATTENTION.
I WISH HE WOULDN'T PUT ME IN SUCH AN AWKWARD SITUATION...
IF YOU WANT PEOPLE TO FOCUS ON YOU, YOU HAVE TO WORK ON IT, SO YOU CAN SHINE.
BY HAVING OTHER PEOPLE LOOK AT YOU, YOU SHINE EVEN MORE.
UNLOCKING THE PASSION DEEP INSIDE YOU WILL ALSO HELP YOU SHINE.
IZUMI-KUN AND OTHER WOULD-BE STARS SHOULD UNDERSTAND THIS AND USE IT TO CAPTURE THE PUBLIC'S HEART.
EVEN IF STARDOM ISN'T YOUR GOAL, YOU STILL NEED TO SHINE IF YOU WANT SOMEONE TO PAY ATTENTION TO YOU.
THE WAY AYASE-SENSEI STARES AT IZUMI-SAN...
ACHE
YOUR FRIEND IZUMI-KUN COULD BE A REAL STAR...
...BUT SOMETHING IS HOLDING HER BACK. SHE KEEPS HER PASSION LOCKED DEEP INSIDE.

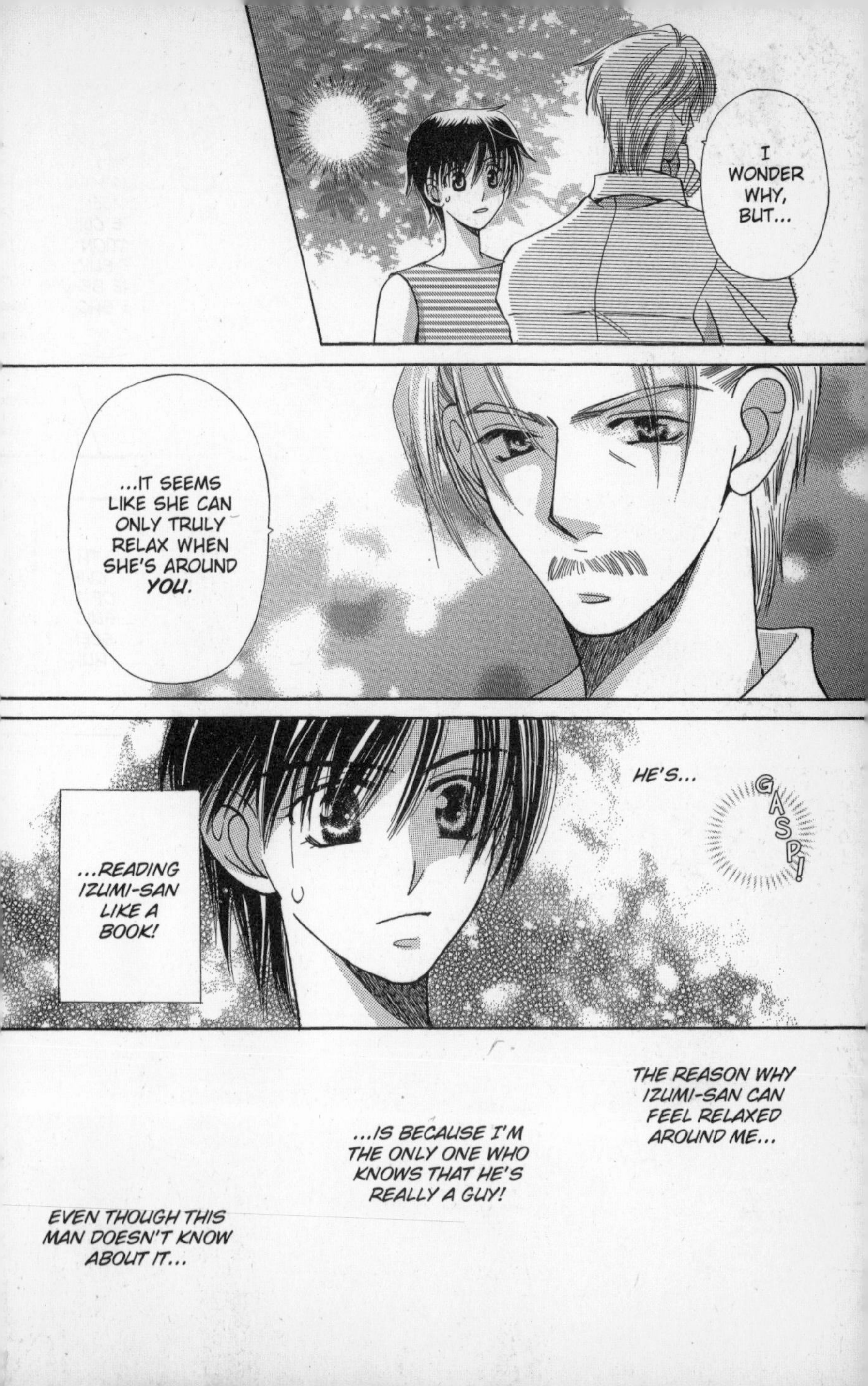
I WONDER WHY, BUT...
...IT SEEMS LIKE SHE CAN ONLY TRULY RELAX WHEN SHE'S AROUND YOU.
HE'S...
GASP!
...READING IZUMI-SAN LIKE A BOOK!
THE REASON WHY IZUMI-SAN CAN FEEL RELAXED AROUND ME...
...IS BECAUSE I'M THE ONLY ONE WHO KNOWS THAT HE'S REALLY A GUY!
EVEN THOUGH THIS MAN DOESN'T KNOW ABOUT IT...

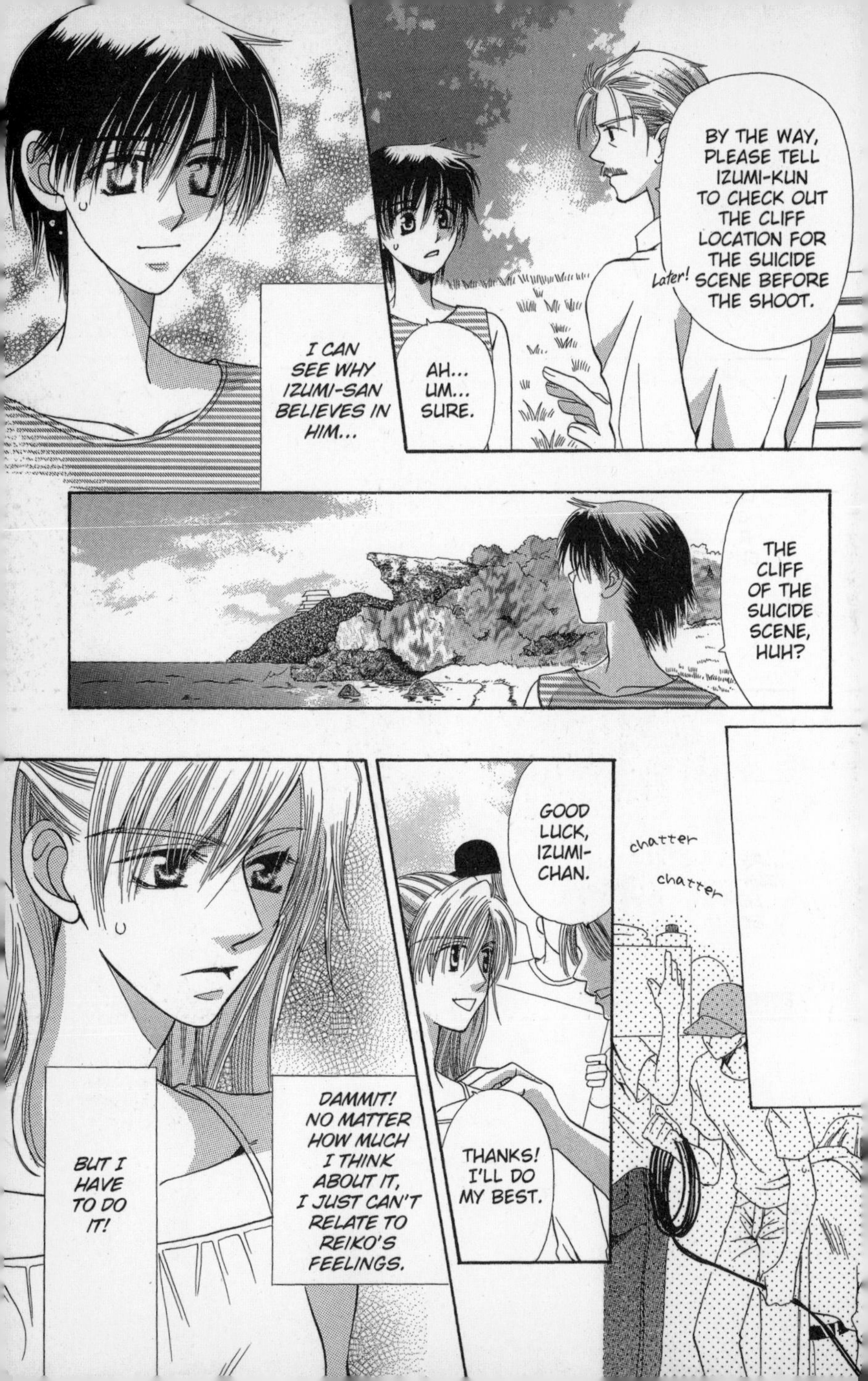
BY THE WAY, PLEASE TELL IZUMI-KUN TO CHECK OUT THE CLIFF LOCATION FOR THE SUICIDE SCENE BEFORE THE SHOOT.
Later!
AH... UM... SURE.
I CAN SEE WHY IZUMI-SAN BELIEVES IN HIM...
THE CLIFF OF THE SUICIDE SCENE, HUH?
chatter
chatter
GOOD LUCK, IZUMI-CHAN.
THANKS! I'LL DO MY BEST.
DAMMIT! NO MATTER HOW MUCH I THINK ABOUT IT, I JUST CAN'T RELATE TO REIKO'S FEELINGS.
BUT I HAVE TO DO IT!

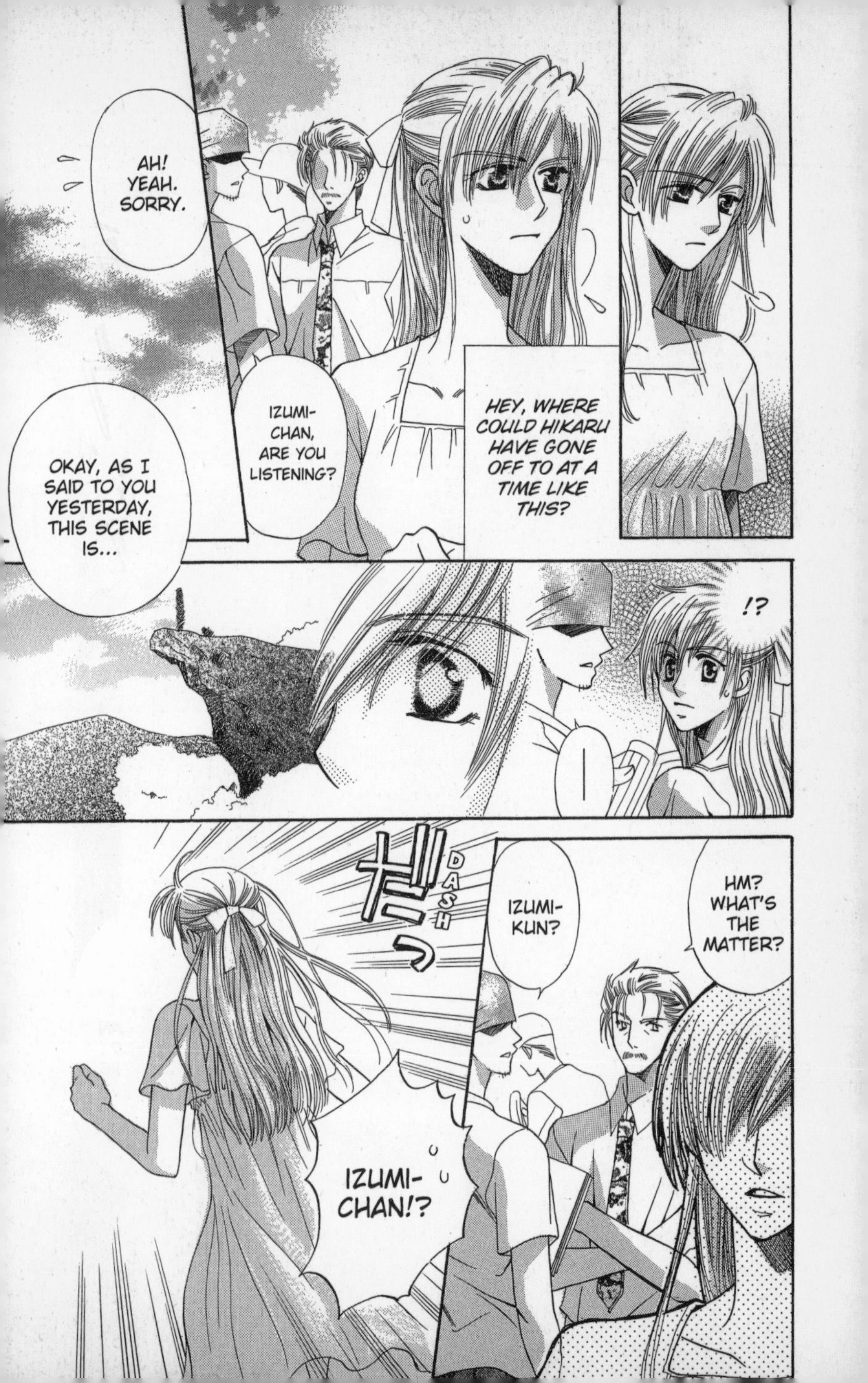
HEY, WHERE COULD HIKARU HAVE GONE OFF TO AT A TIME LIKE THIS?
IZUMI-CHAN, ARE YOU LISTENING?
AH! YEAH. SORRY.
OKAY, AS I SAID TO YOU YESTERDAY, THIS SCENE IS...
!?
HM? WHAT'S THE MATTER?
IZUMI-KUN?
DASH
IZUMI-CHAN!?

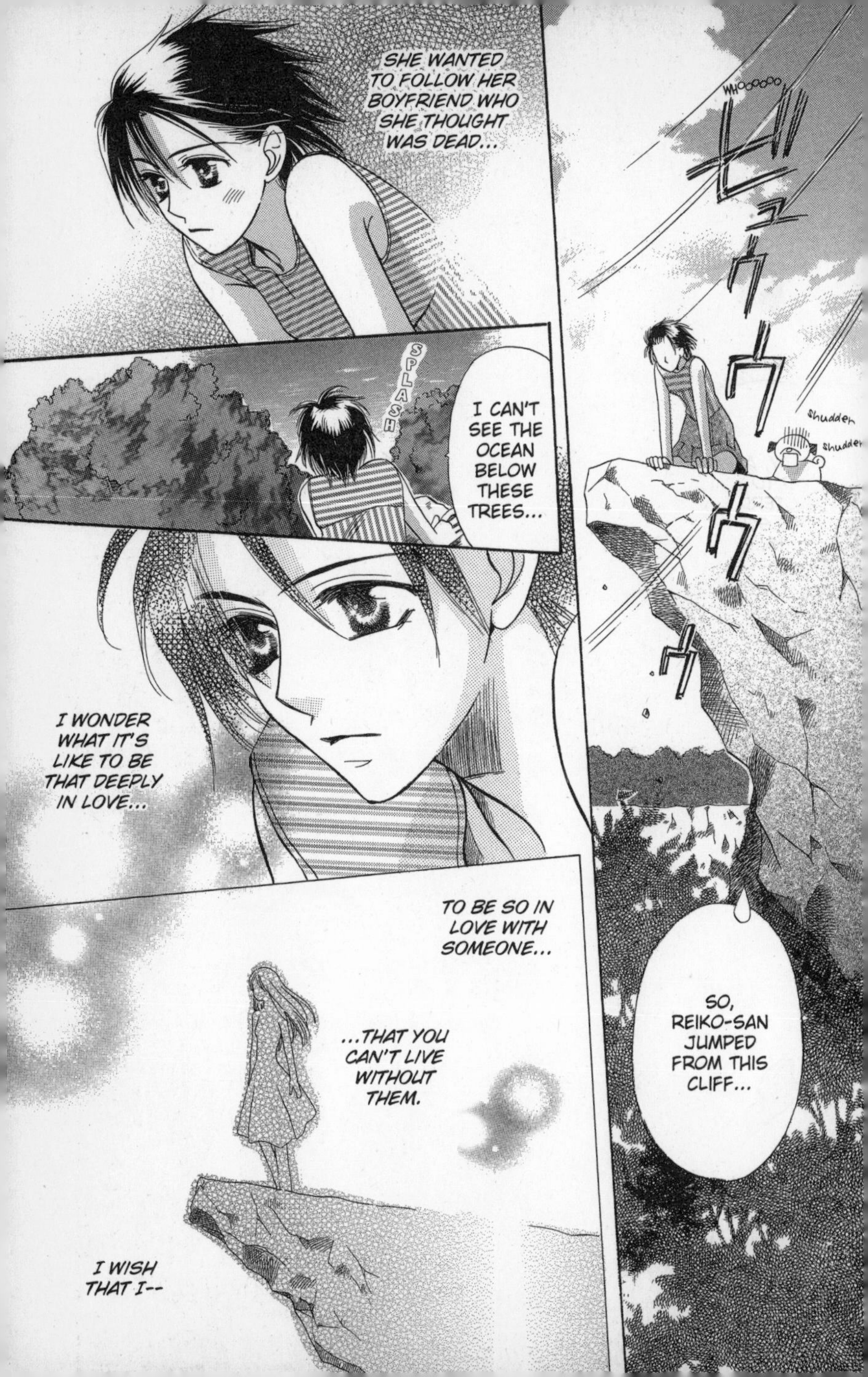
WHOOOOOO
shudder
shudder
SO, REIKO-SAN JUMPED FROM THIS CLIFF...
SHE WANTED TO FOLLOW HER BOYFRIEND WHO SHE THOUGHT WAS DEAD...
SPLASH
I CAN'T SEE THE OCEAN BELOW THESE TREES...
I WONDER WHAT IT'S LIKE TO BE THAT DEEPLY IN LOVE...
TO BE SO IN LOVE WITH SOMEONE...
...THAT YOU CAN'T LIVE WITHOUT THEM.
I WISH THAT I--

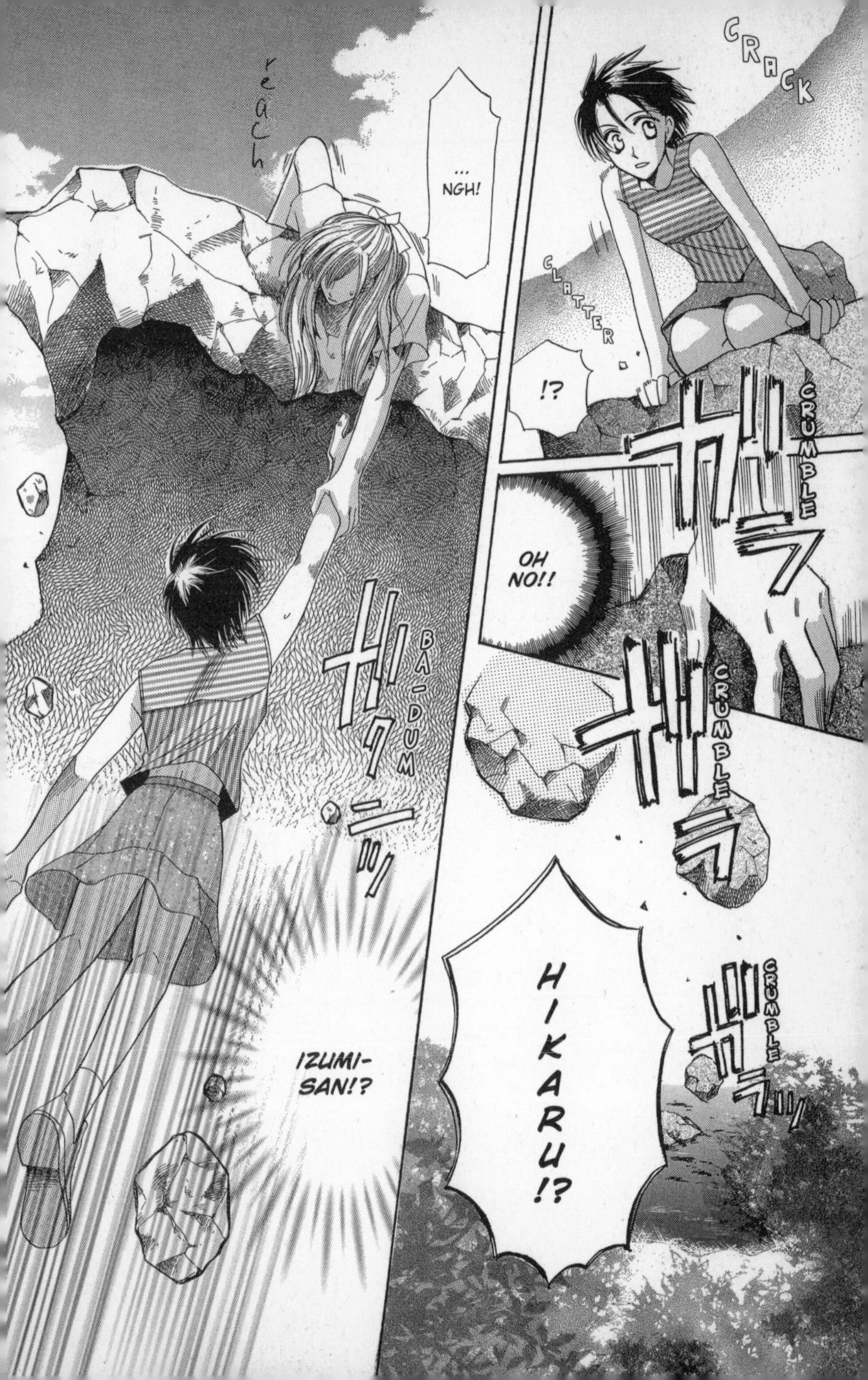
CRACK
CLATTER
!?
CRUMBLE
OH NO!!
CRUMBLE
HIKARU!?
CRUMBLE
reach
... NGH!
BA-DUM
IZUMI-SAN!?

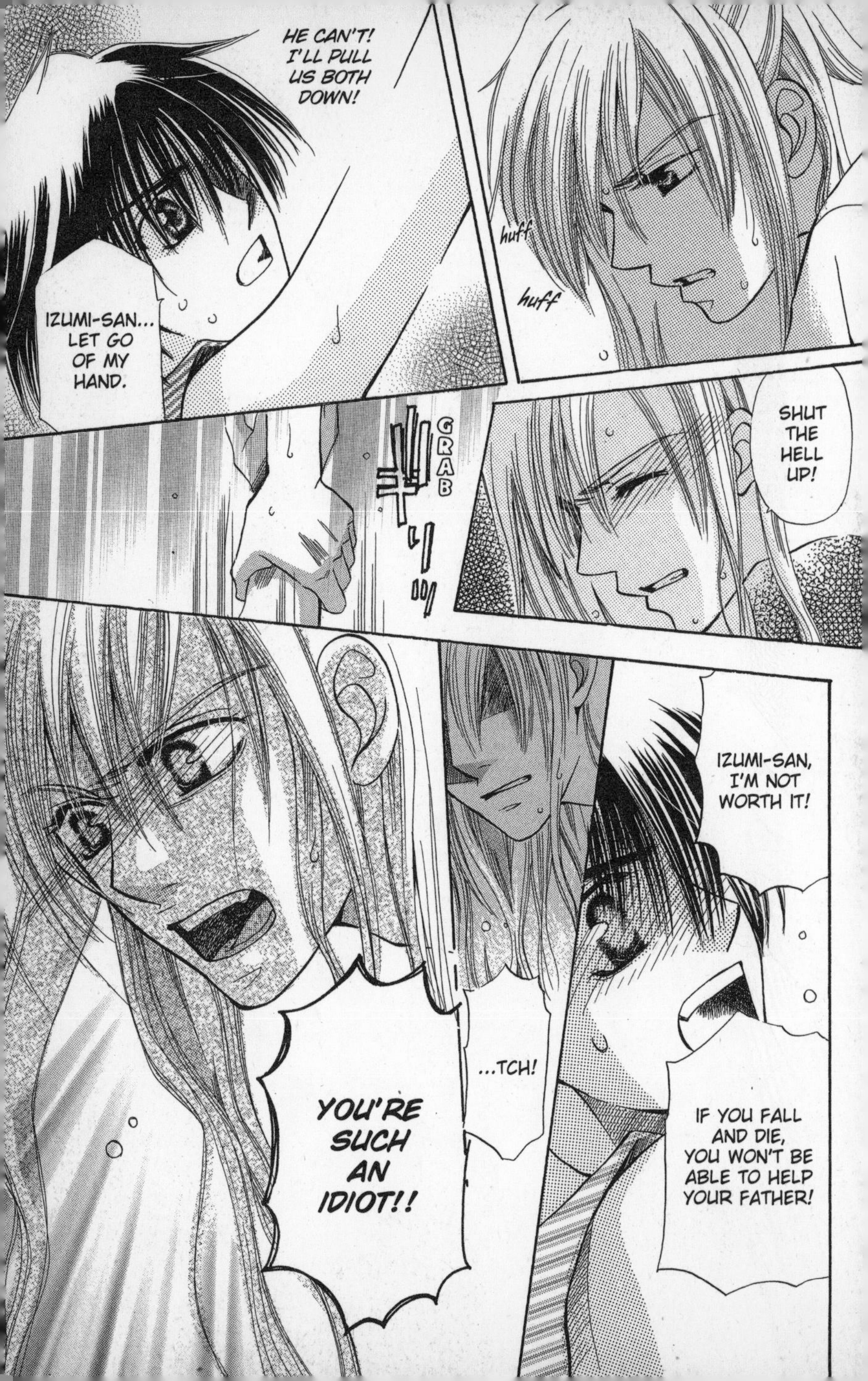
huff
huff
HE CAN'T! I'LL PULL US BOTH DOWN!
IZUMI-SAN... LET GO OF MY HAND.
SHUT THE HELL UP!
GRAB
IZUMI-SAN, I'M NOT WORTH IT!
IF YOU FALL AND DIE, YOU WON'T BE ABLE TO HELP YOUR FATHER!
...TCH!
YOU'RE SUCH AN IDIOT!!

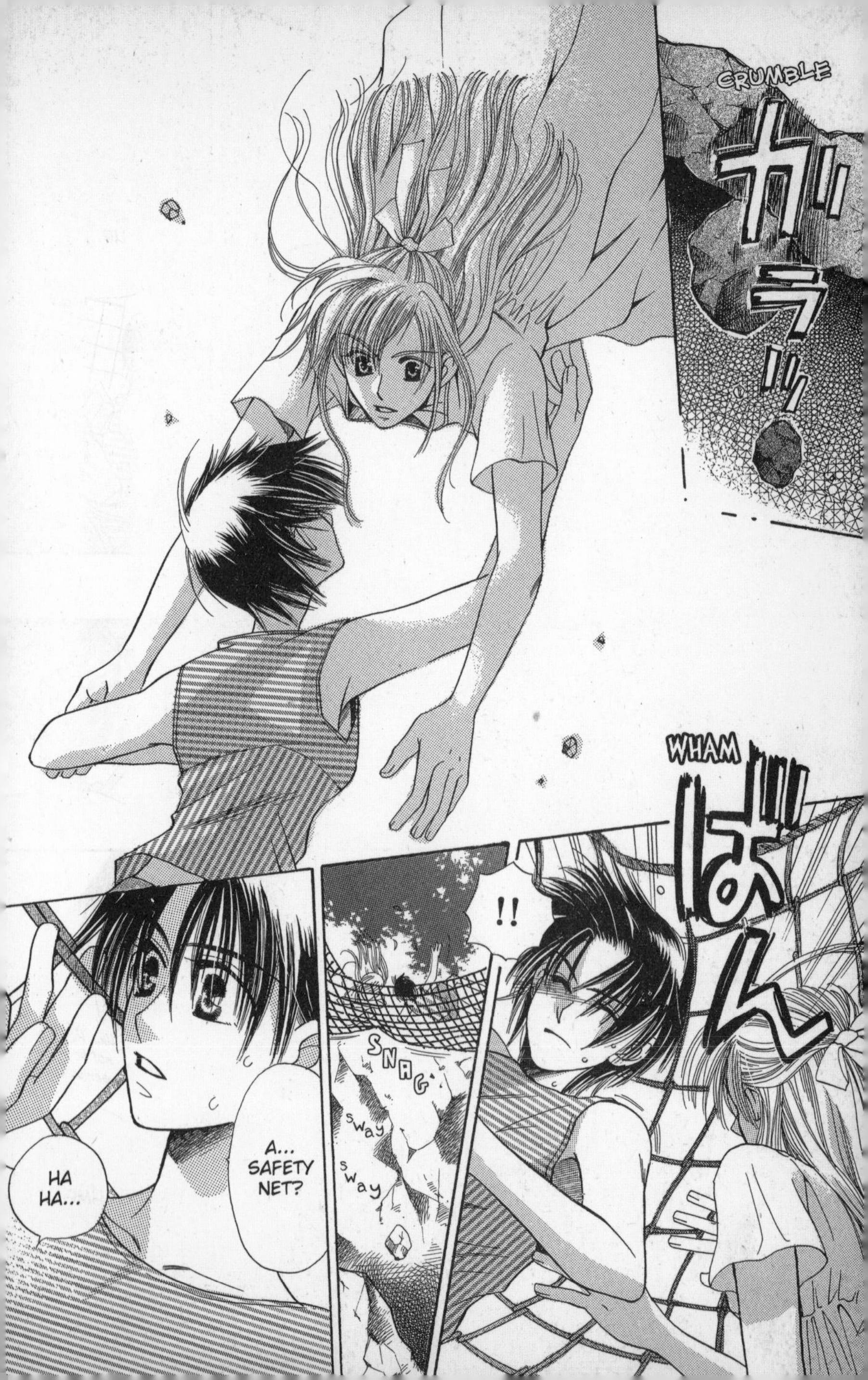
CRUMBLE
ガラッ
WHAM
ばん
!!
SNAG
sway
sway
A... SAFETY NET?
HA HA...

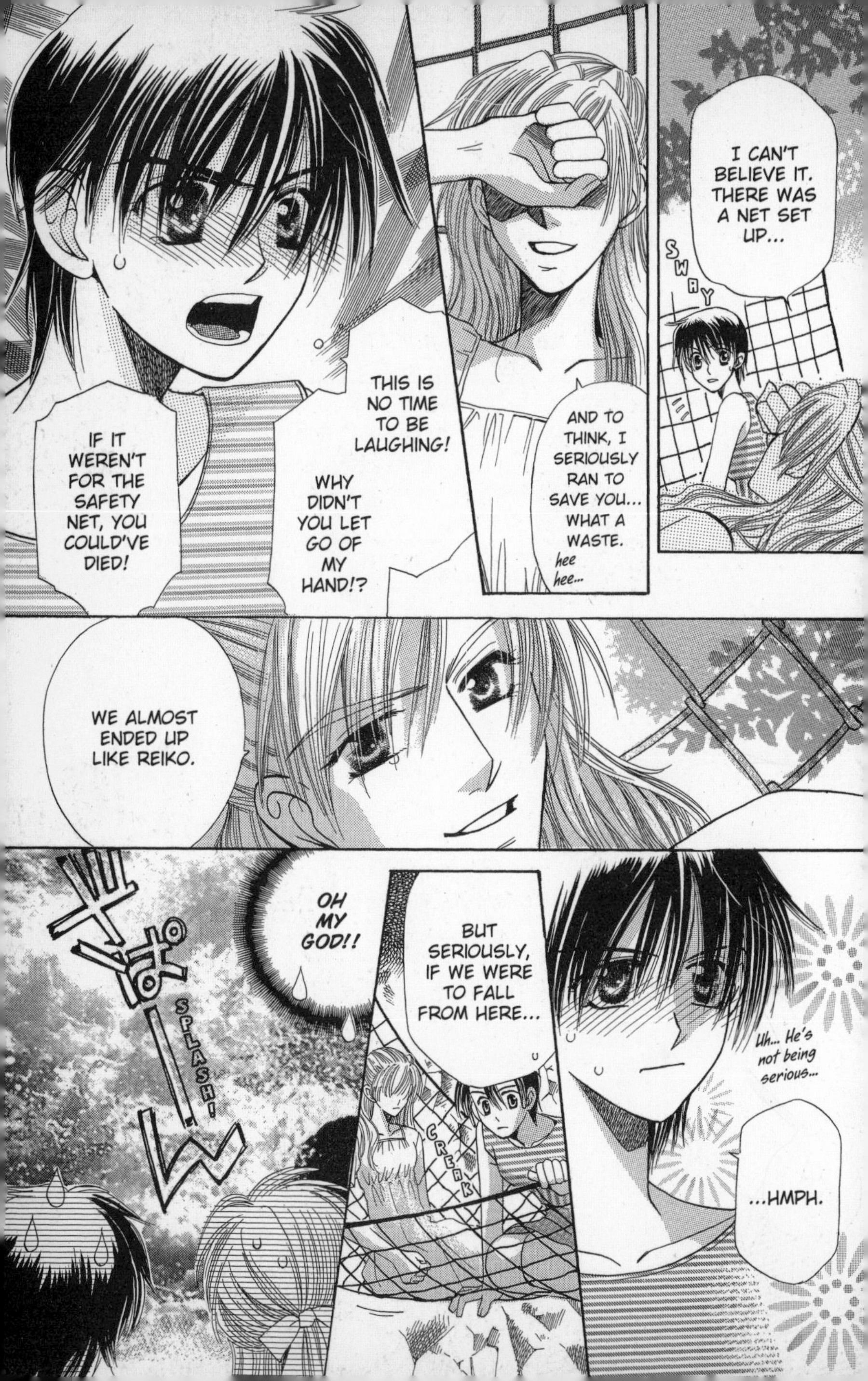
I CAN'T BELIEVE IT. THERE WAS A NET SET UP...
SWAY
AND TO THINK, I SERIOUSLY RAN TO SAVE YOU... WHAT A WASTE.
hee hee...
THIS IS NO TIME TO BE LAUGHING!
WHY DIDN'T YOU LET GO OF MY HAND!?
IF IT WEREN'T FOR THE SAFETY NET, YOU COULD'VE DIED!
WE ALMOST ENDED UP LIKE REIKO.
BUT SERIOUSLY, IF WE WERE TO FALL FROM HERE...
CREAK
Uh... He's not being serious...
...HMPH.
OH MY GOD!!
SPLASH!

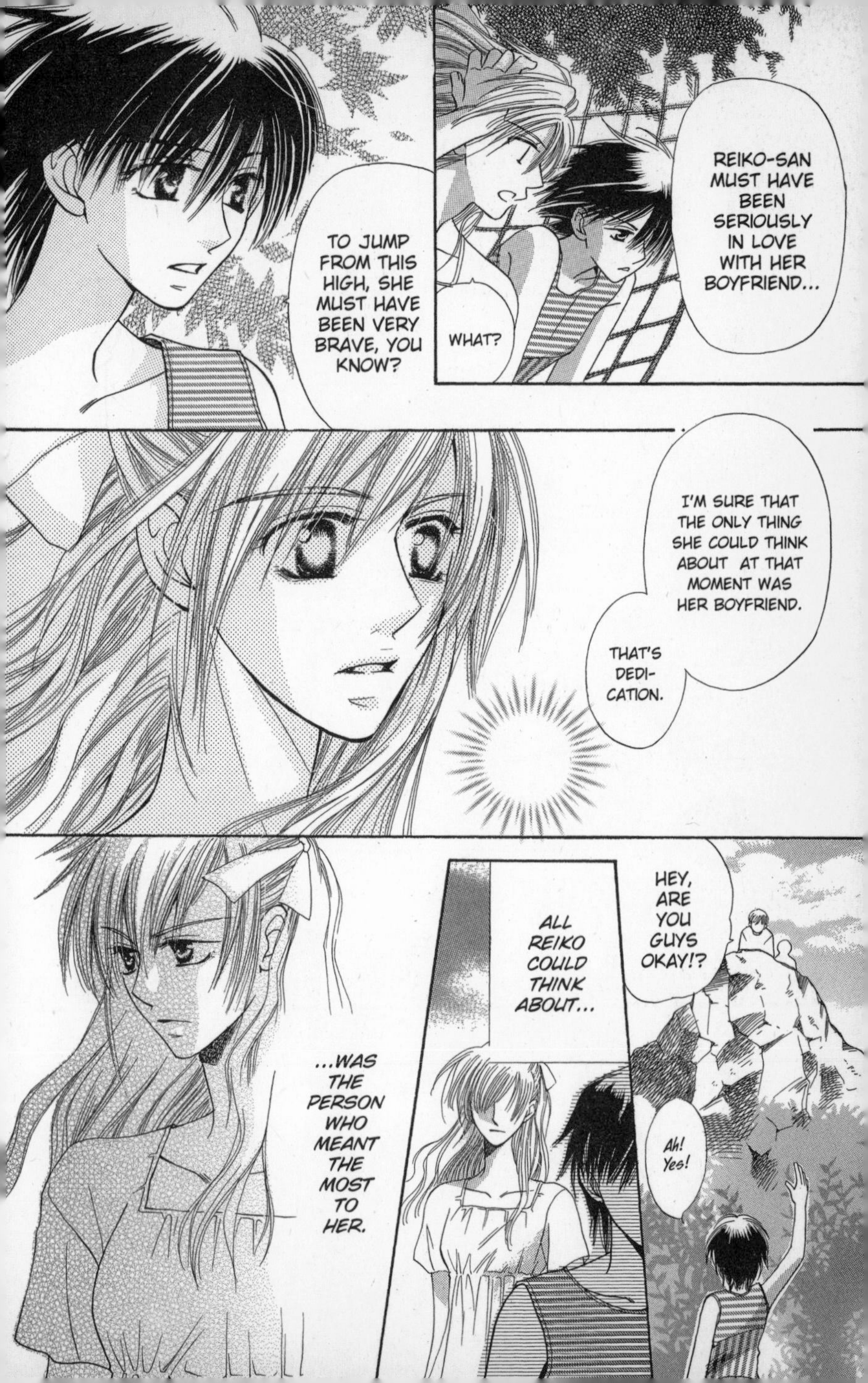
REIKO-SAN MUST HAVE BEEN SERIOUSLY IN LOVE WITH HER BOYFRIEND...
WHAT?
TO JUMP FROM THIS HIGH, SHE MUST HAVE BEEN VERY BRAVE, YOU KNOW?
I'M SURE THAT THE ONLY THING SHE COULD THINK ABOUT AT THAT MOMENT WAS HER BOYFRIEND.
THAT'S DEDI-CATION.
HEY, ARE YOU GUYS OKAY!?
ALL REIKO COULD THINK ABOUT...
Ah! Yes!
...WAS THE PERSON WHO MEANT THE MOST TO HER.

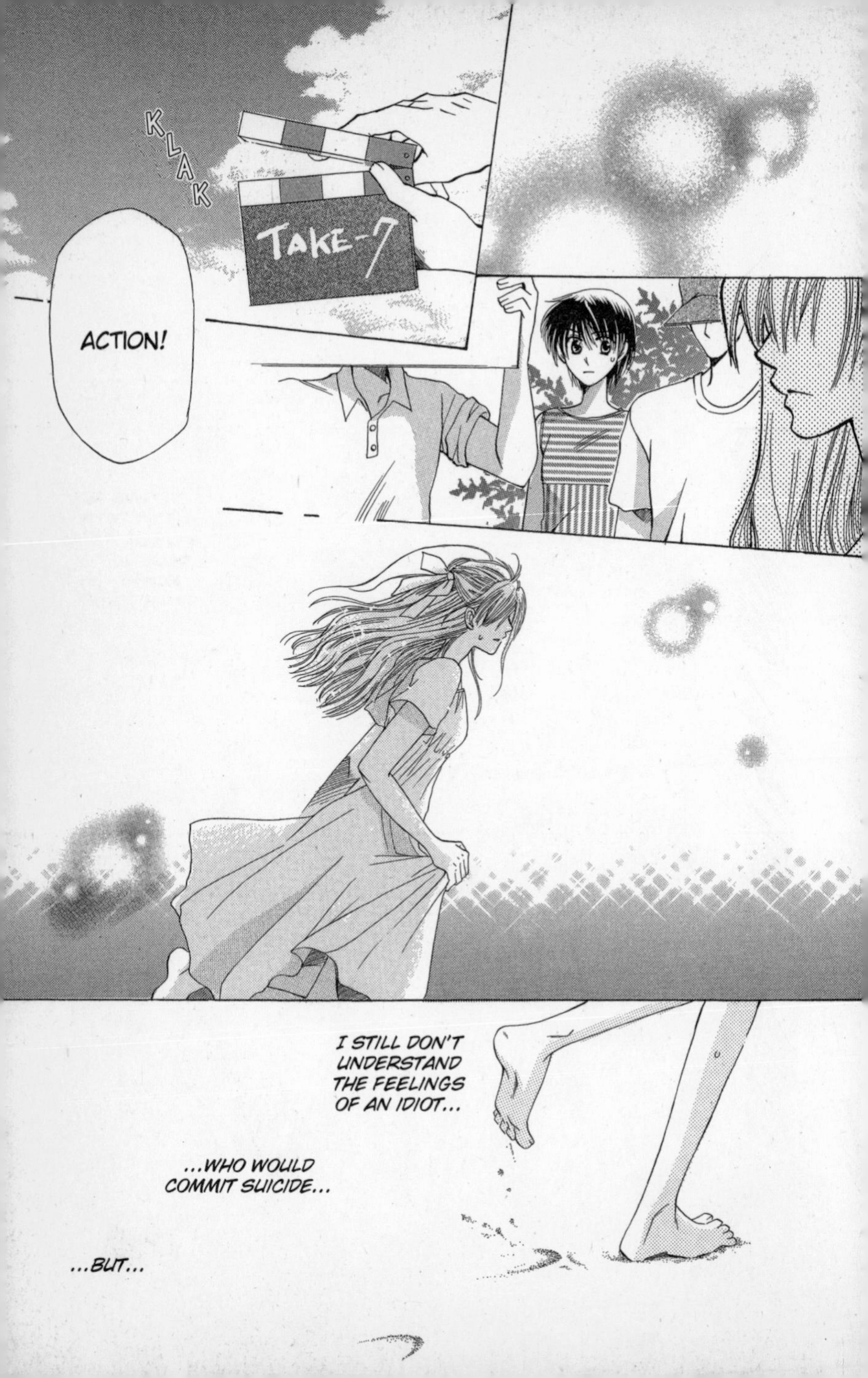
TAKE-7
KLAK
ACTION!
I STILL DON'T UNDERSTAND THE FEELINGS OF AN IDIOT...
...WHO WOULD COMMIT SUICIDE...
...BUT...

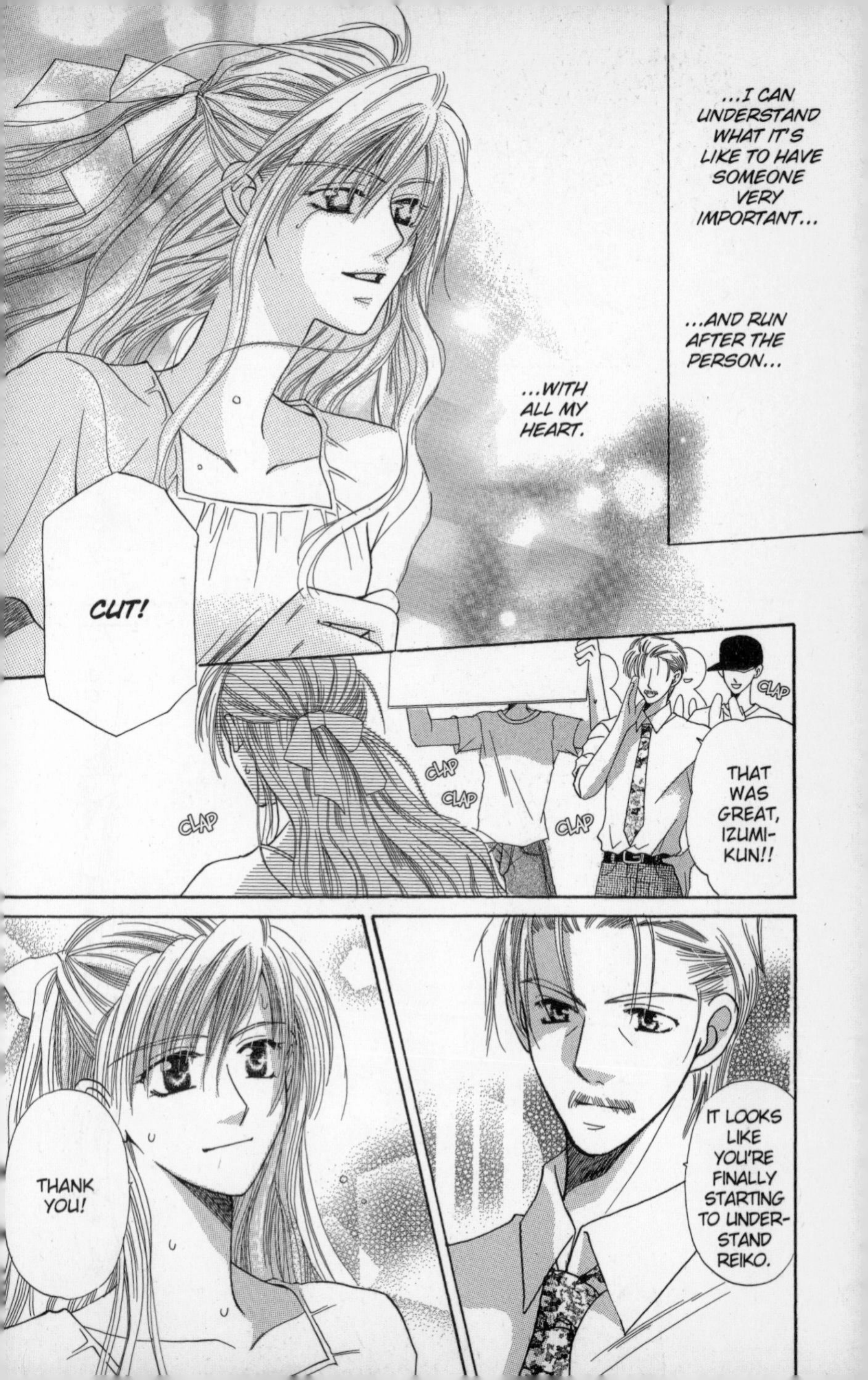
...I CAN UNDERSTAND WHAT IT'S LIKE TO HAVE SOMEONE VERY IMPORTANT...
...AND RUN AFTER THE PERSON...
...WITH ALL MY HEART.
CUT!
CLAP
THAT WAS GREAT, IZUMI-KUN!!
CLAP
CLAP
CLAP
CLAP
IT LOOKS LIKE YOU'RE FINALLY STARTING TO UNDER-STAND REIKO.
THANK YOU!

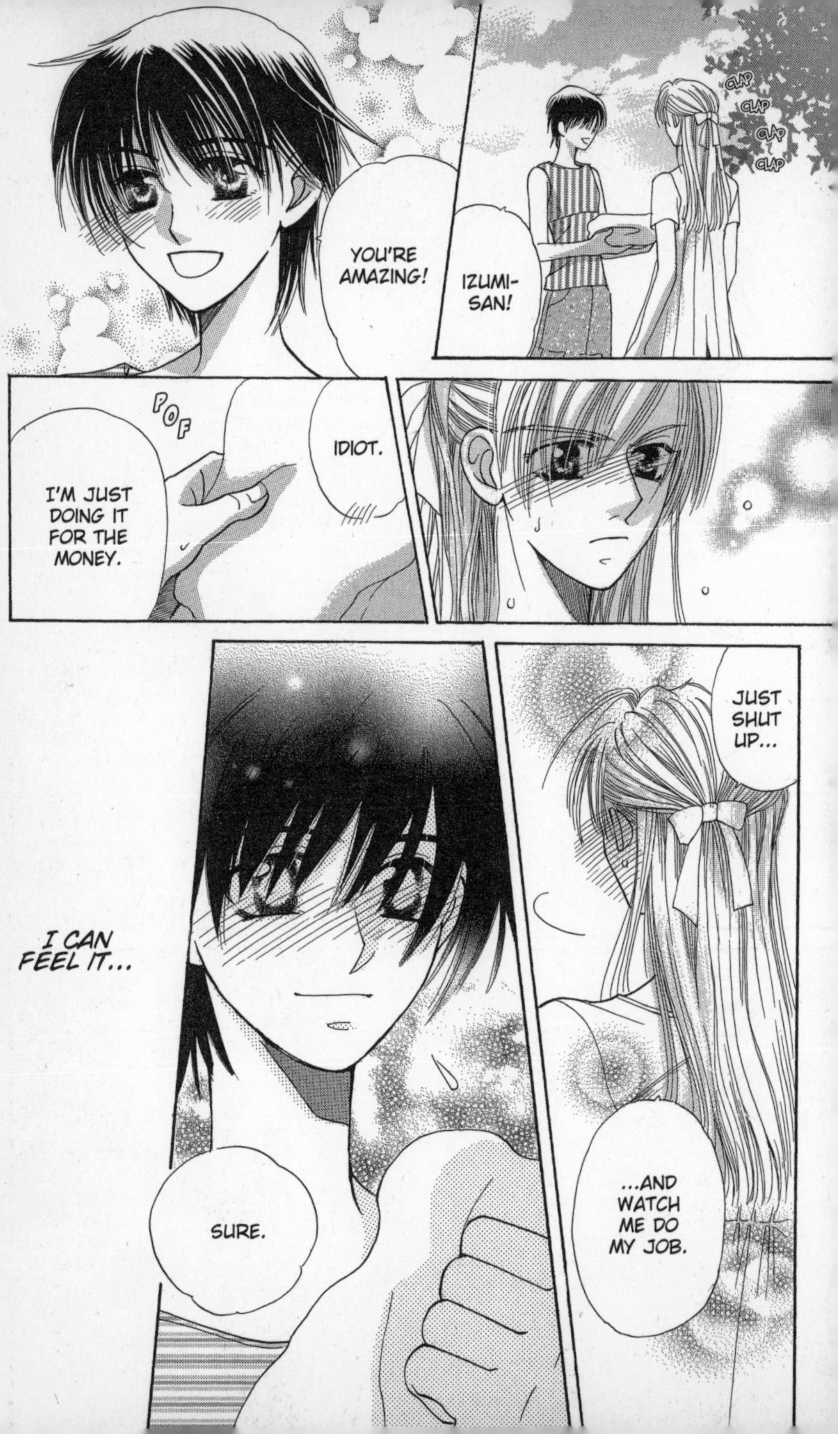
CLAP
CLAP
CLAP
CLAP
IZUMI-SAN!
YOU'RE AMAZING!
IDIOT.
POF
I'M JUST DOING IT FOR THE MONEY.
JUST SHUT UP...
...AND WATCH ME DO MY JOB.
I CAN FEEL IT...
SURE.

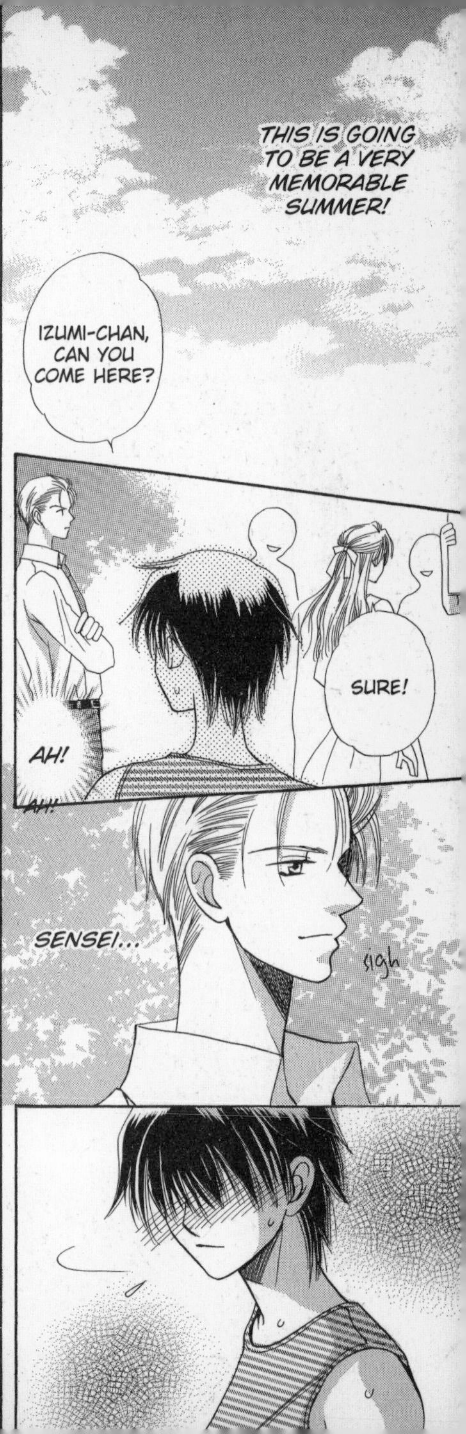
THIS IS GOING TO BE A VERY MEMORABLE SUMMER!
IZUMI-CHAN, CAN YOU COME HERE?
SURE!
AH!
AH!
SENSEI...
sigh

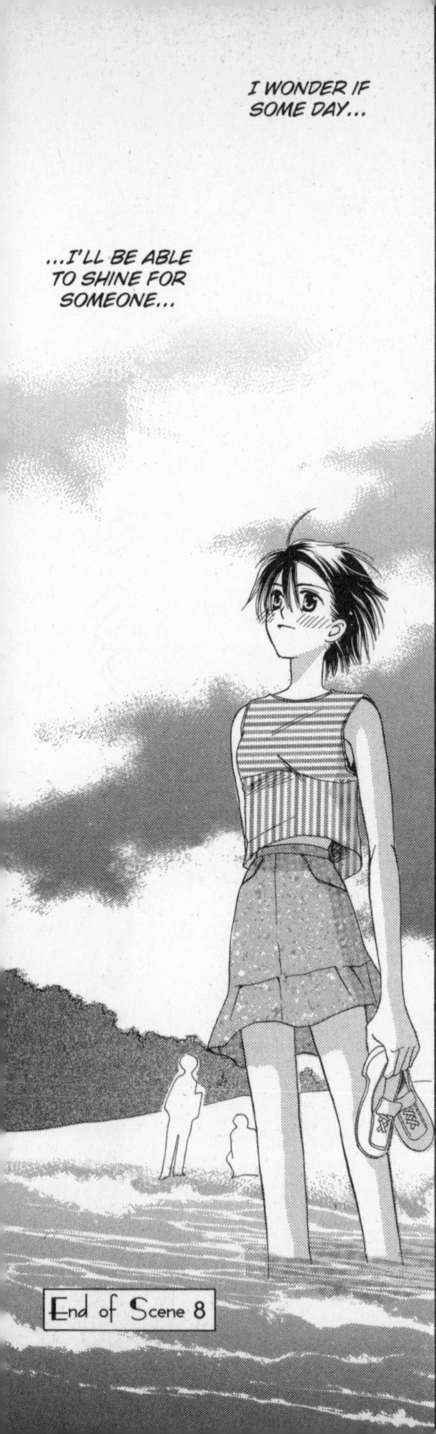
I WONDER IF SOME DAY...
...I'LL BE ABLE TO SHINE FOR SOMEONE...

End of Scene 8

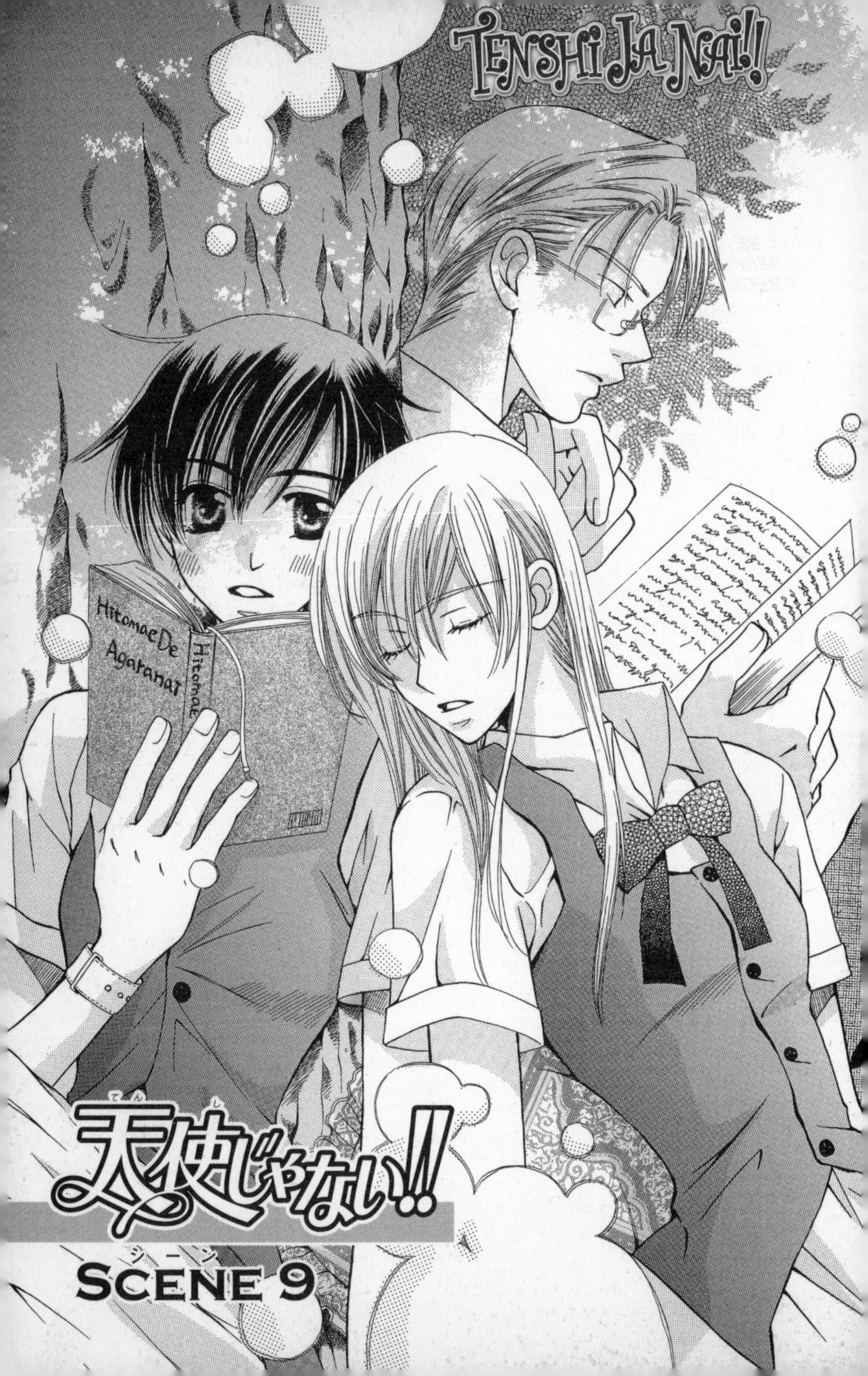
TENSHI JA NAI!!
HitomaeDe Agaranai
Hitomae
てんし
天使じゃない!!
シーン
SCENE 9

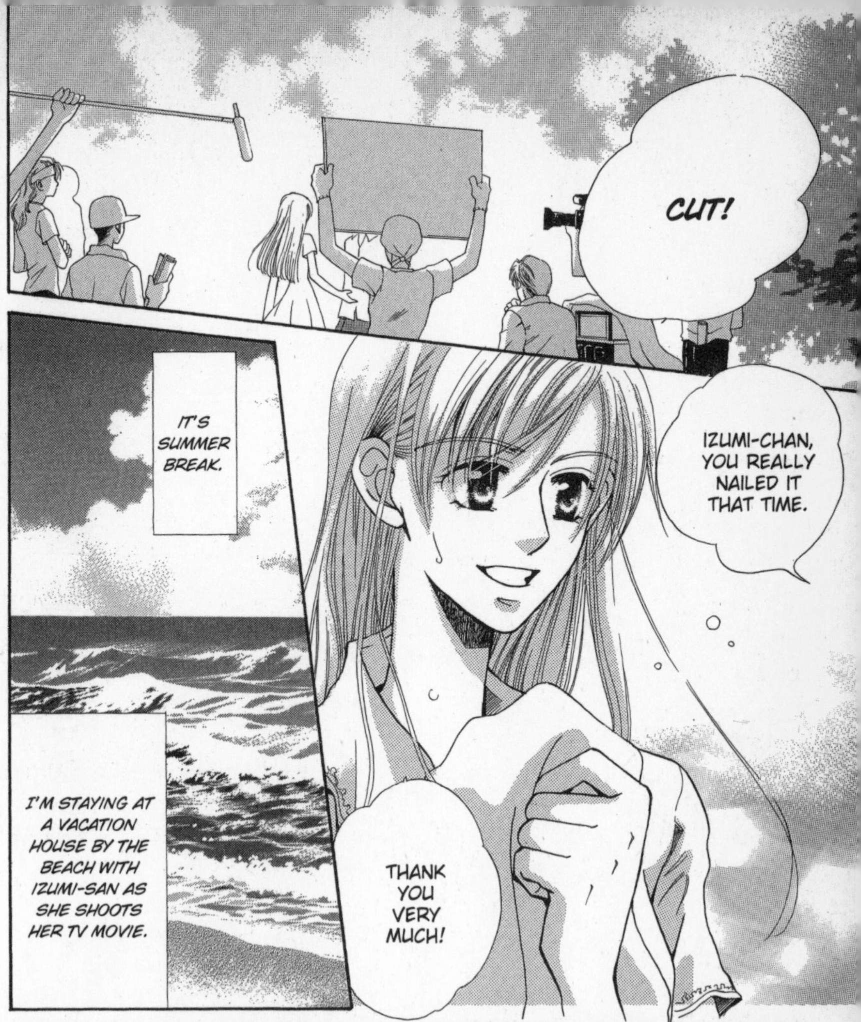
CUT!
IZUMI-CHAN, YOU REALLY NAILED IT THAT TIME.
THANK YOU VERY MUCH!
IT'S SUMMER BREAK.
I'M STAYING AT A VACATION HOUSE BY THE BEACH WITH IZUMI-SAN AS SHE SHOOTS HER TV MOVIE.

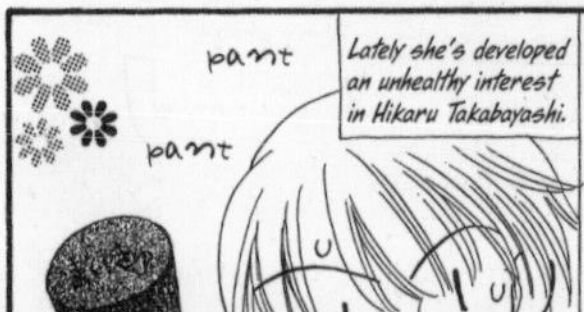
pant
pant
Lately she's developed an unhealthy interest in Hikaru Takabayashi.

Kaoru Momochi (15 years old)

Birthday: March 3rd Blood type: O

Reporter-type. She's kind of cute and perky but tends to hover around people like a hyena. Even though she belongs to the A.V. club and the school paper, because of her unusual personality, no one seems to want to work with her so she usually ends up working by herself. Even a lonely girl like her has concerns of her own. (Although the author isn't sure if she'll ever get to those concerns...)

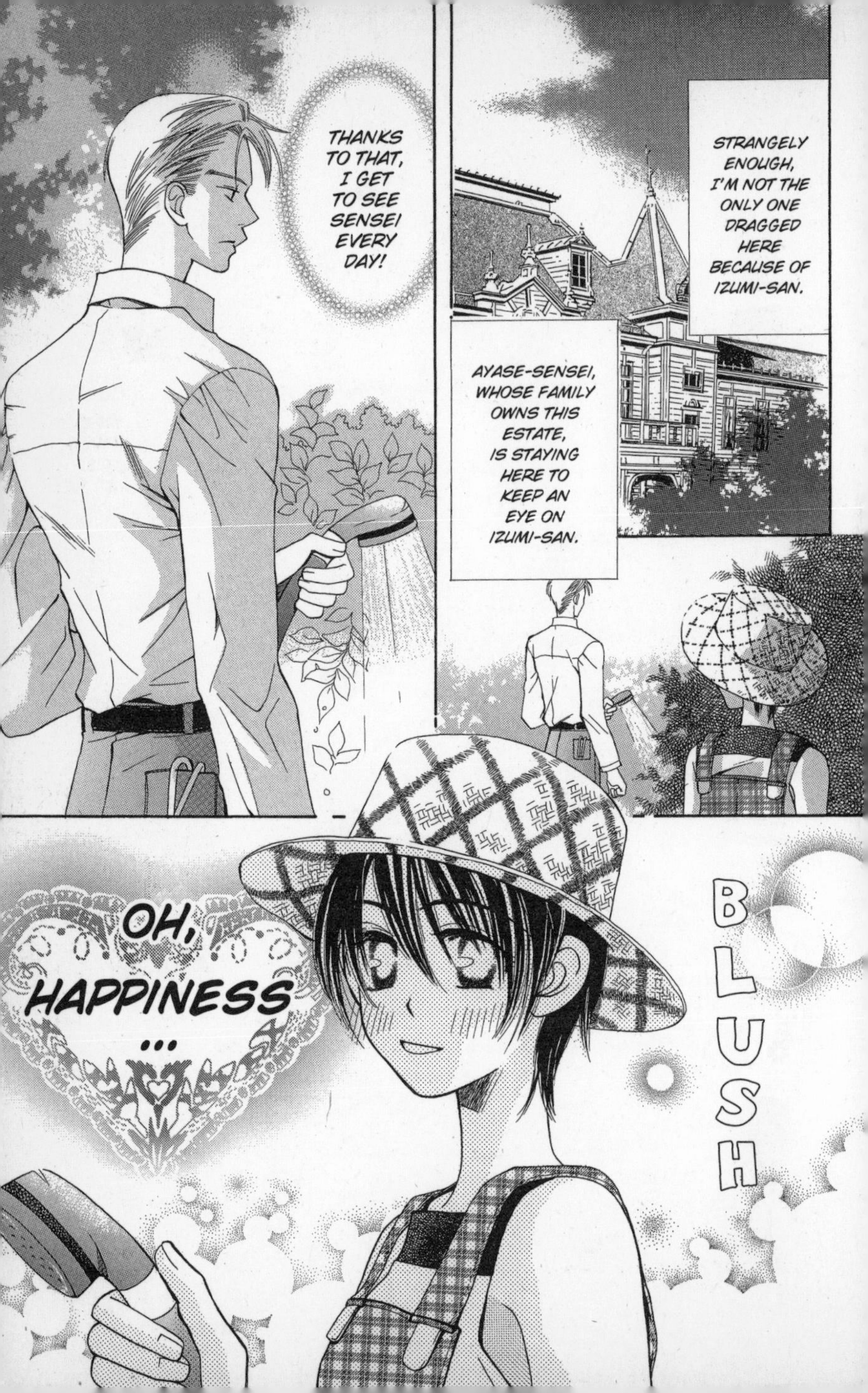
STRANGELY ENOUGH, I'M NOT THE ONLY ONE DRAGGED HERE BECAUSE OF IZUMI-SAN.
AYASE-SENSEI, WHOSE FAMILY OWNS THIS ESTATE, IS STAYING HERE TO KEEP AN EYE ON IZUMI-SAN.
THANKS TO THAT, I GET TO SEE SENSEI EVERY DAY!
BLUSH
OH, HAPPINESS ...

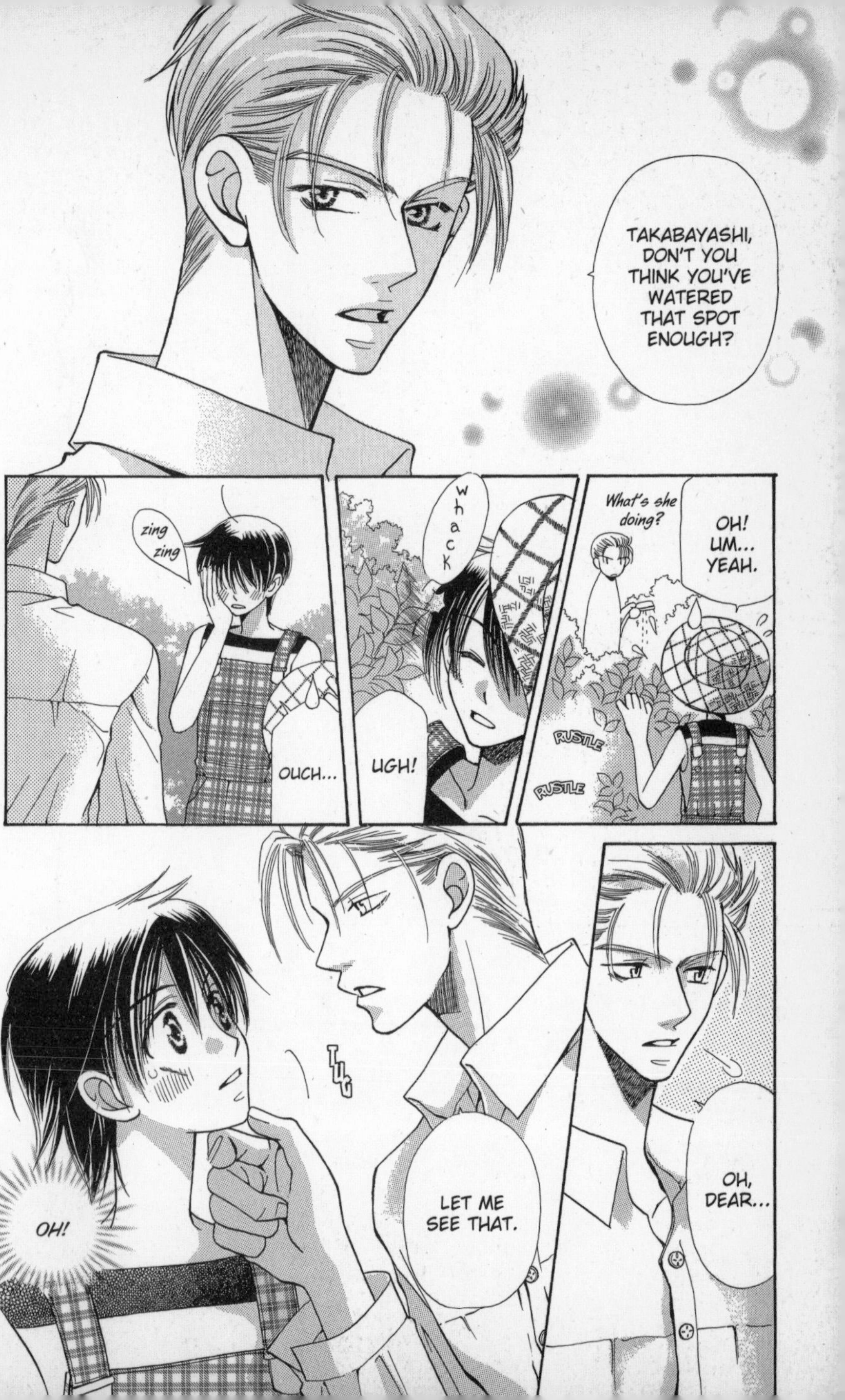
TAKABAYASHI, DON'T YOU THINK YOU'VE WATERED THAT SPOT ENOUGH?
What's she doing?
OH! UM... YEAH.
RUSTLE
RUSTLE
whack
UGH!
zing zing
OUCH...
OH, DEAR...
TUG
LET ME SEE THAT.
OH!

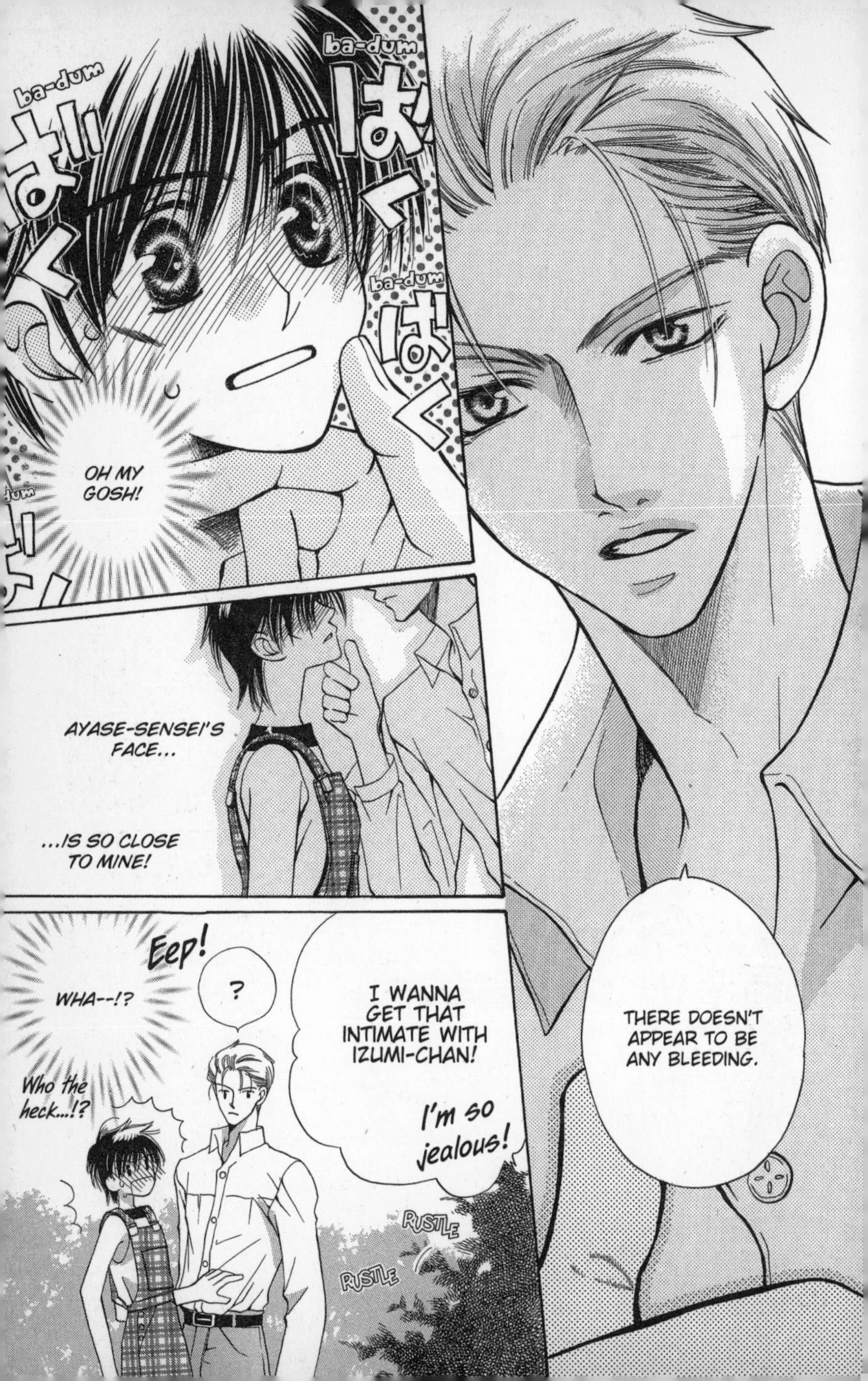

THERE DOESN'T APPEAR TO BE ANY BLEEDING.
ba-dum
ba-dum
ba-dum
OH MY GOSH!
AYASE-SENSEI'S FACE...
...IS SO CLOSE TO MINE!
I WANNA GET THAT INTIMATE WITH IZUMI-CHAN!
I'm so jealous!
?
Eep!
WHA--!?
Who the heck...!?
RUSTLE
RUSTLE

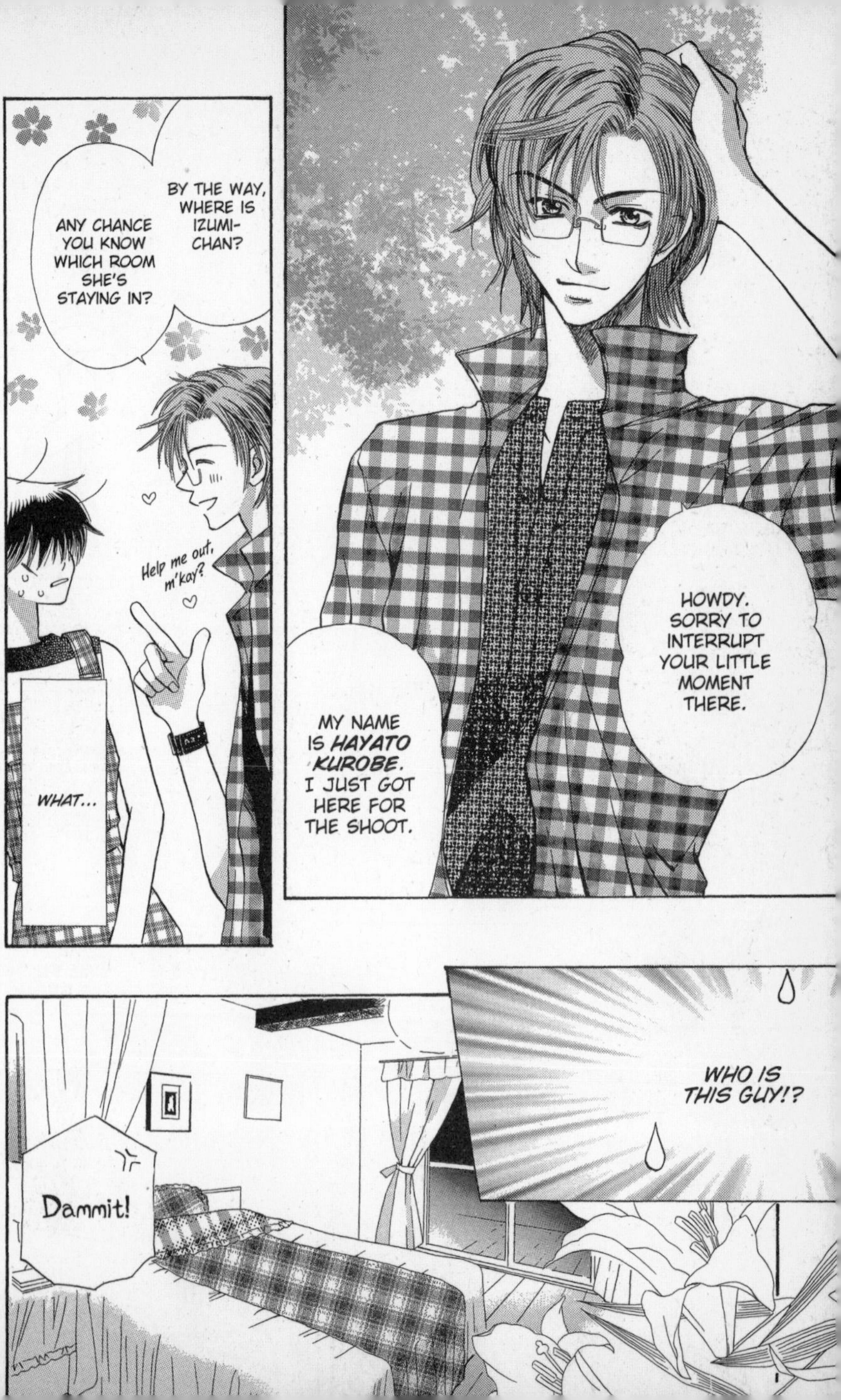
HOWDY. SORRY TO INTERRUPT YOUR LITTLE MOMENT THERE.
MY NAME IS *HAYATO KUROBE*. I JUST GOT HERE FOR THE SHOOT.
BY THE WAY, WHERE IS IZUMI-CHAN?
ANY CHANCE YOU KNOW WHICH ROOM SHE'S STAYING IN?
Help me out, m'kay?
WHAT...
WHO IS THIS GUY!?
Dammit!

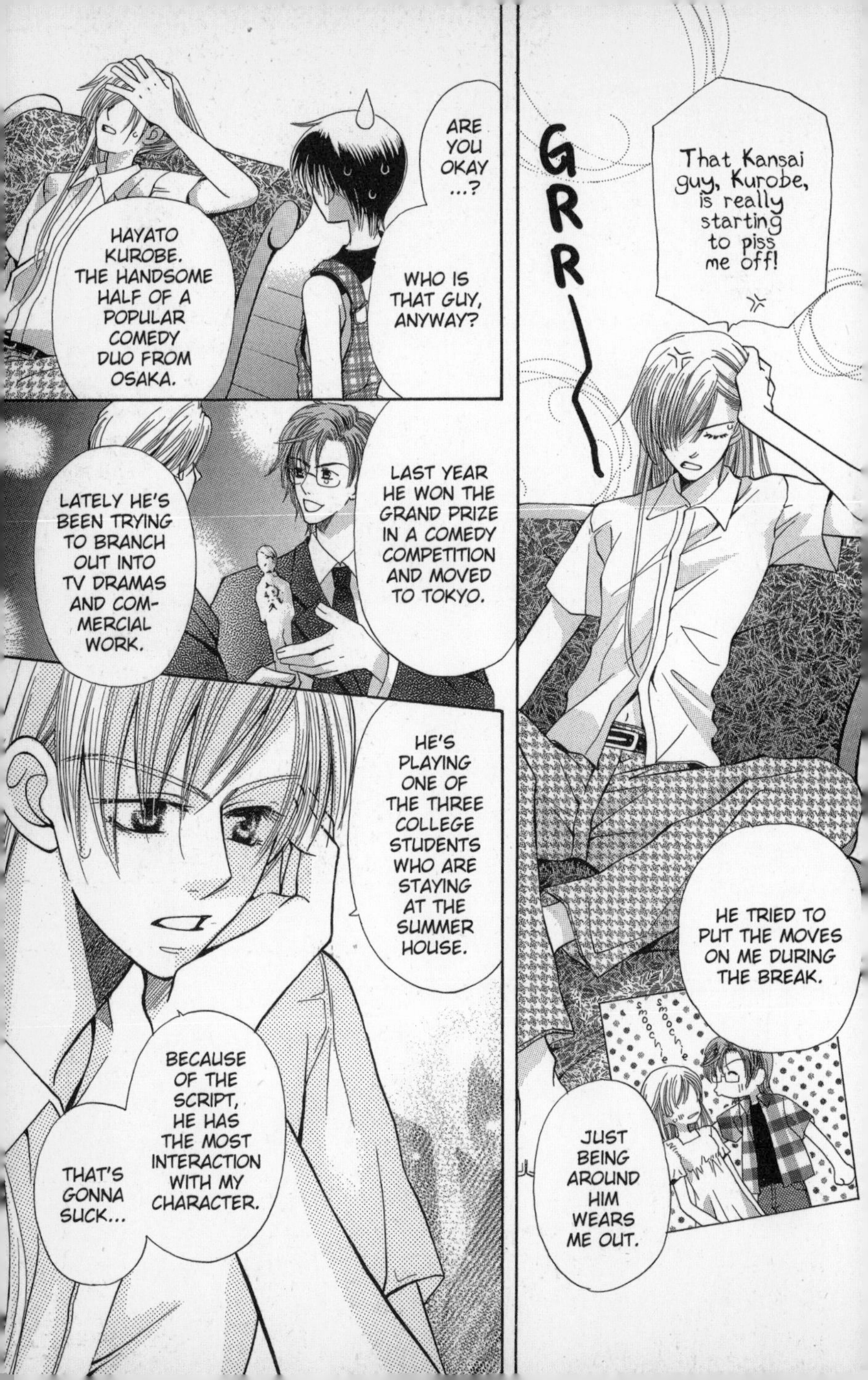
GRR
That Kansai guy, Kurobe, is really starting to piss me off!
HE TRIED TO PUT THE MOVES ON ME DURING THE BREAK.
smoochie smoochie
JUST BEING AROUND HIM WEARS ME OUT.
ARE YOU OKAY ...?
WHO IS THAT GUY, ANYWAY?
HAYATO KUROBE. THE HANDSOME HALF OF A POPULAR COMEDY DUO FROM OSAKA.
LAST YEAR HE WON THE GRAND PRIZE IN A COMEDY COMPETITION AND MOVED TO TOKYO.
LATELY HE'S BEEN TRYING TO BRANCH OUT INTO TV DRAMAS AND COM-MERCIAL WORK.
HE'S PLAYING ONE OF THE THREE COLLEGE STUDENTS WHO ARE STAYING AT THE SUMMER HOUSE.
BECAUSE OF THE SCRIPT, HE HAS THE MOST INTERACTION WITH MY CHARACTER.
THAT'S GONNA SUCK...

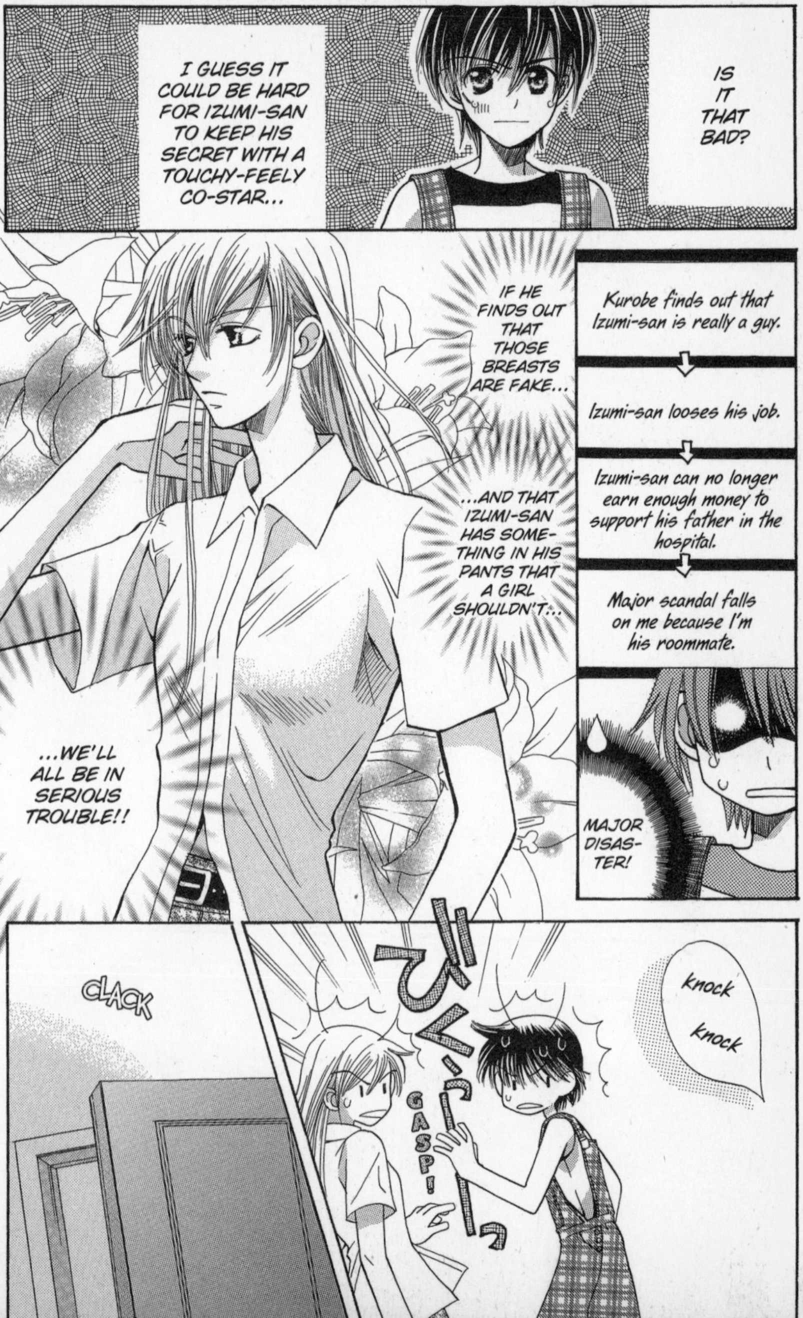
IS IT THAT BAD?
I GUESS IT COULD BE HARD FOR IZUMI-SAN TO KEEP HIS SECRET WITH A TOUCHY-FEELY CO-STAR...
Kurobe finds out that Izumi-san is really a guy.
Izumi-san looses his job.
Izumi-san can no longer earn enough money to support his father in the hospital.
Major scandal falls on me because I'm his roommate.
MAJOR DISASTER!
IF HE FINDS OUT THAT THOSE BREASTS ARE FAKE...
...AND THAT IZUMI-SAN HAS SOMETHING IN HIS PANTS THAT A GIRL SHOULDN'T...
...WE'LL ALL BE IN SERIOUS TROUBLE!!
knock knock
GASP!
CLACK

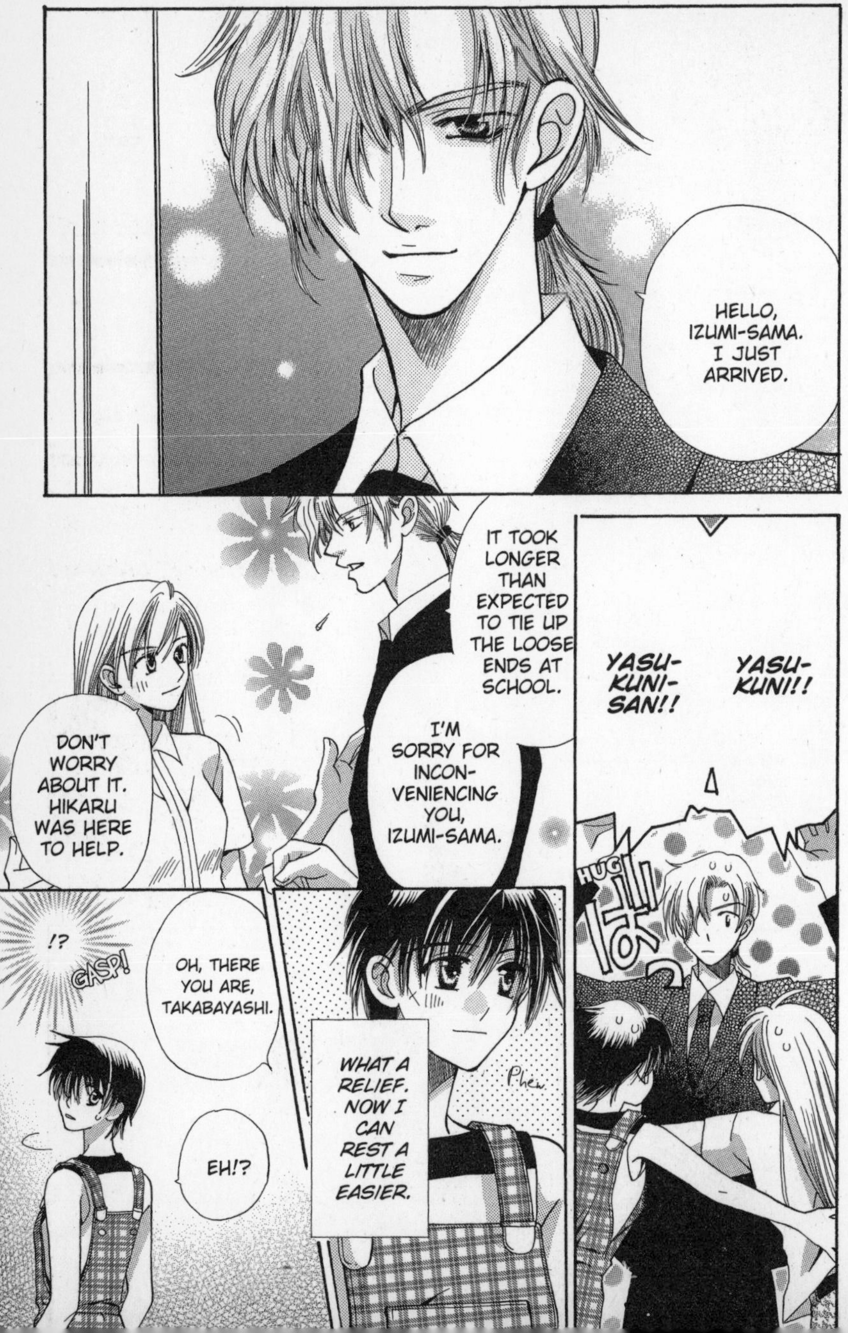
HELLO, IZUMI-SAMA. I JUST ARRIVED.
YASU-KUNI!!
YASU-KUNI-SAN!!
HUG
ぱっ
IT TOOK LONGER THAN EXPECTED TO TIE UP THE LOOSE ENDS AT SCHOOL.
I'M SORRY FOR INCON-VENIENCING YOU, IZUMI-SAMA.
DON'T WORRY ABOUT IT. HIKARU WAS HERE TO HELP.
WHAT A RELIEF. NOW I CAN REST A LITTLE EASIER.
Phew
!?
GASP!
OH, THERE YOU ARE, TAKABAYASHI.
EH!?

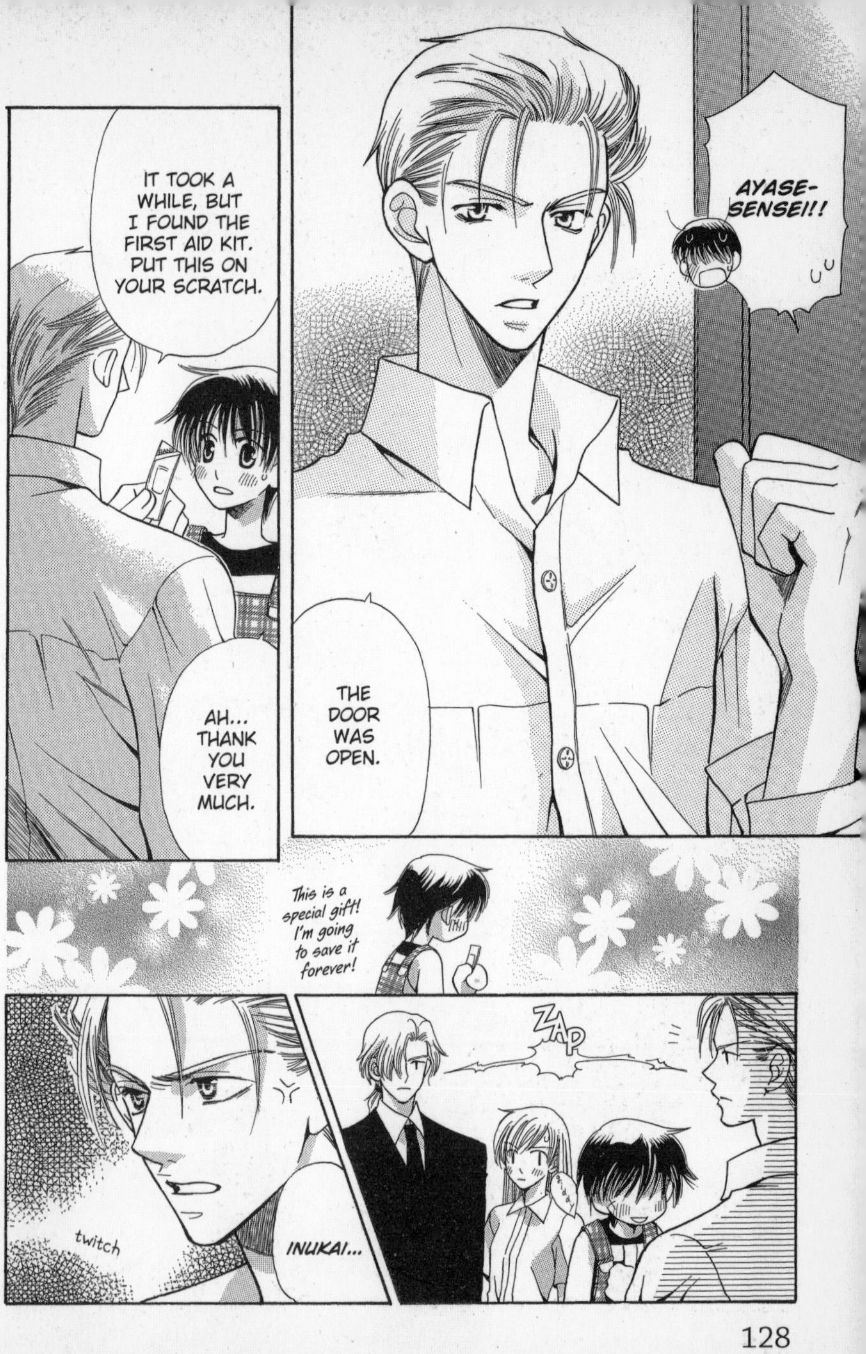
AYASE-SENSEI!!
THE DOOR WAS OPEN.
IT TOOK A WHILE, BUT I FOUND THE FIRST AID KIT. PUT THIS ON YOUR SCRATCH.
AH... THANK YOU VERY MUCH.
This is a special gift! I'm going to save it forever!
ZAP
INUKAI...
twitch

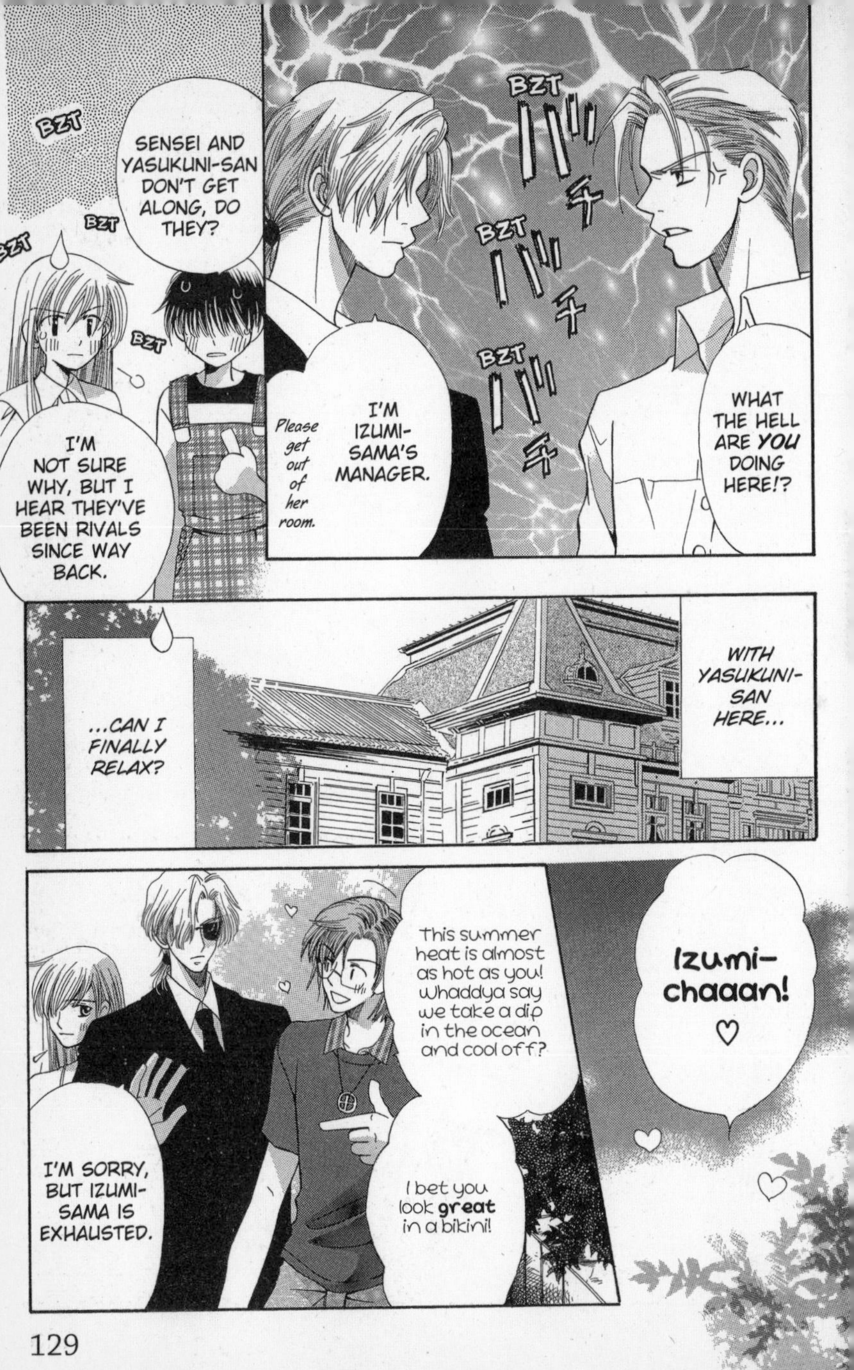
BZT
BZT
BZT
WHAT THE HELL ARE YOU DOING HERE!?
I'M IZUMI-SAMA'S MANAGER.
Please get out of her room.
BZT
SENSEI AND YASUKUNI-SAN DON'T GET ALONG, DO THEY?
BZT
BZT
BZT
I'M NOT SURE WHY, BUT I HEAR THEY'VE BEEN RIVALS SINCE WAY BACK.
WITH YASUKUNI-SAN HERE...
...CAN I FINALLY RELAX?
Izumi-chaaan! ♡
This summer heat is almost as hot as you! Whaddya say we take a dip in the ocean and cool off?
I bet you look great in a bikini!
I'M SORRY, BUT IZUMI-SAMA IS EXHAUSTED.

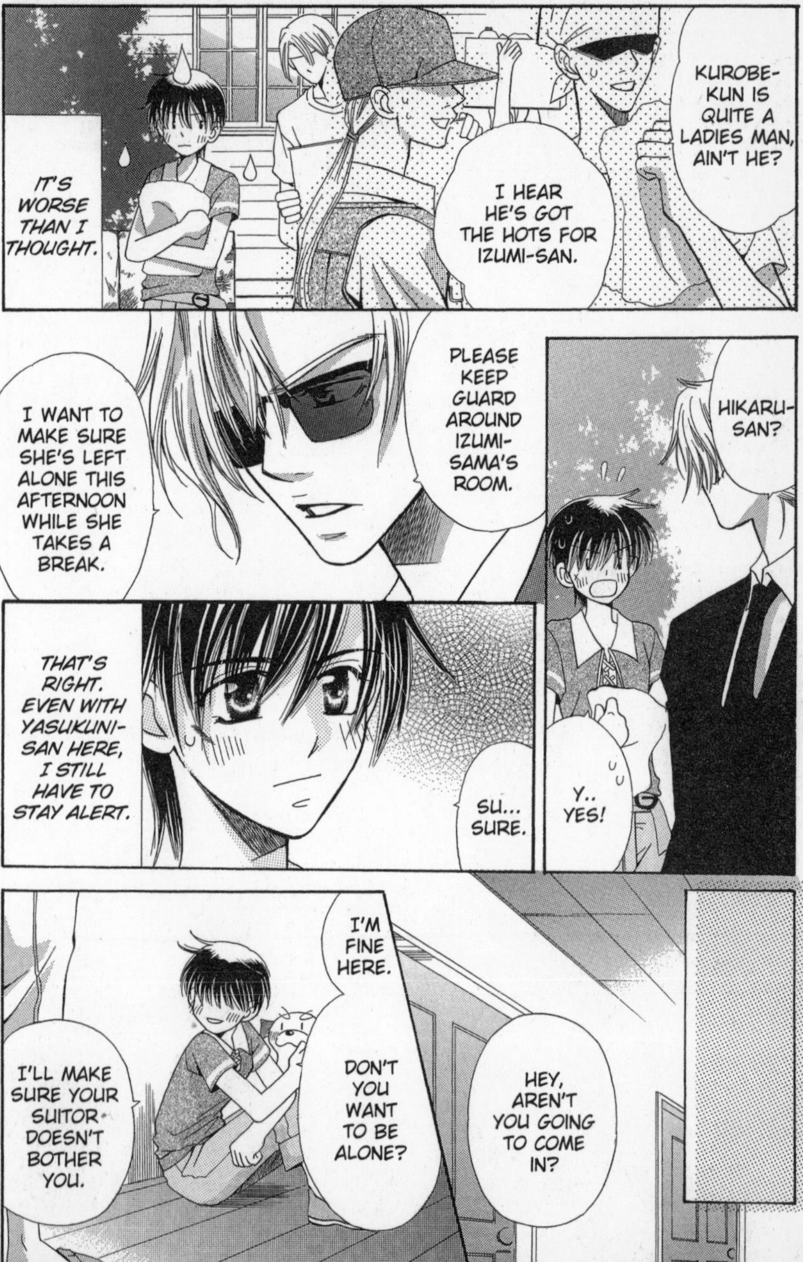
KUROBE-KUN IS QUITE A LADIES MAN, AIN'T HE?
I HEAR HE'S GOT THE HOTS FOR IZUMI-SAN.
IT'S WORSE THAN I THOUGHT.
HIKARU-SAN?
Y.. YES!
PLEASE KEEP GUARD AROUND IZUMI-SAMA'S ROOM.
I WANT TO MAKE SURE SHE'S LEFT ALONE THIS AFTERNOON WHILE SHE TAKES A BREAK.
SU... SURE.
THAT'S RIGHT. EVEN WITH YASUKUNI-SAN HERE, I STILL HAVE TO STAY ALERT.
HEY, AREN'T YOU GOING TO COME IN?
I'M FINE HERE.
DON'T YOU WANT TO BE ALONE?
I'LL MAKE SURE YOUR SUITOR DOESN'T BOTHER YOU.

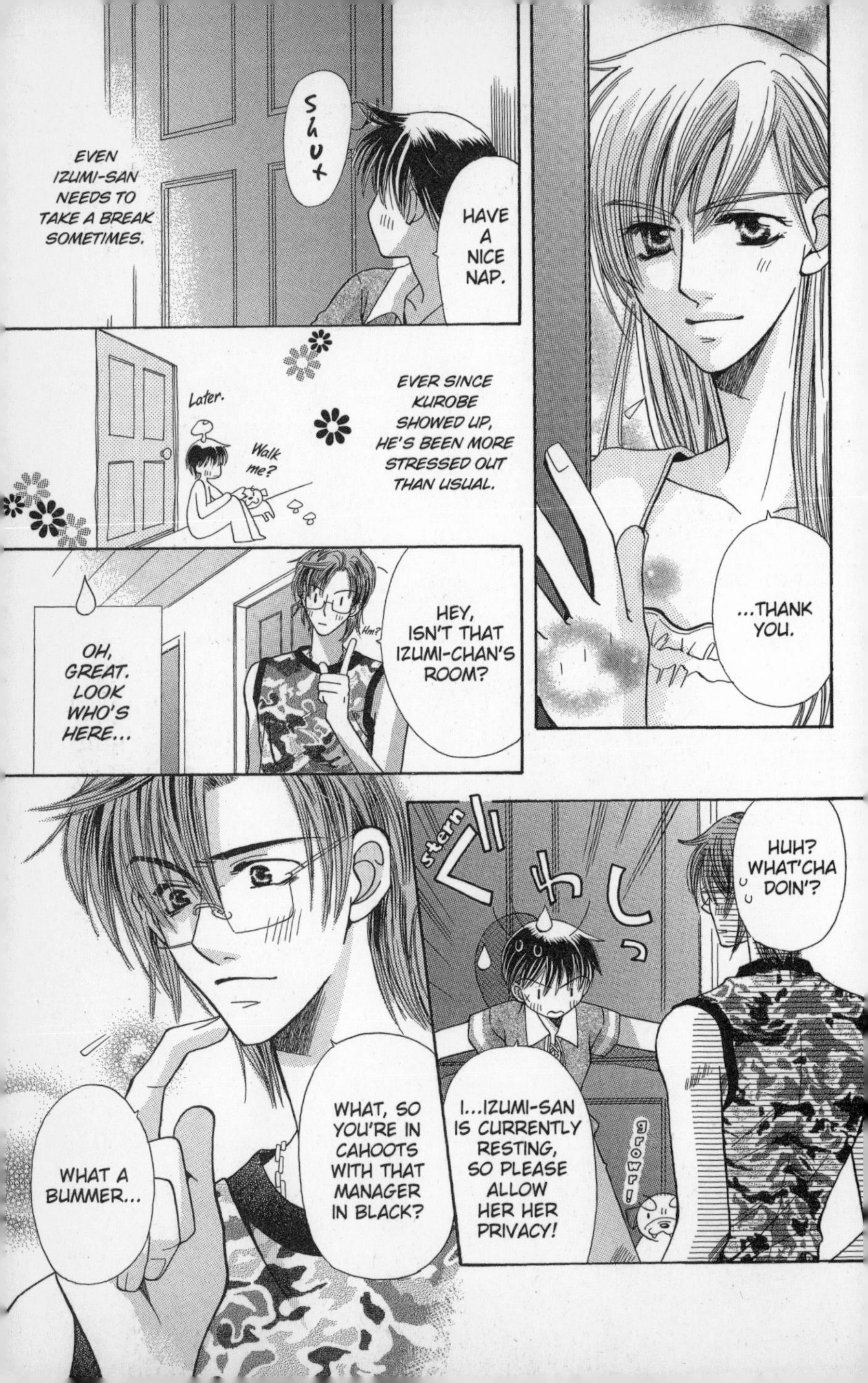
...THANK YOU.
HAVE A NICE NAP.
Shut
EVEN IZUMI-SAN NEEDS TO TAKE A BREAK SOMETIMES.
EVER SINCE KUROBE SHOWED UP, HE'S BEEN MORE STRESSED OUT THAN USUAL.
Walk me?
Later.
HEY, ISN'T THAT IZUMI-CHAN'S ROOM?
Hm?
OH, GREAT. LOOK WHO'S HERE...
HUH? WHAT'CHA DOIN'?
stern
I...IZUMI-SAN IS CURRENTLY RESTING, SO PLEASE ALLOW HER HER PRIVACY!
growl!
WHAT, SO YOU'RE IN CAHOOTS WITH THAT MANAGER IN BLACK?
WHAT A BUMMER...

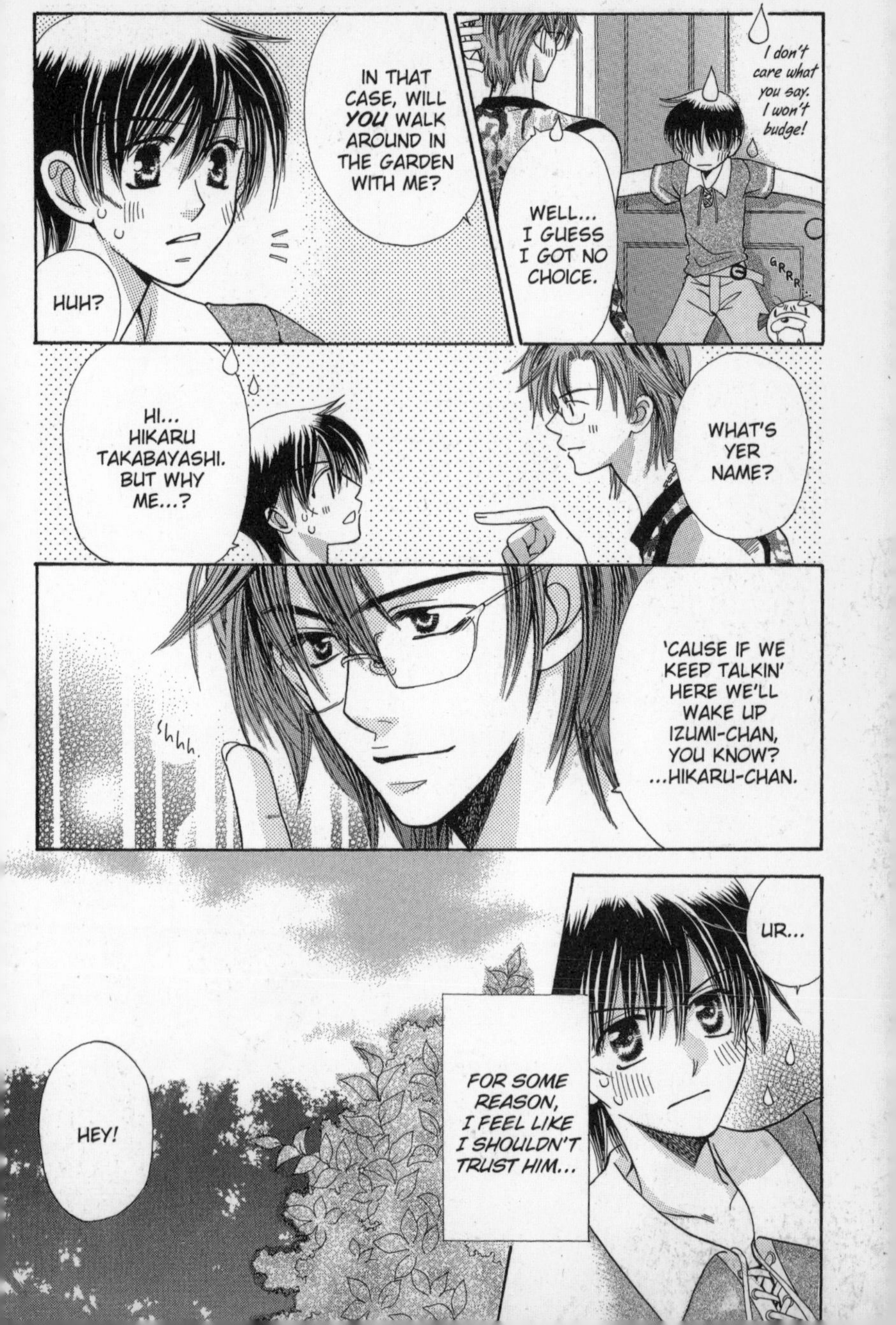
I don't care what you say. I won't budge!
WELL... I GUESS I GOT NO CHOICE.
IN THAT CASE, WILL YOU WALK AROUND IN THE GARDEN WITH ME?
HUH?
WHAT'S YER NAME?
HI... HIKARU TAKABAYASHI. BUT WHY ME...?
'CAUSE IF WE KEEP TALKIN' HERE WE'LL WAKE UP IZUMI-CHAN, YOU KNOW? ...HIKARU-CHAN.
shhh.
UR...
FOR SOME REASON, I FEEL LIKE I SHOULDN'T TRUST HIM...
HEY!

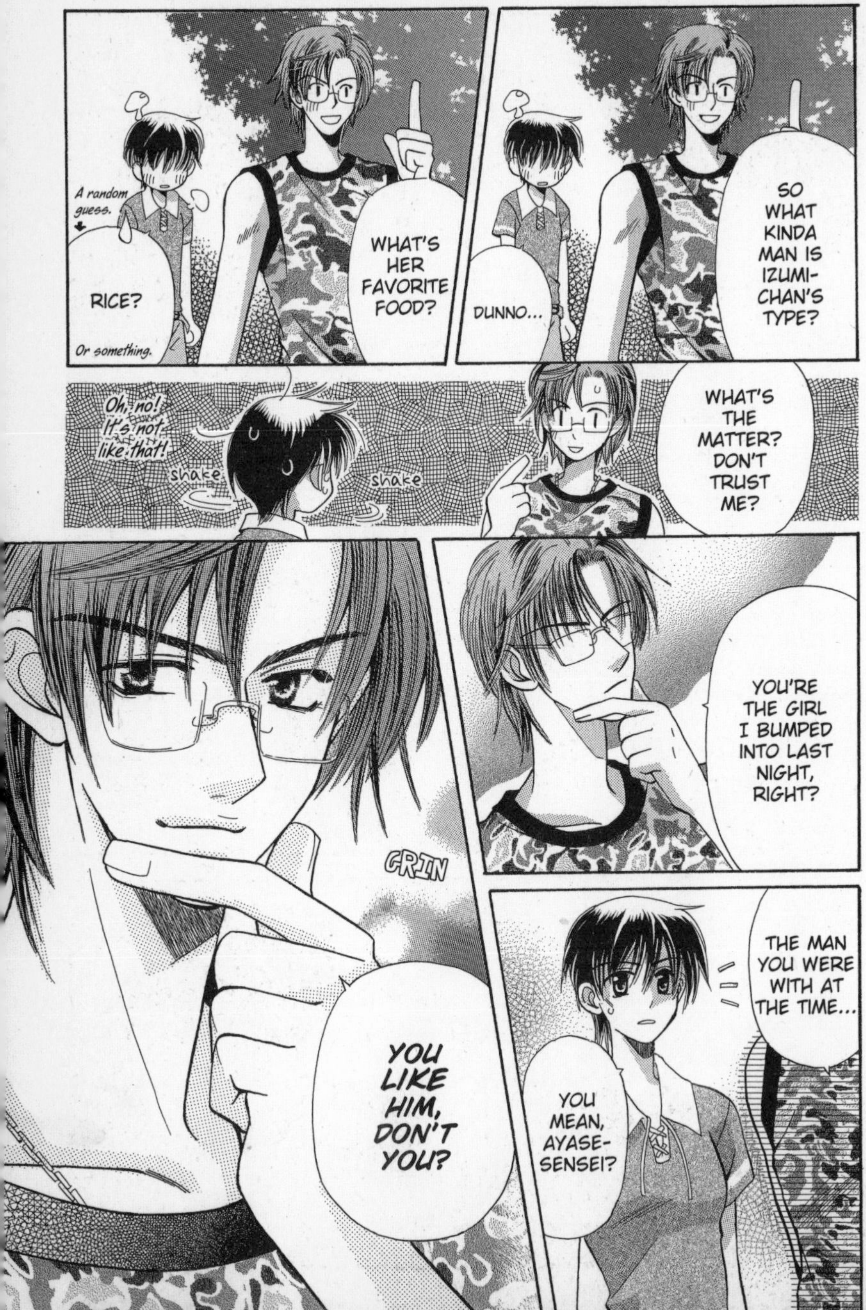
SO WHAT KINDA MAN IS IZUMI-CHAN'S TYPE?
DUNNO...
WHAT'S HER FAVORITE FOOD?
A random guess.
RICE?
Or something.
WHAT'S THE MATTER? DON'T TRUST ME?
Oh, no! It's not like that!
shake
shake
YOU'RE THE GIRL I BUMPED INTO LAST NIGHT, RIGHT?
THE MAN YOU WERE WITH AT THE TIME...
YOU MEAN, AYASE-SENSEI?
GRIN
YOU LIKE HIM, DON'T YOU?

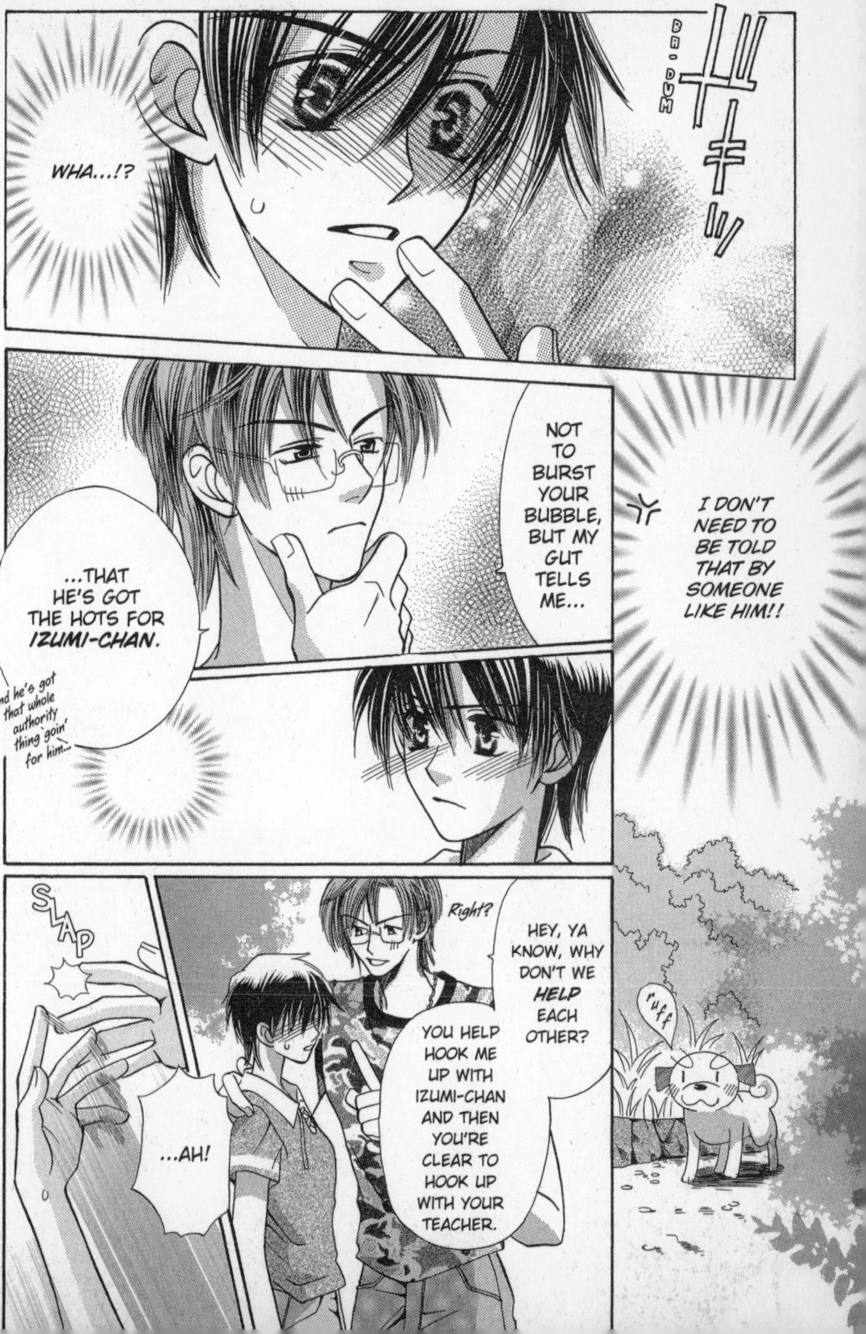
BA-DUM
WHA...!?
NOT TO BURST YOUR BUBBLE, BUT MY GUT TELLS ME...
...THAT HE'S GOT THE HOTS FOR ***IZUMI-CHAN***.
And he's got that whole authority thing 'goin' for him...
I DON'T NEED TO BE TOLD THAT BY SOMEONE LIKE HIM!!
ruff
HEY, YA KNOW, WHY DON'T WE ***HELP*** EACH OTHER?
Right?
YOU HELP HOOK ME UP WITH IZUMI-CHAN AND THEN YOU'RE CLEAR TO HOOK UP WITH YOUR TEACHER.
...AH!
SLAP

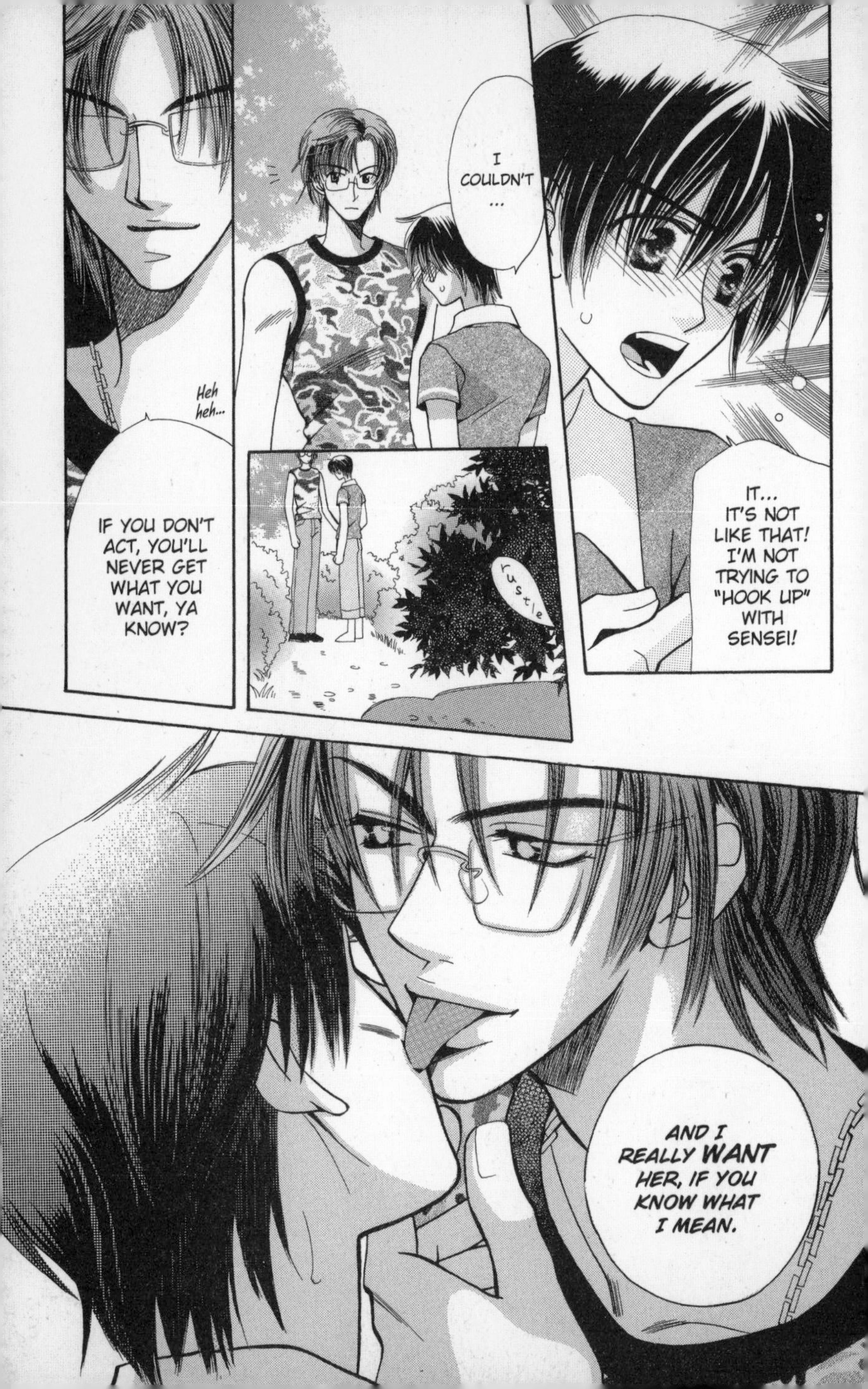
IT... IT'S NOT LIKE THAT! I'M NOT TRYING TO "HOOK UP" WITH SENSEI!
I COULDN'T ...
rustle
Heh heh...
IF YOU DON'T ACT, YOU'LL NEVER GET WHAT YOU WANT, YA KNOW?
AND I REALLY **WANT** HER, IF YOU KNOW WHAT I MEAN.

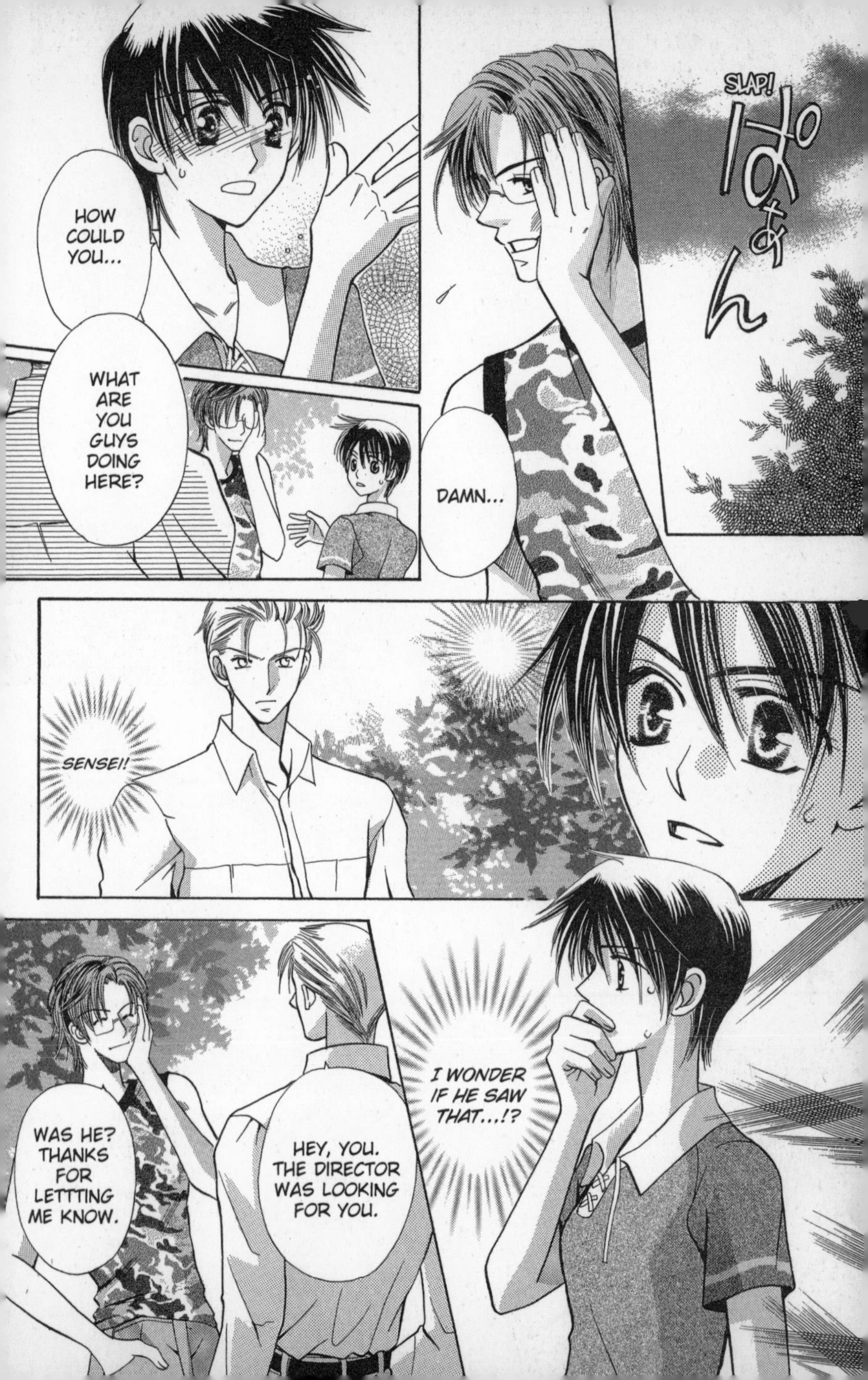
SLAP!
ぱぁん
DAMN...
HOW COULD YOU...
WHAT ARE YOU GUYS DOING HERE?
SENSEI!
I WONDER IF HE SAW THAT...!?
HEY, YOU. THE DIRECTOR WAS LOOKING FOR YOU.
WAS HE? THANKS FOR LETTTING ME KNOW.

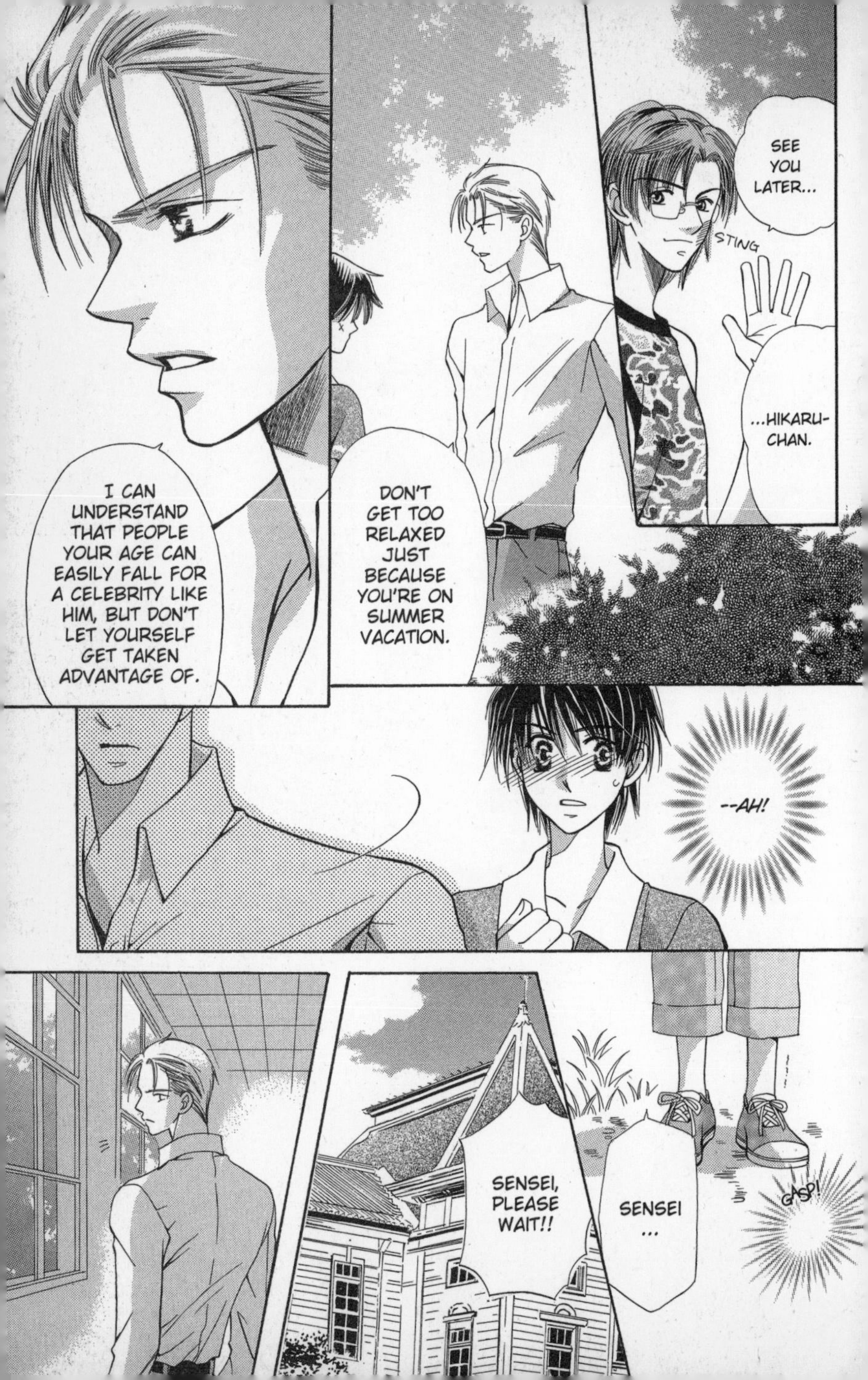
SEE YOU LATER...
STING
...HIKARU-CHAN.
DON'T GET TOO RELAXED JUST BECAUSE YOU'RE ON SUMMER VACATION.
I CAN UNDERSTAND THAT PEOPLE YOUR AGE CAN EASILY FALL FOR A CELEBRITY LIKE HIM, BUT DON'T LET YOURSELF GET TAKEN ADVANTAGE OF.
--AH!
GASP!
SENSEI ...
SENSEI, PLEASE WAIT!!

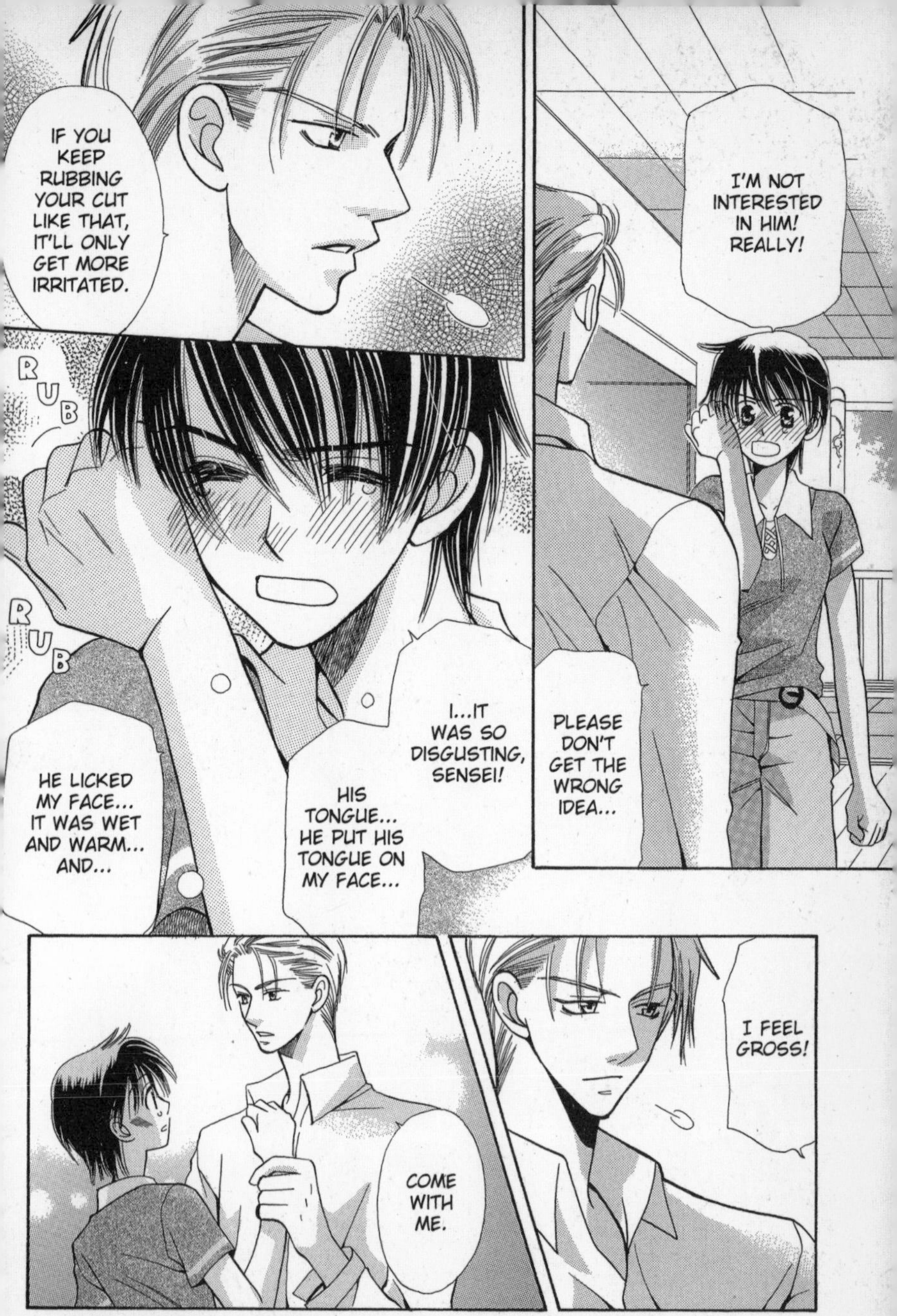
I'M NOT INTERESTED IN HIM! REALLY!
PLEASE DON'T GET THE WRONG IDEA...
IF YOU KEEP RUBBING YOUR CUT LIKE THAT, IT'LL ONLY GET MORE IRRITATED.
RUB
RUB
I...IT WAS SO DISGUSTING, SENSEI!
HIS TONGUE... HE PUT HIS TONGUE ON MY FACE...
HE LICKED MY FACE... IT WAS WET AND WARM... AND...
I FEEL GROSS!
COME WITH ME.

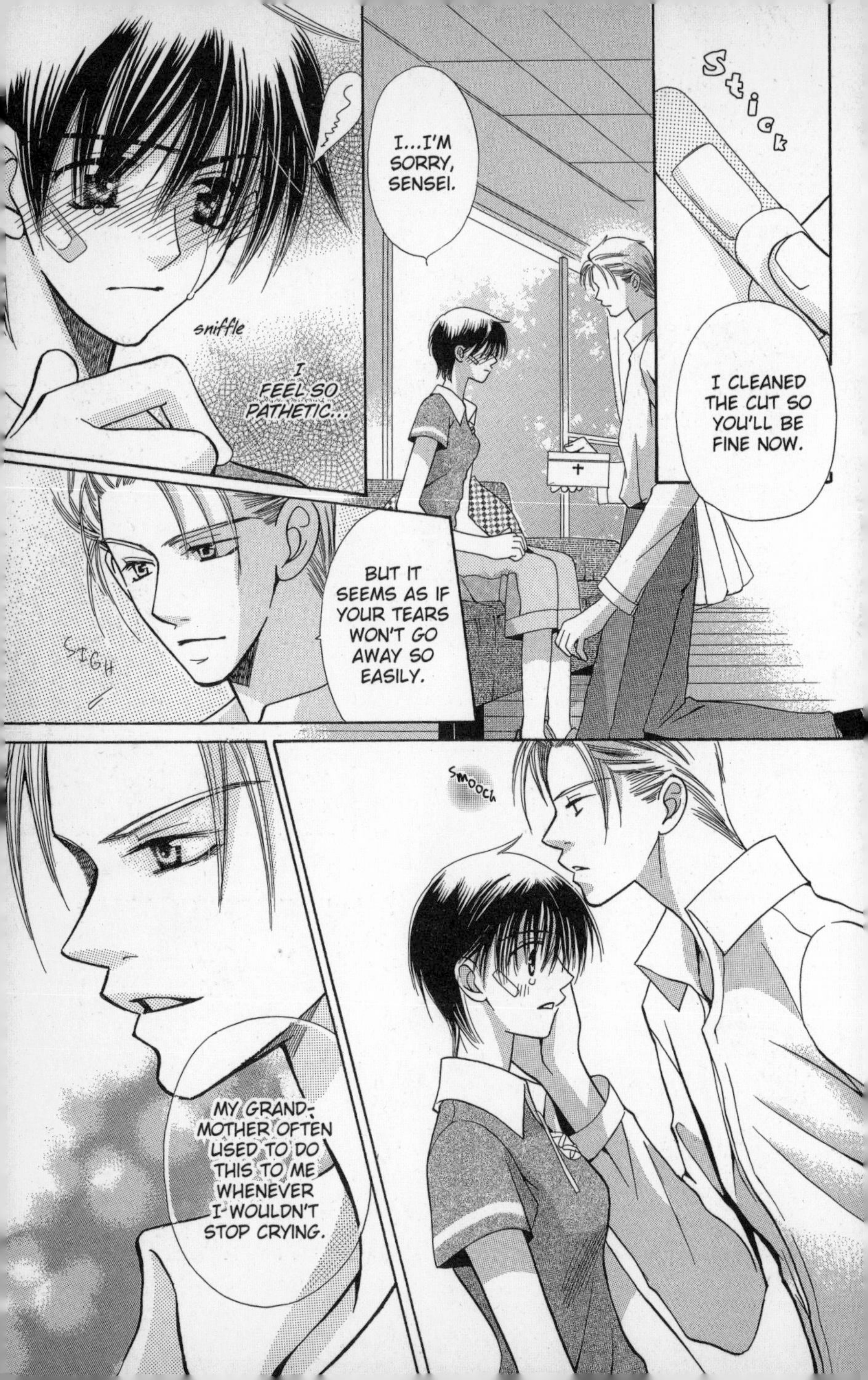
Stick
I CLEANED THE CUT SO YOU'LL BE FINE NOW.
I...I'M SORRY, SENSEI.
sniffle
I FEEL SO PATHETIC...
BUT IT SEEMS AS IF YOUR TEARS WON'T GO AWAY SO EASILY.
SIGH
Smooch
MY GRAND-MOTHER OFTEN USED TO DO THIS TO ME WHENEVER I WOULDN'T STOP CRYING.

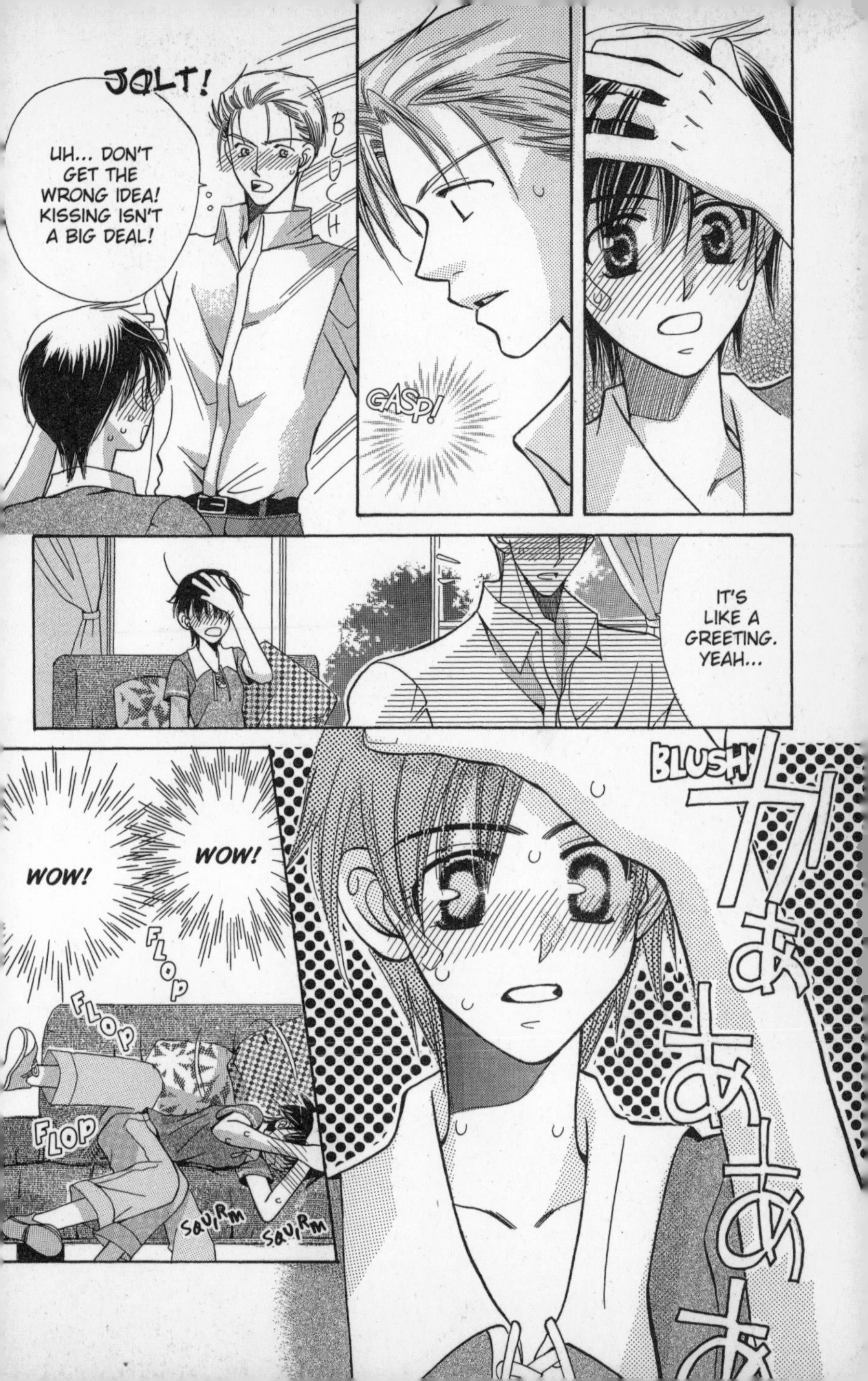
GASP!
JOLT!
BLUSH
UH... DON'T GET THE WRONG IDEA! KISSING ISN'T A BIG DEAL!
IT'S LIKE A GREETING. YEAH...
BLUSH
WOW!
WOW!
FLOP
FLOP
FLOP
SQUIRM
SQUIRM

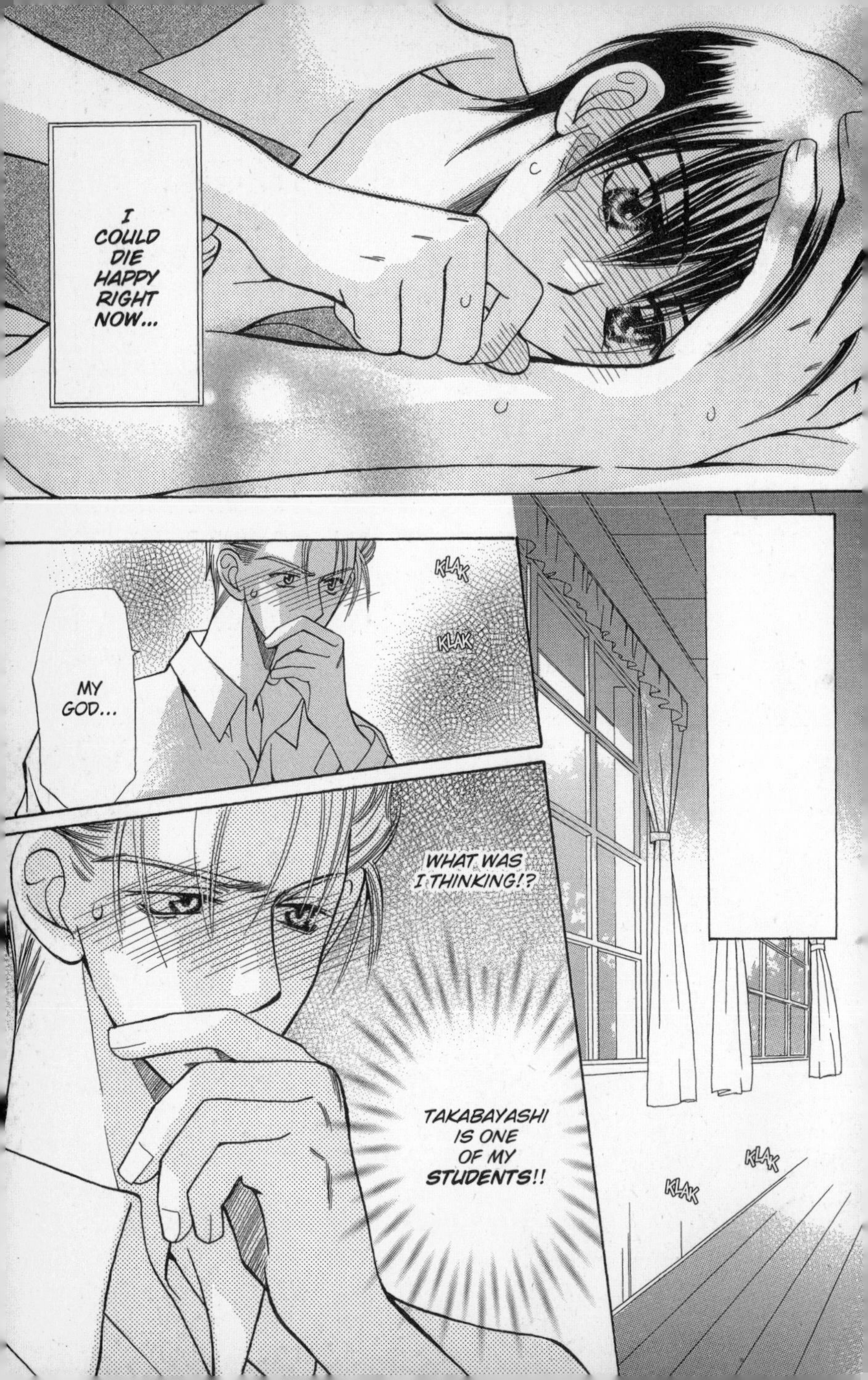
I COULD DIE HAPPY RIGHT NOW...
KLAK
KLAK
MY GOD...
WHAT WAS I THINKING!?
TAKABAYASHI IS ONE OF MY STUDENTS!!
KLAK
KLAK

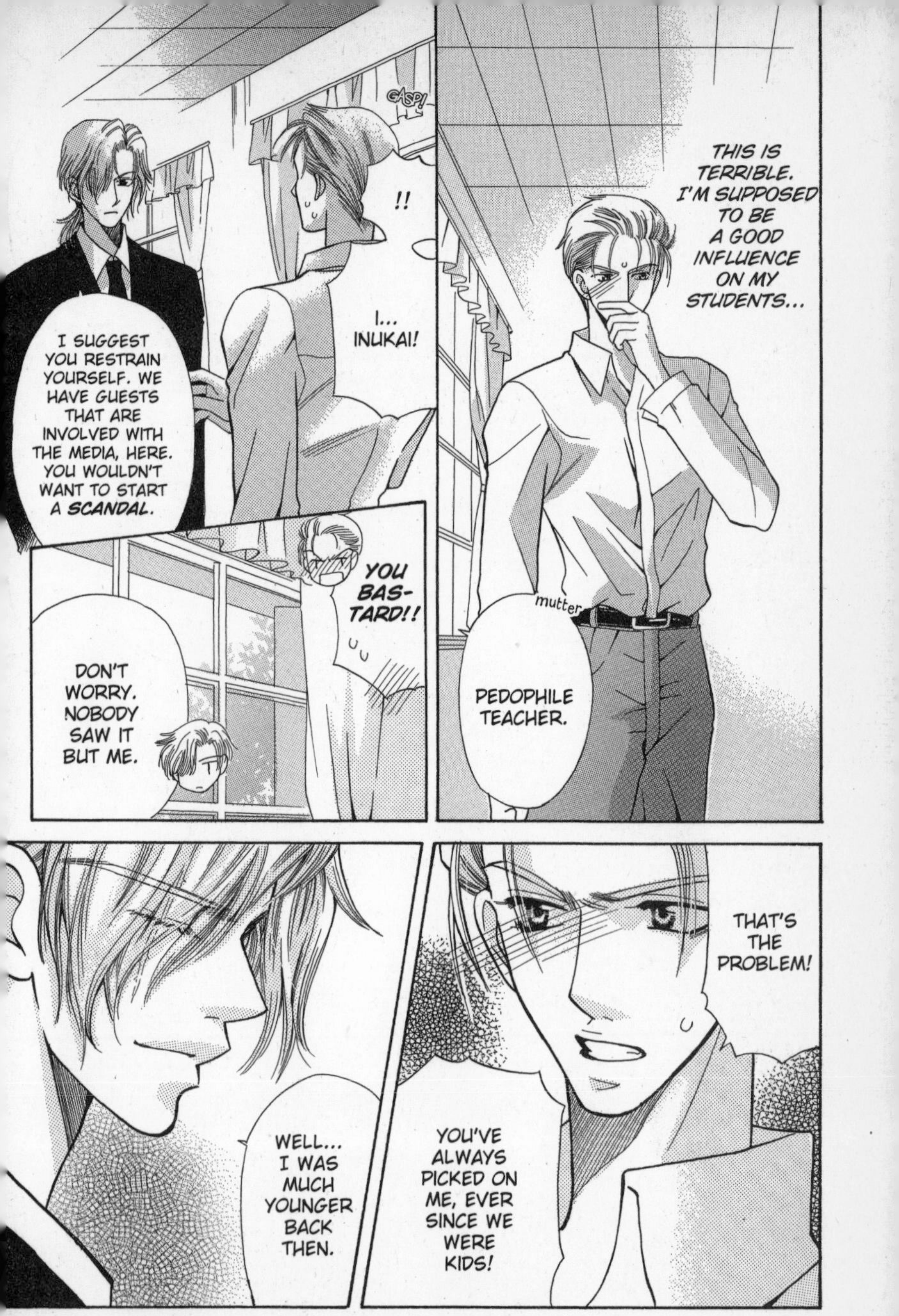
THIS IS TERRIBLE. I'M SUPPOSED TO BE A GOOD INFLUENCE ON MY STUDENTS...
mutter
PEDOPHILE TEACHER.
GASP!
!!
I... INUKAI!
I SUGGEST YOU RESTRAIN YOURSELF. WE HAVE GUESTS THAT ARE INVOLVED WITH THE MEDIA, HERE. YOU WOULDN'T WANT TO START A SCANDAL.
YOU BASTARD!!
DON'T WORRY. NOBODY SAW IT BUT ME.
THAT'S THE PROBLEM!
YOU'VE ALWAYS PICKED ON ME, EVER SINCE WE WERE KIDS!
WELL... I WAS MUCH YOUNGER BACK THEN.

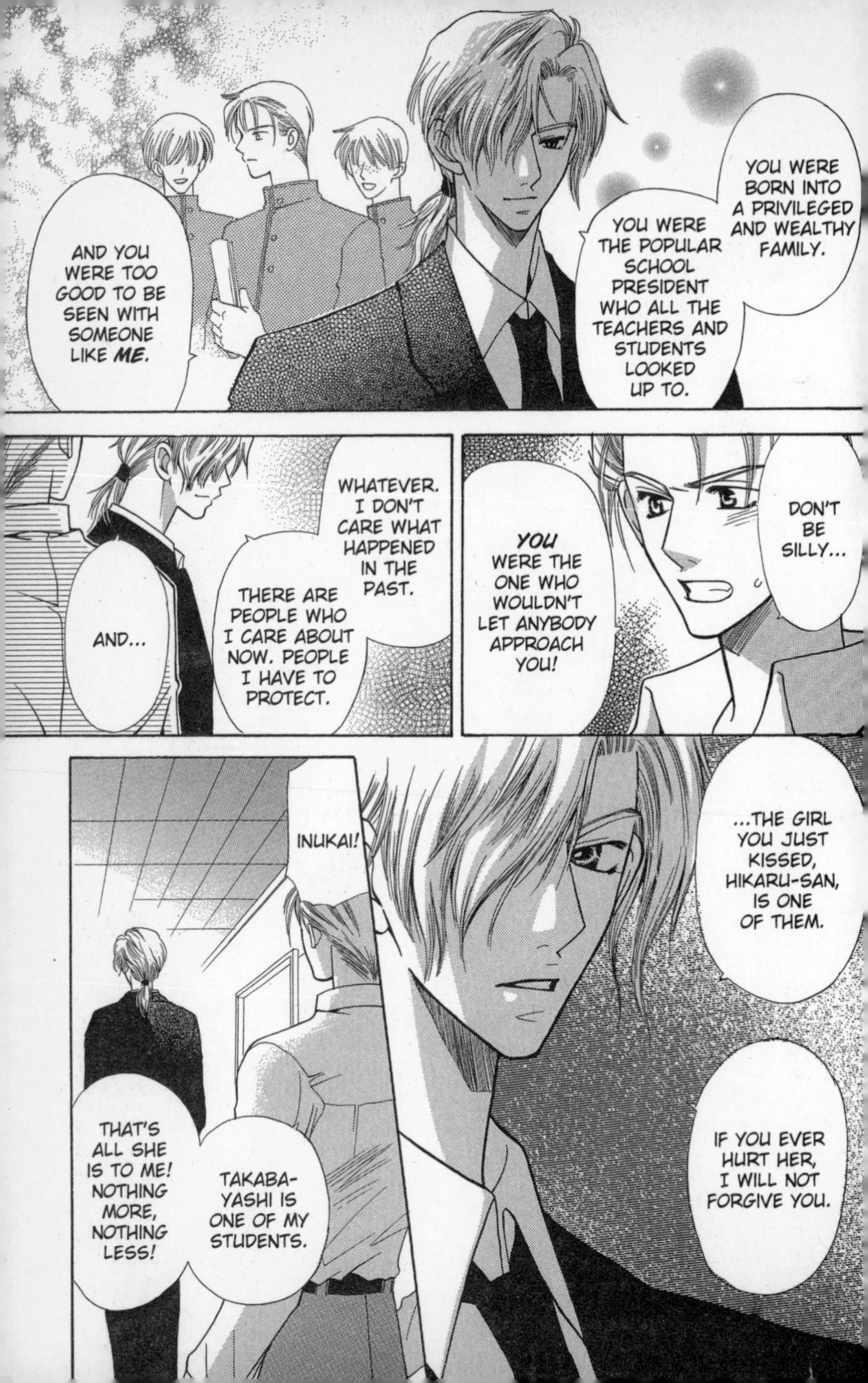
YOU WERE BORN INTO A PRIVILEGED AND WEALTHY FAMILY.
YOU WERE THE POPULAR SCHOOL PRESIDENT WHO ALL THE TEACHERS AND STUDENTS LOOKED UP TO.
AND YOU WERE TOO GOOD TO BE SEEN WITH SOMEONE LIKE *ME.*
DON'T BE SILLY...
YOU WERE THE ONE WHO WOULDN'T LET ANYBODY APPROACH YOU!
WHATEVER. I DON'T CARE WHAT HAPPENED IN THE PAST.
THERE ARE PEOPLE WHO I CARE ABOUT NOW. PEOPLE I HAVE TO PROTECT.
AND...
...THE GIRL YOU JUST KISSED, HIKARU-SAN, IS ONE OF THEM.
IF YOU EVER HURT HER, I WILL NOT FORGIVE YOU.
INUKAI!
TAKABA-YASHI IS ONE OF MY STUDENTS.
THAT'S ALL SHE IS TO ME! NOTHING MORE, NOTHING LESS!

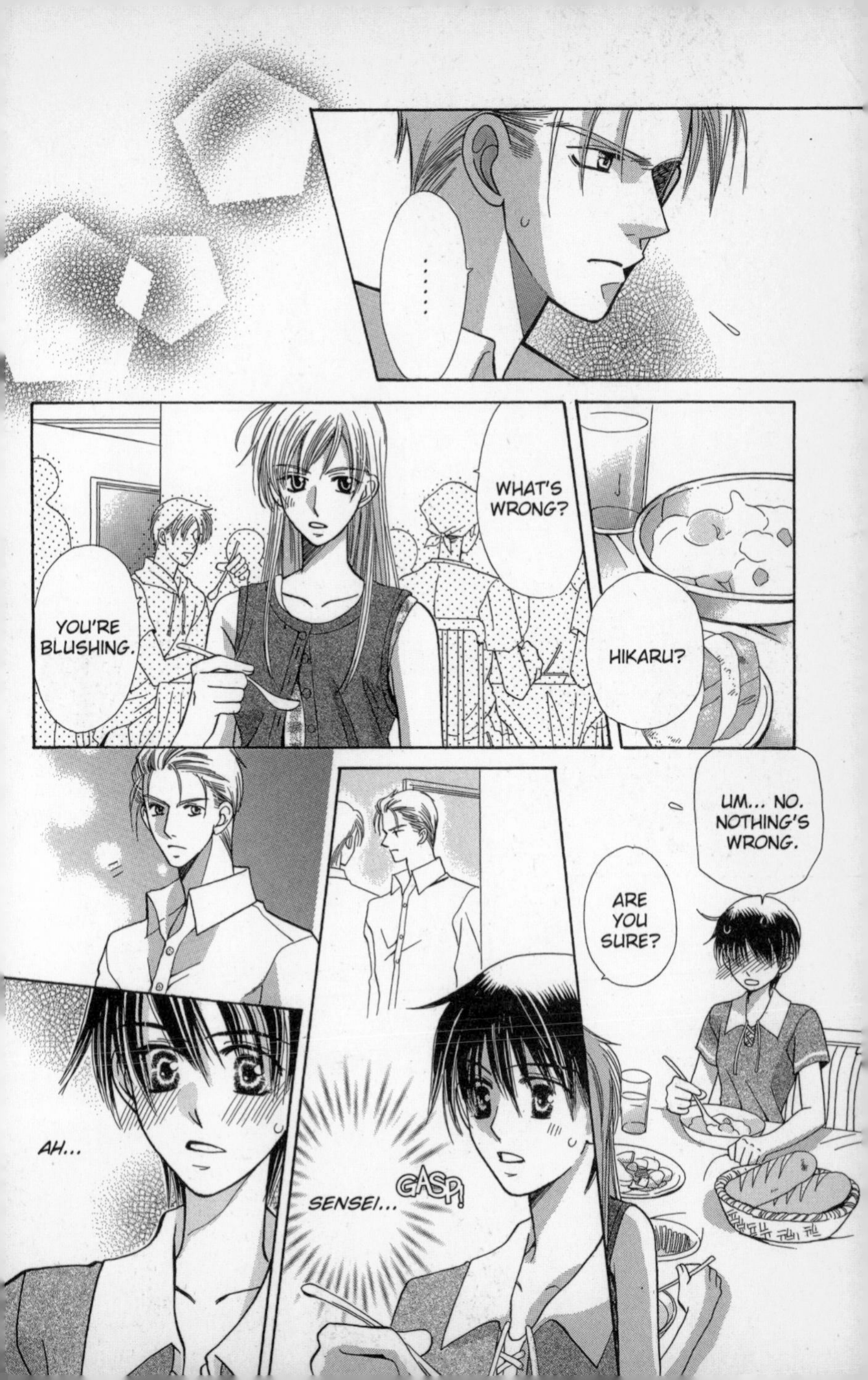
......
HIKARU?
WHAT'S WRONG?
YOU'RE BLUSHING.
UM... NO. NOTHING'S WRONG.
ARE YOU SURE?
GASP!
SENSEI...
AH...

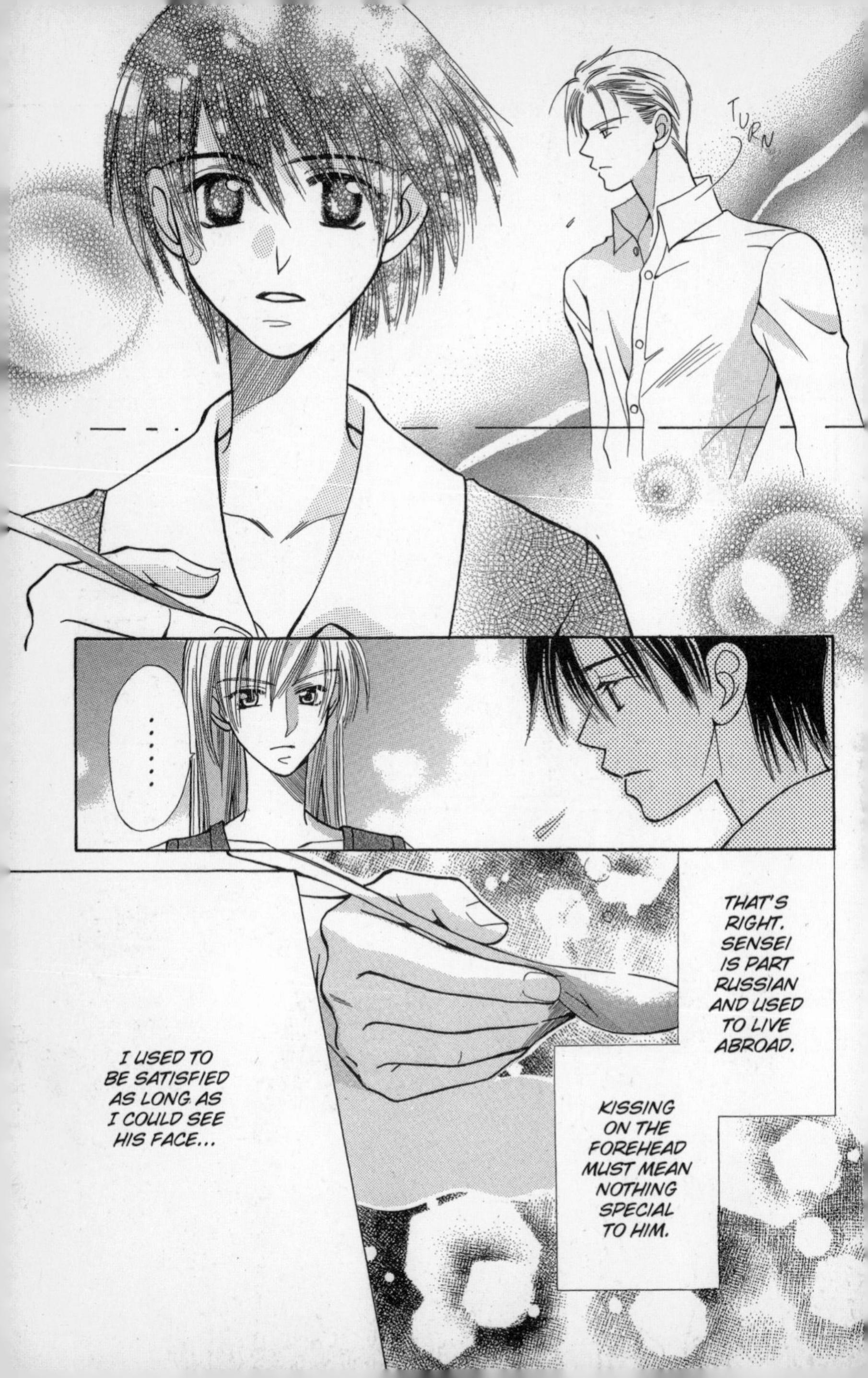
TURN
......
THAT'S RIGHT. SENSEI IS PART RUSSIAN AND USED TO LIVE ABROAD.
KISSING ON THE FOREHEAD MUST MEAN NOTHING SPECIAL TO HIM.
I USED TO BE SATISFIED AS LONG AS I COULD SEE HIS FACE...

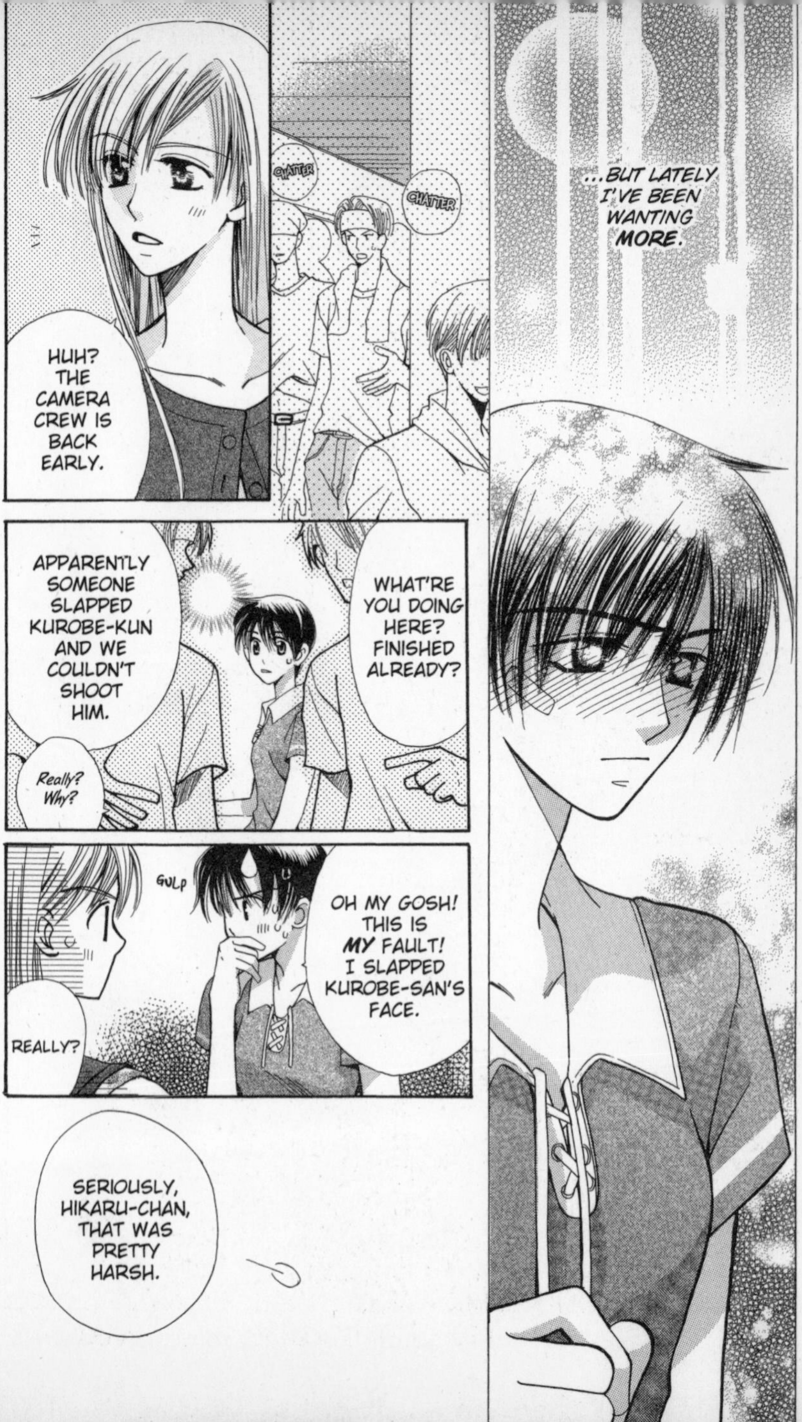
...BUT LATELY I'VE BEEN WANTING MORE.
CHATTER
CHATTER
HUH? THE CAMERA CREW IS BACK EARLY.
WHAT'RE YOU DOING HERE? FINISHED ALREADY?
APPARENTLY SOMEONE SLAPPED KUROBE-KUN AND WE COULDN'T SHOOT HIM.
Really? Why?
OH MY GOSH! THIS IS MY FAULT! I SLAPPED KUROBE-SAN'S FACE.
GULP
REALLY?
SERIOUSLY, HIKARU-CHAN, THAT WAS PRETTY HARSH.

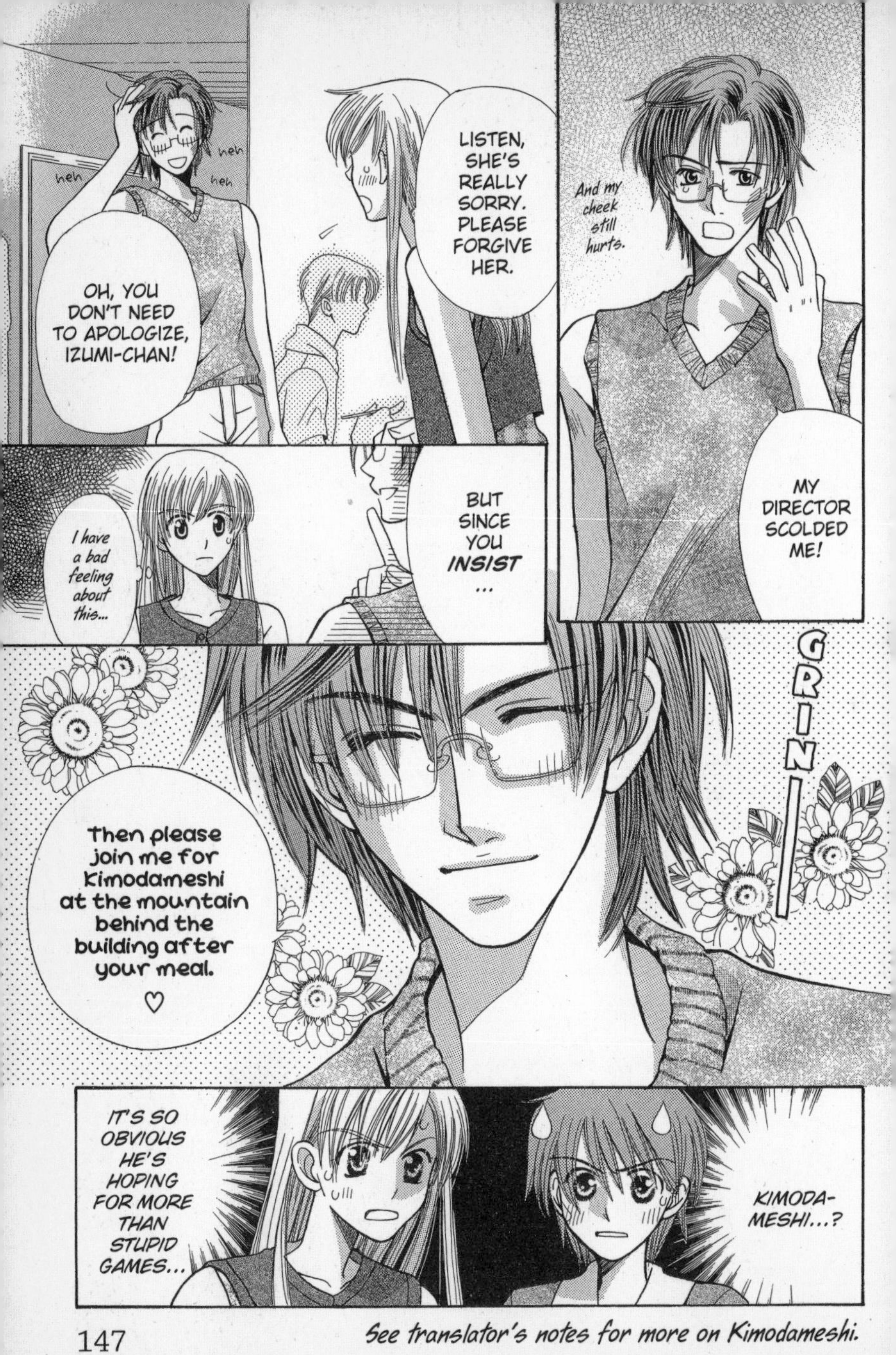
And my cheek still hurts.
MY DIRECTOR SCOLDED ME!
LISTEN, SHE'S REALLY SORRY. PLEASE FORGIVE HER.
heh heh heh
OH, YOU DON'T NEED TO APOLOGIZE, IZUMI-CHAN!
BUT SINCE YOU INSIST...
I have a bad feeling about this...
GRIN
Then please join me for Kimodameshi at the mountain behind the building after your meal. ♡
KIMODA-MESHI...?
IT'S SO OBVIOUS HE'S HOPING FOR MORE THAN STUPID GAMES...

See translator's notes for more on Kimodameshi.

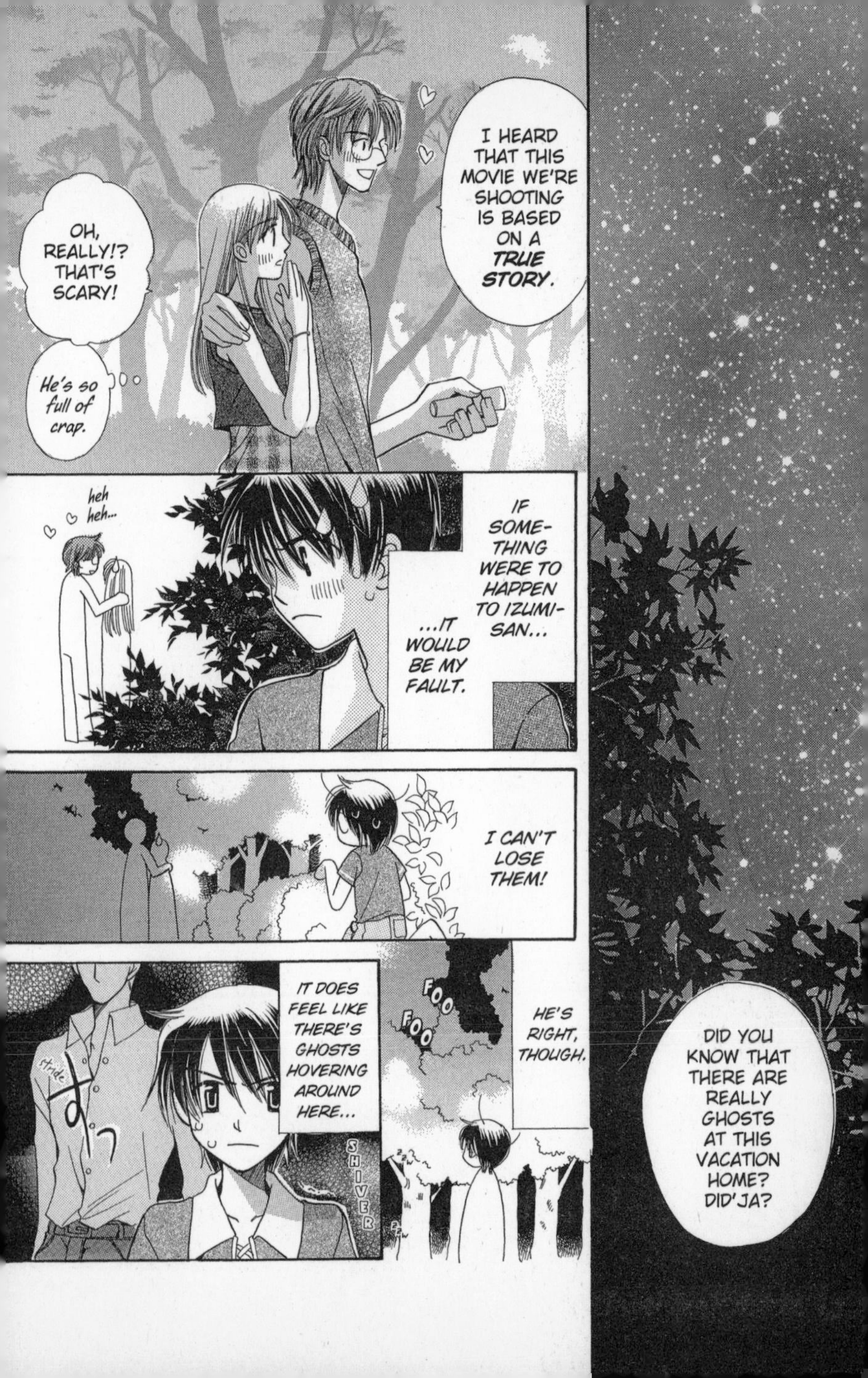
DID YOU KNOW THAT THERE ARE REALLY GHOSTS AT THIS VACATION HOME? DID'JA?
I HEARD THAT THIS MOVIE WE'RE SHOOTING IS BASED ON A TRUE STORY.
OH, REALLY!? THAT'S SCARY!
He's so full of crap.
IF SOMETHING WERE TO HAPPEN TO IZUMI-SAN...
...IT WOULD BE MY FAULT.
heh heh...
I CAN'T LOSE THEM!
HE'S RIGHT, THOUGH.
FOO
FOO
IT DOES FEEL LIKE THERE'S GHOSTS HOVERING AROUND HERE...
SHIVER
stride

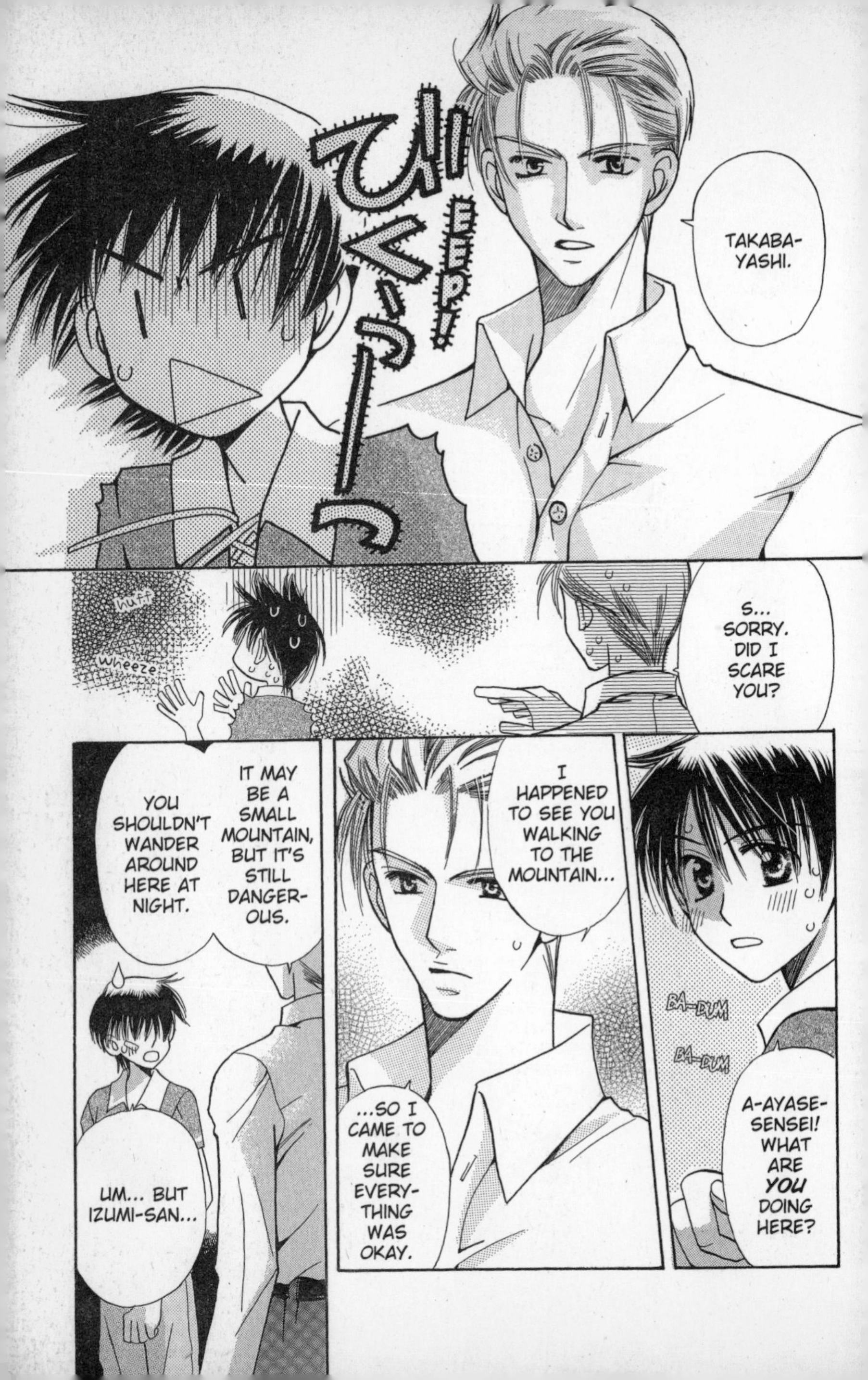
TAKABA-YASHI.
びくぅーっ
EEP!
S... SORRY. DID I SCARE YOU?
huff
wheeze
A-AYASE-SENSEI! WHAT ARE *YOU* DOING HERE?
BA-DUM
BA-DUM
I HAPPENED TO SEE YOU WALKING TO THE MOUNTAIN...
...SO I CAME TO MAKE SURE EVERY-THING WAS OKAY.
IT MAY BE A SMALL MOUNTAIN, BUT IT'S STILL DANGER-OUS.
YOU SHOULDN'T WANDER AROUND HERE AT NIGHT.
UM... BUT IZUMI-SAN...

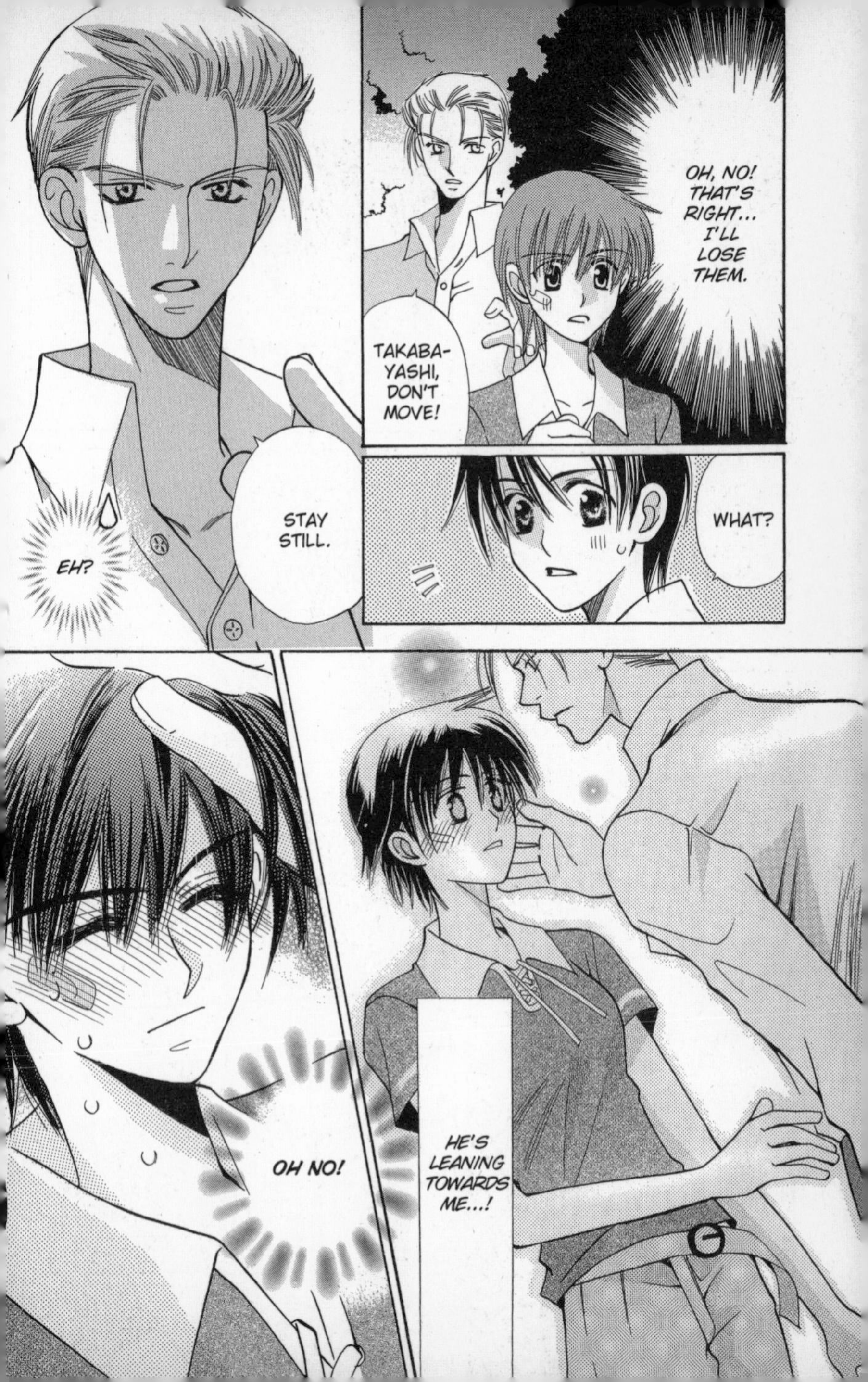
OH, NO! THAT'S RIGHT... I'LL LOSE THEM.
TAKABA-YASHI, DON'T MOVE!
WHAT?
STAY STILL.
EH?
HE'S LEANING TOWARDS ME...!
OH NO!

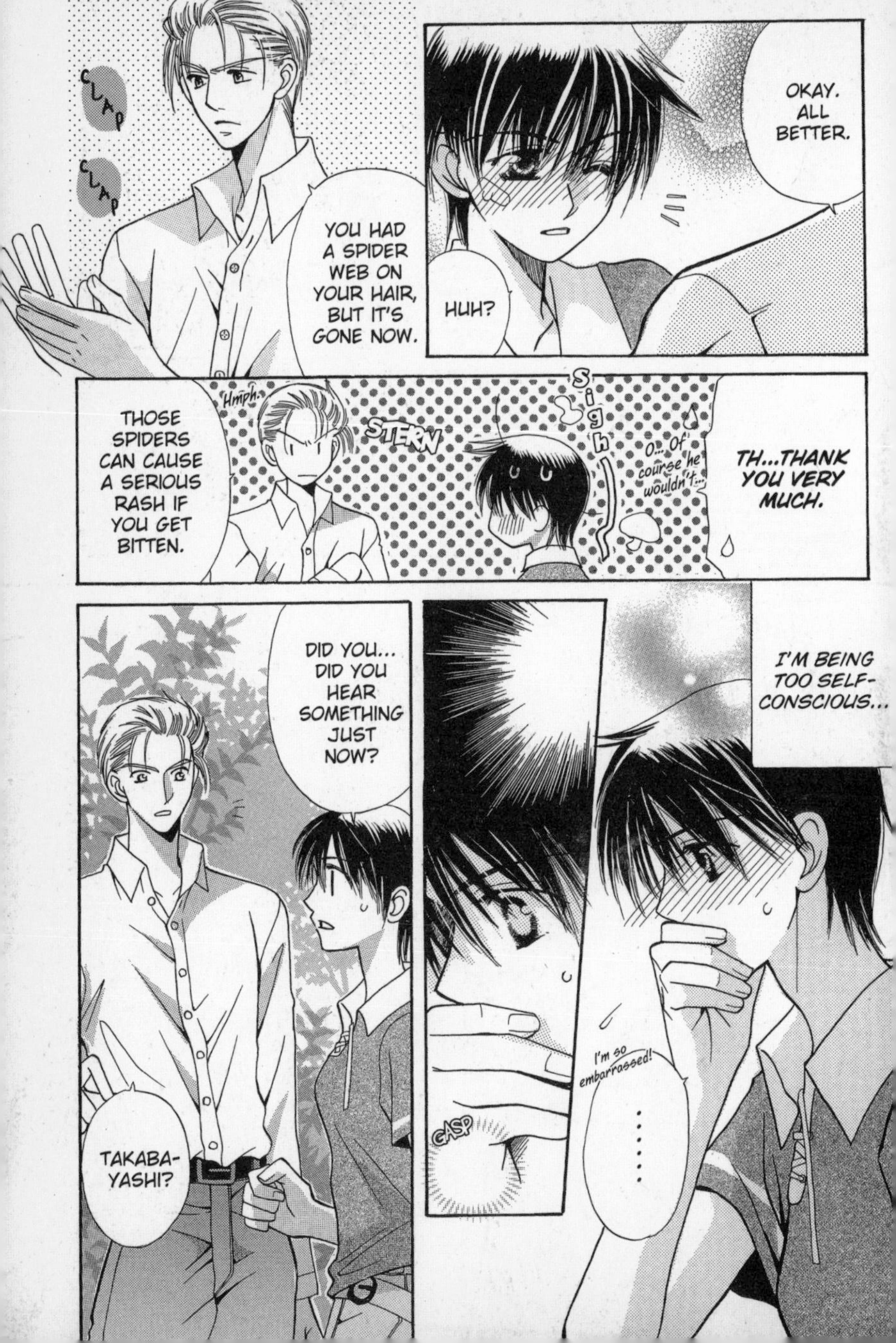
OKAY. ALL BETTER.
HUH?
CLAP
CLAP
YOU HAD A SPIDER WEB ON YOUR HAIR, BUT IT'S GONE NOW.
TH...THANK YOU VERY MUCH.
O... Of course he wouldn't...
Sigh
STERN
Hmph.
THOSE SPIDERS CAN CAUSE A SERIOUS RASH IF YOU GET BITTEN.
I'M BEING TOO SELF-CONSCIOUS...
I'm so embarrassed!
......
GASP
DID YOU... DID YOU HEAR SOMETHING JUST NOW?
TAKABA-YASHI?

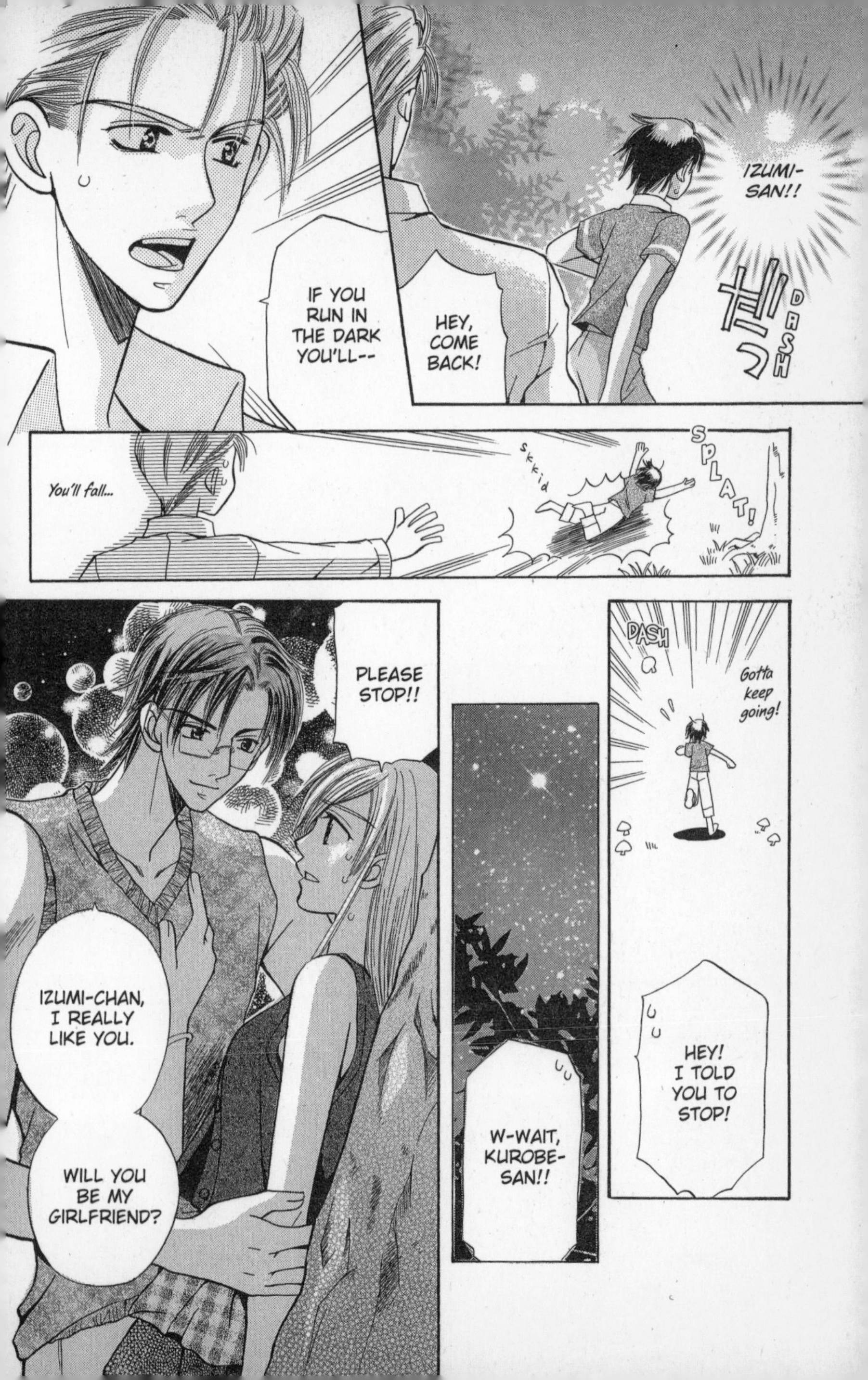
IZUMI-SAN!!
DASH
HEY, COME BACK!
IF YOU RUN IN THE DARK YOU'LL--
SPLAT!
skkid
You'll fall...
DASH
Gotta keep going!
HEY! I TOLD YOU TO STOP!
W-WAIT, KUROBE-SAN!!
PLEASE STOP!!
IZUMI-CHAN, I REALLY LIKE YOU.
WILL YOU BE MY GIRLFRIEND?

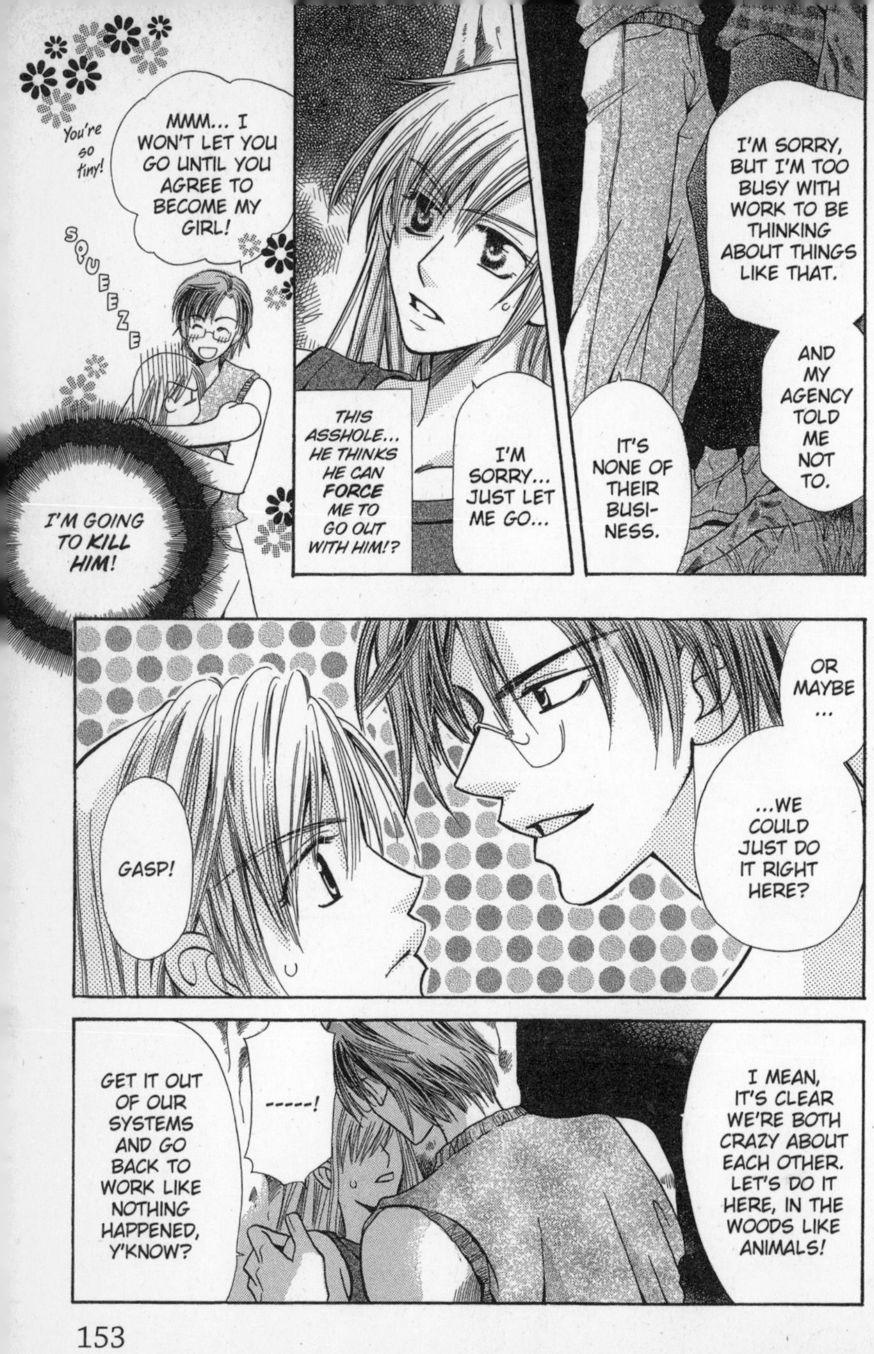
I'M SORRY, BUT I'M TOO BUSY WITH WORK TO BE THINKING ABOUT THINGS LIKE THAT.
AND MY AGENCY TOLD ME NOT TO.
IT'S NONE OF THEIR BUSI-NESS.
I'M SORRY... JUST LET ME GO...
THIS ASSHOLE... HE THINKS HE CAN FORCE ME TO GO OUT WITH HIM!?
MMM... I WON'T LET YOU GO UNTIL YOU AGREE TO BECOME MY GIRL!
You're so tiny!
SQUEEZE
I'M GOING TO KILL HIM!
OR MAYBE ...
...WE COULD JUST DO IT RIGHT HERE?
GASP!
I MEAN, IT'S CLEAR WE'RE BOTH CRAZY ABOUT EACH OTHER. LET'S DO IT HERE, IN THE WOODS LIKE ANIMALS!
-----!
GET IT OUT OF OUR SYSTEMS AND GO BACK TO WORK LIKE NOTHING HAPPENED, Y'KNOW?

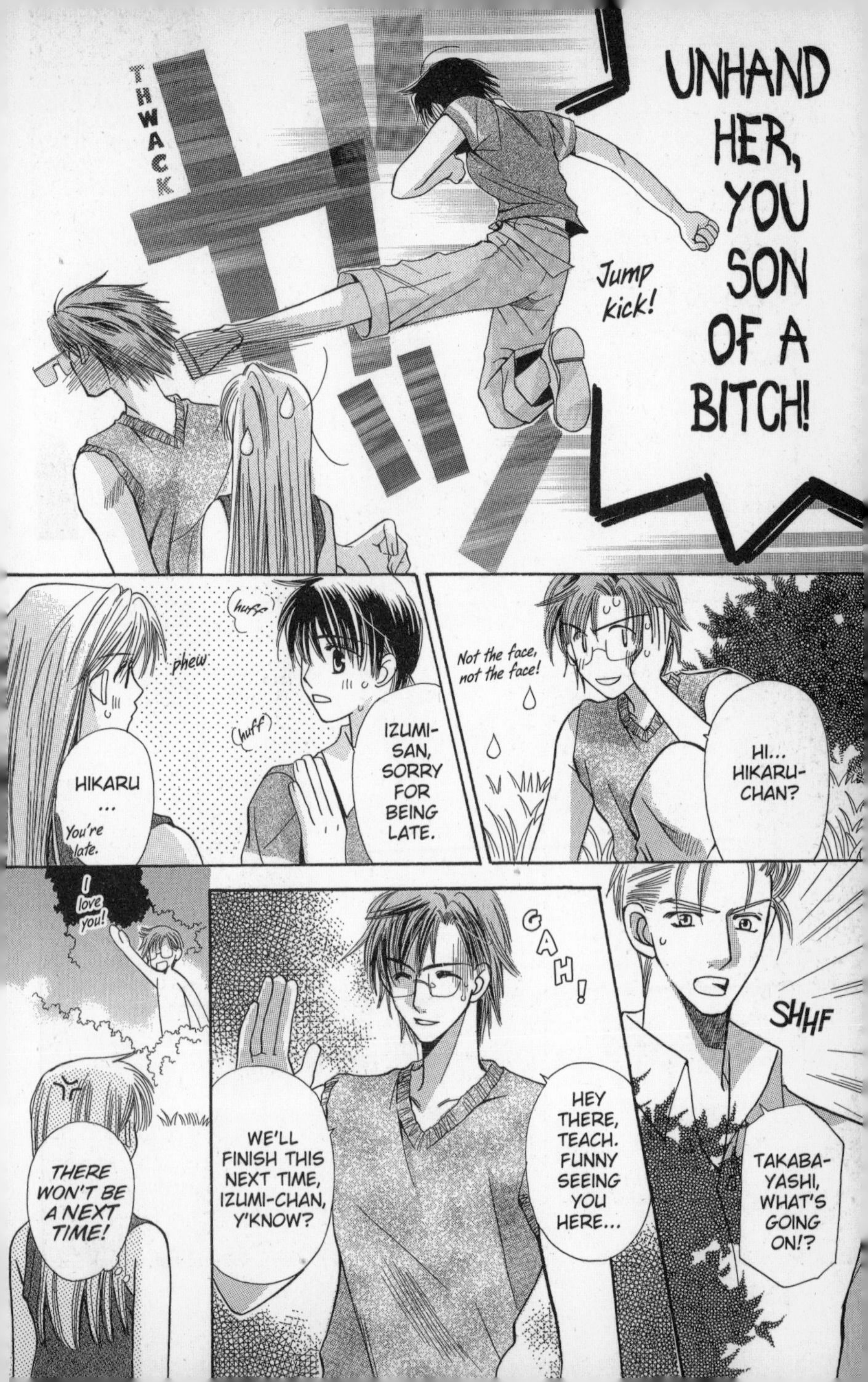
UNHAND HER, YOU SON OF A BITCH!
Jump kick!
THWACK
HI... HIKARU-CHAN?
Not the face, not the face!
IZUMI-SAN, SORRY FOR BEING LATE.
(huff)
phew
(huff)
HIKARU ...
You're late.
SHHF
TAKABA-YASHI, WHAT'S GOING ON!?
HEY THERE, TEACH. FUNNY SEEING YOU HERE...
GAH!
WE'LL FINISH THIS NEXT TIME, IZUMI-CHAN, Y'KNOW?
I love you!
THERE WON'T BE A NEXT TIME!

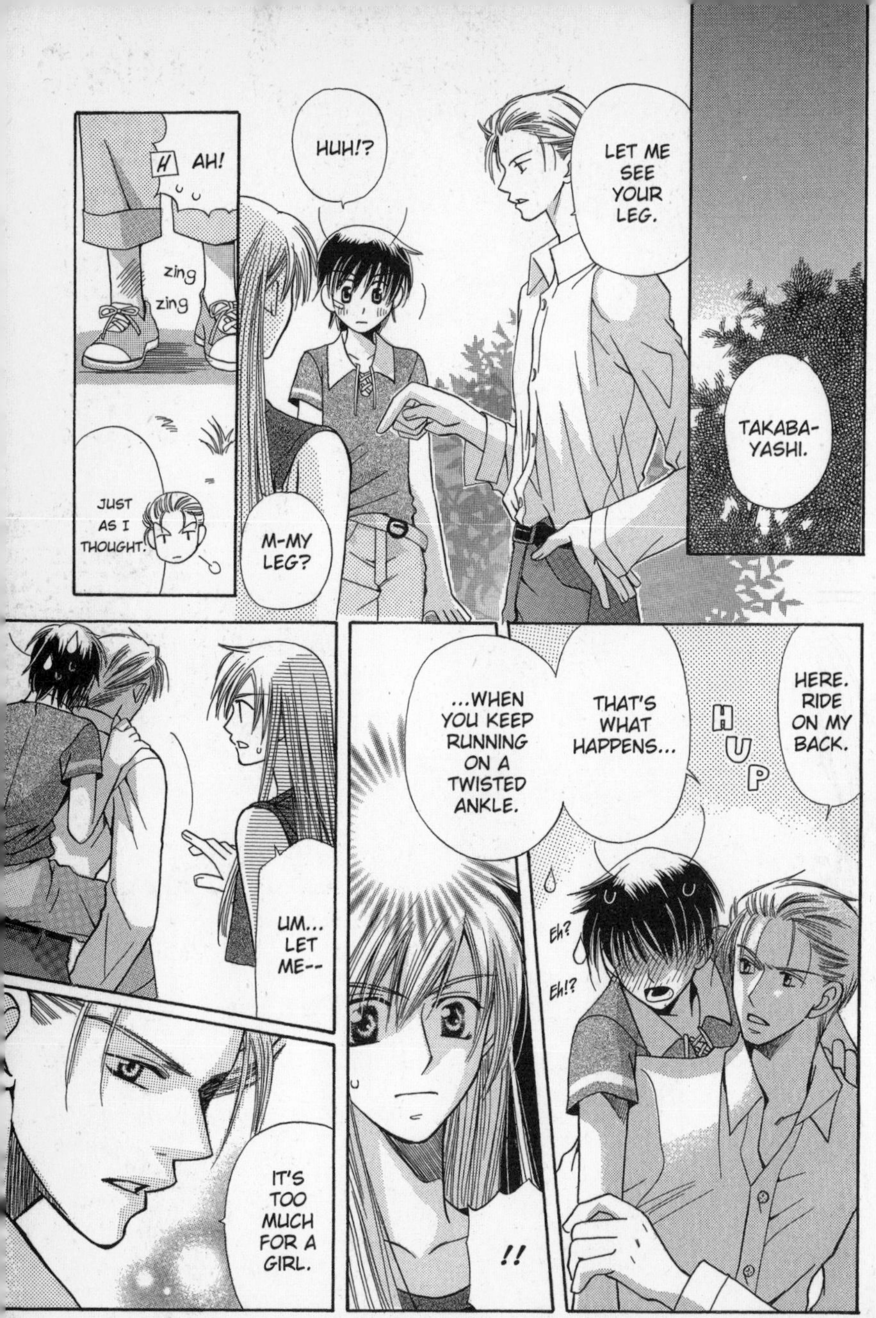
TAKABA-
YASHI.
LET ME SEE YOUR LEG.
HUH!?
M-MY LEG?
H AH!
zing
zing
JUST AS I THOUGHT.
HERE. RIDE ON MY BACK.
HUP
Eh?
Eh!?
THAT'S WHAT HAPPENS...
...WHEN YOU KEEP RUNNING ON A TWISTED ANKLE.
!!
UM... LET ME--
IT'S TOO MUCH FOR A GIRL.

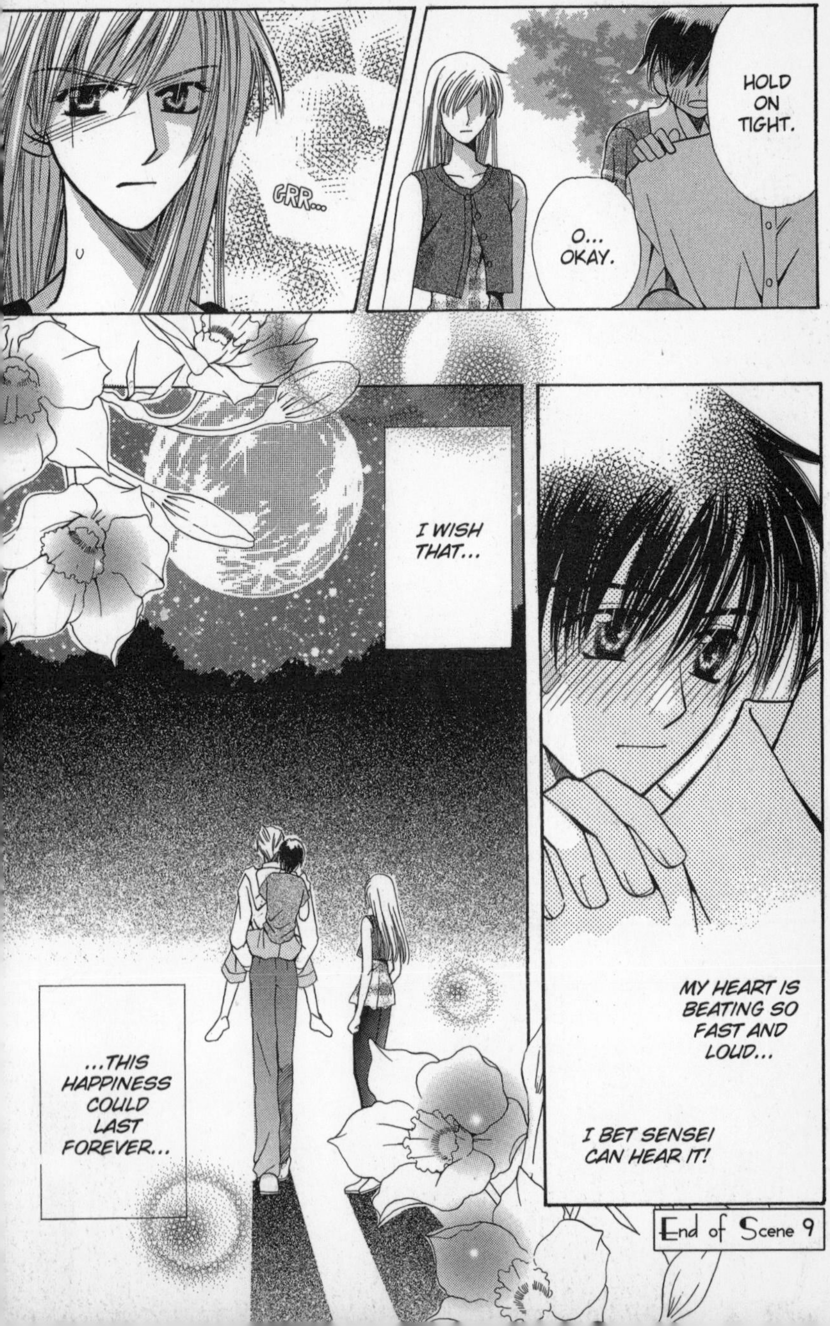
HOLD ON TIGHT.
O... OKAY.
GRR...
MY HEART IS BEATING SO FAST AND LOUD...
I BET SENSEI CAN HEAR IT!
I WISH THAT...
...THIS HAPPINESS COULD LAST FOREVER...

End of Scene 9

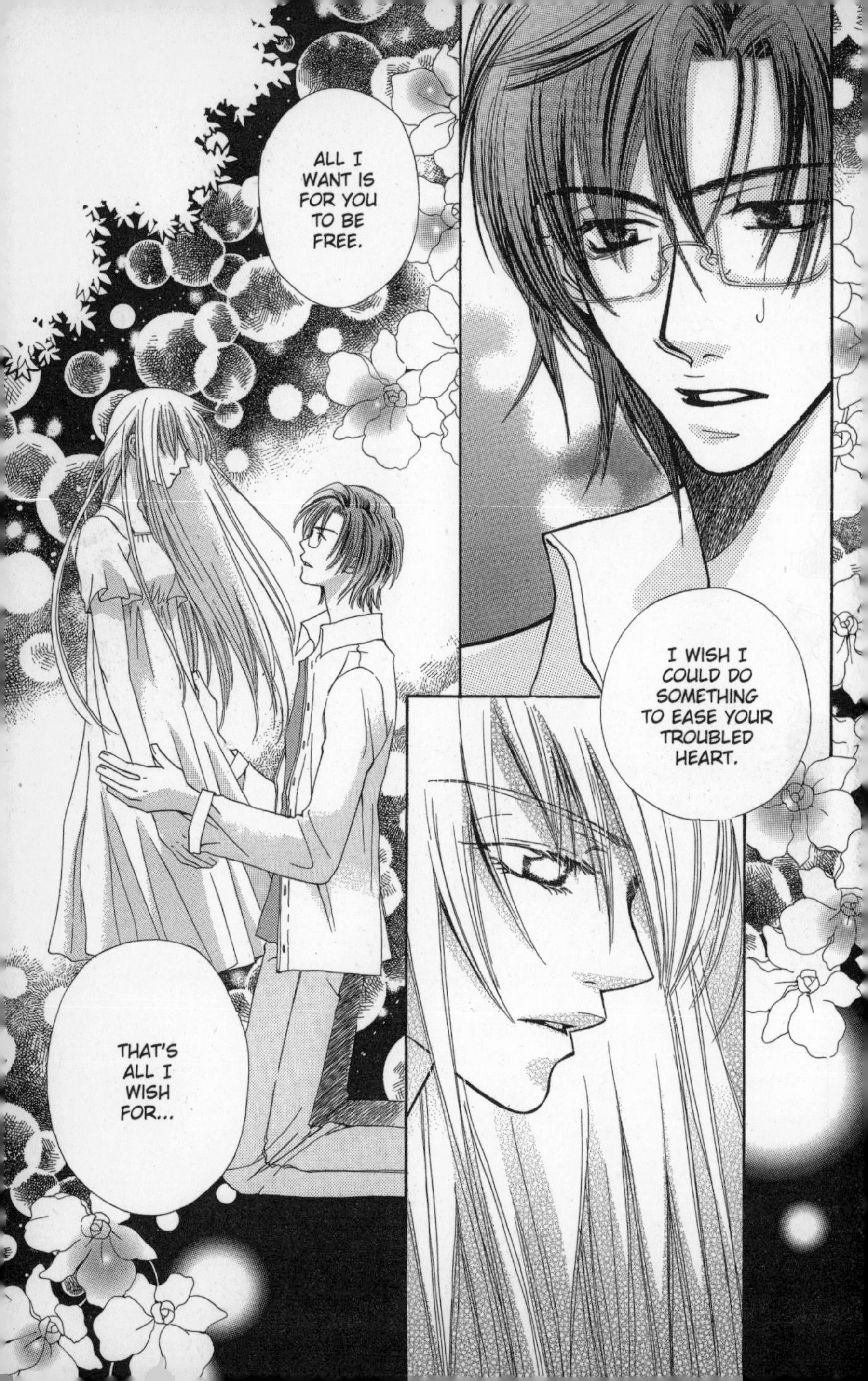
I WISH I COULD DO SOMETHING TO EASE YOUR TROUBLED HEART.
ALL I WANT IS FOR YOU TO BE FREE.
THAT'S ALL I WISH FOR...

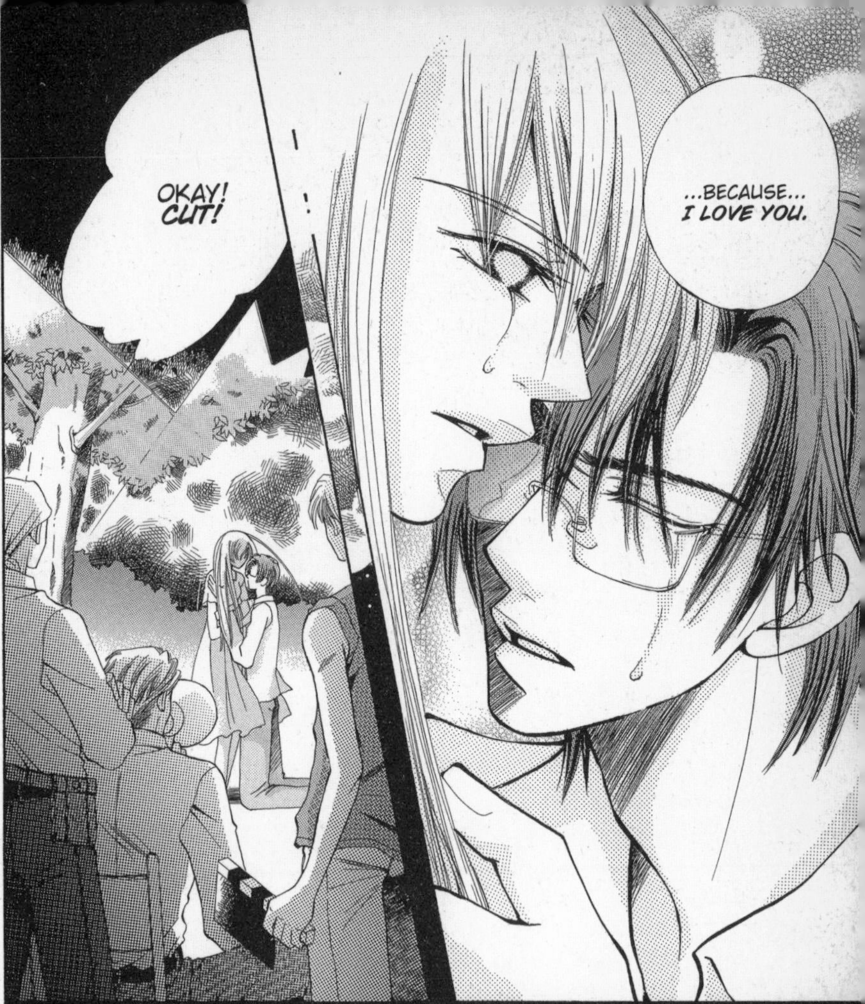
...BECAUSE...
I LOVE YOU.
OKAY!
CUT!

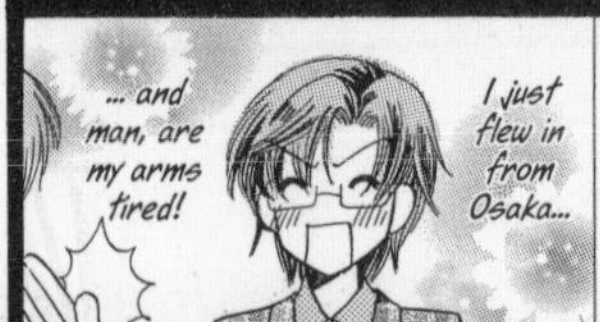
I just flew in from Osaka...
... and man, are my arms tired!

Hayato Kurobe (20 years old)
Kansai Comedian-type.

In his personal life he comes off as silly, but in his comedy duo, he's the straight man. He has a tendency to fall for many girls at once but lately he's been head-over-heels for Izumi, even though "she" doesn't return his advances. Secretly he takes pleasure in this rejection—he's a bit of a masochist.

(The author isn't sure whether or not Izumi and Hayato will ever get along...)

*More on Kansai Comedy in the Translator's Notes.

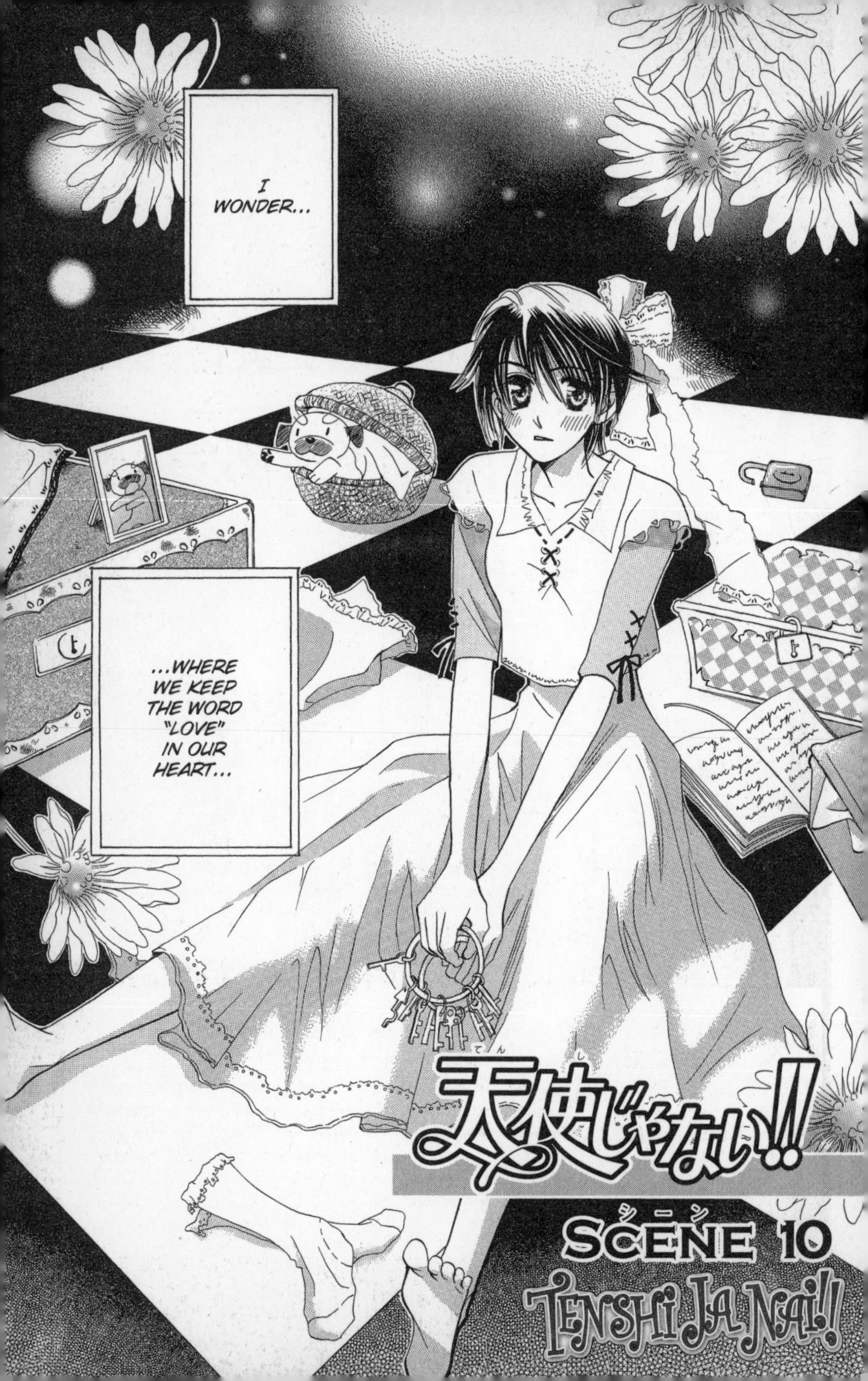
I WONDER...
...WHERE WE KEEP THE WORD "LOVE" IN OUR HEART...
天使じゃない!!
SCENE 10
TENSHI JA NAI!!

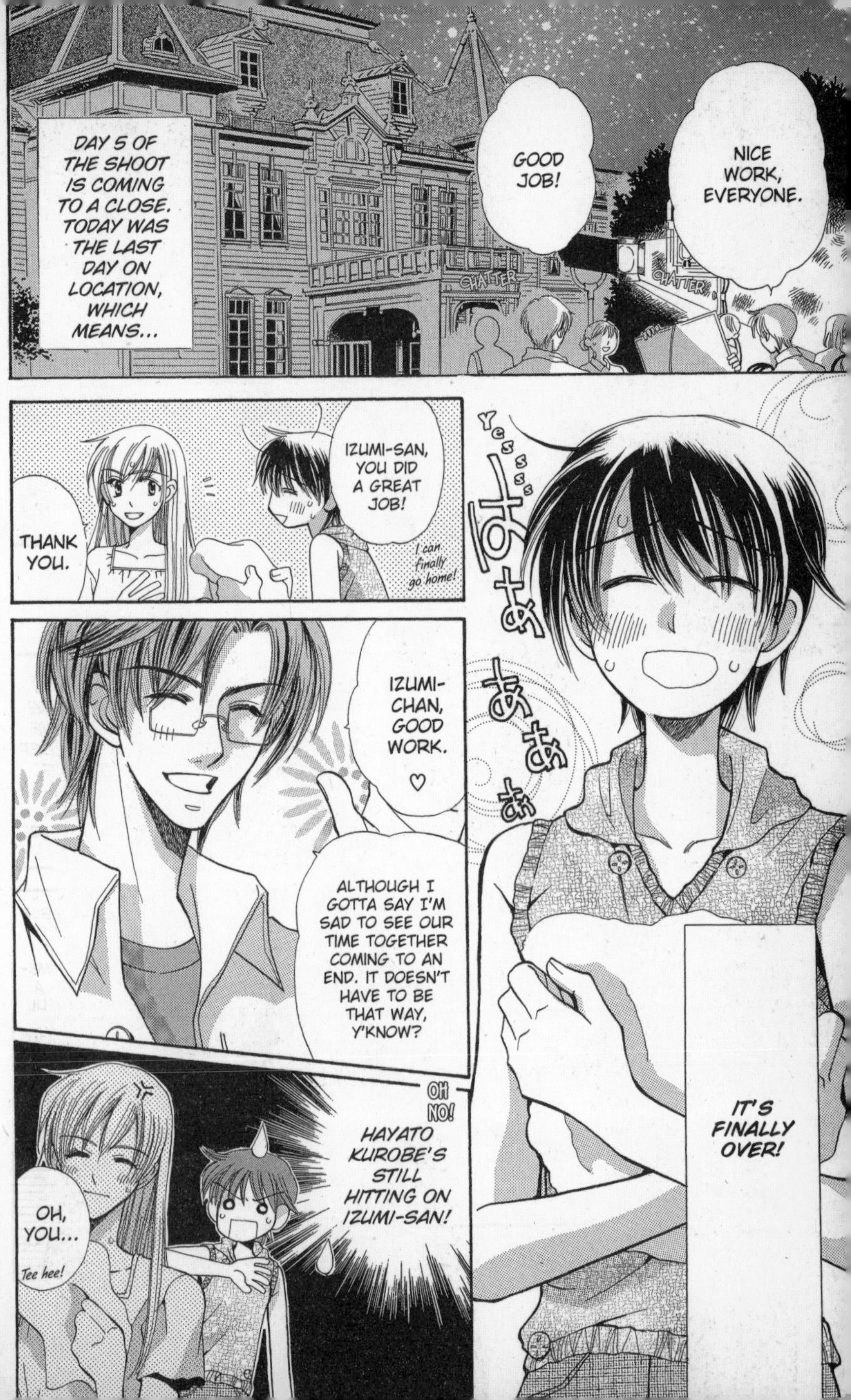
NICE WORK, EVERYONE.
GOOD JOB!
CHATTER
CHATTER
DAY 5 OF THE SHOOT IS COMING TO A CLOSE. TODAY WAS THE LAST DAY ON LOCATION, WHICH MEANS...
Yessss
すああああ
IT'S FINALLY OVER!
IZUMI-SAN, YOU DID A GREAT JOB!
I can finally go home!
THANK YOU.
IZUMI-CHAN, GOOD WORK. ♡
ALTHOUGH I GOTTA SAY I'M SAD TO SEE OUR TIME TOGETHER COMING TO AN END. IT DOESN'T HAVE TO BE THAT WAY, Y'KNOW?
OH NO!
HAYATO KUROBE'S STILL HITTING ON IZUMI-SAN!
OH, YOU...
Tee hee!

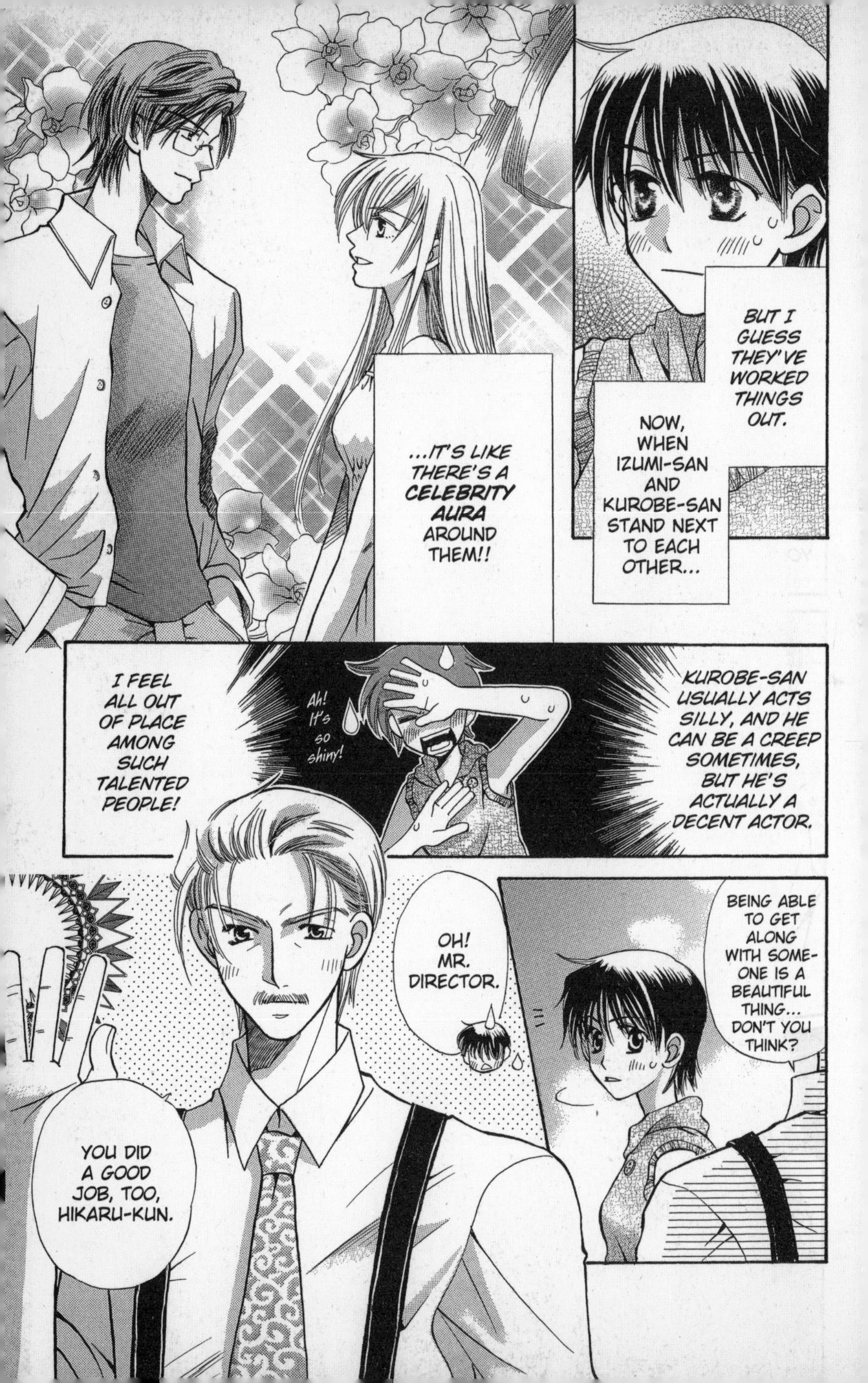
BUT I GUESS THEY'VE WORKED THINGS OUT.
NOW, WHEN IZUMI-SAN AND KUROBE-SAN STAND NEXT TO EACH OTHER...
...IT'S LIKE THERE'S A CELEBRITY AURA AROUND THEM!!
KUROBE-SAN USUALLY ACTS SILLY, AND HE CAN BE A CREEP SOMETIMES, BUT HE'S ACTUALLY A DECENT ACTOR.
Ah! It's so shiny!
I FEEL ALL OUT OF PLACE AMONG SUCH TALENTED PEOPLE!
BEING ABLE TO GET ALONG WITH SOME-ONE IS A BEAUTIFUL THING... DON'T YOU THINK?
OH! MR. DIRECTOR.
YOU DID A GOOD JOB, TOO, HIKARU-KUN.

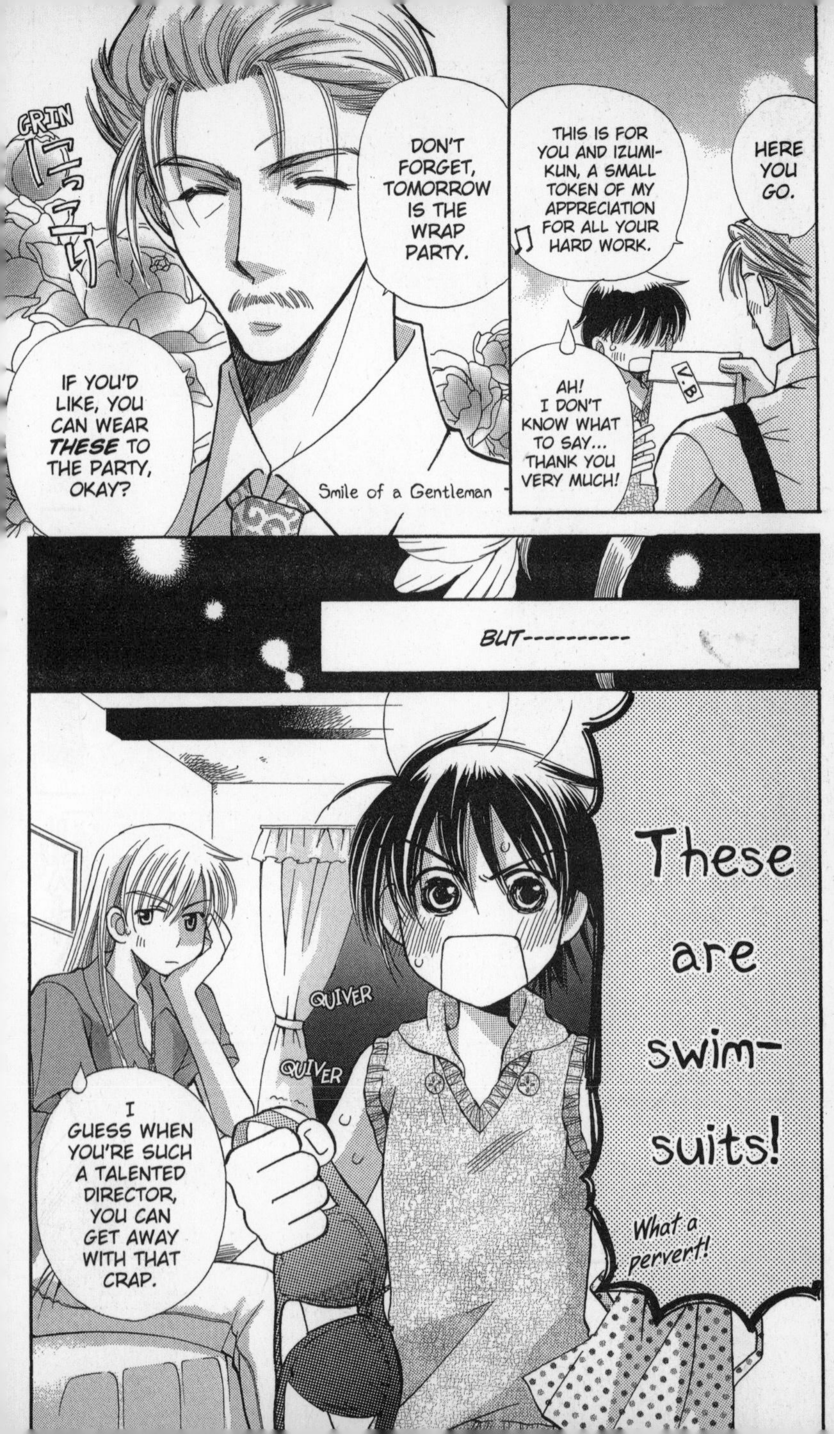
HERE YOU GO.
THIS IS FOR YOU AND IZUMI-KUN, A SMALL TOKEN OF MY APPRECIATION FOR ALL YOUR HARD WORK.
AH! I DON'T KNOW WHAT TO SAY... THANK YOU VERY MUCH!
DON'T FORGET, TOMORROW IS THE WRAP PARTY.
GRIN
IF YOU'D LIKE, YOU CAN WEAR ***THESE*** TO THE PARTY, OKAY?
Smile of a Gentleman
BUT----------
These are swim-suits!
What a pervert!
QUIVER
QUIVER
I GUESS WHEN YOU'RE SUCH A TALENTED DIRECTOR, YOU CAN GET AWAY WITH THAT CRAP.

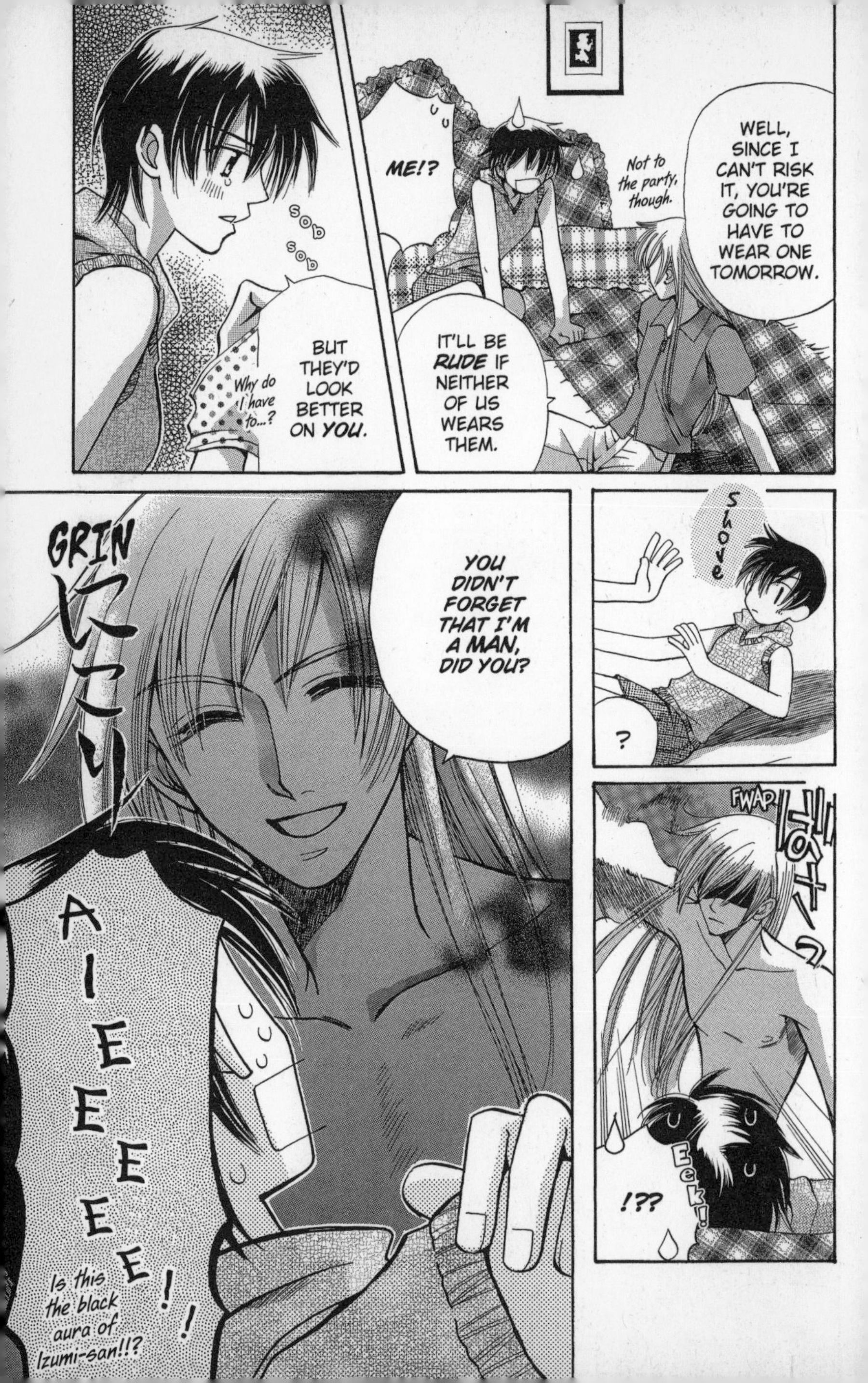
WELL, SINCE I CAN'T RISK IT, YOU'RE GOING TO HAVE TO WEAR ONE TOMORROW.
Not to the party, though.
ME!?
IT'LL BE RUDE IF NEITHER OF US WEARS THEM.
sob sob
BUT THEY'D LOOK BETTER ON YOU.
Why do I have to...?
Shove
?
FWAP
Eek!
!??
YOU DIDN'T FORGET THAT I'M A MAN, DID YOU?
GRIN
にっこり
AIEEEEE!!
Is this the black aura of Izumi-san!!?

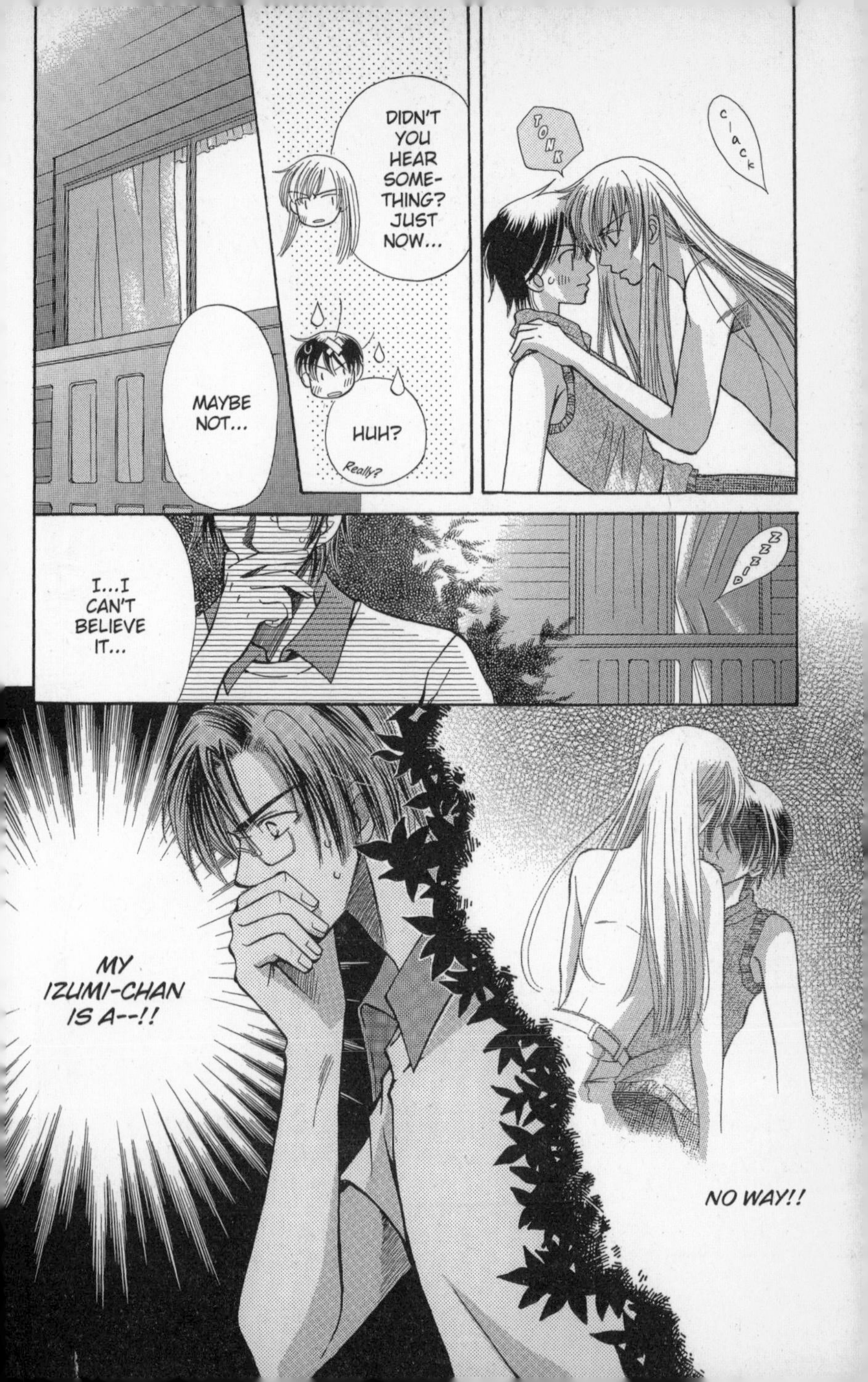
TONK
clack
DIDN'T YOU HEAR SOME-THING? JUST NOW...
HUH?
Really?
MAYBE NOT...
ZZZID
I...I CAN'T BELIEVE IT...
NO WAY!!
MY IZUMI-CHAN IS A--!!

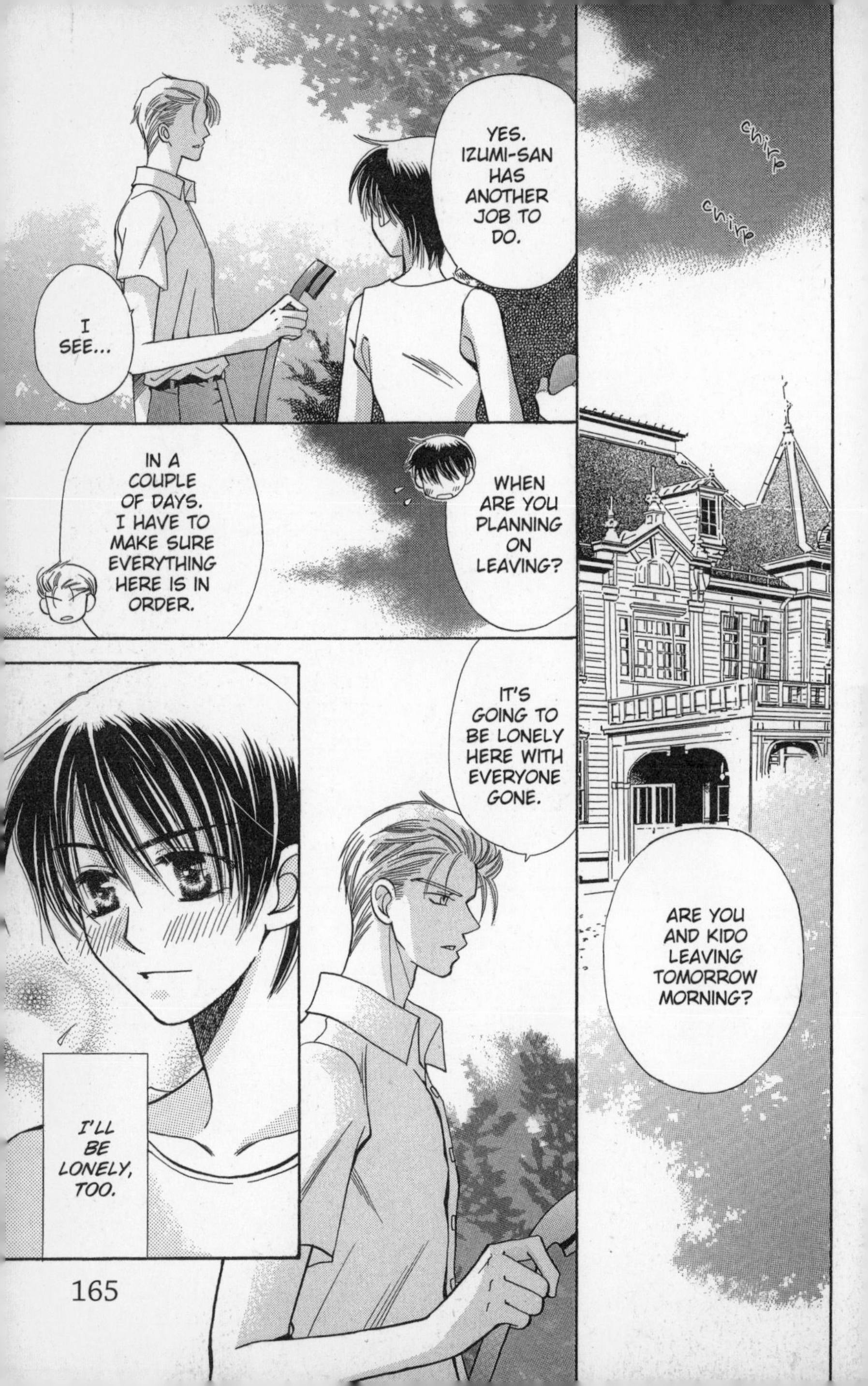
chirp
chirp
ARE YOU AND KIDO LEAVING TOMORROW MORNING?
YES. IZUMI-SAN HAS ANOTHER JOB TO DO.
I SEE...
WHEN ARE YOU PLANNING ON LEAVING?
IN A COUPLE OF DAYS. I HAVE TO MAKE SURE EVERYTHING HERE IS IN ORDER.
IT'S GOING TO BE LONELY HERE WITH EVERYONE GONE.
I'LL BE LONELY, TOO.

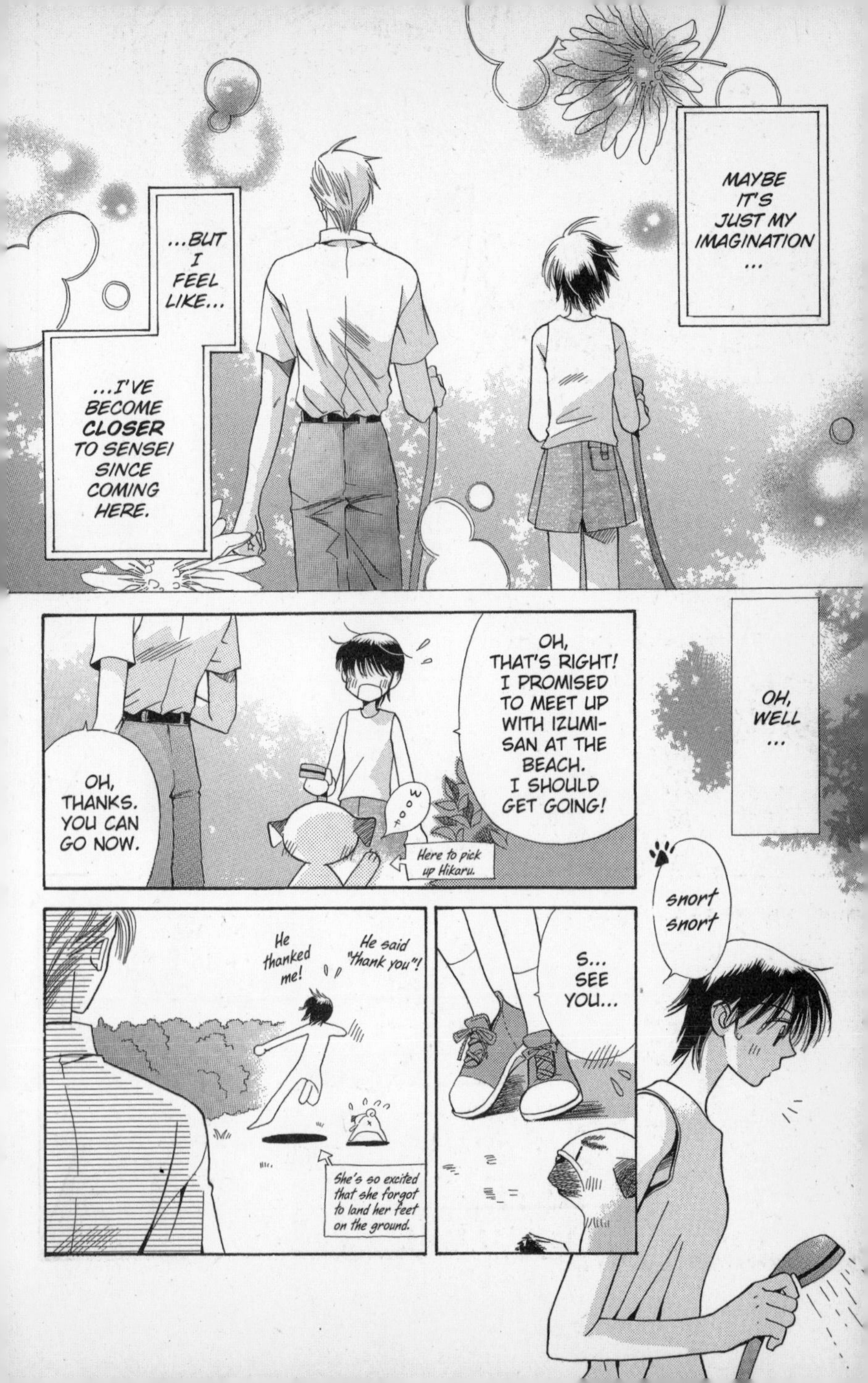
MAYBE IT'S JUST MY IMAGINATION ...
...BUT I FEEL LIKE...
...I'VE BECOME CLOSER TO SENSEI SINCE COMING HERE.
OH, WELL ...
snort snort
OH, THAT'S RIGHT! I PROMISED TO MEET UP WITH IZUMI-SAN AT THE BEACH. I SHOULD GET GOING!
OH, THANKS. YOU CAN GO NOW.
woof
Here to pick up Hikaru.
S... SEE YOU...
He said "thank you"!
He thanked me!
She's so excited that she forgot to land her feet on the ground.

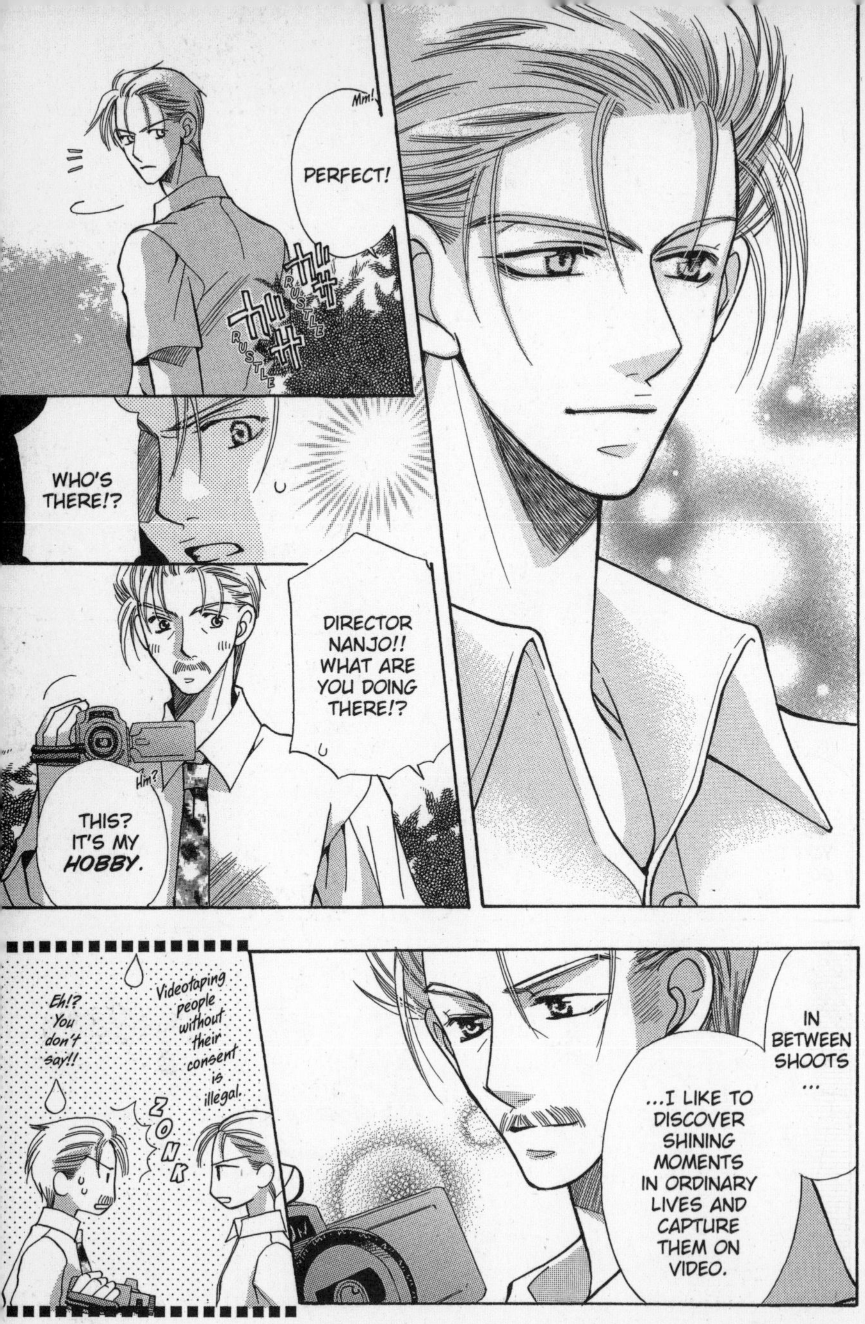
Mm!
PERFECT!
RUSTLE
RUSTLE
WHO'S THERE!?
DIRECTOR NANJO!! WHAT ARE YOU DOING THERE!?
Hm?
THIS? IT'S MY HOBBY.
IN BETWEEN SHOOTS...
...I LIKE TO DISCOVER SHINING MOMENTS IN ORDINARY LIVES AND CAPTURE THEM ON VIDEO.
Videotaping people without their consent is illegal.
ZONK
Eh!? You don't say!!

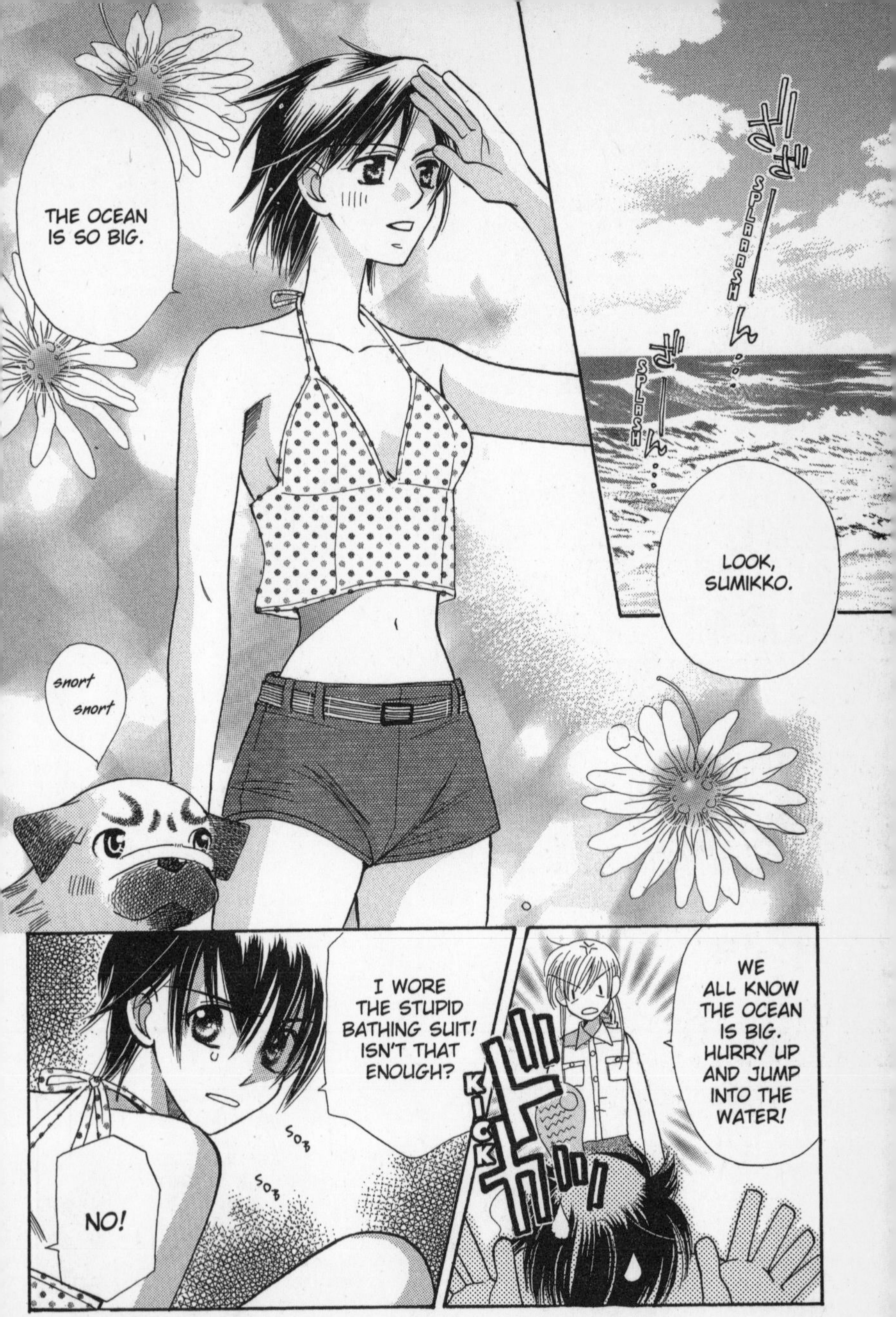
SPLAAASH
SPLASH
LOOK, SUMIKKO.
THE OCEAN IS SO BIG.
snort snort
WE ALL KNOW THE OCEAN IS BIG. HURRY UP AND JUMP INTO THE WATER!
KICK
I WORE THE STUPID BATHING SUIT! ISN'T THAT ENOUGH?
sob
sob
NO!

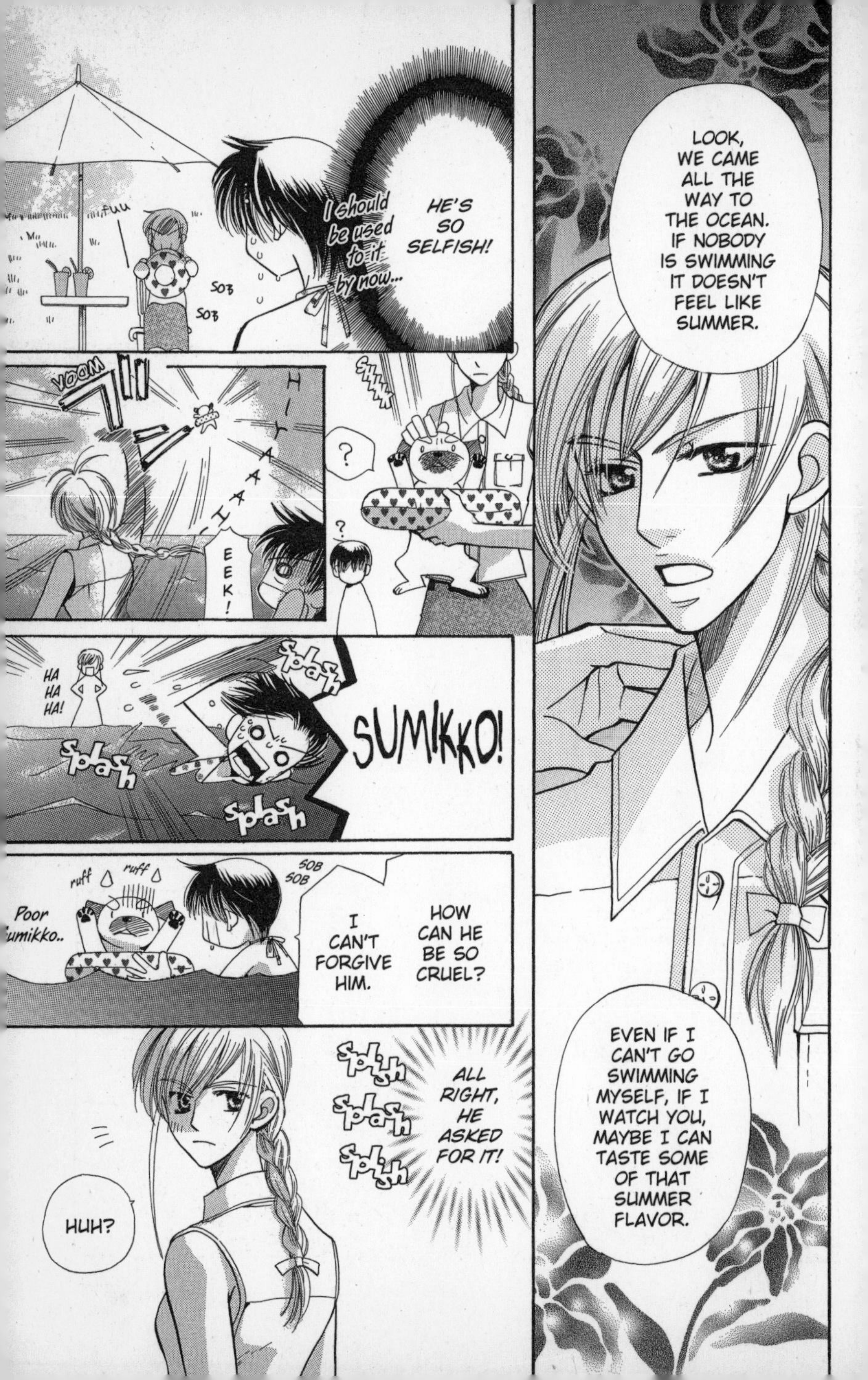
LOOK, WE CAME ALL THE WAY TO THE OCEAN. IF NOBODY IS SWIMMING IT DOESN'T FEEL LIKE SUMMER.
EVEN IF I CAN'T GO SWIMMING MYSELF, IF I WATCH YOU, MAYBE I CAN TASTE SOME OF THAT SUMMER FLAVOR.
HE'S SO SELFISH!
I should be used to it by now...
fuu
SOB
SOB
SHHK
?
?
VOOM
HIYAAAAH!
EEK!
splash
SUMIKKO!
HA HA HA!
splash
splash
SOB SOB
HOW CAN HE BE SO CRUEL?
I CAN'T FORGIVE HIM.
ruff
ruff
Poor Sumikko..
splish
splash
splish
ALL RIGHT, HE ASKED FOR IT!
HUH?

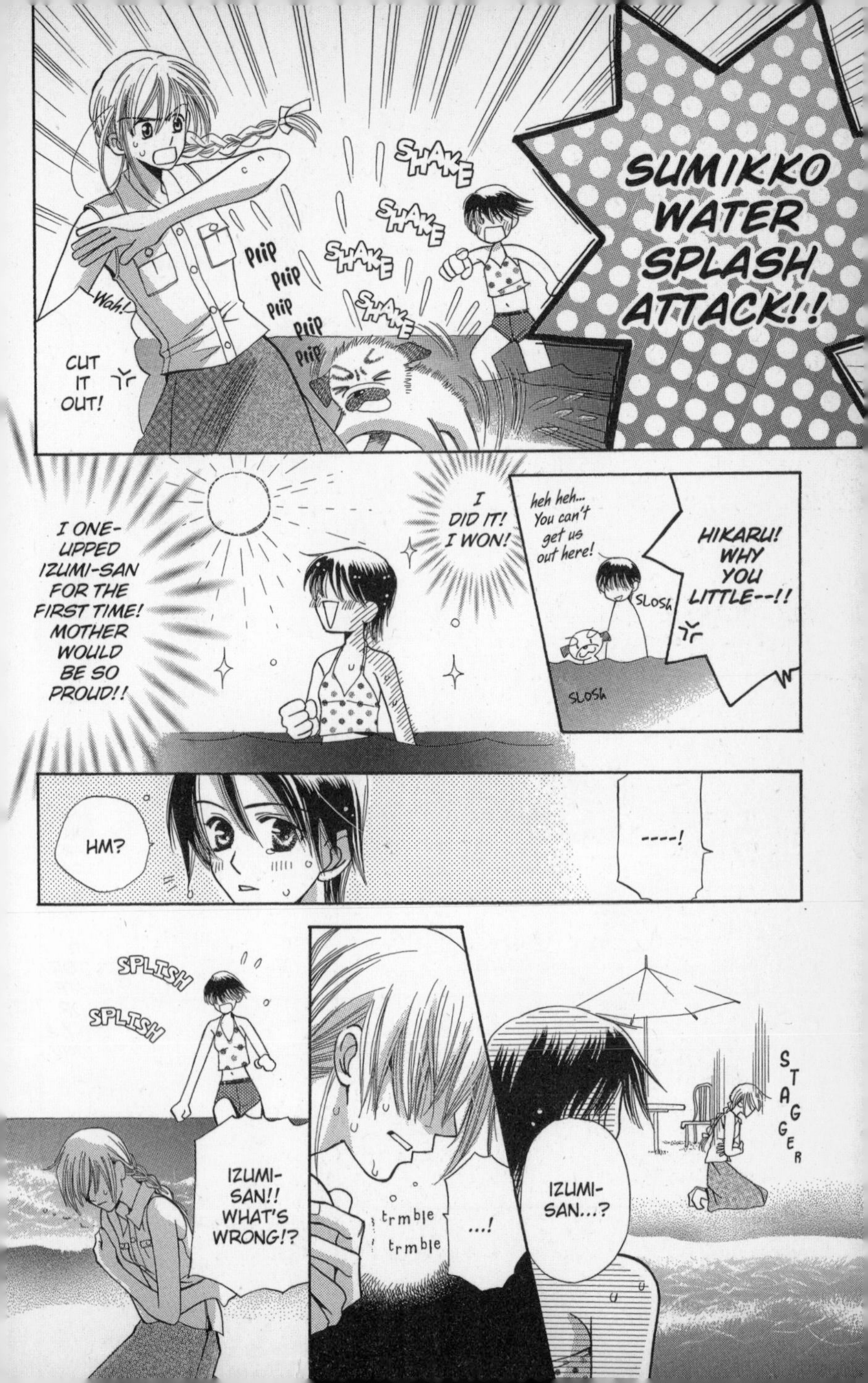
SUMIKKO WATER SPLASH ATTACK!!
SHAKE
SHAKE
SHAKE
SHAKE
piip
piip
piip
piip
piip
Wah!
CUT IT OUT!
heh heh... You can't get us out here!
HIKARU! WHY YOU LITTLE--!!
SLOSH
SLOSH
I DID IT! I WON!
I ONE-UPPED IZUMI-SAN FOR THE FIRST TIME! MOTHER WOULD BE SO PROUD!!
----!
HM?
STAGGER
IZUMI-SAN...?
...!
trmble
trmble
SPLISH
SPLISH
IZUMI-SAN!! WHAT'S WRONG!?

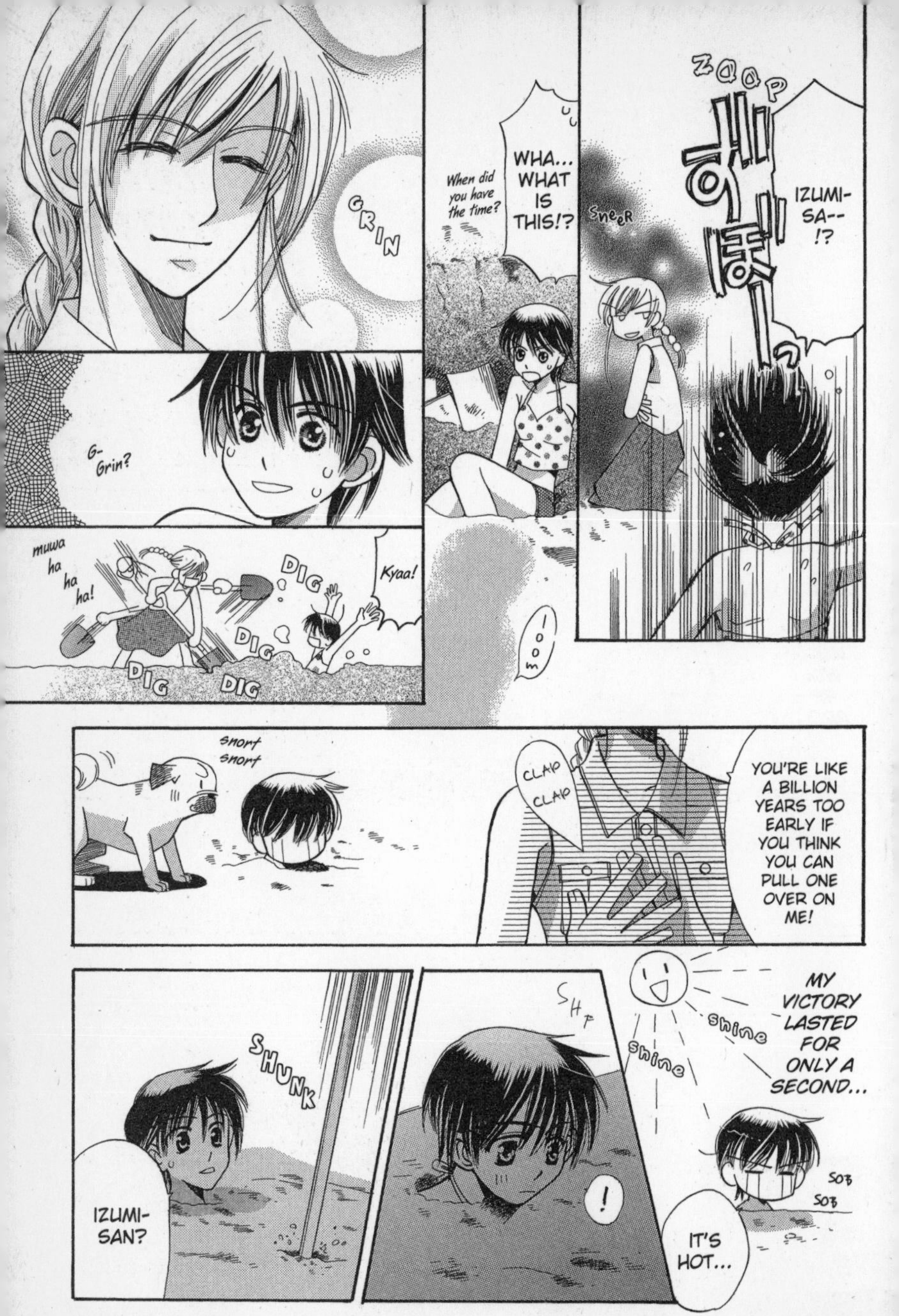
ZAAP
ずぼーっ
IZUMI-SA--!?
Sneer
WHA... WHAT IS THIS!?
When did you have the time?
moo!
GRIN
G-Grin?
Kyaa!
DIG
DIG
muwa ha ha ha!
DIG
DIG
YOU'RE LIKE A BILLION YEARS TOO EARLY IF YOU THINK YOU CAN PULL ONE OVER ON ME!
CLAP CLAP
snort snort
MY VICTORY LASTED FOR ONLY A SECOND...
shine
shine
SOB SOB
IT'S HOT...
!
SHP
SHUNK
IZUMI-SAN?

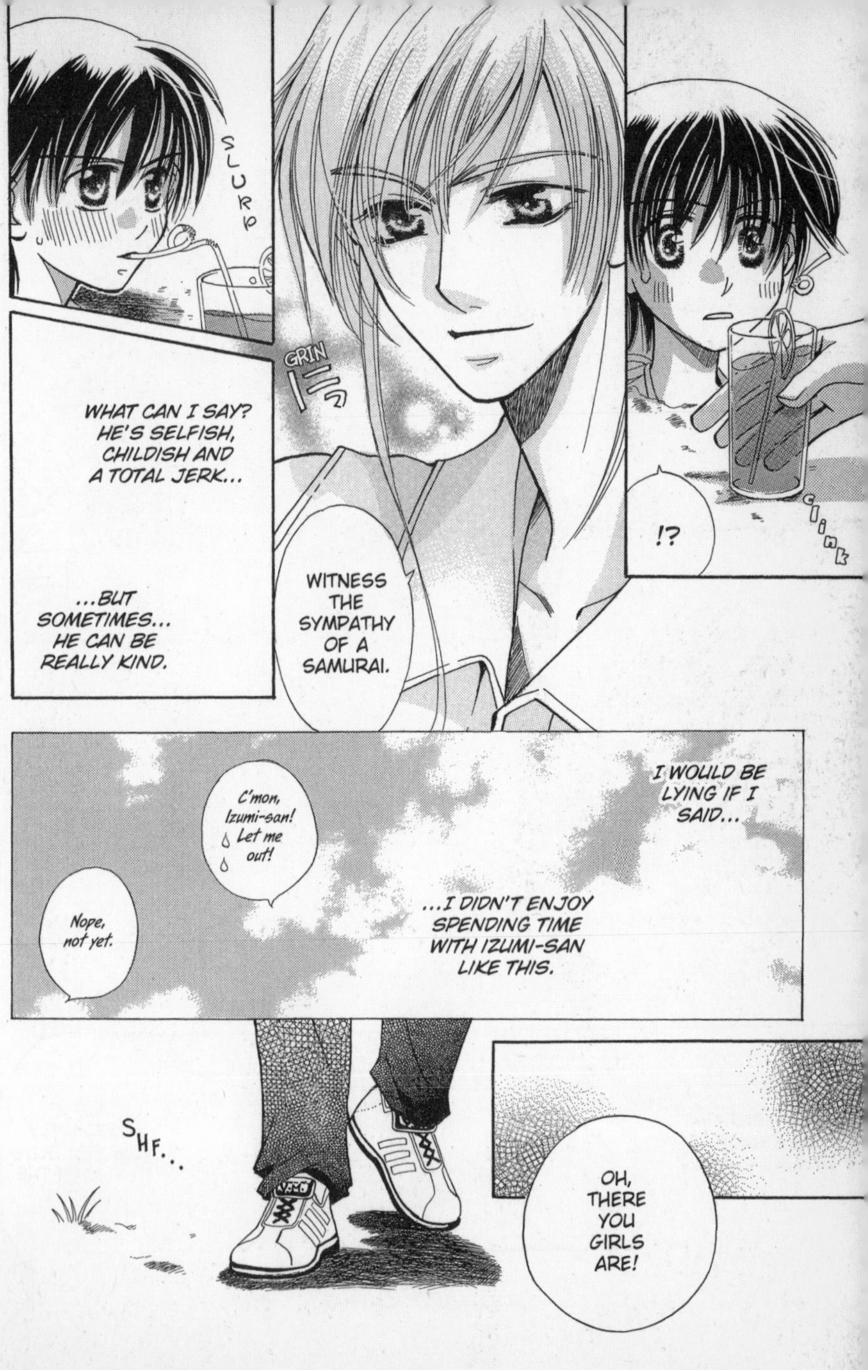
!?
clink
GRIN
WITNESS THE SYMPATHY OF A SAMURAI.
SLURP
WHAT CAN I SAY? HE'S SELFISH, CHILDISH AND A TOTAL JERK...
...BUT SOMETIMES... HE CAN BE REALLY KIND.
I WOULD BE LYING IF I SAID...
...I DIDN'T ENJOY SPENDING TIME WITH IZUMI-SAN LIKE THIS.
C'mon, Izumi-san! Let me out!
Nope, not yet.
OH, THERE YOU GIRLS ARE!
SHF...

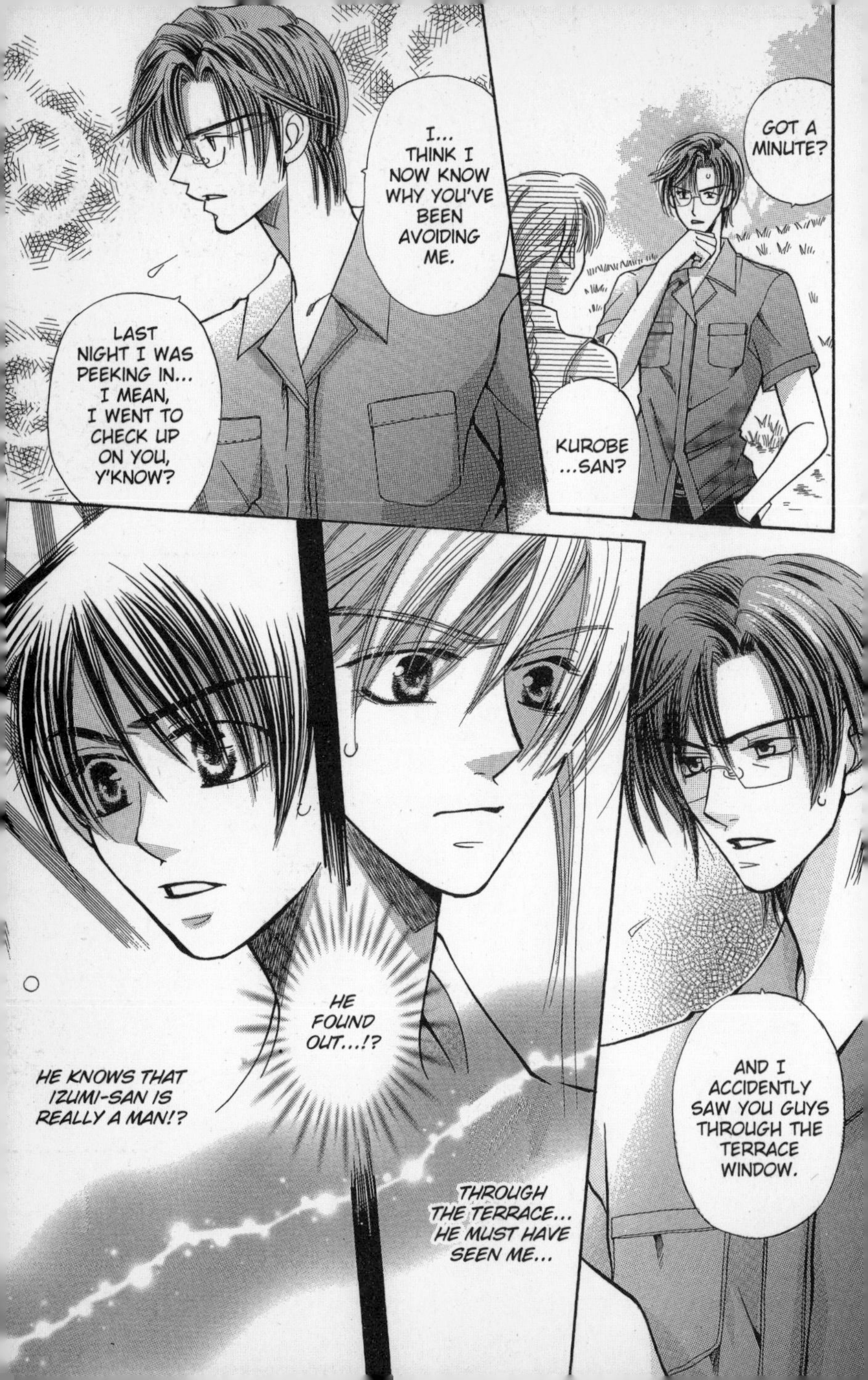
GOT A MINUTE?
KUROBE ...SAN?
I... THINK I NOW KNOW WHY YOU'VE BEEN AVOIDING ME.
LAST NIGHT I WAS PEEKING IN... I MEAN, I WENT TO CHECK UP ON YOU, Y'KNOW?
AND I ACCIDENTLY SAW YOU GUYS THROUGH THE TERRACE WINDOW.
THROUGH THE TERRACE... HE MUST HAVE SEEN ME...
HE FOUND OUT...!?
HE KNOWS THAT IZUMI-SAN IS REALLY A MAN!?

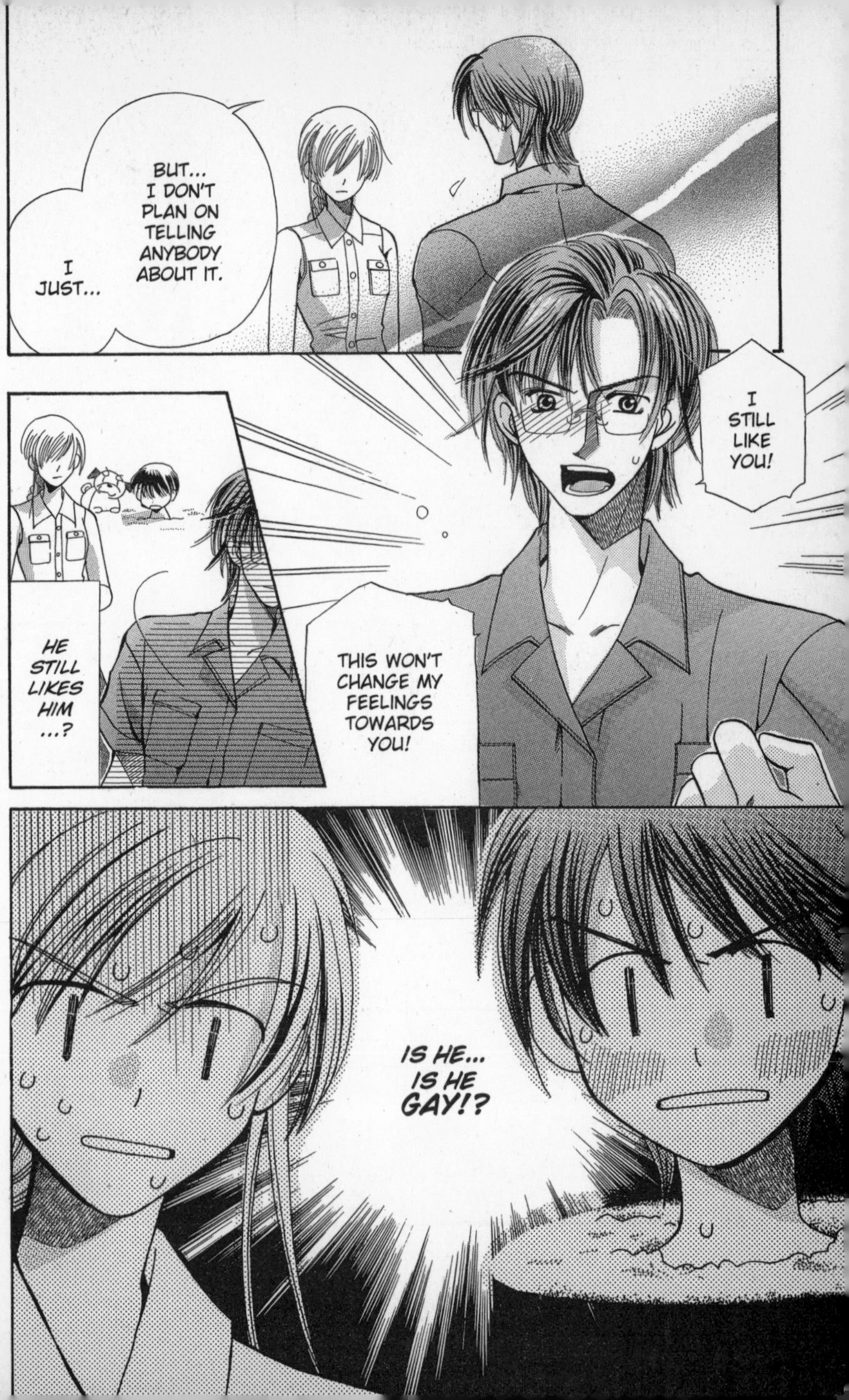
BUT... I DON'T PLAN ON TELLING ANYBODY ABOUT IT. I JUST...
I STILL LIKE YOU!
THIS WON'T CHANGE MY FEELINGS TOWARDS YOU!
HE STILL LIKES HIM ...?
IS HE... IS HE GAY!?

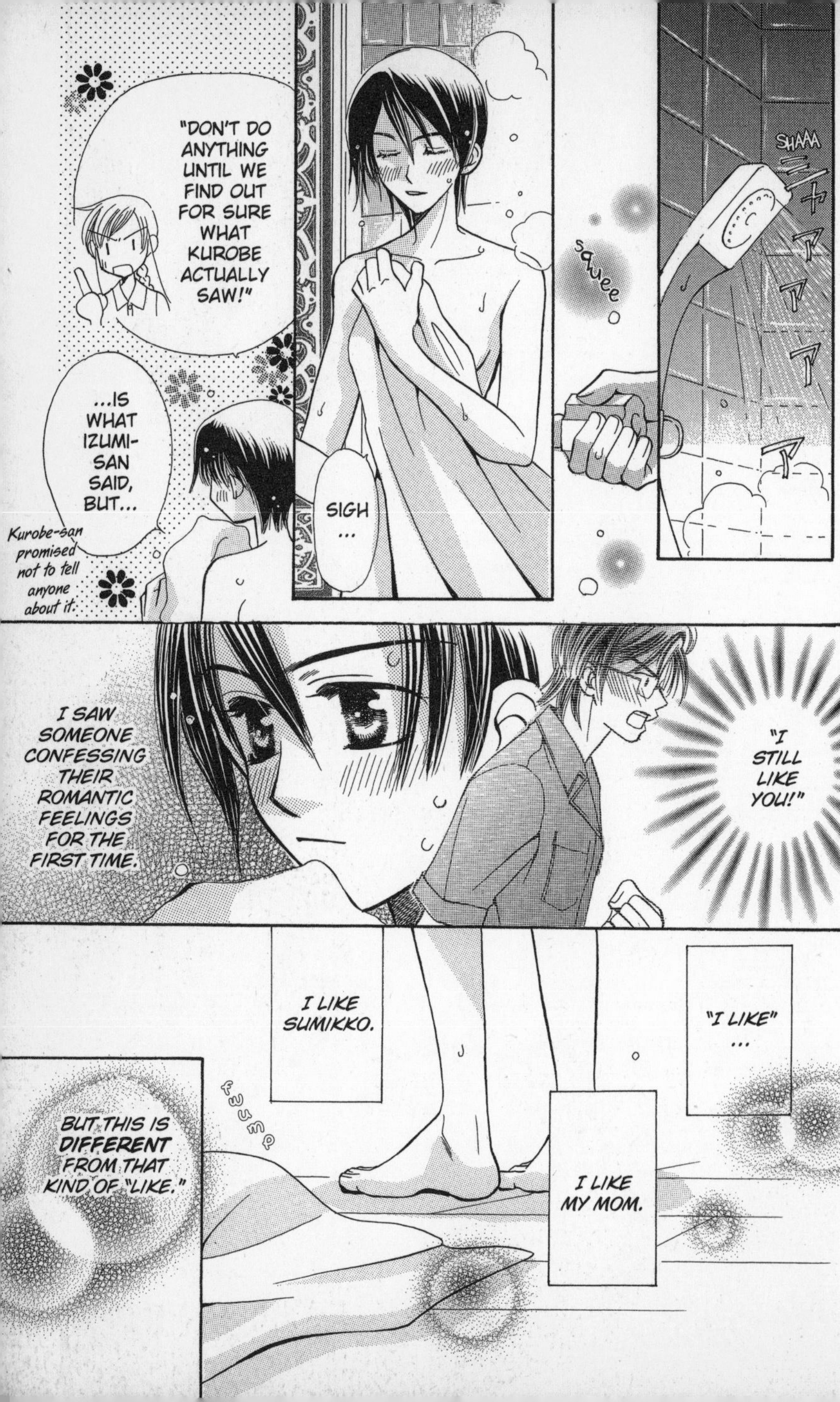
SHAAA
squee
SIGH ...
"DON'T DO ANYTHING UNTIL WE FIND OUT FOR SURE WHAT KUROBE ACTUALLY SAW!"
...IS WHAT IZUMI-SAN SAID, BUT...
Kurobe-san promised not to tell anyone about it.
"I STILL LIKE YOU!"
I SAW SOMEONE CONFESSING THEIR ROMANTIC FEELINGS FOR THE FIRST TIME.
"I LIKE" ...
I LIKE MY MOM.
I LIKE SUMIKKO.
fwump
BUT THIS IS DIFFERENT FROM THAT KIND OF "LIKE."

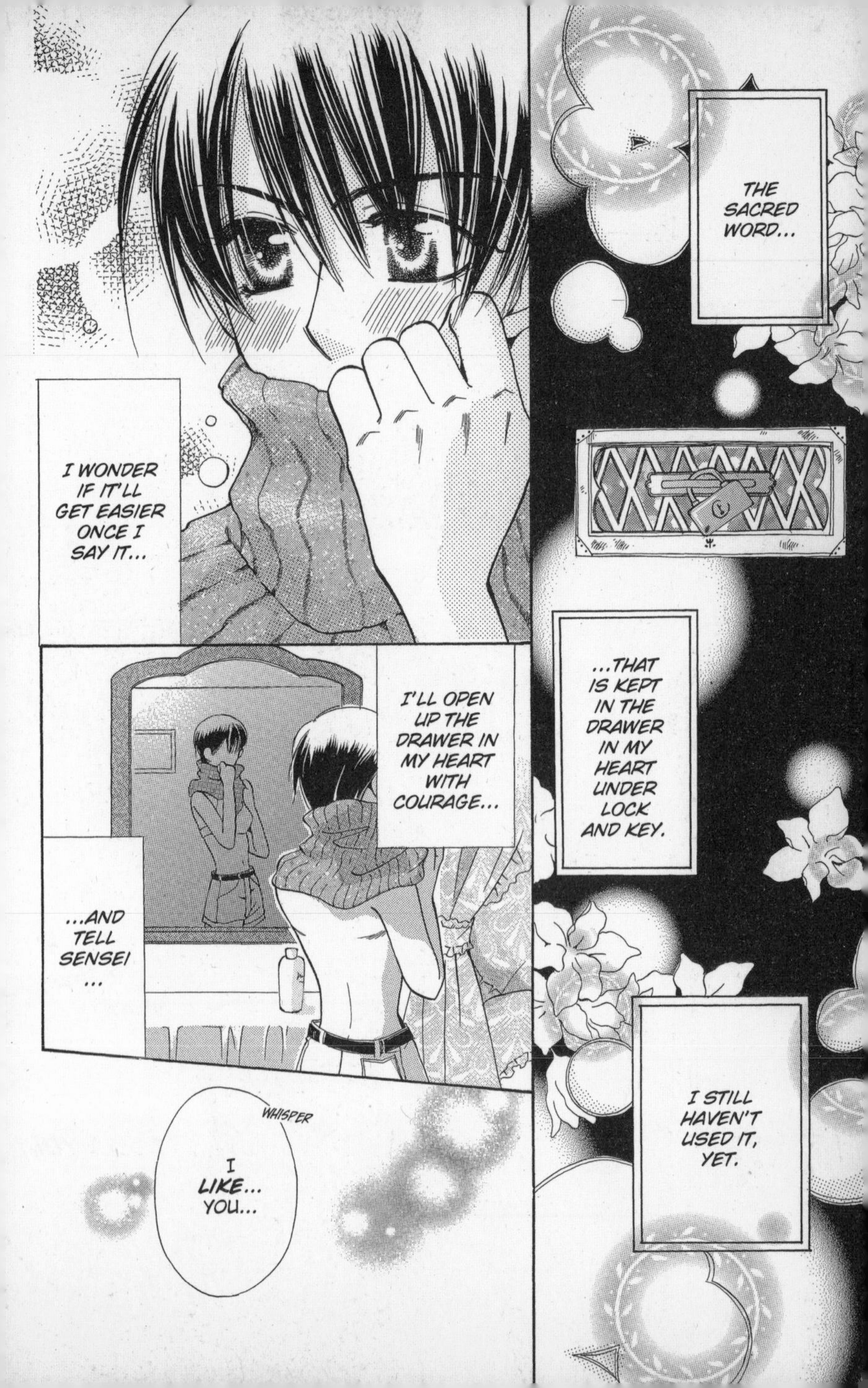
THE SACRED WORD...
...THAT IS KEPT IN THE DRAWER IN MY HEART UNDER LOCK AND KEY.
I STILL HAVEN'T USED IT, YET.
I WONDER IF IT'LL GET EASIER ONCE I SAY IT...
I'LL OPEN UP THE DRAWER IN MY HEART WITH COURAGE...
...AND TELL SENSEI...
WHISPER
I LIKE... YOU...

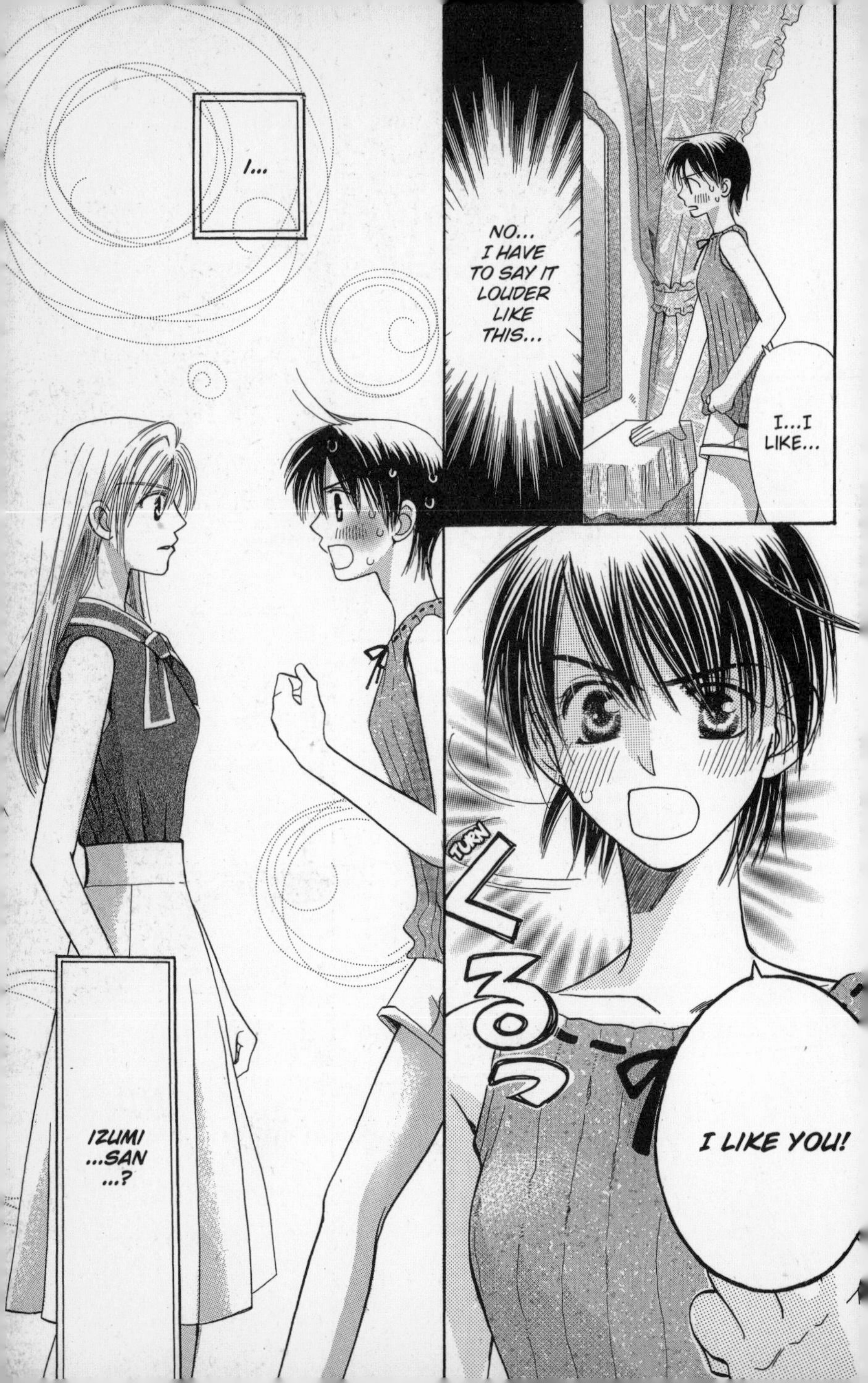
I...I LIKE...
NO... I HAVE TO SAY IT LOUDER LIKE THIS...
I LIKE YOU!
TURN
くるっ
I...
IZUMI ...SAN ...?

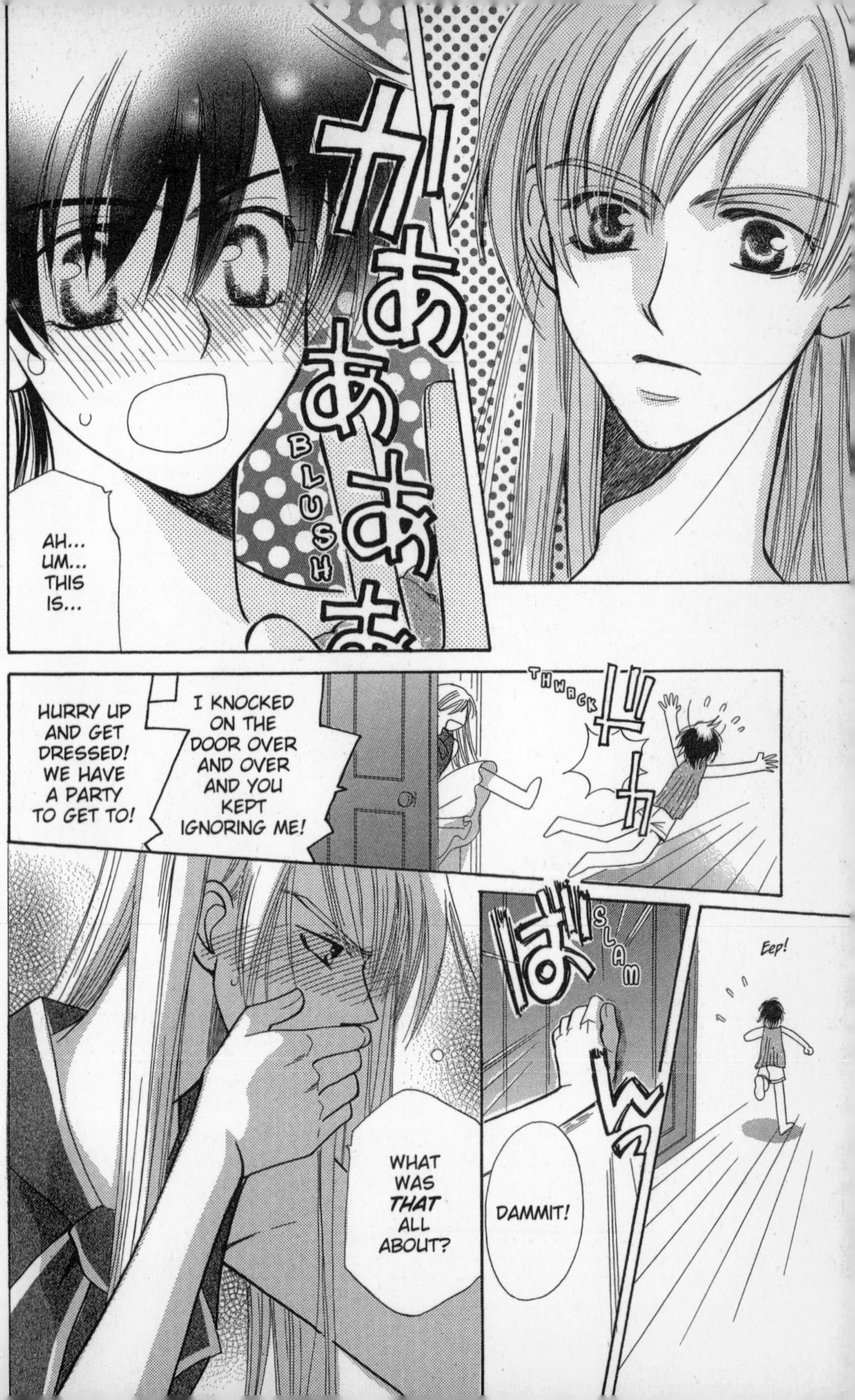

かあああ
BLUSH
AH... UM... THIS IS...
THWACK
I KNOCKED ON THE DOOR OVER AND OVER AND YOU KEPT IGNORING ME!
HURRY UP AND GET DRESSED! WE HAVE A PARTY TO GET TO!
SLAM
Eep!
DAMMIT!
WHAT WAS *THAT* ALL ABOUT?

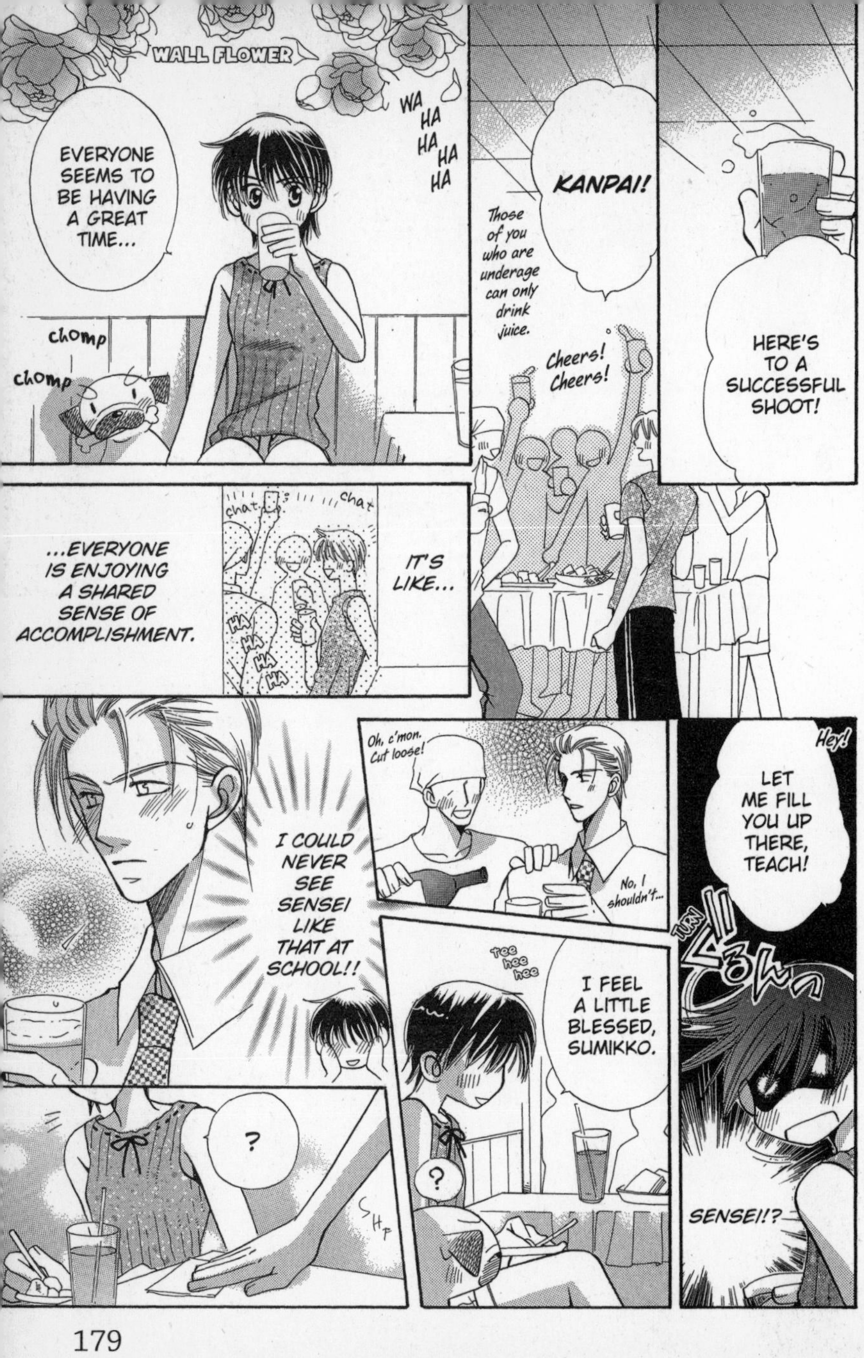
HERE'S TO A SUCCESSFUL SHOOT!
KANPAI!
Those of you who are underage can only drink juice.
Cheers! Cheers!
WALL FLOWER
WA HA HA HA HA
EVERYONE SEEMS TO BE HAVING A GREAT TIME...
chomp
chomp
chat
chat
HA HA HA HA
IT'S LIKE...
...EVERYONE IS ENJOYING A SHARED SENSE OF ACCOMPLISHMENT.
Hey!
LET ME FILL YOU UP THERE, TEACH!
TURN
SENSEI!?
Oh, c'mon. Cut loose!
No, I shouldn't...
I COULD NEVER SEE SENSEI LIKE THAT AT SCHOOL!!
tee hee hee
I FEEL A LITTLE BLESSED, SUMIKKO.
?
?
SHP

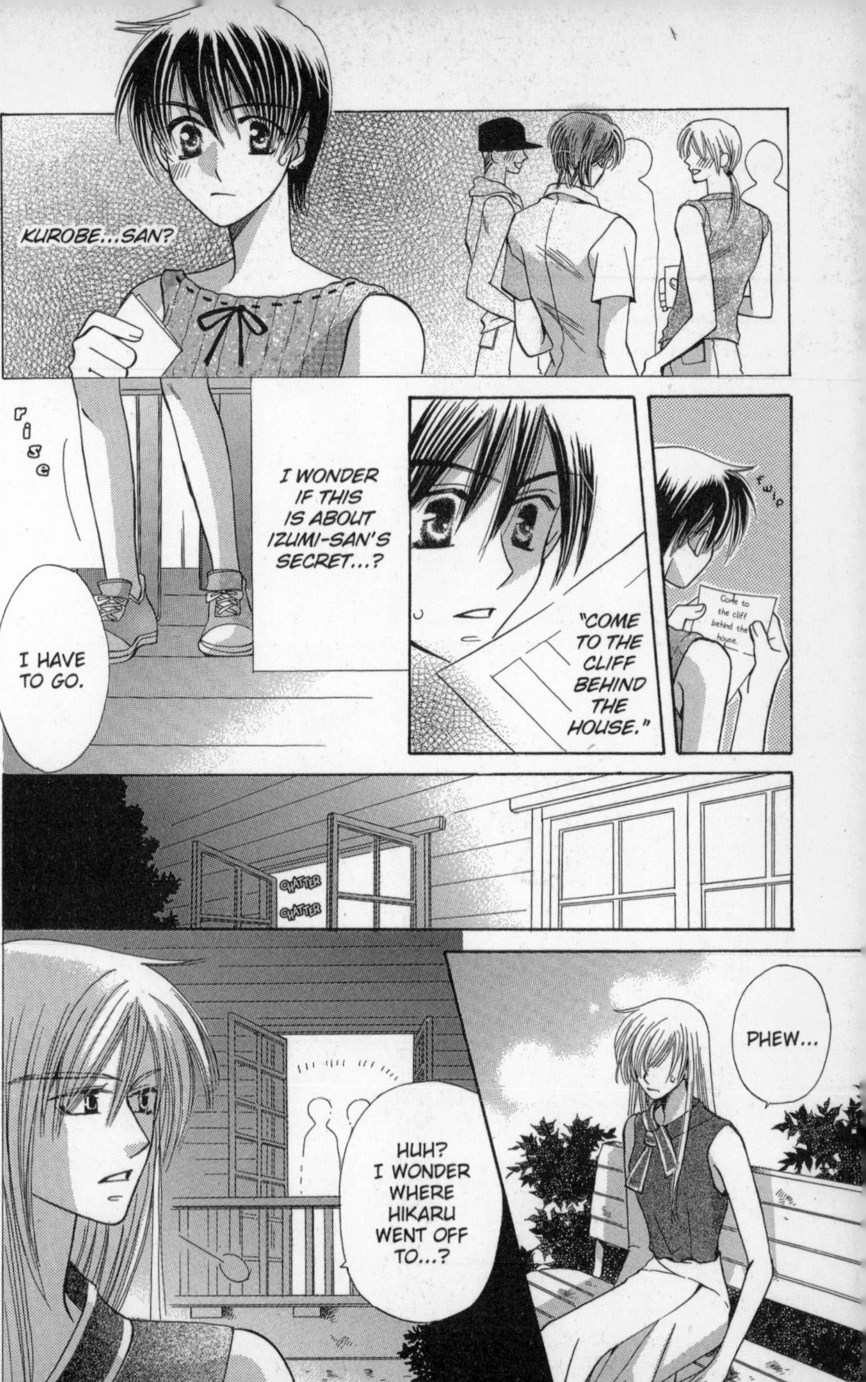
KUROBE...SAN?
twip
Come to the cliff behind the house.
"COME TO THE CLIFF BEHIND THE HOUSE."
I WONDER IF THIS IS ABOUT IZUMI-SAN'S SECRET...?
rise
I HAVE TO GO.
CHATTER
CHATTER
PHEW...
HUH? I WONDER WHERE HIKARU WENT OFF TO...?

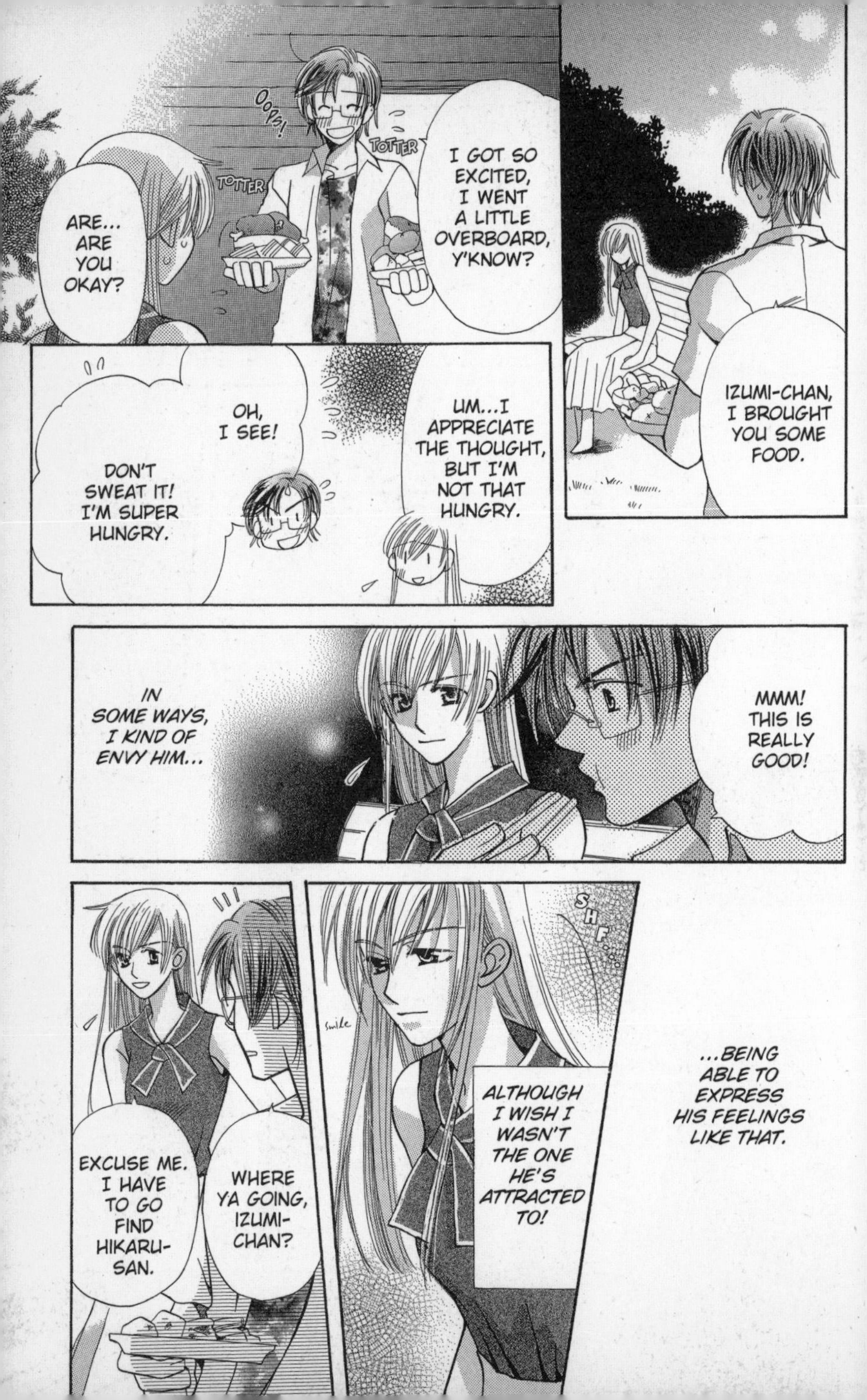
IZUMI-CHAN, I BROUGHT YOU SOME FOOD.
OOPS!
TOTTER
TOTTER
I GOT SO EXCITED, I WENT A LITTLE OVERBOARD, Y'KNOW?
ARE... ARE YOU OKAY?
UM...I APPRECIATE THE THOUGHT, BUT I'M NOT THAT HUNGRY.
OH, I SEE!
DON'T SWEAT IT! I'M SUPER HUNGRY.
MMM! THIS IS REALLY GOOD!
IN SOME WAYS, I KIND OF ENVY HIM...
...BEING ABLE TO EXPRESS HIS FEELINGS LIKE THAT.
SHF...
ALTHOUGH I WISH I WASN'T THE ONE HE'S ATTRACTED TO!
smile
WHERE YA GOING, IZUMI-CHAN?
EXCUSE ME. I HAVE TO GO FIND HIKARU-SAN.

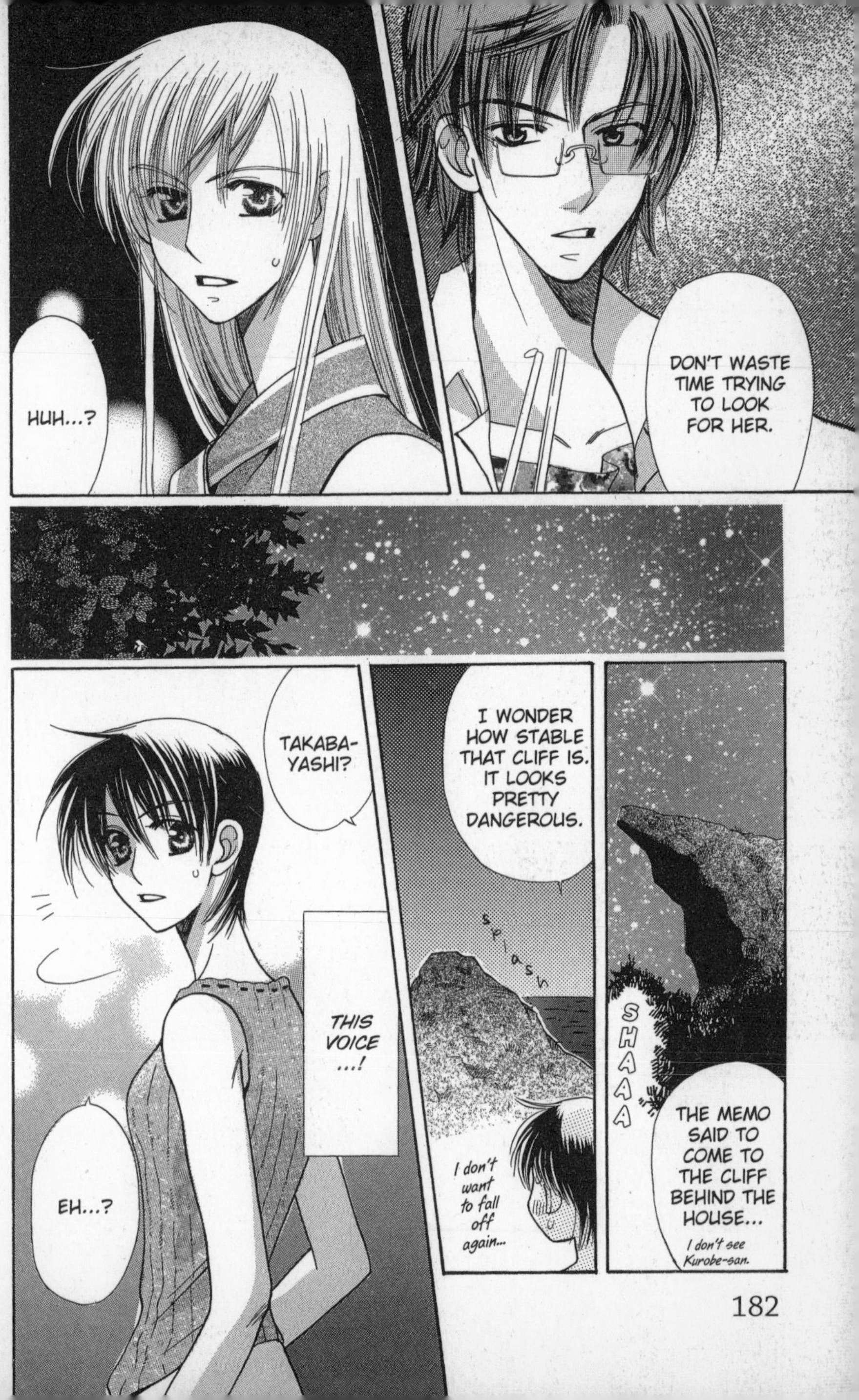
DON'T WASTE TIME TRYING TO LOOK FOR HER.
HUH...?
SHAAA
THE MEMO SAID TO COME TO THE CLIFF BEHIND THE HOUSE...
I don't see Kurobe-san.
I WONDER HOW STABLE THAT CLIFF IS. IT LOOKS PRETTY DANGEROUS.
splash
I don't want to fall off again...
TAKABA-YASHI?
THIS VOICE ...!
EH...?

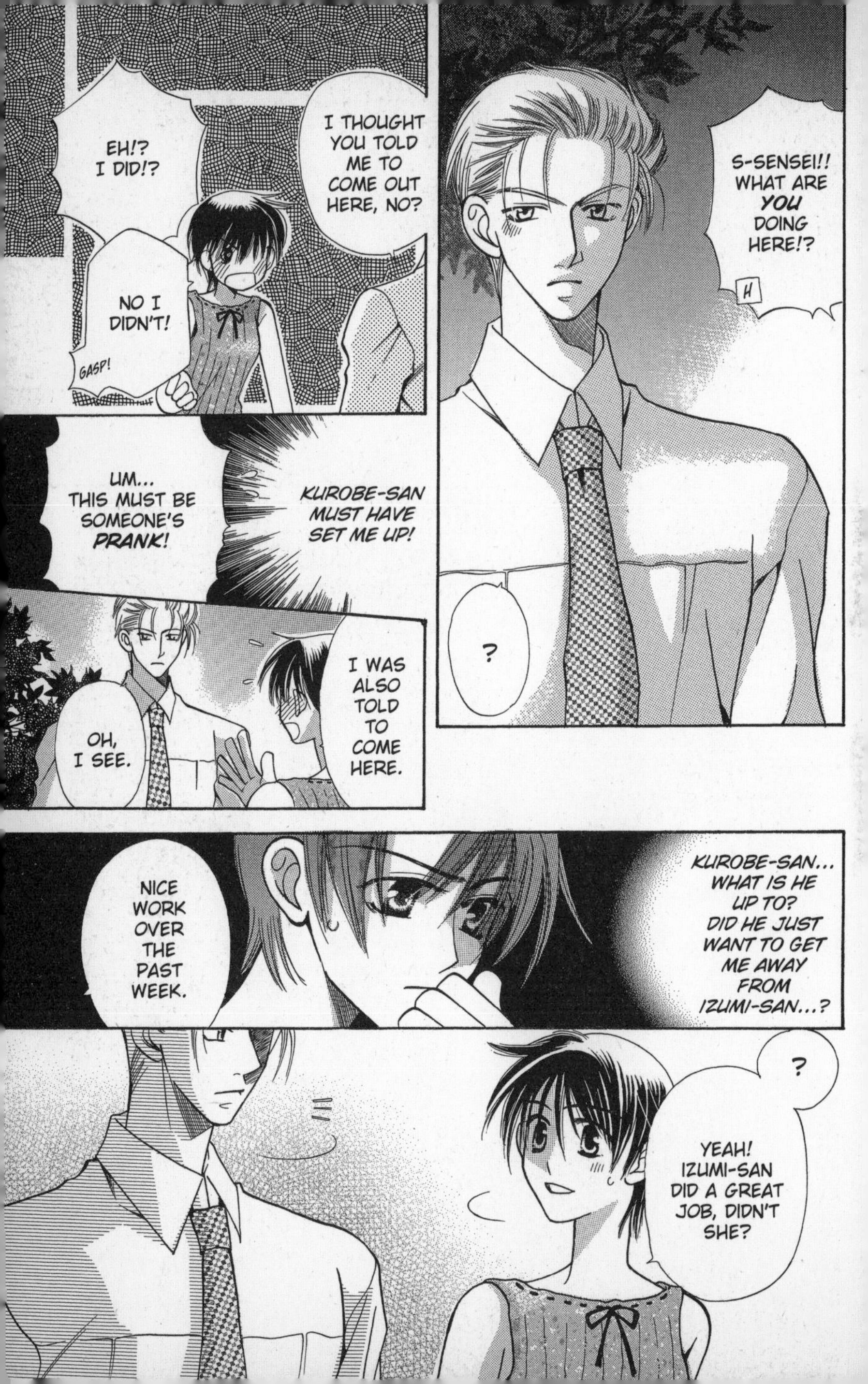
S-SENSEI!! WHAT ARE *YOU* DOING HERE!?
H
?
I THOUGHT YOU TOLD ME TO COME OUT HERE, NO?
EH!? I DID!?
NO I DIDN'T!
GASP!
KUROBE-SAN MUST HAVE SET ME UP!
UM... THIS MUST BE SOMEONE'S **PRANK!**
I WAS ALSO TOLD TO COME HERE.
OH, I SEE.
KUROBE-SAN... WHAT IS HE UP TO? DID HE JUST WANT TO GET ME AWAY FROM IZUMI-SAN...?
NICE WORK OVER THE PAST WEEK.
?
YEAH! IZUMI-SAN DID A GREAT JOB, DIDN'T SHE?

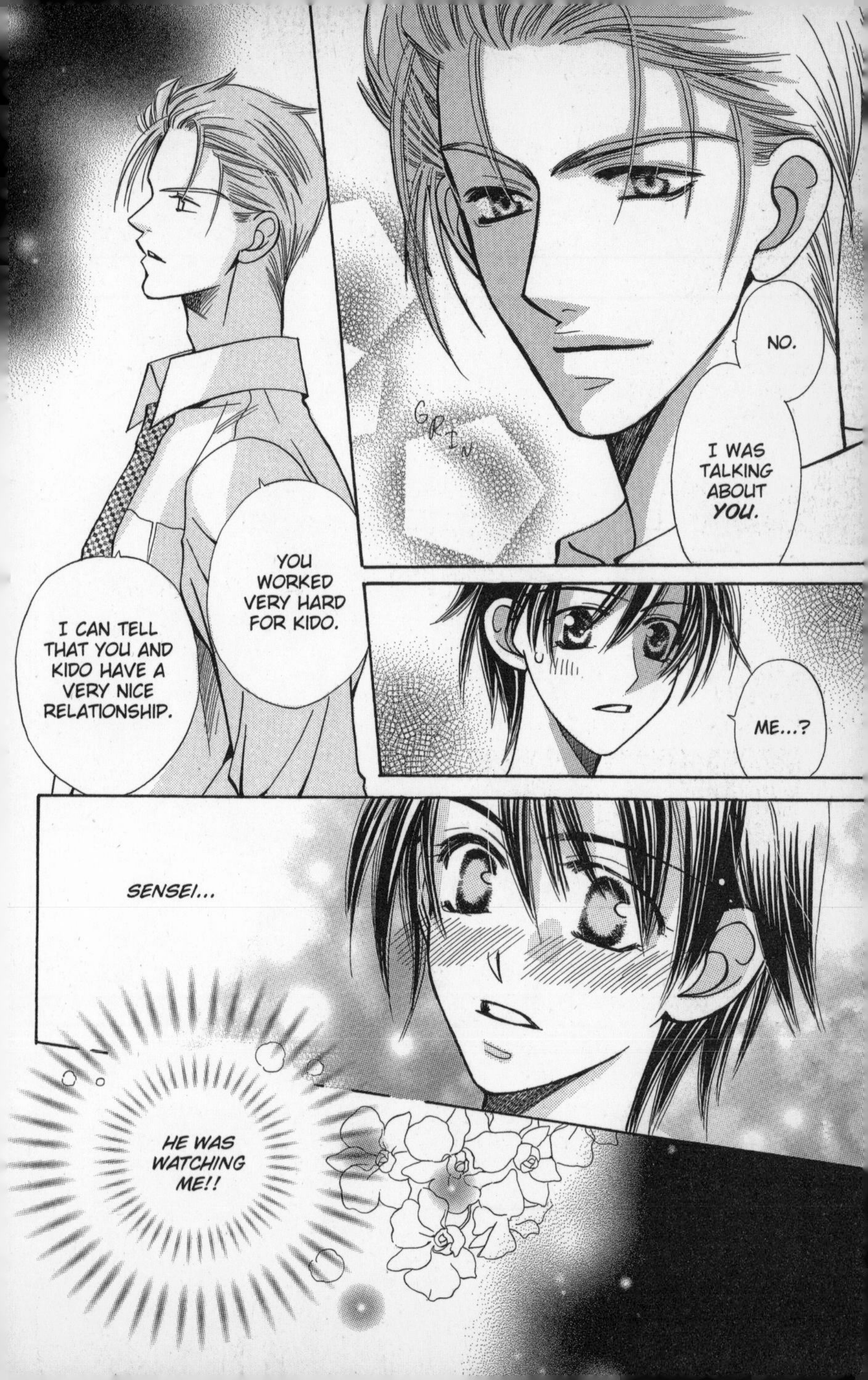
GRIN
NO.
I WAS TALKING ABOUT YOU.
ME...?
YOU WORKED VERY HARD FOR KIDO.
I CAN TELL THAT YOU AND KIDO HAVE A VERY NICE RELATIONSHIP.
SENSEI...
HE WAS WATCHING ME!!

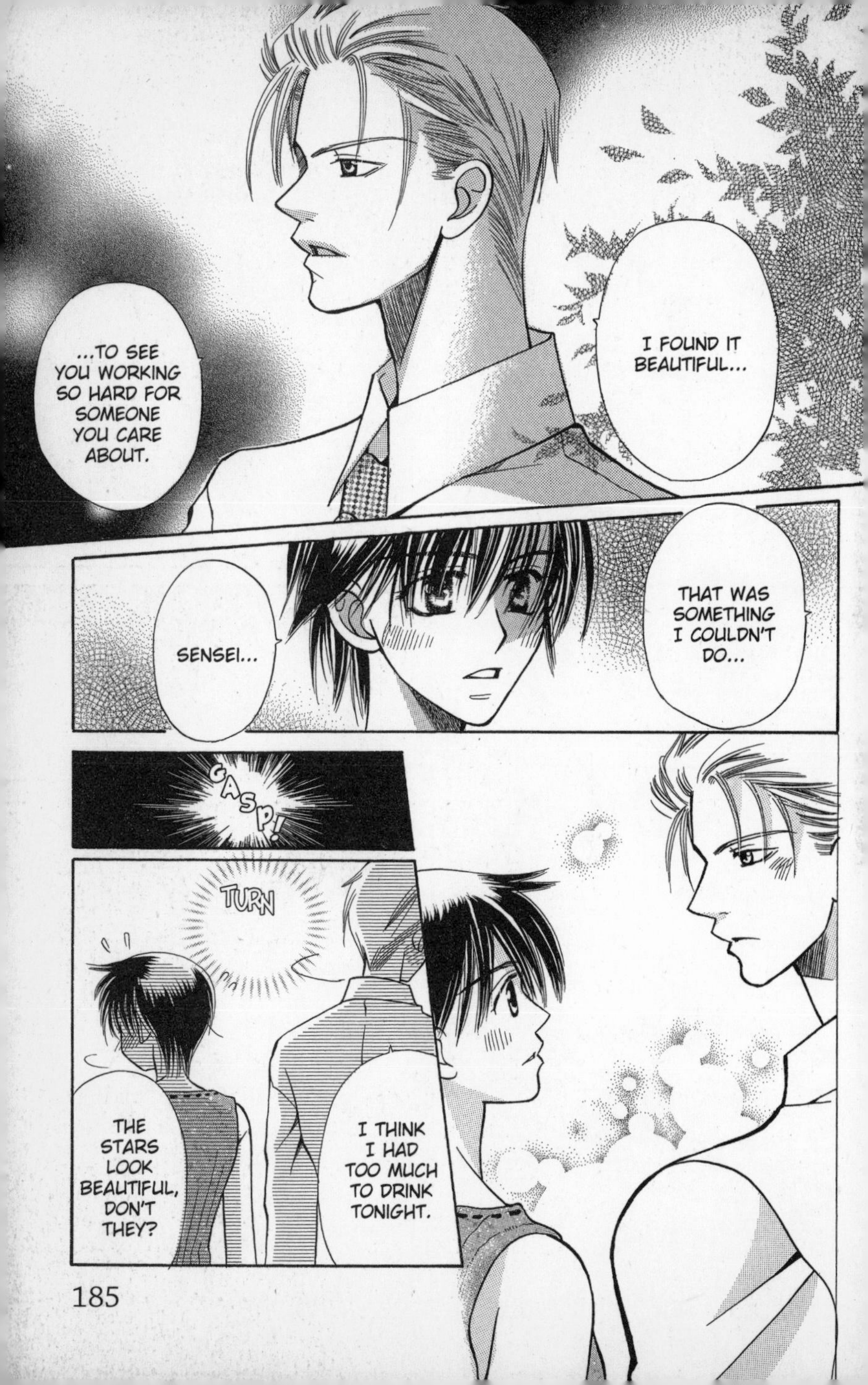
I FOUND IT BEAUTIFUL...
...TO SEE YOU WORKING SO HARD FOR SOMEONE YOU CARE ABOUT.
THAT WAS SOMETHING I COULDN'T DO...
SENSEI...
GASP!
TURN
I THINK I HAD TOO MUCH TO DRINK TONIGHT.
THE STARS LOOK BEAUTIFUL, DON'T THEY?

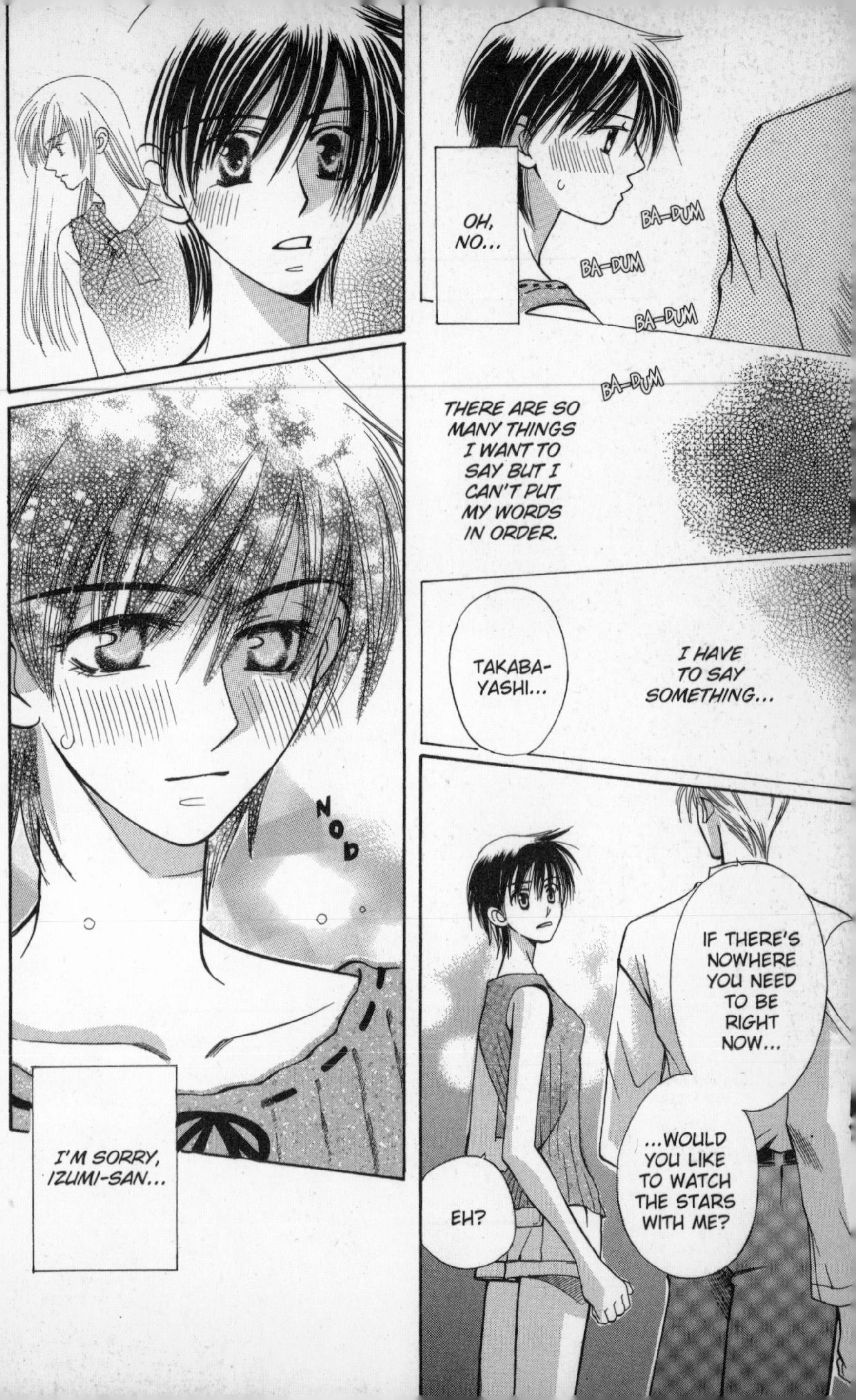
OH, NO...
BA-DUM
BA-DUM
BA-DUM
BA-DUM
THERE ARE SO MANY THINGS I WANT TO SAY BUT I CAN'T PUT MY WORDS IN ORDER.
I HAVE TO SAY SOMETHING...
TAKABA-YASHI...
IF THERE'S NOWHERE YOU NEED TO BE RIGHT NOW...
...WOULD YOU LIKE TO WATCH THE STARS WITH ME?
EH?
NOD
I'M SORRY, IZUMI-SAN...

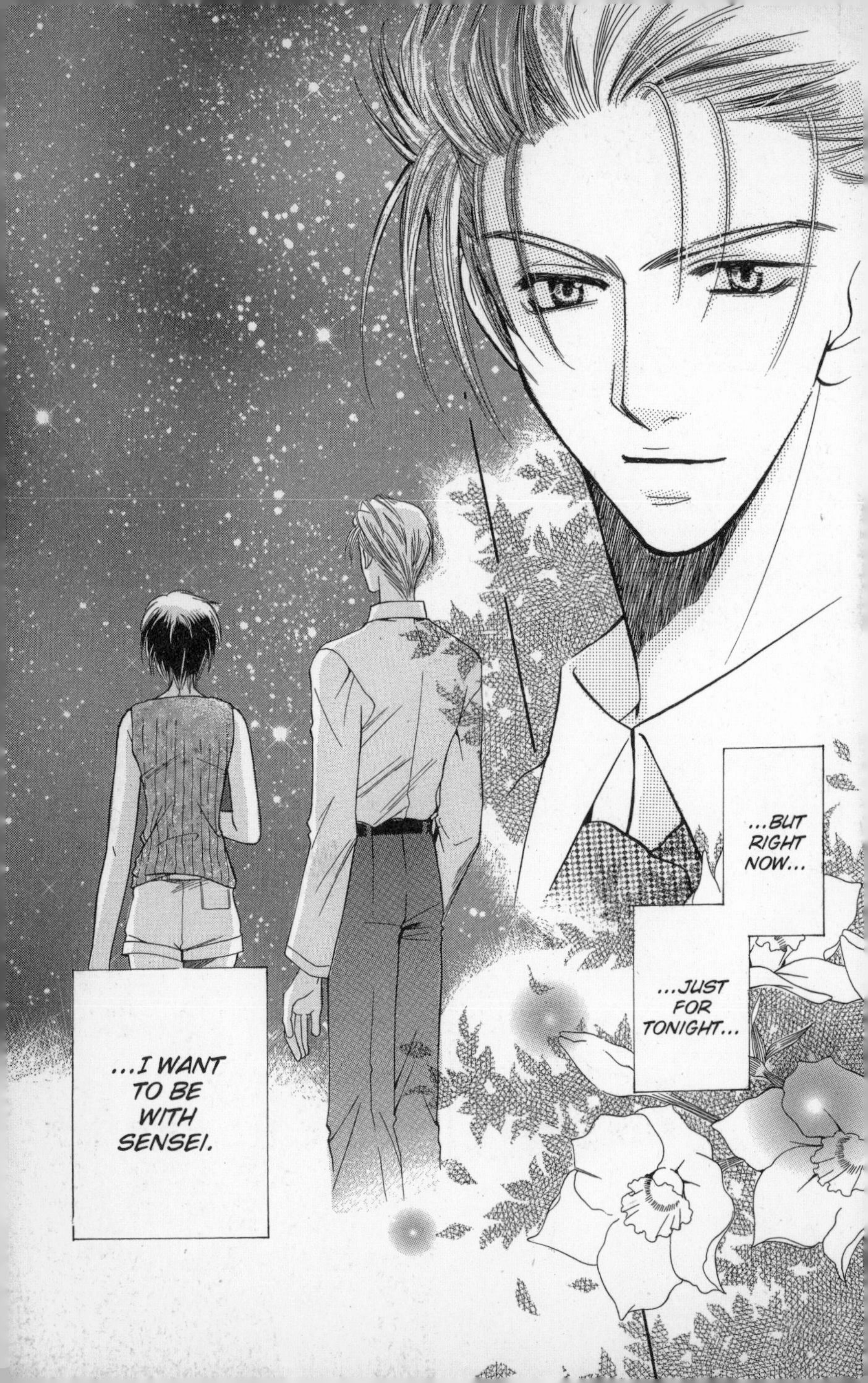
...BUT RIGHT NOW...
...JUST FOR TONIGHT...
...I WANT TO BE WITH SENSEI.

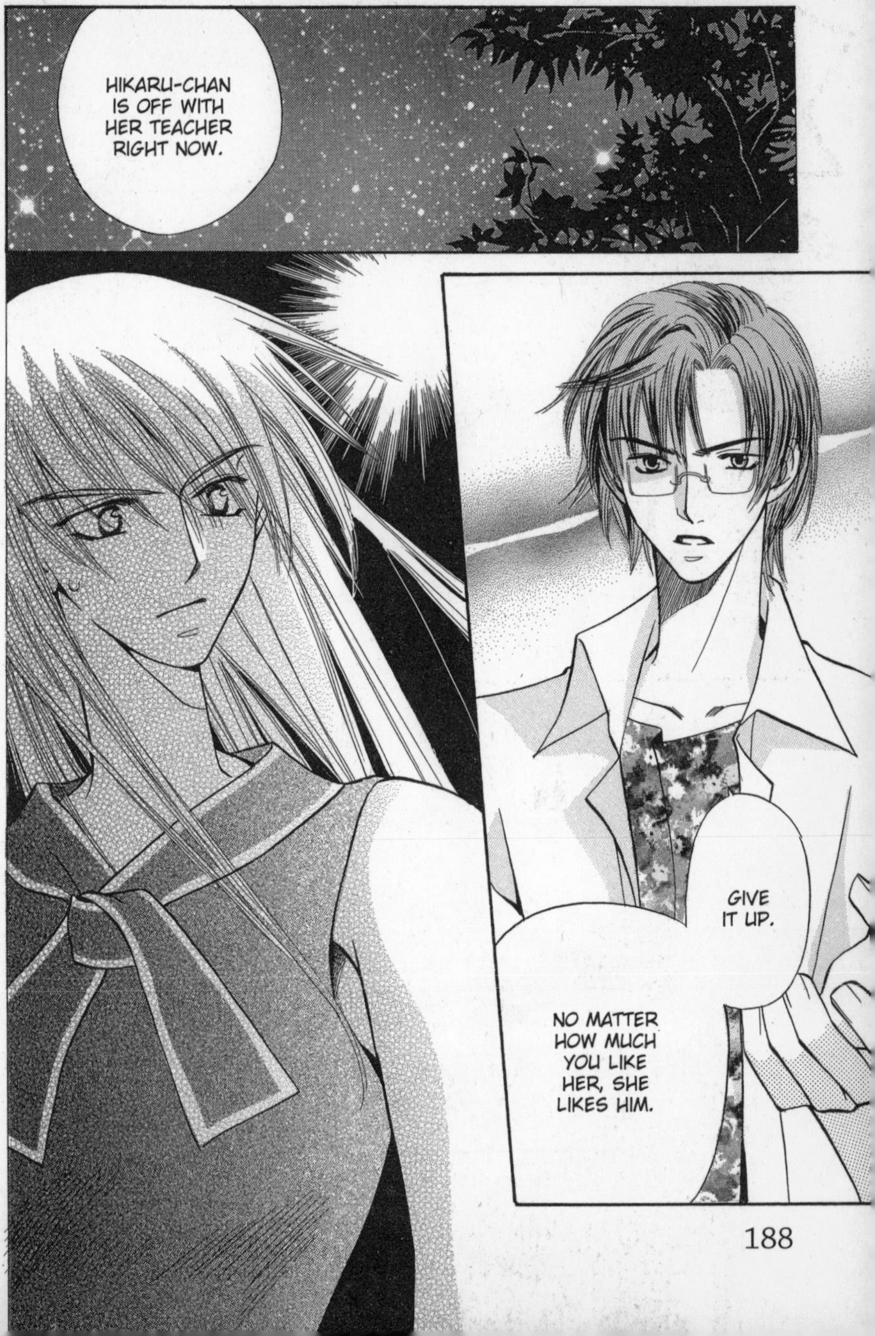
HIKARU-CHAN IS OFF WITH HER TEACHER RIGHT NOW.
GIVE IT UP.
NO MATTER HOW MUCH YOU LIKE HER, SHE LIKES HIM.

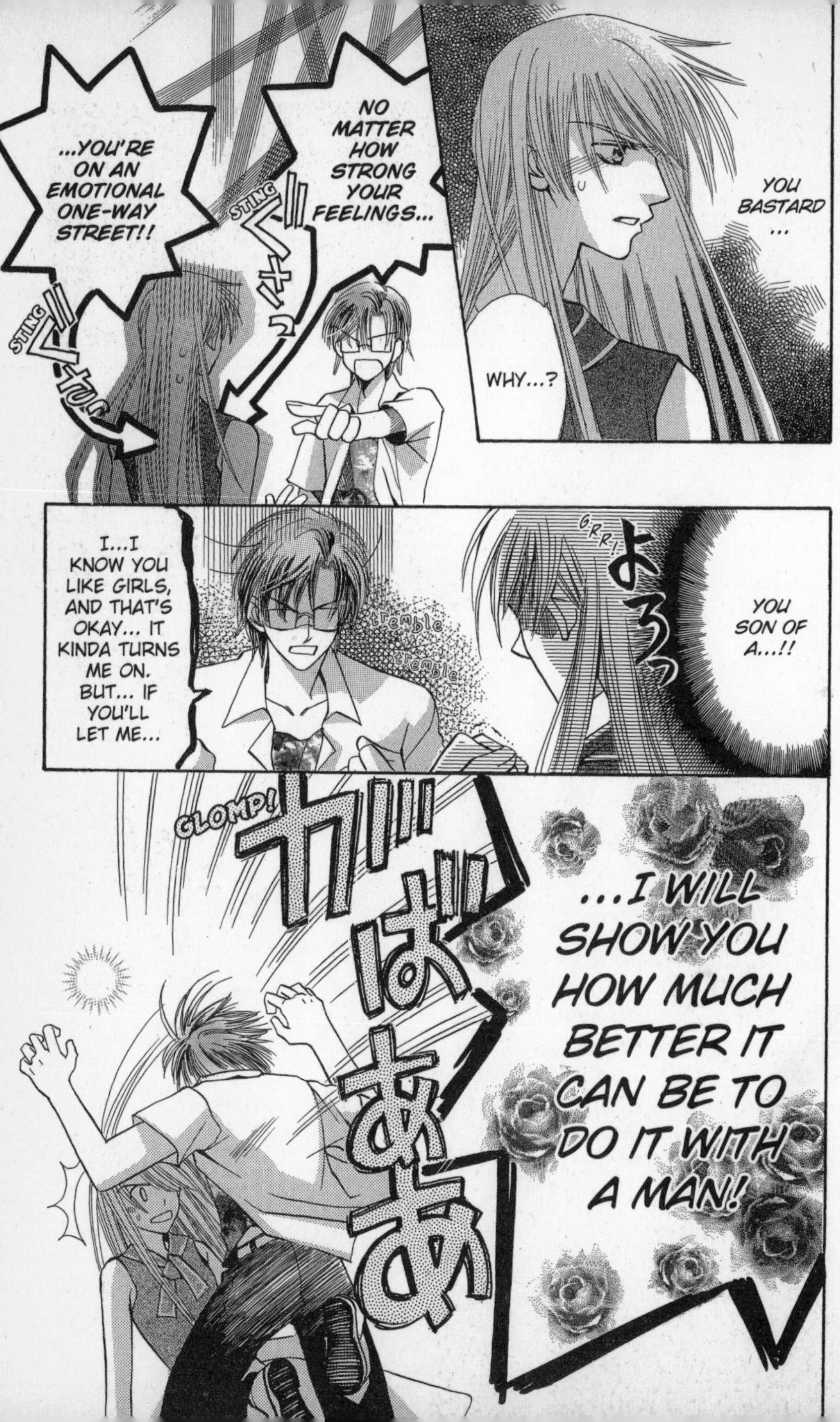
YOU BASTARD ...
WHY...?
NO MATTER HOW STRONG YOUR FEELINGS...
STING
...YOU'RE ON AN EMOTIONAL ONE-WAY STREET!!
STING
GRR!
YOU SON OF A...!!
I...I KNOW YOU LIKE GIRLS, AND THAT'S OKAY... IT KINDA TURNS ME ON. BUT... IF YOU'LL LET ME...
tremble tremble
GLOMP!
...I WILL SHOW YOU HOW MUCH BETTER IT CAN BE TO DO IT WITH A MAN!

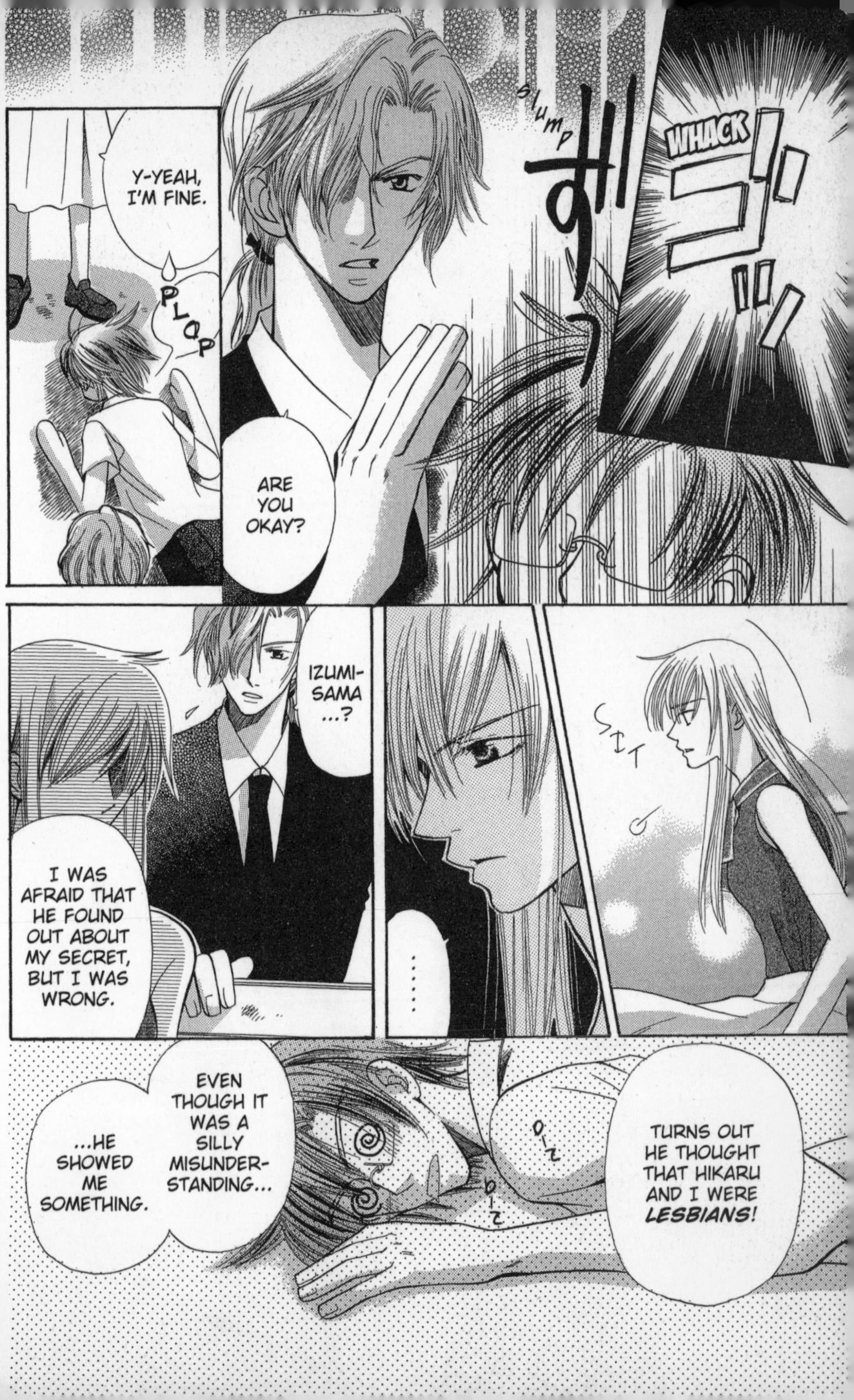
slump
WHACK
ARE YOU OKAY?
Y-YEAH, I'M FINE.
PLOP
SIT
......
IZUMI-SAMA ...?
I WAS AFRAID THAT HE FOUND OUT ABOUT MY SECRET, BUT I WAS WRONG.
TURNS OUT HE THOUGHT THAT HIKARU AND I WERE *LESBIANS!*
EVEN THOUGH IT WAS A SILLY MISUNDER-STANDING...
...HE SHOWED ME SOMETHING.

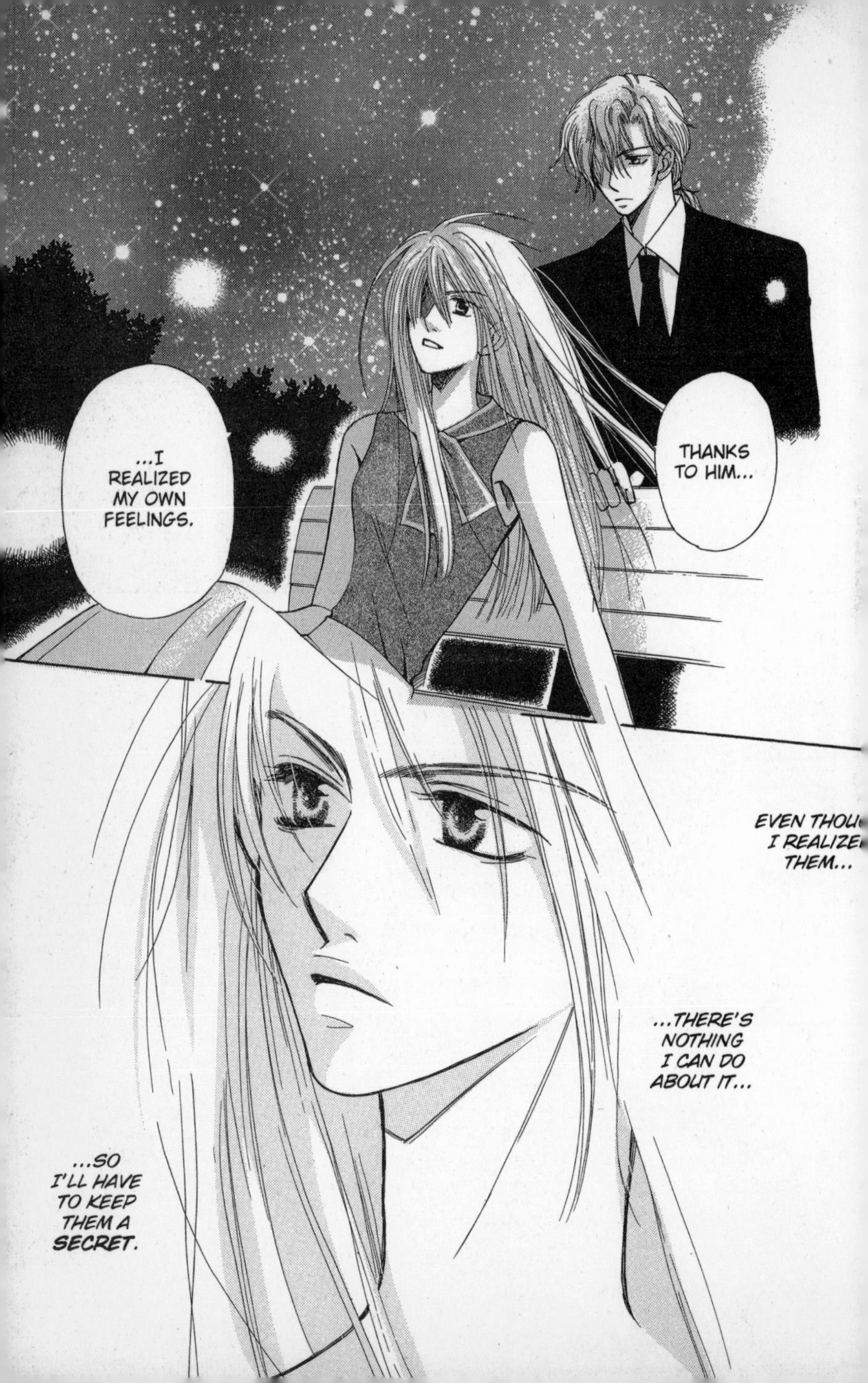
THANKS TO HIM...
...I REALIZED MY OWN FEELINGS.
EVEN THOU
I REALIZE
THEM...
...THERE'S NOTHING I CAN DO ABOUT IT...
...SO I'LL HAVE TO KEEP THEM A SECRET.

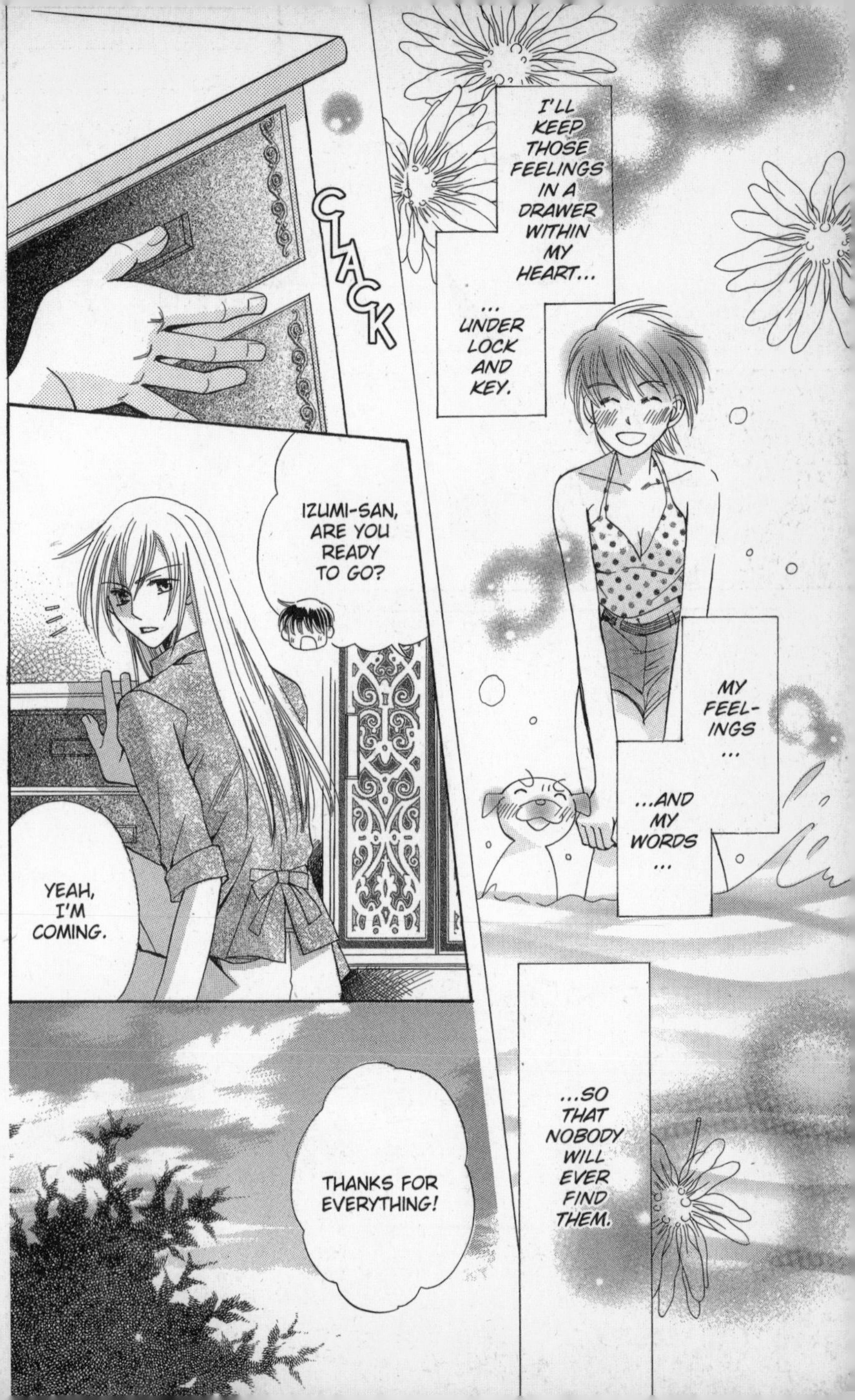
I'LL KEEP THOSE FEELINGS IN A DRAWER WITHIN MY HEART...
...UNDER LOCK AND KEY.
MY FEEL-INGS...
...AND MY WORDS...
...SO THAT NOBODY WILL EVER FIND THEM.
CLACK
IZUMI-SAN, ARE YOU READY TO GO?
YEAH, I'M COMING.
THANKS FOR EVERYTHING!

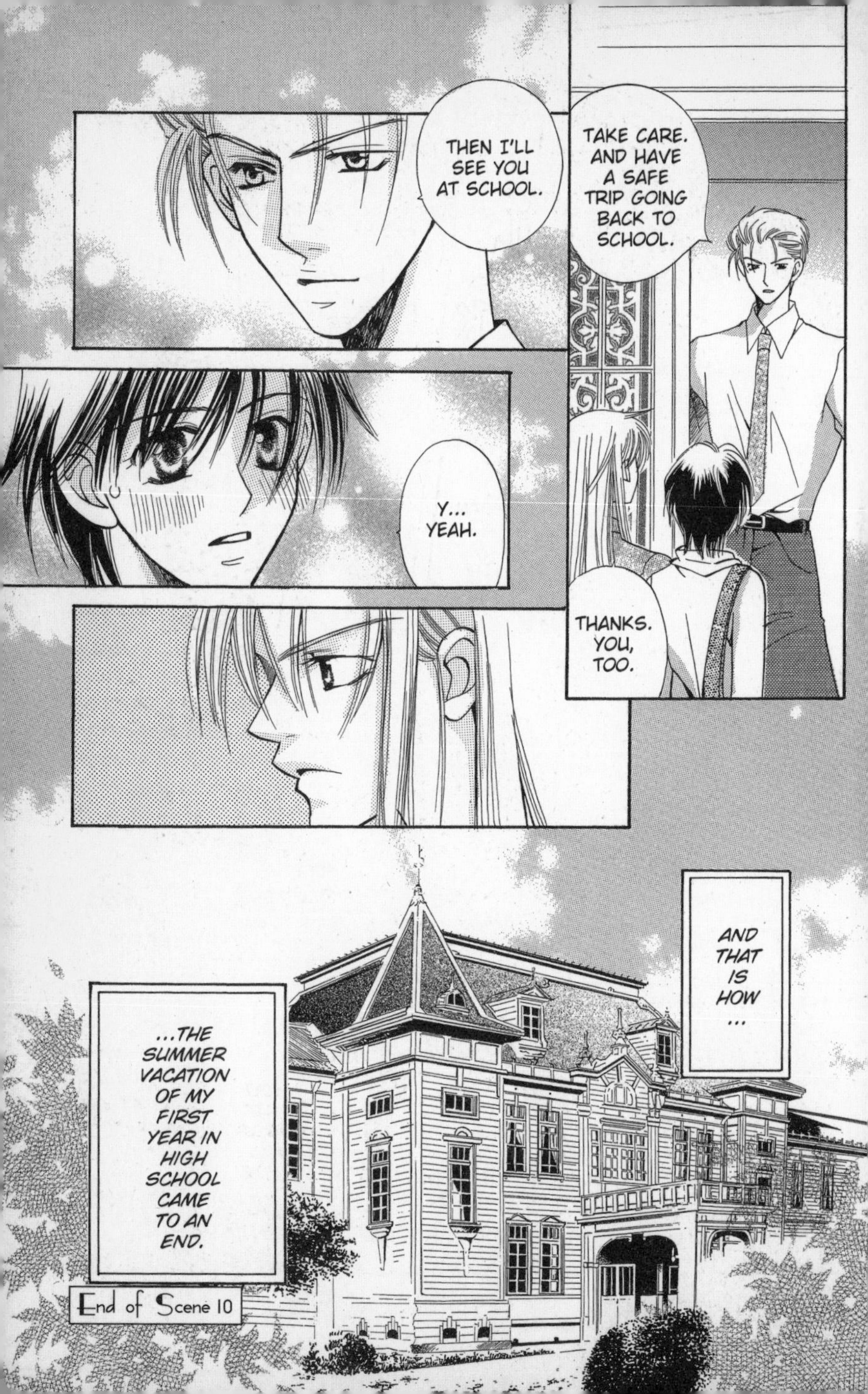
TAKE CARE. AND HAVE A SAFE TRIP GOING BACK TO SCHOOL.
THANKS. YOU, TOO.
THEN I'LL SEE YOU AT SCHOOL.
Y... YEAH.
AND THAT IS HOW...
...THE SUMMER VACATION OF MY FIRST YEAR IN HIGH SCHOOL CAME TO AN END.
End of Scene 10

To all of you who read Tenshi Ja Nai!! Volume 1, thanks for coming back! I truly appreciate all of you who have been supporting me from the beginning. I will continue to work harder to become a better manga creator.

To all of my readers, my assistants, Hariguchi-san, Aihara-san, my supportive family, my 2 pets 🐾 (laugh), and my editor, Kijima-san, thank you so much! I hope that you'll continue to support me in the future as well!!

December 29, 2003

Like what you read? Is there anything we can do to make your manga reading experience even better? Send your feedback, fan art and letters to:

Go! Media Entertainment, LLC
5737 Kanan Rd., #591
Agoura Hills, CA 91301

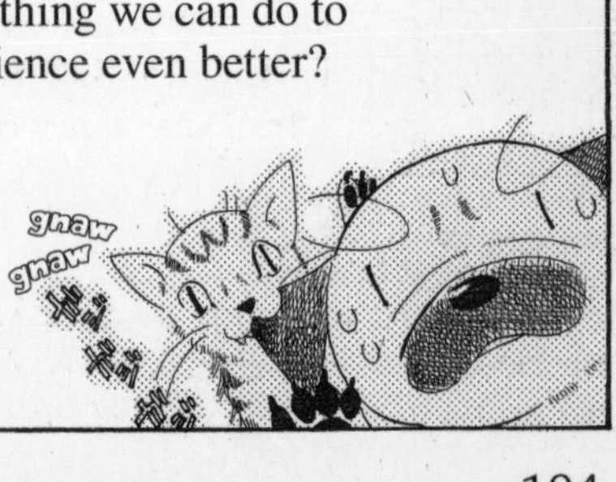
gnaw
gnaw

Translator's Notes

Page 25--*Sanpakugan*

A rare condition in which the iris is located at the top of the eye so that the whites of the eye surround it on three sides. In physiognomy, *sanpakugan* eyes are believed to be a sign of bad luck.

Page 37--Giant

Giant is a big bully from the classic manga series *Doraemon* (the most popular kids' series in Japan). He dreams of becoming a singer and likes to "treat" other kids to his "concerts," but has a singing voice like nails on a chalkboard. For Ayase-sensei's singing to be compared to Giant's it must be awful!

Page 74--Bloomers

No, the girls aren't running in their underwear! Those ultra-short shorts, called Bloomers ("*Buruma*"), matched with white T-shirts, are the standard girls' P.E. uniform.

Page 84--Summer Vacation

In Japan, the school year is divided into three terms. Summer Vacation falls between the first and second term, so when Hikaru and Izumi go back to school in the next volume, they'll still be in the middle of their first year. As it is in America, Summer Vacation is the longest break in the school year at just over a month.

Page 125--Kansai

Kansai is a region in the west part of Japan where Kyoto, Kobe and Osaka are located. The Kansai dialect is quite distinctive and more slangy than the Japanese spoken in Tokyo. Kurobe speaks with a pretty thick Kansai accent.

Page 147--*Kimodameshi*

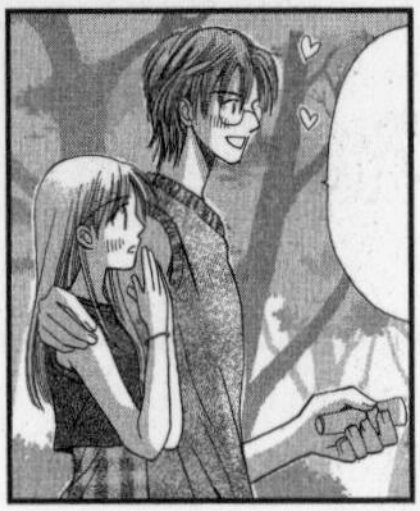

Kimodameshi, literally means "a test of courage." In the game *kimodameshi*, someone is challenged to face their fears and reach a goal in a scary location. It is often played on summer nights around haunted houses or cemeteries. Sometimes other people will pretend to be ghosts in order to scare the participants away from reaching the goal.

Page 158--*Manzai*

Manzai is a Japanese stand-up comedy double act, like Abbot and Costello. The *boke* (funny man) sets up punchlines and *tsukkomi* (straight man) shoots them down in rapid succession. *Manzai* developed in Osaka so most performers speak in Kansai dialect. Like comedians in U.S., it is not unusual for successful manzai comedians to break out into acting and TV hosting. "Beat" Takeshi Kitano, a well-known actor/director/writer, got his start as a *manzai* entertainer.

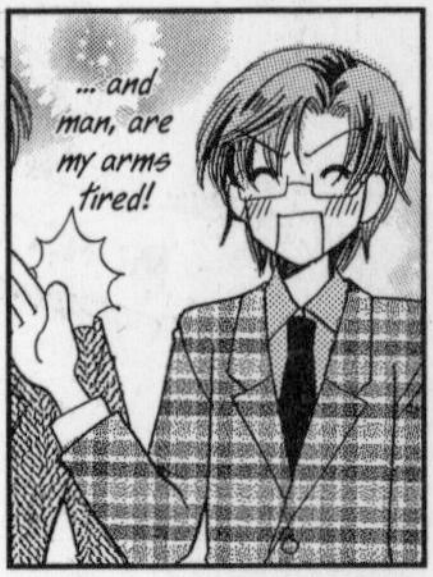
...and man, are my arms tired!

Page 160--*Otsukaresan*

At the wrap party, everyone uses the phrase "*otsukaresan*" (or, less formally, "*Otsukare*"). This is a set phrase used to thank someone for their hard work or among coworkers or teammates after a job is complete.

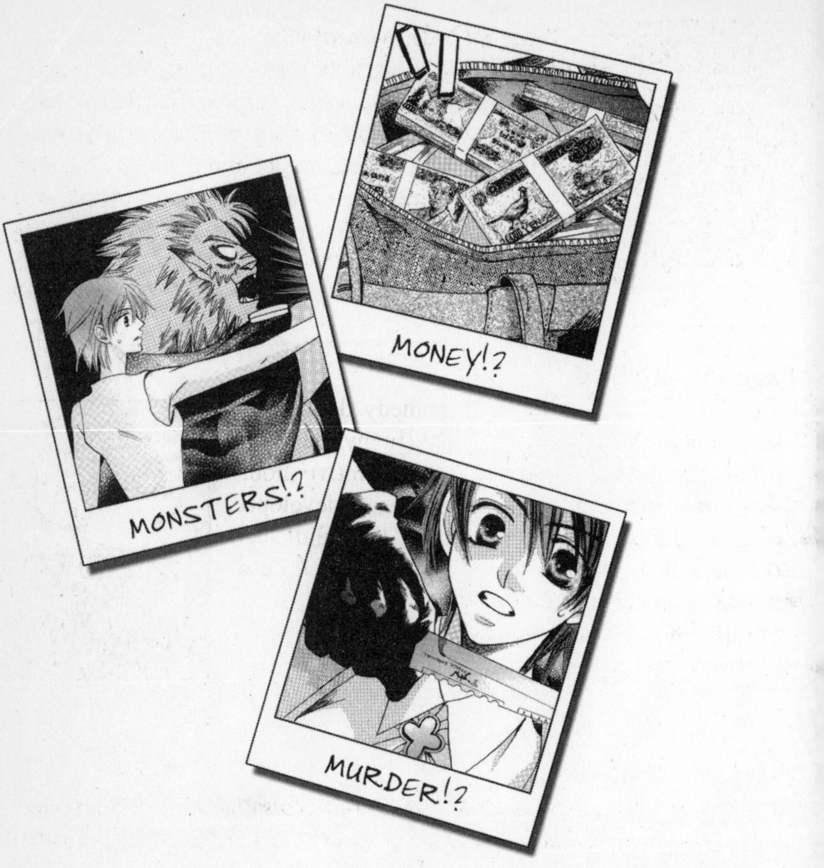
MONEY!?
MONSTERS!?
MURDER!?

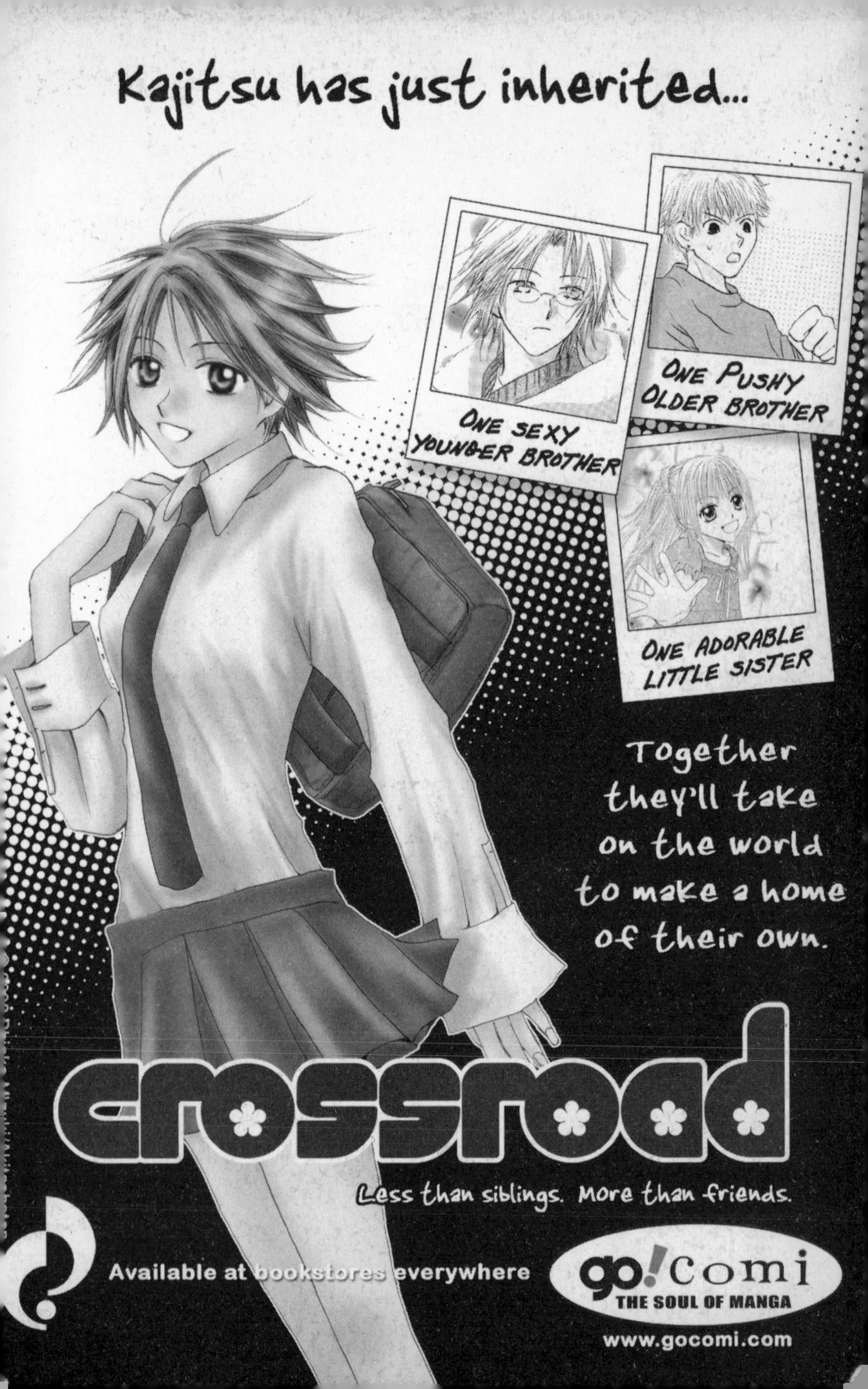

Kajitsu has just inherited...
One sexy younger brother
One pushy older brother
One adorable little sister
Together they'll take on the world to make a home of their own.
crossroad
Less than siblings. More than friends.
Available at bookstores everywhere
go!comi
THE SOUL OF MANGA
www.gocomi.com

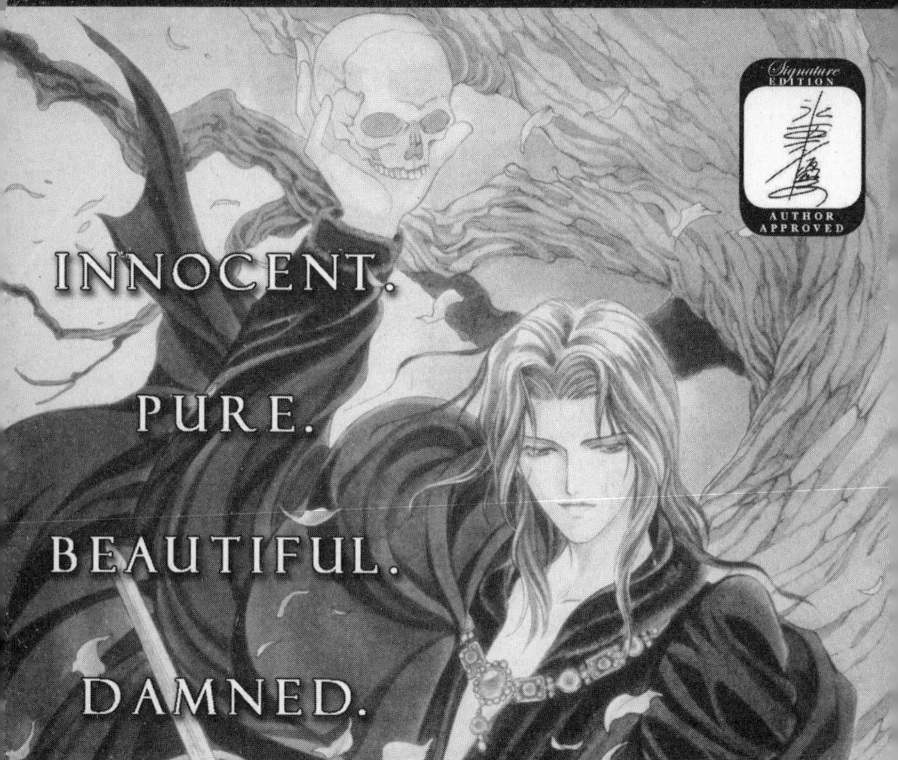
Signature EDITION
AUTHOR APPROVED
INNOCENT.
PURE.
BEAUTIFUL.
DAMNED.
Cantarella
© 2001 You Higuri/Akitashoten

Author's Note

There's no turning back now--Volume 2 is out! I'm so happy to see you all again. Remember Reggie? She's celebrating the fact that she's no longer a stray kitten. She and I both thank you for your ongoing support. (meow)

-Takako Shigematsu

Visit Shigematsu-sensei online at
http://www5b.biglobe.ne.jp/~taka_s/